GÖSTA REHN, THE SWEDISH MODEL AND LABOUR MARKET POLICIES

Gösta Rehn, the Swedish Model and Labour Market Policies

International and national perspectives

Edited by

HENRY MILNER
University Laval, Canada and University of Umeå, Sweden

ESKIL WADENSJÖ
Stockholm University, Sweden

Ashgate

Aldershot • Burlington USA • Singapore • Sydney

Published by
Ashgate Publishing Limited
Gower House
Croft Road
Aldershot
Hants GU11 3HR
England

Ashgate Publishing Company
131 Main Street
Burlington, VT 05401-5600 USA

Ashgate website: http://www.ashgate.com

British Library Cataloguing in Publication Data
Gösta Rehn, the Swedish model and labour market policies :
international and national perspectives
1.Rehn, Gösta 2. Manpower policy
I.Milner, Henry II.Wadensjö, Eskil, 1944-
331.1'2042

Library of Congress Control Number: 2001088786

ISBN 0 7546 1454 9

Printed and bound in Great Britain by
Antony Rowe Ltd., Chippenham, Wiltshire

Contents

Part 3. Nordic Perspectives

Part 4. European Perspectives

List of Figures

List of Tables

Acknowledgements

This book is the result of collaboration between a Canadian political scientist and a Swedish economist. It was the absence of any single English-language publication setting out Gösta Rehn's ideas and their contemporary relevance that led us both to seek a way to ensure that Gösta's legacy be secure. The result is this book. Of course, we could not have done this alone. Many of the contributors to this volume helped this project along in different ways.

Beyond the contributors, the efforts of several people in particular helped make this project possible. First and foremost are Frances Boylston, Jean Parr and Helena Orrje. Frances Boylston, as well as Jean Parr and Nicholas Aylott, helped make sure the text was in readable English. Helena Orrje painstakingly checked for consistency within and among the chapters. Jean Parr and Helena Orrje made important contributions to the production of the bibliography included in this volume. Equally indispensable, though in a different way, has been Gösta's widow Danielle Legoux-Rehn. Without her determination to see it reach fruition, the project may well have foundered on more than one occasion.

Thanks go out to as well to the many people who contributed to the success of the SASE (The Society for the Advancement of Socio-Economics) where it all began, for making it possible to stage the gathering that started it all in Vienna in July 1998. Special mention should go to Mary Grossman, executive director, and Jerry Hage, then President of SASE. We also wish to thank Björn Skala, (then Swedish Ambassador to Austria), who graciously sponsored a reception in honour of Gösta at the Embassy to coincide with the conference. Others who helped along the way include Gösta's son, Lars-Göran Larsson, Katherine Hodkinson of Ashgate Publishing, and Mats Lindahl of MediaMontage in Stockholm who skillfully prepared the camera-ready copy.

Stockholm, November 2003

Henry Milner   Eskil Wadensjö

Preface
Gösta Rehn 1913-1996

Gösta Rehn's career – in his writing, his teaching and his actions – was dedicated to improving working life. Beginning in his student days, through his early teaching days in the 1930s, his work on labour movement and governmental committees in the 1940s, and throughout his long career as a leading labour economist, he sought to link social betterment with improving working conditions – theoretically and practically.

Gösta Rehn was one of the fathers of the 'Swedish Model'. During the late 1940s and early 1950s, in collaboration with economist Rudolf Meidner, his colleague at the Swedish Confederation of Labour (LO), Rehn developed the economic model which carries their names. They saw that, especially in the context of the post-war economic context, Keynesian non-selective macroeconomic stimulation was a long-term prescription for job-destroying inflation; moreover, there was an alternative. Under centralized bargaining, non-inflationary growth was achievable through tight fiscal and monetary policies combined with 'active labour-market policies' to enhance the demand for and supply of appropriately trained workers, and with mobility underpinned by solid welfare state guarantees. Key among the active labour market policies was the establishment of retraining programs to enable workers to move from declining to expanding industries. Gösta Rehn and Rudolf Meidner did not invent active labour market policy or solidaristic wage policy and never claimed to have done so. But they combined these two elements with a restrictive economic policy into a new model with the intent to make it possible to combine price stability and full employment.

Swedish policy in the 1950s and 60s especially, in many ways embodied this 'Rehn-Meidner model', combining growth, full employment, and redistribution. The influence of Rehn's ideas was enormous, guiding a generation of labour economists and policy-makers in the Nordic countries, and influencing others in many countries.

Because he directed his theoretical contributions to mainstream economic-policy debates in Sweden and internationally, Gösta Rehn's influence on economic theory came largely through a series of articles, papers and debates on these policies published in both the specialized and lay literature. During his years at the OECD and Stockholm University, his many publications and lectures argued notably for tax incentives to encourage hiring of workers at the margin as the appropriate application of 'non-inflationary expansion policies'. Yet Gösta Rehn could never rest content with writing academic papers: endless hours in his later years were dedicated to making the case before decision makers and winning over public opinion through op-ed pieces, letters to the editor, etc.

A social reformer, who sought to improve life for the less fortunate today, and change the world tomorrow, Gösta Rehn devoted no small measure of his considerable energies to causes he believed in. He took part as a volunteer in the Finnish Winter War 1939/40 on the Finnish side and was also much engaged in occupied Norway. During the war, he organized youth groups to support the insurgents in Norway and Finland. Later, he was also involved in the integration of immigrants in Sweden, serving for many years as president of the Foundation for Immigrants and Minorities.

What counted for Gösta Rehn were ideas. Ready to discuss the issues with anyone interested, he would marshal facts and arguments to back up his views, and force his interlocutors to do the same. His very personality made him distinctly uncomfortable with ambiguity and fine theoretical distinctions distant from immediate practical choices: Social Democracy would succeed through the practical choices of real people in the real world or not at all.

Hence, without abandoning his commitment to a better, more equal society and world, Gösta Rehn would never let his ideals cloud his thinking about policies. Policies stand or fall by whether their implementation could attain concrete, measurable objectives under known conditions. He was quite ready and willing to criticize his political allies if they failed the test. Consider his attitude toward working time. He shared the preoccupation of the Swedish labour movement with redistribution through work rather than income. Yet he denounced as poor economics the programs of continental social democrats that assumed that the amount of work was fixed so that unemployment could be fought by reducing the workweek or forcing early retirement upon everyone. Gösta Rehn's alternative approach, 'life-long flexibility' sought to maximize freedom of choice for individuals based on differing needs at different stages in their working lives.

Gösta Rehn's career

After graduating from secondary school and completing his military service, Gösta Rehn studied at the School of Social Work in Stockholm between the years 1933 and 1936. At the same time he studied at the Stockholms Högskola (now Stockholm University). After graduating from the School of Social Work he held a number of short-term jobs – teaching, conducting studies for various organizations and working as assistant at the Ministry of Trade. He combined those jobs with further studies at Stockholms Högskola until he left in the spring of 1940 to volunteer in the Winter War. After returning to Stockholm he continued with his combination of studies and various small jobs, now more and more for LO, the powerful trade union confederation. In 1943 he was employed full time at LO's research department. At that time Richard Sterner was head of the department but Rudolf Meidner succeeded him later in the 1940s. By agreement with LO Gösta Rehn was allowed to devote a third of his working hours to studies, but he was soon fully absorbed by work at LO. In the 1940s he took part in various governmental committees. From 1952 to 1958 he was on leave from LO working for two governmental committees on the problem of combining price stability and full employment. Part of his work was presented as a Licentiate thesis in economics at Stockholms Högskola. He came back to LO in August 1958 but did not find it easy to work together with the new LO leader Arne Geijer, and he left LO permanently in 1959.

From 1959 to 1962, he was Head of the Economic Affairs Branch of the Swedish Ministry of Finance, afterwards leaving Sweden to take up the position of Director of the Employment and Social Affairs Secretariat at the OECD in Paris, which he held until 1973. From 1974 to 1979, he was professor of labour market policy at the Institute of Social Research (SOFI) at Stockholm University and also Director of the institute. There he remained to continue his research and lecturing even after his formal retirement.

Gösta Rehn worked in different places and in different positions, but he never stopped writing; he also never stopped doing other things to exclusively write. His writings are numerous and varied. A complete bibliography at the end of this volume reveals that no small part of his output was in languages other than Swedish – English, German, French and Spanish. Gösta Rehn was very concerned to take into account the prevailing situation in other countries so that his ideas could be applied anywhere there was interest in considering them. On the other hand, widespread interests and activities meant that, despite the large and impressive list of articles he published, nowhere were his ideas presented in a single comprehensive form.

How this book came about

Gösta Rehn died on November 30th, 1996. It was not unexpected since he had been suffering from a serious deterioration of both his physical and mental capacities following his suffering a broken hip two years earlier. Yet it came as a shock nonetheless. Until his accident, though already in his 80s, Gösta Rehn had retained the vibrancy and remarkable intellectual and even physical vigour that made his presence so powerful among his colleagues and friends.

One of the editors of this collection, Henry Milner, was in New Zealand at the time of Gösta Rehn's death and could therefore not attend the funeral in Stockholm. In his absence he, in a sense, represented the many individuals who had been affected by Gösta Rehn the man and his ideas in different countries around the world and who were unable to appropriately pay their respects. Clearly something was needed on the occasion of Gösta Rehn's passing to draw wider attention to the ideas and contributions that he, along with his colleagues, had made over half a century.

With the encouragement of Gösta Rehn's widow Danielle Legoux-Rehn and son Lars-Göran Larsson, Milner undertook to organize a conference for this purpose. At its summer 1997 meeting in Montreal, the leadership of SASE (The Society for the Advancement of Socio-Economics) agreed that at its next conference, slated for the following July in Vienna, there would be a special event honouring Gösta Rehn. Milner began the work of planning a one-day conference, which would highlight the work and contribution of Gösta Rehn in a series of papers sessions and a plenary presentation. One of those invited to participate in the conference was Eskil Wadensjö who succeeded Gösta Rehn as professor in labour market policy at SOFI in 1980. Eskil Wadensjö had earlier edited a collection in Swedish of Gösta Rehn's writing and also a collection of comments on the achievements of Gösta Rehn on the occasion of Gösta Rehn's 75th birthday and taken charge of the Rehn archives.

The success of the Vienna conference naturally led to a discussion of whether the papers that had been given there could serve as a basis for the book. It was clear that, with some additions, they could do so admirably. Henry Milner and Eskil Wadensjö decided to proceed with the project. The presenters were asked to revise their papers for a book, while additional scholars were solicited by the editors to contribute in order to fill in the gaps. During this process, Katherine Hodkinson of Ashgate Publishing in the United Kingdom came on board and Ashgate undertook to publish the edited volume. What follows is the result of that process.

An outline of the chapters

The first part of the book sets out the key elements of Rehn's ideas and places them in historical context. Eskil Wadensjö shows how acceptance of the Rehn-Meidner model was by no means inevitable. It faced competition in the form of the Rubbestad programme, which had been endorsed by a parliamentary commission mandated in 1948 to investigate the functioning of existing labour market policies. The article compares the two programmes and offers an explanation for the victory for Rehn-Meidner. Next, Lennart Erixon carefully sets out the logic of the Rehn-Meidner model, stressing where it differed from the then dominant Keynesian model and policy prescriptions. After considering relevant recent developments, he concludes that, despite certain limitations, the model can make a useful contribution to the formulation of economic policy today.

The next section focuses directly on how Rehn's ideas have fared in Sweden. Klas Eklund argues that though Swedish economic and political developments were strongly influenced by Rehn and his colleagues, the Rehn-Meidner model and the subsequent proposals of Gösta Rehn were, in important respects, better suited to conditions in the 1970s and 80s than the policies actually followed by the 'Swedish Model' with which they were – rightly or wrongly – associated. Had the actual Swedish model been more like Gösta Rehn's program and proposals, Eklund suggests, it would have been more flexible and resistant to external shocks, with higher growth and lower inflation.

Anders Bäckström focuses on the labour market policies, a key component of the Rehn-Meidner model. After describing how the labour market differs significantly today from when the policy was first set out, he argues that the policy prescriptions under the Rehn-Meidner model are still relevant, though the emphasis has changed. Special attention must be paid to those aspects of Rehn-Meidner linked to enhanced training and mobility.

Henry Milner's contribution takes up his contention that the Scandinavian welfare states have proven able to adapt to changes in the wider economic environment due to a distinctive set of institutions associated with high levels of 'civic literacy'. These institutions, he argues, are the product of a series of policy prescriptions associated with no one more than Gösta Rehn. Milner analyses the recent evolution of the institutions of the Scandinavian welfare state, stressing the importance of information-enhancing policies as they were incorporated into the Swedish model generally, and the Rehn-Meidner model in particular.

Axel van den Berg brings to bear the results of a decade-long research project investigating the sources of industrial resistance to change and flexibility in Sweden, using Canada as the contrasting case. The question posed is whether Swedish workers in fact lived up to the Rehn-Meidner model's expectations that, in Rehn's words, 'on the basis of this active labour market policy the trade unions could moderate any tendencies towards "Luddite" reluctance to technical progress or a protectionist resistance to structural change among their members.' Are Swedish workers more open to technical and structural change affecting their present jobs when compared to workers and trade unionists in Canada who do not enjoy the same degree of security?

The next two parts of the book assesses the impact of Rehn and Rehn-Meidner abroad. Part three focuses on Sweden's Nordic cousins. Heikki Ervasti looks at Finland, a country with a strong centralized trade union movement and an egalitarian tradition. The solidaristic wage policy aspect of Rehn-Meidner has had wide support in the Finnish society, he notes. With the labour market increasingly fragmented, Ervasti analyses Finnish data from the International Survey of Economic Attitudes to ask if support for the policy is as strong as in earlier decades of the post-war period. Geir Høgsnes and Frode Longva focus on recent Norwegian developments affecting centralized wage bargaining, another key element of Rehn-Meidner. They maintain that Norway has developed a unique form of collective bargaining that takes place not on one level but in co-ordinated fashion at both central and local levels. The actual mechanisms under which the model achieves this co-ordination are, however, not apparent. Using the 1996/97 wage bargaining round as an illustration, they try to show that, despite appearances, Norway lives up to the basic expectations of the model.

Denmark is the focus of the next article in which Sven Jochem suggests that, overall, other Nordic countries conformed better to the expectations of Rehn than did Sweden. The success of the model, argues Jochem, depends upon concertation amongst interest organizations and state actors. In a globalizing economy, employers are less concerned with national systems of interest mediation, and thus new forms of concertation must develop to adapt to these conditions. In comparing the positions of the employers' associations in the 1980s, he shows that, unlike the Swedish SAF, the Danish DA renewed co-operation with Labour. A major reason for this divergence, Jochem argues, lies in the burden the welfare state places on employers in Denmark as opposed to Sweden. For his part, Christian Toft examines Danish post-war traditions of active labour market policy. He explains why, in contrast to the Swedish trade unions, Danish trade unions formally rejected the active labour market programme. Despite this, he argues further, once we take into account the fact that industrial training and education in Denmark is placed in the Ministry of Education rather than in a Labour Market Board as in Sweden, the differences in labour market policies in practice shrink to insignificance.

The final part of the book addresses the rest of Europe. We begin with Austria, a continental bastion of social democracy. Markus Marterbauer compares the 'Austro-Keynesian' and Rehn-Meidner models. While the main purpose of both was to combine full employment with price stability, the former, he finds, differed significantly from the latter, borrowing those aspects that were suited to Austrian conditions and the goals of its policy makers. One core element of Austro-Keynesianism, macroeconomically oriented incomes policy, contrasts especially sharply with the Swedish solidarity wage policy. Comparing the relative success of both models, Marterbauer contrasts the mechanisms used to stabilize the expectations of investors, aggregate demand, and co-ordinate wage policy.

Next, Jelle Visser asks if Gösta Rehn would have approved of the policies underlying the 'Dutch miracle' in the Netherlands of the 1990s. After describing recent changes in the Dutch labour market, and analyzing the policies underlying them, Visser investigates to what extent they are compatible with the assumptions, prescriptions and expectations of the Swedish Model as articulated by Rehn. For their part, Dominique Anxo, Christine Brossier and Bernard Gazier assess the influence of Gösta Rehn in France, a country in which he lived for 12 years, and to which he returned frequently. After identifying the various channels through which Rehn and his ideas contributed to the French policy debates and decisions, they look in detail at the influence of specific aspects of active labour market and working-time policies, the latter a matter of much controversy in France.

Finally, Mark Wickham-Jones looks at the labour market policies of the British Labour Party in the 1950s and early 60s, the heyday of Rehn-Meidner. He notes that Labour's 'revisionist' approach to social democracy essentially confined itself to Keynesian macroeconomic instruments – in marked contrast to the core features of the Rehn-Meidner model with its emphasis on active labour market policies and solidaristic wage bargaining. The failure of these ideas to make headway within the party, despite studies undertaken by British labour economists of the Swedish model, he concludes, is linked to the insular and atheoretical nature of British social democracy during much of the post-war era.

PART 1
Gösta Rehn's Contribution

Chapter 1

The Labour Market Policy – Rehn or Rubbestad

Eskil Wadensjö

Sweden has had an active labour market policy for many years. Its administrative structure gradually changed over the first half of the 20th century and until its form was determined for the decades to come with the establishment of the National Labour Market Board (AMS) in 1948. When the LO economists discussed how to formulate a policy for making it possible to combine full employment with price stability in the late 1940s and early 1950s, a substantial labour market policy already existed. A new feature was that this policy would be combined with a restrictive fiscal and monetary policy and a solidaristic wage policy.[1] Although the solidaristic wage policy had been formulated, discussed and accepted at earlier LO congresses, it had not come into enactment yet. Another new feature was the proposal that the labour market policy should be extensive not only in times of depression but even in periods of prosperity. The LO economists also advocated that the labour market policy should be expanded.

The LO model, or Rehn-Meidner model as it came to be known, was not immediately accepted by the Social Democratic party and therefore not by the Government and the Riksdag. The model was accepted only at the end of the 1950s and then the active labour market policy rapidly expanded. In hindsight it may appear to have been an inevitable learning process, but the outcome was not given in advance. Influential politicians inside, as well as outside the Social Democratic party, were strongly against the policy and had suggested alternatives. In this chapter the situation at the time and the alternatives to an expansion of the labour market policy will be in focus.

The founding of the Swedish labour market policy[2]

Industrialization occurred late in Sweden, but developed very rapidly in the decades following 1870. The first significant economic decline and considerable unemployment came in the late 1890s. One of the policy measures in response to this crisis was state support of municipal employment agencies. The first municipal employment offices were established already in 1902 and began to receive state support in 1907. The number of offices quickly increased from 9 in 1906 to 118 in 1916. This measure won widespread approval and support. Liberal economists such as Gustav Cassel and Eli Heckscher supported it and viewed it as a measure which would enable the labour market to function better as a market.

During the First World War other important steps were taken towards what was to become the Swedish labour market policy. First, one of the things which was later to characterize the labour market policy was tried: that is, public relief works as a means to combat unemployment. Trade barriers during the war led to structural unemployment. For a short period of time, cash allowances were paid out to those who were affected. Soon, however, it was decided that work should have priority over cash support, and public relief works were set up for the unemployed.

Secondly, the question of support to the union unemployment insurance funds or the establishment of a state-organized unemployment insurance system was investigated. In the end it was decided that no support would go to unemployment insurance – instead priority would be given to public relief works and then to need-tested cash support. The wages paid for these public works were set low so that no one would be tempted to stay on, if any other job became available. The public relief works were also used as a test of the willingness of the unemployed to work before cash support was paid out. If a person refused to take public relief work, he could not receive cash support.

The two main features of Swedish labour market policy were already evident at this point:

1) A strong emphasis on work and a discouragement of cash allowances and support. An unemployed person was expected to either get a job on the open labour market through the employment agencies, or would be directed to a (poorly paid) public works job. The work principle is preferred, not the cash support principle.

2) That it is a question of labour *market* policy is also emphasized. By means of the measures taken, the labour market should come to work better (via the employment agencies) or at least not function worse (the formation of the public relief works with low wages).

During the depression period of the early 1920s the public relief works expanded to a very great extent. They were organized by a special authority, the Unemployment Commission. The labour market policy of the 1920s was very unpopular in the labour movement. The low pay in the public relief works and their use for testing the willingness to take a job led to political conflict between the Social Democratic party and the non-socialist parties.

During the 1930s the policy was partially changed. Due to the influence of Keynes and the contemporary (and in some respects earlier) Stockholm School, and with a Social Democratic government in power since 1932, a new form of public works that paid the market wage was initiated. Public works were also more consciously integrated into, and became an important part of, economic policy. This new form of public works was organized by the National Board of Welfare and not by the Unemployment Commission. The Unemployment Commission continued with the earlier form of public works, but the extent of those works gradually declined.

Dating from 1935, state support of the union unemployment insurance funds was granted. This support was limited, however, and the accompanying conditions so strict that only a small part of the insurance funds accepted it during the 1930s.

At the same time, it was made compulsory for the counties and the larger cities to establish employment offices in order to be able, among other things, to test the willingness on the part of those who received benefits from unemployment insurance funds to accept work.

In the years before the Second World War a committee was working with the formulation of the future labour market policy, '1937 års arbetslöshetssakkunniga'.[3] This study was never completed due to the outbreak of the war. But the committee had formulated a preliminary version of the final report where it is apparent that they intended to propose a larger role for labour market policy, with a central authority to be made responsible for it. Even though not published, the results of the committee work were not forgotten. The chairman, Gustav Möller, was Minister of Social Affairs, the minister in charge of labour market policy. The secretary of the committee, Arthur Thomson, was appointed head of the new temporary authority, Arbetsmarknadskommissionen (The Labour Market Commission).[4] This authority, which was intended to be in force during the war, replaced the Unemployment Commission and also became responsible for the public relief works organized by the National Welfare Board and the employment offices, which had been temporarily nationalised after the outbreak of the Second World War. County labour market boards were constituted for all counties and also for Stockholm. Many labour market programs were tested during the war, among them labour market training and mobility allowances. Special programs were also developed for disabled workers.

The labour market policy was an important issue for the Labour Movement's committee for the Program for the Post-war Period.[5] The program, which was published before the war ended, had three main aims: 1) full employment, 2) a fair income distribution and a higher standard of living, and 3) higher efficiency and greater democracy in the economy. Below the three headings 27 special issues or points were identified, and in practice the program was named after those issues 'De 27 punkterna'. Two of the 27 points dealt with labour market policy: '7. Public works should be expanded when employment in the public sector declines' and '8. Efficient labour exchange and labour market retraining. A better vocational education and vocational guidance. More jobs for disabled people.' The solidaristic wage policy, which, like the active labour market policy, later became a part of the Rehn-Meidner model, was also included in the program: '10. A solidaristic wage policy. Equal pay for equal work, both with a comparison between agriculture and other industries and between men and women.' The first issue of the program stated that the economic policy should aim at avoiding inflation (and deflation). Head of the committee was Ernst Wigforss, Minster of Finance. Richard Sterner, head of LO's research department, was secretary and Gösta Rehn, also from LO's research department, was deputy secretary.

After the war a governmental committee studied the future organisation of the labour market policy. It proposed that the nationalisation of the employment offices should be made permanent and that a central authority in charge of the employment offices and the labour market policy should be established. The Riksdag acted on this in 1947 and the new authority, the National Labour Market Board (Arbetsmarknadsstyrelsen (AMS)), started in 1948. This meant that when discussion of a new and expanded role for the labour market policy started in the late 1940s, there were both labour market programmes and an organisation that was well-equipped for implementing them.

The Rubbestad alternative[6]

As mentioned earlier, the new organisation of the labour market administration started in 1948. This did not mean that the Government had a plan for the further development of the labour market policy. On the contrary, the opposition criticized this. As a response to the criticism a governmental committee was appointed: the '1950 års Arbetsförmedlingsutredning'. Its main task was to evaluate the new organisation of the employment offices. The committee became known under the name 'Rubbestadsutredningen' after its most well-known member, Axel Rubbestad, a leading member of Bondeförbundet (the 'Farmers party', presently the Center Party (Centerpartiet)).[7] Rubbestad was very critical of public spending and big government. The other members were Gustaf Karlsson (chairman, representing the Social Democratic party in the parliament), Gösta Åqvist (representing the Liberal party (Folkpartiet) in the parliament) and Leif Hultström (from the National Board of Welfare). The committee was appointed in January, started to work in March and after intensive work, with 40 meetings between March 1 and November 16, wrote a report that covered the county and local organisation, with the exception of Stockholm, and which was presented in December the same year.[8]

The report was critical of most things concerning the employment offices. It accepted the nationalisation of the employment offices but was critical of how priorities were established and thought that the labour market policy was too extensive.

The committee stressed that many vacancies were only short-term vacancies and that the effort and cost of finding applicants for those positions in many cases was not worth the money. The committee also stressed that the existence of the employment offices probably led to too high mobility in the labour market. This 'excessive mobility' of the labour force was a concern not only for this committee but also for various participants in the political debate. The committee did not want to stop all service for those who already had jobs but were looking for another. It could lead to the employment offices gaining a reputation for being places where only the unemployed and disabled went to seek jobs and therefore become less popular among the employers. The service for those looking for new jobs should be reduced, however, thereby making it possible to reduce the number of offices and personnel at the employment offices.

The proposal of the committee meant a reduction in the number of employment offices by 43 from 251 to 208. This reduction and the elimination of some positions in the county councils meant that the staff of the labour market administration would diminish by around 100. One member of the committee, Rubbestad, made a formal reservation against the proposal. He wished to reduce the size of personnel even further and proposed 30 more without further argumentation.

As customary with reports from governmental committees, it was sent out to various authorities and organisations for comments. LO was one of those on the list. In its answer, LO strongly argued against a reduction of the public employment service. 'The only rule which should be of guidance [for determining the size of the employment service] is that the labour exchange shall deliver and expand its services as long as there are valid arguments for that the losses in time and other forms in working life will be reduced by the services of the employment offices.' (LO 1951, p.5)

The LO answer to the report concludes with the following words: 'Landsorganisationen cannot support a reduction of the organisation, which results in the public employment service being deprived of the possibility to fulfil its labour market policy tasks in a satisfactory manner.' (LO 1951, pp. 7-8.) The answer was formulated by Nils Kellgren, and signed by him and the deputy chairman of LO Einar Norrman. Nils Kellgren was one of the four members of LO's research department who wrote the main part of the report to the LO congress 1951.[9] The other three were Rudolf Meidner, Gösta Rehn and Arne Henriksson.

A second committee report was completed a few months after the first one (1950 års Arbetsförmedlingsutredning 1951). This report dealt with that part of the organisation, which was added to the labour market administration during the war – the crisis organisation (which handled building regulation and the employment of foreigners (refugees)). Even this report proposed a reduction of personnel, and Rubbestad once again dissented favouring a larger reduction of the personnel.

The government made a proposal to the Riksdag based on the first two reports of the committee (Government 1951), more or less ignoring the objections of LO. Instead of reducing the number of employment offices from 251 to 208, they were reduced to 217. Instead of reducing the number of personnel by 77, in the part of the labour market administration this proposal dealt with, it was reduced by 60. The

Rubbestad policy of reducing the employment offices was followed even if not to the extent Rubbestad wanted. Of the Rehn-Meidner model, at this time known from the first articles, no traces are to be found in the Government proposal and in the decisions taken by the Riksdag.

The committee continued its work and met 26 times from December 1950 to November 1951. In addition to the two reports already mentioned, the committee presented three reports. One dealt with the organisation of the employment offices in Stockholm (1950 års Arbetsförmedlingsutredning 1951a), one with the National Labour Market Board (1950 års Arbetsförmedlingsutredning 1951b), and one with some remaining issues (1950 års Arbetsförmedlingsutredning 1951c). Rubbestad left the committee in the end of May and for the last few months of the committee's existence was replaced by Ivar Johansson, a member of the same political party as Rubbestad. This replacement did not change the main ideas of the committee, also these reports argued for a reduction of the staff and by that of a lowering of the ambitions of the labour market policy. There was one exception, however, the committee advocated an expansion of the labour market programs for disabled workers.

The Government followed the recommendations of these reports. The committee proposed a decline of the personnel of the Labour Market Board from 390 to 345. In a proposal to the Riksdag put forward in February 1952 (Government 1952), the Government set the number to 348, almost the same as the committee. This proposal was presented and accepted by the Government after the report to the LO congress in 1951 had proposed a more ambitious and thus an expanded labour market policy.

The size of the personnel at the employment offices stabilised after the decline in the early 1950s but it was not until the early 1960s that it was restored to the size of the early post-war years.[10] The number of people in labour training was low (it had been higher in the 1930s and during the war). The number of people in public relief jobs was very low until the end of the 1950s. The only exception was in accordance with the proposal of the committee that the programs for disabled workers expanded.

In looking at the political decisions that were made, and to the actual development of the labour market policy, the main part of the 1950s was the decade of the 'Rubbestad model' for labour market policy, not of the LO or the Rehn model. But most things changed in the late 1950s. In the next section this development will be presented.

The Rehn-Meidner model and the government[11]

The 1951 LO congress accepted the Report to congress which outlined the Rehn-Meidner policy. However, it took a long time before the Government and the Riksdag accepted it. The Minister of Finance, Per Edvin Sköld, strongly opposed the program and he held a strong position in the government regarding economic policy formulation. Another obstacle was that the Social Democratic government in 1951 changed to a coalition government between the Social Democratic and the Farmers' party. The Farmers'party (Rubbestad's party) did not favour an active labour market policy.

The situation changed in the mid-1950s. Prime Minister Tage Erlander gradually became a supporter of the Rehn-Meidner policy and therefore of an active labour market policy.[12] More important was probably that Per Edvin Sköld left as minister of finance and that his successor, Gunnar Sträng, was much more supportive of the ideas behind the Rehn-Meidner model.[13] That Arne Geijer, new LO chairman from 1956, was much less in favour of the Rehn-Meidner program and active labour market policy was of less importance.

Another factor working for the Rehn-Meidner model was that the political conflict regarding the supplementary pension scheme led to that the Farmers' party left the government in 1957 and that the Social Democratic party formed a one party-government. Also important was that the new General Director of National Labour Market Board, Bertil Ohlsson (from August 1957), was strongly in favour of an active labour market policy and that he was strong-willed and resourceful. The unemployment rate rose in 1957 and 1958 making it politically easier to expand the volume of the labour market programs. The labour market policy continued to expand even more rapidly in the early 1960s when the unemployment was very low. By this time it is clear that the Rehn-Meidner policy had replaced the Rubbestad policy as the guideline for the Swedish labour market policy.

When looking back from the 1970s to the 1950s, Tage Erlander described this development in the following way: 'The new labour market policy was launched after thorough discussions with LO, discussions which above all were stimulated primarily by Meidner and Rehn. The new labour market policy of the 1950s was a further development of the line of thought which the [Social Democratic] party fought for under Wigforss-Möller's days of glory, but when weak support by the Parliament made it impossible to realize those ideas to their full extent.' (Erlander 1979, p. 38).

Conclusions

As shown in chapters in this volume, the Rehn-Meidner model and its advocacy of an active labour market policy has had an impact of the labour market policy outside Sweden. The first requisite for this of course is that the model was formulated, but a second requisite is that the model was actually implemented in Sweden. It is not very likely that the model would have had the same influence if it had not been tested in its home country.

In this chapter two aspects of the implementation of an active labour market policy in Sweden as a part of the Rehn-Meidner model have been stressed. The first one is the long history of active labour market policy and the development of a strong central administration of the employment offices and the various programmes completed by the founding of the National Labour Market Board (AMS) in 1948. The second aspect is that the implementation of the active labour market of the Rehn-Meidner model was not inevitable. There was an alternative, the Rubbestad policy of a contraction of the labour market administration and policy. This alternative was initially successful, and it was only after a long political process in the 1950s that the policy came to be changed, and the active labour market policy became the policy preferred by the Government and the Riksdag.

Notes

1 See Erixon (this volume) for a detailed presentation of the Rehn-Meidner model.
2 See for example Öhman (1974) and Ohlsson and Olofsson (1998) for the long run development of labour market policy in Sweden. Edebalk (1974) contains an analysis of the development of the unemployment insurance system up to 1935.
3 See Rothstein (1989).
4 It was set up as an advisory body September 15, 1939 and was made a governmental authority in May 1940.
5 See Arbetarrörelsens efterkrigsprogram (1944) for the plan and Ohlsson (1998) for a detailed account of the committee's work. The committee had its first meeting on April 29, 1943 and the report was published on July 19, 1944. The parts on labour market policy were presented in a first version already at an extended meeting on July 25-31, 1943.
6 Thoursie in Delander, Thoursie and Wadensjö (1991) discusses the 'Rubbestad committee' and its effects. Rehn (1977) mentioned that the Rubbestad committee delayed the implementation of an active labour market policy.
7 Rubbestad was a member of the Riksdag and had been minister 1943-45 in the wartime coalition government.
8 See 1950 års Arbetsförmedlingsutredning (1950).
9 See LO (1951a).
10 See Olli (1996) for figures over the development of participation in the labour market programs and of the number of people employed in the labour market administration.
11 Rehn (1977) contains a vivid description of his attempts to sell the Rehn-Meidner model to the Government.
12 See Erlander (1976).
13 See Rehn (1977) and Johansson (1992).

References

Arbetarrörelsens efterkrigsprogram. De 27 punkterna med motivering (1944), Stockholm.

Delander, Lennart, Ragnar Thoursie and Eskil Wadensjö (1991), *Arbetsförmedlingens historia,* Allmänna förlaget, Stockholm.

Edebalk, Per Gunnar (1974), *Arbetslöshetsförsäkringsdebatten. En studie i svensk socialpolitik 1892-1934,* Skrifter utgivna av Ekonomisk-historiska Föreningen i Lund.

Erlander, Tage (1976), *1955-1960,* Tiden, Stockholm.

Erlander, Tage (1979), *Sjuttiotal,* Tiden, Stockholm.

Government (1951), Proposition 135 to the Riksdag, 'Angående anslag för budgetåret 1951/52 till arbetsmarknadsstyrelsen och den offentliga arbetsförmedlingen'.

Government (1952), Proposition 127 to the Riksdag, 'Angående anslag för budgetåret 1952/53 till arbetsmarknadsstyrelsen och den offentliga arbetsförmedlingen m.m.'.

Johansson, Anders L. (1992), *Gunnar Sträng Landsvägsagitatorn,* Tiden, Stockholm.

LO (1951), Answer to the Government's referral for consideration of '1950 års arbetsförmedling'.

LO (1951a), *Fackföreningsrörelsen och den fulla sysselsättningen,* Stockholm.

Ohlsson, Björn (1958), 'Tillkomsten av arbetarrörelsens efterkrigsprogram', *Statsvetenskaplig tidskrift,* pp. 38-55.

Ohlsson, Rolf and Jonas Olofsson (1998), *Arbetslöshetens dilemma,* SNS Förlag, Stockholm.

Öhman, Berndt (1970), Svensk arbetsmarknadspolitik 1900-1947, Prisma, Stockholm.

Olli, Åsa (1996), *Arbetsmarknadspolitiskt kalendarium,* Report from EFA, no. 44.

Rehn, Gösta (1977), 'Finansministrarna, LO-ekonomerna och arbetsmarknadspolitiken', in Jan Herin and Lars Werin (eds), *Ekonomisk debatt och ekonomisk politik, nationalekonomiska föreningen 100 år,* Norstedts, Stockholm, pp. 201-27.

Rothstein, Bo (1989), 'Att organisera arbetsmarknadspolitik' in Eskil Wadensjö, Åke Dahlberg and Bertil Holmlund (eds), *Vingarnas trygghet,* Dialogos, Lund, pp. 108-30.

1937 års arbetslöshetssakkunnigas betänkande (1939), Draft version of final report, 363 pages (Riksarkivet).

1950 års Arbetsförmedlingsutredning (1950), Del I. Den offentliga arbetsförmedlingens organisation, mimeo, December 1950.

1950 års Arbetsförmedlingsutredning (1951), Del II. Den offentliga arbetsförmedlingens krisorganisation, mimeo, January 31, 1951.

1950 års Arbetsförmedlingsutredning (1951a), Del III. Arbetsförmedlingsorganisationen i Stor-Stockholm, mimeo, June 20, 1951.

1950 års Arbetsförmedlingsutredning (1951b), Del IV. Arbetsmarknadsstyrelsens organisation, mimeo, November 11, 1951.

1950 års Arbetsförmedlingsutredning (1951c), Vissa detaljfrågor, mimeo, December 28, 1951.

Chapter 2

A Swedish Economic Policy – The Rehn-Meidner Model's Theory, Application and Validity*

Lennart Erixon

Introduction

The Swedish economists Gösta Rehn and Rudolf Meidner made a unique contribution to macroeconomics in developing the Rehn-Meidner model (R-M model). Their model is one of the few coherent visions of economic policy beyond Keynesianism. Its scope, where means and priorities of economic policy are concerned, has not been fully acknowledged even by friendly observers of the Swedish system. The R-M model is both an economic and wage policy programme and a theory of wages, profits, inflation and growth. In this discussion I shall briefly describe the content of the policy programme and its comprehensiveness and attempt to show its reliance on market-conforming measures to achieve full employment, price stability, growth and equity. I will then outline the positive economic theory behind the R-M policy model with a particular eye to the strategic role of profits in its theory of wages and inflation. A cursory comparison is made with modern wage theories (for a more detailed comparison, as well as findings from studies in the 1980s and 90s that put the hypotheses of the model to test see Erixon 2000).

The components of the Rehn-Meidner policy model, which are analyzed here, are identical to the original with one exception: the use of marginal employment subsidies. In the 1970s Rehn considered these subsidies to be effective measures in achieving full employment with price stability. However, it should be noted that, wage-earner funds are not understood as a component of the R-M model.

We begin with a description of the macroeconomic conditions and predominant economic policy ideas in Sweden at the time of the formulation of the R-M model. We see the provocative character of the model in the age of Keynesianism as well as the economic circumstances that shaped the model. The main part of this chapter will be devoted to a discussion of the applications of the R-M model in Sweden. Labour market policy and solidaristic wage policy would hardly have expanded to their current scope in Sweden if Rehn and Meidner had not placed them in a larger economic and political context. The final section of the chapter contains comments on the current validity of the R-M model. Its relevance is discussed in terms of new economic and political circumstances and priorities in economic policy. Though not necessarily directly referring to the R-M model, politicians in the EU countries are attracted today by its belief that an ambitious employment policy is possible within the framework of a restrictive macroeconomic policy.

Sweden's overheated economy post-World War II

Whereas Keynesian ideas about stabilization policy gained widespread acceptance in the Western world after World War II, in Sweden the Keynesian revolution had begun even earlier. In the early 30s, the Stockholm School of Economics, which included Gunnar Myrdal and Bertil Ohlin, supported an active employment policy. Upon winning the 1932 election, the Swedish Social Democratic Party, with the agreement of the Agrarian Party, pursued a Keynesian deficit policy aimed at bringing Sweden out of the depression.[1] From 1932-76 the Social Democrats formed the government, although in coalition with the Agrarian Party during 1936-39 and 1951-57.

At the end of World War II, Swedish politicians and economists were convinced that the Western economy was on its way into a depression, just as it had been after World War I. The labour movement devised a radical Keynesian post-war programme for full employment in 1944. (Gösta Rehn was one of the secretaries of the committee that developed the programme.) But the post-war depression failed to materialize. Rapid reconstruction of Western Europe with the help of the Marshall plan favoured Swedish industry, which specialized in raw materials, semi-finished goods and investment goods. Furthermore, the end of the war unleashed a demand in Sweden for housing and consumer durable goods. Domestic companies could not expand their production capacity fast enough to meet the demand with the result that Sweden's economy became severely overheated.

In the early post-war period inflationary tendencies were reinforced by expansive economic policies. It was really not until the mid-1950s that monetary policy was used to stabilize the Swedish economy when the country strongly pursued a policy of low interest rates. From the end of the war to the middle of the 1950s fiscal policy was the prime instrument used to achieve full employment and economic stability. Although mainly counter-cyclical, fiscal policy was expansive, at least from 1947 to 1960 (Matthiessen 1971, p. 176, and Lindbeck 1975, pp. 102-6). The Social Democratic commitment to full employment meant using fiscal and monetary restraints to stabilize the Swedish economy. However, it should be noted that in some of the early post-war years expansionary fiscal policy was not a part of a conscious strategy to maintain high aggregate demand.

The government introduced in the late 1940s a number of *ad hoc* measures to curb inflation and its negative effects in line with the British Beveridge plan and the labour movement's post-war programme. To eliminate foreign inflation, the Swedish krona (SEK) was revalued by 17 per cent in 1946. Domestic inflation was tackled in 1946-48 by price controls, specific taxes on consumer goods and petroleum, higher statutory corporate taxes, and regulations placed on the construction sector. However, demand remained high and imports increased sharply, which had an adverse effect on Sweden's balance of payments. Imports were regulated in 1947, the trade unions agreed to a wage freeze in 1949-50 and the SEK was devalued by a full 30 per cent in relation to the US dollar in 1949.[2]

Devaluation, together with favourable export prices during the Korean conflict, brought about a profit boom in Sweden's industries at the beginning of the 1950s, particularly in raw materials industries. Despite the high rate of inflation, the government avoided a revaluation of the SEK and attempted instead to dampen the overheated economy by price controls, stricter rules of inventory valuation, profit freezes, by regulations affecting the construction sector and by levying duties and taxes on investments and exports. After the Korean conflict, the pace of price increases in Sweden slowed significantly as a result of a reduction in the international inflation rate coupled with high and steady productivity growth. Yet, to mitigate the economic boom in 1955-56, monetary restraints were combined with new duties on investments and increases in statutory corporate taxes and with a phasing out of the use of free depreciation allowances for machinery and equipment (Bergström 1969, pp. 66-7 and 117-23, Södersten and Lindberg 1983, p. 43 and Jonung 1993, pp. 295-300).

Swedish economic policy could be termed "Keynesian" from the end of World War II up until the late 1950s. Political decision-makers laid a strong emphasis on full employment, which was then defined in a more policy-demanding manner than in the 1930s. They pursued a counter-cyclical general economic policy with a bias towards expansionism in order to maintain full employment and used *ad hoc* measures to fight inflation and its negative effects. In addition, fiscal rather than monetary instruments were used to stabilize the economy in line with Keynes' recommendations in the *General Theory*.[3]

In those early post-war years, Swedish politicians were convinced that in the Keynesian model they had at their disposal a superior political instrument for economic stabilization. But the model had been designed, in spite of its advocacy of counter-cyclical measures, for an economy in depression and not for an overheated economy with virtually full employment.

The content of the Rehn-Meidner model

Working as LO economists, Gösta Rehn and Rudolf Meidner became more and more critical of the Keynesian policy in the early post-war period. A general policy of expansion lead to "over-employment" resulting in high absenteeism and staff turnover and a greater risk of accidents at work. It also meant inflation and negative effects on resource allocation and growth. Moreover, Keynesianism was inflationary in its effects not only on aggregate demand but also by its unpredictable and unintentional effects on distribution. An expansionary monetary and fiscal policy generates tensions between different wage earner groups and challenges the cohesion within the labour movement. A high demand for, and limited availability of, specific skills causes 'wage drift', i.e., pay in excess of those negotiated in central agreements.[4] Wage drift gives rise to demands for compensation from other groups of employees to maintain their relative wage positions: a Keynesian policy of full employment aggravates the conflict between wage earners who benefit and those who do not benefit from market forces, resulting in inflationary wage-wage spirals.

Rehn and Meidner thought that Keynesianism was a threat even to full employment. Expansive monetary or fiscal policy causes inflation and current account deficits. These problems call for a restrictive economic policy, which, in turn, causes unemployment. The two LO economists wanted to replace a Keynesian stop-go policy with a policy that permanently kept the rate of inflation under control.

According to them, in the context of Keynesian full employment policy, inflation cannot be curbed by means of regulations. Regulations can hardly be comprehensive, and from a growth and employment viewpoint, it is often the 'wrong' companies and sectors that suffer their effects. Incomes policy agreements are difficult to achieve and also ineffective in an overheated economy. They will also threaten the independent position of labour market organisations[5] and weaken the legitimacy of trade unions in the eyes of their members. Declarations of 'wage restraint' are incompatible with the main task of a trade union, which is to achieve the highest possible pay rises for their members.

In a report presented to the 1951 LO Congress entitled *The Trade Union Movement and Full Employment* (Meidner, Rehn et al. 1953), Rehn and Meidner set forth their alternative to Keynesianism. (Hereafter I equate the R-M model and the LO report, as the subsequent work of Rehn and Meidner did not add anything to the original model apart from Rehn's proposal of marginal employment subsidies and Meidner's proposal of wage earner funds.)

A salient purpose of the R-M model is to combine full employment with price stability. But the model also took as its point of departure other objectives of economic policy in the post-war period, namely growth and equity. The means and objectives of the model are shown in Figure 2.1.

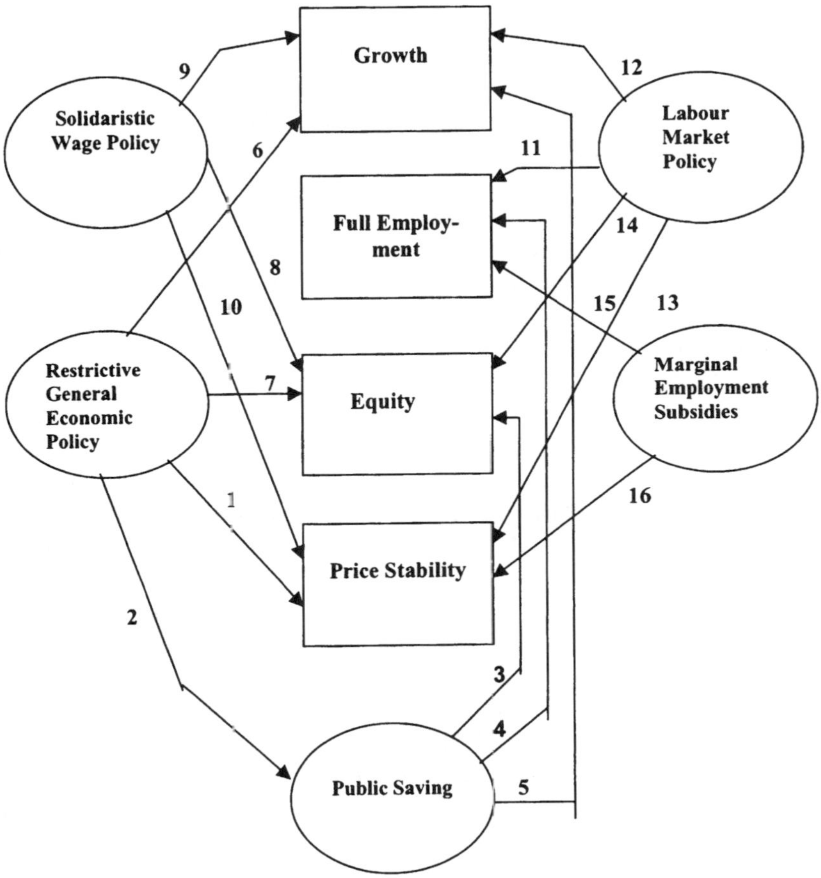

Figure 2.1 Means and objectives in the Rehn-Meidner economic and wage policy model

A restrictive fiscal policy

The R-M model advocates a restrictive general economic policy to curb the rate of inflation (arrow 1 in Figure 2.1). Rehn and Meidner gave priority to fiscal rather than monetary restraints in the 1951 LO report, but later included revaluations as appropriate tools to achieve price stability in an open economy.[6] The central idea was that fiscal policy should be predominantly tight over the business cycle. Hence, their programme for stabilization is, unlike the Keynesian strategy, more than a recommendation of fiscal restraint near full employment. Another purpose of fiscal restraint over the business cycle is to create a public saving surplus (arrow 2). In the model public saving is an intermediate goal. It is preferable to private saving in terms of income and wealth distribution (arrow 3) but also in the achievement of certain employment and growth objectives in industrial policy (arrow 4 and 5 respectively). These ambitions make public saving the least market-conforming component of the R-M model.

Rehn and Meidner also expected that a restrictive general economic policy would foster rationalizations in companies and structural change through forcing the closing of unproductive firms (arrow 6). A further objective of the tight economic policy was to support the equity principles of their model (arrow 7). By keeping down wage drift, the policy reduces the risk of wages reflecting differences in profitability between companies rather than the content of work.

Solidaristic wage policy

Solidaristic wage policy implies equal pay for equal work irrespective of the profitability of companies (arrow 8). The policy is sometimes confused with a policy of equal wages for unequal work. But it is governed by an ambition to establish fair wage differentials rather than wage equalisation in general. Wage differentials between different groups of wage earners are permitted but they should reflect 'objective' differences in working environment, responsibility, experience and education, not short-run profit or labour market conditions.

Solidaristic wage policy seems to be an example of a crude planning device, typical for the early post-war period. The policy requires a systematic comparison of jobs by central trade unions, possibly in collaboration with central employer organisations. But it can also be considered as an attempt to simulate perfect market equilibrium. This is obvious in the case of identical jobs. But wage differentials in a long-run market equilibrium can also be seen as 'fair' since they reflect real differences in work content and worker qualifications.

The equity principle of solidaristic wages had already been adopted by LO in the 1930s. But Rehn and Meidner also considered solidaristic wage policy as a mean of encouraging overall economic growth, primarily through structural change, and of alleviating inflationary wage-wage races (arrow 9 and 10 respectively).

Solidaristic wage policy, together with a restrictive general economic policy, threatens to obliterate the least profitable companies and industries. The threat leads to closures, which make it possible to transfer resources to dynamic sectors, or to rationalizations of the least profitable companies and industries. At the same time, solidaristic wage policy results in 'excess profits' in the most profitable companies and industries, which otherwise would have had to pay higher wages. These profits increase the self-financing capabilities of established profitable firms and strengthen the motivation to set up new companies in dynamic sectors. Further, larger profit differences due to solidaristic wage policy strengthens the incentives to transfer resources from low-profitability sectors to high-profitability ones.

By solidaristic wage policy, a pull mechanism is replaced by a push mechanism, or better, a rationing mechanism, in labour markets. Labour mobility is maintained by the threatened unemployment in unprofitable sectors but also by greater number of vacancies in profitable sectors. The inflow of job applicants and vacancies is seen as counter-balancing the negative effects on structural change caused by weaker pay incentives. Rehn and Meidner's preference for solidaristic wage policy was based on a conviction that wage differentials must grow large to create a significant labour mobility due to inertia in the labour market. Large wage differentials between sectors are not only unacceptable from a distribution viewpoint but they are also inflationary by causing wage-wage spirals.

Rehn and Meidner also assumed that the determination of fair wages would slow down inflationary wage races *per se*. They hoped that wage earners' demand to keep up with pay rises for other wage earners would be less intense in the absence of challenging wage differentials (Meidner and Rehn et al. 1953, p. 96, Rehn 1977, p. 216 and 1980, pp. 36 and 39-40). Hence, central bargaining would lead to wage moderation in the R-M model, but only indirectly by creating the conditions for solidaristic wage policy.

Labour market policy

A restrictive general economic policy will, *ceteris paribus*, cause unemployment in some sectors of the economy, especially if profit conditions vary. Further, a tendency to 'structural unemployment' will show up when solidaristic wage policy is pursued. Nonetheless, Rehn and Meidner's main recommendation for achieving full employment is labour market policy measures (arrow 11).

The labour market policy can be divided into three parts, selective demand policy, supply-orientated measures, and actions to improve the matching process on the labour market. Demand-orientated measures should have the smallest possible effects on aggregate demand and therefore be directed towards specific employee groups, companies and regions. The supply side of the labour market was to be affected by the introduction of relocation and retraining grants and occupational training programmes, while public employment services would adjust job applicants to vacancies. I consider the supply- and adjustment-oriented measures as the main elements of labour market policy in the R-M model since they have objectives other than reducing open unemployment in the short run.

One objective of the supply side and matching measures is to increase or reallocate the availability of labour and to improve the labour market's ability to make adjustments. Thus, labour market policy could stimulate economic growth as well by facilitating dynamic sectors' recruitment of labour (arrow 12). In addition, labour market policy is an important weapon in the fight against inflation. Here,

Rehn and Meidner emphasised not only that the alternative employment policy, i.e. an expansionary general economic policy, is inflationary but also that labour market policy has an inflation-dampening effect (arrow 13). Stimulation of labour mobility would moderate the rate of pay rises in sectors with high demand and bottlenecks in the form of labour shortages.

It is wrong to conclude, however, that labour market policy should lead to wage reductions in the R-M model. Labour market policy prevents unemployment and therefore wage reductions in a recession. Rehn and Meidner seem to assume that these wage-increasing effects of labour market policy are decisive over the business cycle. A restrictive general economic policy is meant to counter the inflationary effects of labour market policy.

Labour market policy also plays a role in the effort to achieve greater equity (Meidner 1969, pp. 190-2). Significant wage differentials between sectors will emerge when dynamic companies try to attract labour by higher wages unless measures are undertaken to improve the mobility of labour (arrow 14). In particular, solidaristic wage policy is facilitated by means of government measures to speed up the transfer of labour from stagnating sectors to expanding sectors. By guaranteeing full employment, labour market policy should also change functional income distribution in favour of labour, and thus increase wage earners' share of value added (Rehn 1952, p. 47).

Marginal employment subsidies

Rehn's ambition in advocating marginal employment premiums was to combat unemployment and inflation by reductions in firms' marginal costs (arrow 15 and 16 respectively). The proposal is entirely in line with the supply and matching oriented labour market policy. In the case of labour market policy, expansive companies are relieved of some of the cost of recruiting and up-grading their workforce. However, the intention behind marginal employment subsidies is to introduce a measure that has an immediate price-depressing effect.

Prices will be reduced by a marginal employment subsidy if product markets are competitive or if companies set their prices on the basis of marginal costs. The reduction in prices and the concomitant increase in employment would be greater for a marginal subsidy than for an intra-marginal subsidy, for instance a general reduction in pay-roll taxes. A marginal subsidy will also increase employment and production more than the same amount of an intra-marginal subsidy in an open economy with given world market prices (Layard and Nickell 1980, pp. 57-9, and Johnson and Layard 1986, pp. 946-9). Finally, a marginal subsidy could give new companies more encouragement to form new markets or enter established ones than would an intra-marginal subsidy (Bishop and Haveman 1981, pp. 300-17). A larger number of new companies could result in higher employment but also bring a greater downward pressure on prices.

Marginal employment premiums are not a Swedish innovation, either in practice or in theory. Rehn's contribution was to place the premiums in a stabilization policy context. The proposal induced Rehn to suggest a modification of the R-M model when unemployment rose in Western Europe in the 1970s. He recommended the use of marginal employment subsidies together with labour market programmes and measures aimed at raising effective demand. Rehn also suggested in the 1980s that not only employment but also investments and production increases in general could be given a financial support.

I use the notion of selective employment policy to cover active labour market policies and marginal employment premiums. This notion can give the wrong impression that the employment policy of the R-M model is always directed towards specific firms, regions, sectors and wage-earner groups. Such targeted measures are not included in Rehn's final proposal of marginal employment subsidies. Subsidies should be offered to firms in all regions and sectors and for all kinds of labour. It is the conditional character of marginal subsidies – they are only offered to recruiting firms – which make them selective and therefore distinct from monetary and fiscal policy measures or general reductions in payroll and profit taxes.

The uniqueness of the Rehn-Meidner model

The R-M model was certainly a radical idea in the age of Keynesianism, particularly in a country that had been a precursor of the Keynesian revolution and from a social movement committed to full employment. Two trade union economists dared to recommend a restrictive general economic policy and placed the priority of price stability on an equal footing with the priority of full employment!

The fact that the R-M model was formulated in an overheated economy determined its character. The purpose of labour market policy, including regional policy, was to eliminate the 'islands of unemployment' that was a result of a restrictive general economic policy and a solidaristic wage policy. Rehn and Meidner were not against a traditional public-deficit policy in periods of deep recession or of a counter-cyclical policy in general. But the model's advocacy of a tight fiscal policy goes beyond a qualified Keynesian recommendation that, near full employment, expansionary measures should be cautiously used, or even replaced by fiscal and monetary restraints. Fiscal policy was to be predominantly restrictive throughout the business cycle to set the framework for stabilization policy. The struggle against inflation was not to be called off even in periods of high unemployment; expansionary fiscal and monetary policies had to be complemented with inflation-dampening measures such as marginal employment subsidies.

But the R-M model is also unique in terms of its comprehensive view of economic policy. First, one of the model's advantages is that it embraces all the objectives of post-war economic policy: full employment, price stability, growth and equity. Modern macroeconomic models consider at most two objectives, often price stability and full employment.

Second, the R-M model deviates from most macroeconomic models by allotting at least two tasks to each instrument as illustrated by Figure 1. For instance, labour market policy has four objectives, to achieve full employment, to speed up structural change, to hold back price and wage increases caused by labour-market bottlenecks or high profit margins, and to facilitate solidaristic wage policy. And, according to the model, labour market policy has a further redistribution task – full employment shall alter functional income distribution in favour of labour by increasing its negotiation strength, both collectively and individually.

Third, the instruments of the R-M model are complementary in the sense that some measures must be introduced in the model to alleviate the side effects of other measures. For example, a restrictive economic policy and a solidaristic wage policy will generate unemployment unless labour market policy measures are introduced. But more specifically, a partial application of the model is discouraged by the fact that some measures are effective only when used together with other measures. The principle of solidaristic wage policy must be supported by labour market policy measures and a restrictive economic policy to keep wage drift under control. Further, solidaristic wage policy will only put pressure on 'marginal' firms to rationalize if combined with a restrictive general economic policy. Labour market policy might be a necessary condition for a relationship between a solidaristic wage policy and structural change – labour resources can be released through solidaristic wage policy – but labour market policy may be needed to transfer the resources to expanding firms and sectors. There are other complementarities in the R-M model. Fair wages through solidaristic wage policy will not restrain inflation significantly unless a restrictive economic policy and a labour market policy are launched simultaneously. Moreover, profit margins cannot be reduced permanently by a restrictive general economic policy alone but must be combined with a policy for full employment.

Fourth, the R-M model has the advantage of linking together both short and long-term analysis by assuming that labour market, fiscal and monetary policies all influence growth. Here, the model avoids the one-sided Keynesian view of a positive relationship between profit and demand on the one hand, and productivity growth on the other. Rehn and Meidner did not deny that a restrictive general economic policy might reduce productivity growth if private investments are hampered or if static economics of scale exist (Rehn 1982, pp. 4-5). But according to their model, a restrictive economic policy may quite simply result in high productivity growth through rationalization and structural change.

Of course, none of this proves that the R-M model is still relevant for decisions about economic policy. But we can only address this once we have appreciated the model in its own right, in terms of its logic and all-embracing character.

Wages and inflation in the Rehn-Meidner model

The central role of profits

In the R-M model, the main purpose of the tight fiscal policy is to force down profits and profit margins. Rehn and Meidner expected that a general profit squeeze would speed up rationalizations and structural change. They were also convinced that profits are the significant driving force in the process of inflation. High profits lead to a substantial amount of wage drift, in turn triggering demands for corresponding wage increases from other groups. Profit margins should also be squeezed in the medium and long term to establish a permanent downward pressure on the rate of inflation. Rehn and Meidner envisioned labour market policies and other selective employment measures preventing price reductions under a restrictive general economic policy being met by nominal wage reductions. One could respond that profit margins in a single country can be depressed by a full-employment policy without the support of a tight fiscal policy; the possibilities to mark up wage increases due to labour market policy being limited in an open economy (see Erixon 2000, pp. 38-42).

The 1951 LO report does not state why profits and profit margins are of central importance in wage formation. Rehn has elaborated on this in other writings, for instance in an article he wrote together with Bent Hansen (Hansen and Rehn 1956) where the focus was on firms' competition for scarce labour. Fundamental to the Rehn-Hansen article is the role of marginal productivity theory. Wages are determined in a competitive labour market by prices, adjusted for the degree of monopoly, and physical marginal productivity. A positive demand shock (or a higher marginal productivity) will lead to wage drift since there are anticipated profits from employing more workers at the initial wage rate.

Hence, wage drift is explained by marginal profits, not by average profits in the Rehn-Hansen article. This theoretical approach results in a 'Rehnian paradox' when marginal employment subsidies are included in the R-M model. From the Rehn-Hansen perspective, the aim of a tight economic policy is to squeeze marginal profits. But marginal employment subsidies are an instrument to increase marginal profitability. The 'Rehnian paradox' can only be solved if wage drift is largely determined by actual profits.

There are some ambiguities in Rehn and Meidner's discussion of the relation between actual profits and wages, but my presentation follows the overall spirit of the model concentrating upon those explanations by Rehn and Meidner in which companies and managers, not wage earners, are the main actors. Further, in all explanations except one, higher profits will lead to wage increases by intensifying companies' competition for labour and hence, the relation is associated with an 'upward' shift in the labour demand function.

In the first line of argument, higher actual profits extend the self-financing capacity of companies that in turn stimulate labour demand. There are two possible mechanisms in the R-M model. First, higher actual profits lead to higher investments, as companies' capital costs are reduced. Second, higher actual profits intensify non-investing companies' competition for labour since they have greater financial opportunities to offer higher wages to keep key employees from being hired away by competing firms.

The second Rehn-Meidner argument for a positive relationship between profits and wages is based on the notion of X-inefficiencies. Managers of the companies will reward themselves and their employees higher wages than their efforts merit when actual profits are high. Hence, high profits make employers more careless with regard to wage payments (Hansen and Rehn 1956, p. 89).

These explanations of a relationship between actual profits and wages are distinct from the ones in modern bargaining and fair wage-effort theories. In the latter theories, the 'wage-setting' curve, not the labour-demand curve, shifts upward when profits become higher. In the bargaining theory, higher profits will automatically induce wage increases through a 'rent-sharing' agreement between employees and employers (Cristofides and Oswald 1992, and Blanchflower, Oswald and Sanfey 1996). In the fair wage-effort theory, higher profits accruing to the firms' owners will provoke higher wage claims; wage earners' interest in fair wages is not only based on concerns for wage distribution but also for functional income distribution. These claims are met because employers are afraid that workers otherwise will be less productive (Akerlof and Yellen 1990).

Relative wage preferences, including concerns for functional income distribution, are equally important in the R-M model. In addition, a hypothesis by Rehn and Hansen that high profits make employees more eager to exploit the wage-paying capacity of companies is similar to the fair wage-effort theory. Another hypothesis by Rehn and Hansen that higher average productivity through technical improvements will benefit employees as an 'institutional habit' can be associated with the rent-sharing view (Hansen and Rehn 1956, pp. 89-90 and 96-7). Rehn was strongly influenced by the bargaining theory in the 1980s (Rehn 1982). Yet, I will insist on that the positive relation between actual profits and wages is essentially explained in terms of labour demand and X-inefficiencies in the Rehn-Meidner wage theory. Besides, the hypothesis in the fair wage-effort theory that employers accept higher wage claims since they are afraid that employees will otherwise punish them by a worse performance has no correspondence in the writings of Rehn and Meidner. In their wage model, firms' willingness to offer wages above the competitive level when profits are high reflects that they are X-inefficient.

Relative wage preferences and wage-wage spirals

The hypothesis of a positive relationship between profits and wages forms the basis of the Rehn-Meidner inflation theory. Positive demand shocks will lead to higher nominal wages in competitive labour markets since they will result in (anticipated) gains from recruiting labour and also in higher actual profits that intensify wage competition among firms. Wage drift will later be followed by collective wage increases, reflecting the trade unions' concern about relative wages and the fact that wage increases through market forces are partly captured by the collective wage process.

The assumption that wage earners and their unions care about relative wages is fundamental in the R-M model as in the *General Theory* and the modern theory of fair wages (Akerlof and Yellen 1990). Wage earners compare themselves with wage earners in other occupations within the same firm and in other firms. Rehn and Meidner claimed that incomes policy will be undermined in an overheated economy by the combination of wage drift and compensatory wage claims and by the fact that relative wage preferences are easier to satisfy when unemployment is low and actual profits are high. In good times, it is tempting for trade unions to resist participating in incomes policy agreements and for employers to accept wage increases above the levels of profit maximisation.

The question is why in the R-M model the economy exhibits continued wage rises and inflation. The model never deals explicitly with the reasons why, when its equilibrium is disturbed, an economy changes from a condition of wage and price rises to a condition of galloping inflation. A wage-wage spiral will emerge if employees in the open sector succeed, wholly or partly, to re-establish the wage lead they initially gained through wage drift.

A reasonable hypothesis is that mark up pricing also takes place in the open sector, at least in parts of it. Companies in the exposed sector will accept new wage increases, as they are able to pass them over to customers. An alternative hypothesis is that companies in the exposed sector are forced to accept wage rises or even take initiatives to wage increases that cannot be passed on. In the 'voluntary' case, the behaviour of companies may reflect a lack of information about market conditions, or that the initial profit increase provides scope for 'unearned' rewards for the employees.

It seems, however, that the above arguments offer a weak case for a sustainable wage-wage-price spiral. The process is counter-balanced by monetary restraints unless an accommodating economic policy is pursued. The room for mark up pricing must also be limited in the open sector. Besides, the firms in the open sector will gain information about market conditions and refuse to give 'unearned' wage increases to employees when their profits are depressed. The existence of counter-acting forces in the wage-wage-price process does not exclude the existence of such processes, at least temporarily, in a country like Sweden.

The Rehn-Meidner model in practice

The comparison between the R-M model and the practice of Swedish economic policy is based on my interpretation and not on a systematic analysis of Rehn and Meidner's view of contemporary economic and wage policies. This strategy is not without complications even if the model is relatively unambiguous and the founders never abandoned its central ideas. The model cannot possibly be used as a yardstick under all political and economic conditions. As conditions change, the usefulness of the Rehn-Meidner policy model may diminish. But the model can be used as a normative benchmark for analysing Swedish economic policy in the post-war period.

It is difficult to formulate any definite answers to the question of whether the R-M model was put into practice in Sweden. First, the model consists of five instruments: a restrictive general economic policy, labour market policy, marginal employment premiums, solidaristic wage policy, and public saving. The model has not been applied in all its respects during any post-war period of time. Second, the recommendations in the R-M model have sometimes coincided with those of other models – economic policy only appeared to be inspired by the R-M model, making it often difficult to distinguish the true motives and rudders of economic policy actions. Third, in certain periods, macro policy reflected the difficulties of Keynesian 'fine tuning' rather than an application of the R-M model – a restrictive economic policy was an indication of a wrongly directed Keynesian policy. Yet, despite these reservations, it is possible to discern a 'Golden Age' for the R-M model, from the end of the 1950s until the first oil crisis.

The Golden Age

Sweden showed a relatively good macroeconomic performance in the Golden Age. It is true that neither GDP per capita growth, nor production growth in manufacturing, were exceptionally high in an international perspective, especially from the mid-1960s to 1972 (Historical Statistics, OECD, 1982, table 3.2 and 3.5). But the country succeeded better than most other OECD countries in combining low wage and price rises with low unemployment at the end of the 1960s when the international rate of inflation increased (Historical Statistics, OECD, 1982, table 2.15, 8.11 and 9.8). The Phillips curve became relatively favourable for Sweden, despite a decline in mobility in the Swedish labour market at that time.

Productivity growth in Swedish manufacturing was high, although not exceptional, compared with other OECD countries in the Golden Age (Erixon 1991, p. 245). As well, structural change in manufacturing was rapid in Sweden in the 1960s and early 70s particularly compared with large OECD countries (Fries 1983, pp. 143-7, Nilsson and Zetterberg 1987, pp. 17-19, and Andersson, Gustafsson and Lundberg 1998, pp. 3-4 and 9-10). The extent of structural change is calculated here as an index of movements in employment between industries.

It seems also that the R-M model was a lodestar for economic policy in the Swedish Golden Age. The Social Democratic government pursued a vigorous labour market policy in the recession years of 1957 and 1958. In the 1960s, there was a substantial increase in labour market policy, mostly from the middle of that decade. At the time of the first oil crisis, expenditure on active labour market policy including regional policy measures totalled 2.4 per cent of GDP. The percentage was higher in Sweden than in the other OECD countries (Johannesson 1991, and SOU 1993:43, p. 125).

The development of labour market policy was compatible with the R-M model. From the end of the 1950s to the beginning of the 70s, the greatest increase was in adjustment and supply oriented measures, i.e. measures that aimed to stimulate occupational and geographical mobility. The proportion of the Labour Market Board's budget (excluding cash assistance) spent on these measures increased from 15 per cent in 1960 to one third in fiscal year 1973/74. The Labour Market Board's proportion of government expenditure also increased constantly from 1960 to 1973; during the 1950s this percentage had varied with the business cycle.

Monetary and fiscal policies were counter-cyclical, at least until the mid-1960s.[7] But general economic policy was more restrictive, compared with the preceding post-war period, from the end of the 1950s to the beginning of the 1970s, fully in line with the R-M model as far as fiscal policy is concerned (Matthiessen 1971, p. 176, Lindbeck 1975, p. 104, Jonung 1993, pp. 298-303 and 346-8, and Calmfors 1993, p. 45). The monetary and fiscal policies in the recessions of 1966-68 and 1970-72 were, from a Keynesian viewpoint, far too austere. Fiscal policy in these recessions was, respectively, close to neutral and deflationary. Labour market policy, not Keynesian stimulation policy, prevented a significant increase in Swedish unemployment. Rehn praised the government for countering the trend towards higher unemployment with an active labour market policy rather than using an expansive fiscal policy (Rehn 1977, p. 223). The Minister of Finance, Gunnar Sträng, declared in the midst of the 1970-72 recession that employment policy must by necessity be selective since a Keynesian stimulation policy inevitably would lead to inflation and competitive disadvantages in an open economy (Budget Bill 1971, pp. 19-20, and the Revised Budget Bill 1971, p. 11).

The co-ordination of wage negotiations in the mid-1950s gave the LO the opportunity to pursue a solidaristic wage policy. From the early 1960s until the mid-1970s pay equalisation between and within industries and plants and between the sexes was more far-reaching in Sweden than in any other OECD country (Ohlsson 1980, and Hibbs and Locking 2000).[8] There was not only a widespread pay equalisation among blue-collar workers but also, in the 1970s, among white-collar workers (Jonsson and Siven 1984, pp. 430-1). Market forces alone cannot explain this radical reduction of wage gaps in Sweden, thus central bargaining and wage policies must have been important.

A quantitative study has shown that wage equalisation between industries and plants in Sweden led to a significant increase both in blue-collar labour productivity and in output in the private business sector. Hence, the study confirms a theory that structural change is enhanced by solidaristic wage policy (Hibbs and Locking 2000).[9]

The public sector's share of total savings increased sharply in Sweden, from 35 per cent in 1962 to 44 per cent in 1972. No other OECD country had a corresponding increase in public saving. Further, in the 1960s and the early 1970s, there was a decline in actual rates of return and the profit share of value added in Swedish manufacturing. The fall in profit rates and profit shares was sharper in Sweden than in other OECD countries according to estimates based on national accounts. Table 2.1 shows that the trend coefficients for gross profit shares in manufacturing was higher in Sweden than in eight other OECD countries in 1955-72 – see the first column (Erixon 1987, pp. 49-54; 1991, pp. 285-93). The profit decline and increase in public saving in Sweden was entirely in line with the R-M model.

Table 2.1 Gross operating surplus as a ratio of gross value added in manufacturing. Trend coefficients for 9 OECD countries in 1955-97

	1955-72	1955-90	1955-97
Sweden	-0.6 (-9.3)	-0.2 (-2.6)	0.0 (0.1)
Denmark	-0.1 (-1.5)	0.0 (0.6)	0.2 (4.2)
Finland (1)	-0.4 (-1.8)	0.0 (0.6)	0.2 (3.0)
Netherlands	-0.5 (-4.6)	-0.3 (-3.0)	0 (0.2)
West-Germany	-0.5 (-7.3)	-0.5 (-13.6)	-0.5 (-17.7)
Great Britain	-0.3 (-8.0)	-0.1 (-2.3)	0 (0.1)
United States	0.0 (-0.2)	0.0 (0.0)	0.1 (2.8)
Canada	-0.3 (-4.5)	0.0 (-0.9)	---
Japan	0.2 (2.0)	-0.4 (-7.3)	-0.5 (-11.1)

Notes: (1) Initial year: 1960. t-statistics in brackets.
Sources: OECD, National Accounts, volume II and Eurostat database.

The Social Democratic government was undoubtedly influenced by Rehn and Meidner's ideas in the field of labour market policy (Rehn 1977, pp. 222-4, and Erixon 1997b, p. 640). This policy was not new, either in Sweden or in other countries, but Rehn and Meidner linked it directly to stabilization and growth. Price stability and structural change became important arguments for more expenditures on labour market policy in general and on supply oriented measures in particular.

Similar conclusions may be drawn in the case of the solidaristic wage policy. By the 1930s the LO adopted the principle of a wage policy based on solidarity. The Swedish trade union movement also accepted at an early stage that international competition and structural transformation could eliminate companies and even entire sectors. The R-M model provided the LO with arguments that their own wage policy could accelerate structural change and that its negative effects on employment could be lessened by labour market policy measures.

But the attempts to introduce a uniform evaluation of job content and conditions in the Swedish labour market in the Golden Age were not successful. In the absence of a consensus about fair wage differentials, the LO gave a special priority to the low wage-earner brackets in general from the late 1960s. In practice, solidaristic wage policy followed the principle of 'equal pay for unequal work' as much as the original principle of 'equal pay for equal work' (Arai 1994, Hibbs and Locking 2000). The LO argued that the policy indirectly satisfied the ideal of solidaristic wage policy – actual wage differentials between occupations were too large to be explained or justified by 'objective' job differences. A similar commitment to wage equality in general was made by the central private white-collar union cartel, PTK.

Economic policy in the Golden Age did not satisfy the principles of the R-M model in all respects and its practice during certain recessionary periods was not followed. Fiscal policy was generally expansive from the end of the 1950s to the beginning of the 1970s, just as in the immediate post-war years, rather than predominantly tight as recommended by Rehn and Meidner. Further, the deflationary effects of macro policy in the 1966-68 and 1970-72 recessions mainly reflected the difficulties of implementing Keynesian fine-tuning and not the influence of the R-M model. Actions to counteract the previous economic booms by restrictive policies were taken too late, worsening the effects of the subsequent recessions. Hence, the combination of general restraints and active labour market policy programmes in the recessions is by and large explained by a misdirected countercyclical economic policy (Matthiessen 1971, pp. 205-23, and Söderström 1990, pp. 63-7). The government's fear of public budget deficits, miscalculations of aggregate demand and attempts to reduce current account deficits inherited from the boom periods also explain this policy combination. This Golden Age was characterized by a Keynesian 'stop-go' policy, with alternating economic-political priorities not fulfilling the requirements of the R-M model. Furthermore, the use of price controls in the early 1970s to avoid inflation was not in accordance with the R-M model.

The tendency for profitability to decrease during the Golden Age was not the result of a tougher economic policy, as in the R-M model, but of keener international competition and ever-deeper international recessions. After all, the tendency toward profitability decline was an international phenomenon. Wage adjustments to sharper international competition and deeper recessions might have been prevented by a labour-market policy of full employment in Sweden as predicted by the R-M model. But full employment also prevailed in other OECD countries with low expenditures on labour market policy. We should note that the decline in the rate of return in Swedish manufacturing is halved if profit taxes are accounted for (Erixon 1987, pp. 38-9).[10] Thus, Swedish economic policy actively counter-balanced the tendency to a profit decline, particularly for large companies and capital-intensive industries (Södersten 1971, pp. 324-5 and 329).

Finally, the government's decision to meet deficits in the current account, and in the capital account, during the peaks of the mid and late 1960s by restrictive monetary and fiscal policies, rather than a devaluation of the SEK, was not influenced by the R-M model. Sweden's unwillingness to devalue is better explained by the absence of major external balance problems.

The sharp increase in public savings in Sweden in the 1960s was not a result of a restrictive economic policy. This upswing is largely explained by the introduction of a compulsory service pension scheme (the ATP system) though Rehn's argument for collective capital formation greatly influenced the final shape of the system (Meidner 1988, p. 465).

To summarize, it is possible to demonstrate a direct relationship in terms of labour market policy and solidaristic wage policy between the R-M model and the economic and wage policy pursued in Sweden over a 15-year period beginning in 1957-58. Besides, public saving became more important and profits fell in this period as advocated by the model, and the general economic policy during the last two recessions was shaped as if the model had been used. But public saving, a profit decline, and a contractionary economic policy in the recessions were not the result of a strict application of the model. Moreover, a Rehn-Meidner policy of fair wage differentials was associated with a radical policy of general wage equalisations from the late 1960s.

Departures from the Rehn-Meidner model in the 1970s and 80s

As were other small Western European countries, Sweden was exposed to substantial external pressure from 1973 to 1982 in the form of two oil crises, a restrictive economic policy in major OECD countries and intensive competition from both Japan and the NICs. Sweden's export specialisation in input and investment goods was also disadvantageous in a period of deep international recession. But just as in other OECD countries, Sweden then experienced a prolonged period of high economic activity in the 1980s.

Though Sweden's macroeconomic performance worsened, there is little evidence of a specific Swedish economic disease from the mid-1970s to 1990. The Swedish inflation rate rose above that in the Golden Age and also that in Germany, but until the late 1980s it stayed very close to the OECD and EU average. In the second half of the 1970s and the early 1980s when unemployment rose in the EU countries, however, Sweden managed to avoid high unemployment, and accompanying hysteresis effects in the labour market. The trade-off between unemployment and inflation was therefore still favourable for Sweden in an international perspective at least until the very last years of the 1980s.

As in other OECD countries, productivity growth in Sweden was lower in the period from the mid-1970s to the early 1990s than in the previous period. Labour productivity growth in manufacturing was also lower in Sweden than in competing countries. Sweden's relative welfare position in terms of GDP per capita gradually deteriorated in the 1970s and 80s. The country moved steadily down from fifth to ninth place between 1973 and 1990 in GDP per capita (in purchasing power parities) among OECD countries (OECD National Accounts, Volume I, 1998, p. 162).

There were breaks with the R-M model in the 1970s and 80s but the departure was by no means definitive. The scope of active labour market policy was extensive, irrespective of the level of economic activity and the colour of the government. The Social Democratic government tried to bridge the 1974-76 international recession by a combination of labour market policy and a Keynesian deficit policy. The emphasis on labour market policy continued under non-socialist governments between 1976 and 1982. Expenditure on labour market measures went up from 2 per cent of GDP in fiscal year 1974/75 to 3.7 per cent when unemployment rose in 1977/78. Following a slight reduction, a record share was achieved during the recession of the early 1980s.

Overall, the direction of labour market policy can also not be criticized from the perspective of the R-M model. Possibly some subsidies to firms aimed at 'securing jobs' in the mid-1970s, above all assistance for stockpiling and company training to avoid dismissals, were too defensive to fall within the framework of the R-M model (see however Rehn's defence of the policy, Rehn 1977, p. 226). This defensive labour market policy was a complement to the Employment Security Act, which was applied from 1974. But the share of the supply and adjustment oriented measures of active labour market policy increased steadily in the 1970s with a break only in the middle of the decade. The proportion of demand-oriented measures increased in the economic slump of the early 1980s through extensive relief work programmes. But these programmes were rapidly cut back in favour of measures which targeted 'problem groups' in the labour market during the next economic upswing. In line with the R-M model, the proportion of labour market policy measures aimed at stimulating supply and adjustments in the labour market increased in the boom years of the 1980s.

The general economic policy, including exchange rate policy, was too expansive from 1973 to 1990 according to the R-M model. A 'profit boom' occurred in Swedish manufacturing in 1973 and 1974 caused mainly by an international price increase in raw materials and high international demand for investment goods. The profit and export boom was not mitigated by a revaluation of the SEK. As expected under the R-M model, the profit and export boom caused a 'wage cost crisis' through extensive wage drift and 'collective' demand for compensation in 1974-76. The wage cost crisis contributed to a severe downswing in the rate of return and in profit shares in Swedish manufacturing in 1975-77. Similar cost and profitability crises occurred in other OECD countries especially if they had experienced a sharp increase in profits in the previous years.

The Social Democratic government attempted to bridge the recession after the first oil crisis with a Keynesian deficit policy – a policy that included a reduction in VAT in 1974 and a tax transfer. Next, the non-socialist coalition government devalued the SEK, once in 1976 and twice more (by about 16 per cent) in 1977. The deficit in the current account had increased sharply in Sweden in the mid-1970s as oil prices rose and domestic demand pressure became fairly intense.

The Keynesian aspects of the bridging policies of 1974-76 and the devaluations 1976-77 could possibly pass through the eye of the Rehn-Meidner needle. But fiscal policy was too expansive during the recovery in 1979-80, which helped create a growing central government budget deficit. Although monetary policy became increasingly restrictive, as in many other OECD countries, real rates of interest were negative from the first oil crisis to the second oil crisis in 1979-80.[11]

Sweden managed to avoid high unemployment in the second half of the 1970s and the early 1980s by applying labour market policy measures together with a defensive industrial policy and an expansive fiscal and monetary policy.[12] At the time of the second oil crisis and the recession of the early 1980s, doubts were raised in Sweden about a Keynesian policy aimed at maintaining aggregate domestic demand. But this reassessment did not result in a stricter application of the R-M model. The main purpose of the 'new' economic policy was to eliminate current-account deficits by strengthening cost competitiveness as well as transferring resources to the private sector by stimulating industrial profits. The reorientation of Swedish economic policy was mainly explained by the profitability crisis and the large losses of market shares for Swedish export industry in the second half of the 1970s, the losses largely attributed in the Swedish debate to the 'wage cost crisis'.

A devaluation of the SEK by the new Social Democratic government in 1982, and to some extent by the non-socialist government the year before, were the main expressions of this new economic policy. The devaluation policy was the cornerstone of the Social Democrats' 'Third Way' (Erixon 1989, and Jonung 1999, pp. 191-4). The devaluations by 10 and 16 per cent respectively, taken together with a strong dollar and an international economic upswing (the Reagan boom), lay behind a remarkable profit recovery in Swedish manufacturing in the first half of the 1980s. The rate of return and profit share in Swedish industries became high by international and historical standards in the middle of the 1980s (Erixon 1991, pp. 281-93 and 365).

The profit-oriented stabilization and growth policies did not constitute a clear break with the Keynesian model, as one of their aims was to increase aggregate demand, but were not consistent with the R-M model. The devaluation in 1982 was far too large – Swedish cost competitiveness had already been restored through the 1981 devaluation – and the subsequent fiscal policy not tight enough to meet the requirements of the R-M model. Besides, the SEK was not revaluated in the mid-1980s in spite of favourable external circumstances presented by the absence of a deficit in the current account. A revaluation should have prevented an export-led overheating of the economy.[13]

Measured by the Rehn-Meidner yardstick, the economic policy of the latter 1980s was also too expansive. Automatic depreciations of the SEK, through its strong link to the dollar, maintained cost advantages for Sweden and high profits in the country's exposed sector. Swedish overheating was amplified by a domestic product demand and asset-price boom caused by a deregulation of the credit market and a tax system which made household saving unattractive. Fiscal policy did become more restrictive, and together with built-in stabilizers it eliminated the deficit in the public sector's financial saving in 1987. Public sector financial savings from 1987 to 1990 were equivalent to 4-5 per cent of GDP, a much higher share than in other OECD countries with the exception for Finland. But if the lower rate of household saving and the ongoing export boom are taken into consideration, fiscal policy was not restrictive enough to balance the credit deregulation and the absence of a sufficiently tight interest-rate policy by the Swedish Central Bank.[14]

Sweden's low level of unemployment in the 1980s reflected the priorities set out in the R-M model, but only parts of the model were applied in practice. The main explanation of Sweden's low level of open unemployment during the long peak is excess aggregate demand. Consequently, Sweden's low rates of unemployment were obtained at the expense of a relatively high rate of inflation and it could therefore not be explained by trade-union wage moderation (Calmfors 1993, pp. 44-53, and Lindbeck 1997, pp. 1308-9). Neither is Sweden's low unemployment in the 1980s explained by labour market policies. Expenditures on labour market policies as a ratio of GDP declined steadily from the mid-1980s to 1990 (Calmfors 1993, pp. 28-9, and SOU 1993:43, table 3.1 and 3.2).

The most obvious challenge of the R-M model in the 1980s was the departure from solidaristic wage policy. The trend towards a smaller wage spread in the area covered by agreements between the LO and the Swedish Employers' Confederation (SAF) had ended by the middle of the 1970s, and, in the mid-1980s wage differences between and within industries and plants increased sharply. Wage gaps grew not only among wage earners with different jobs but also for some with identical jobs and skills, which constituted the real challenge of the R-M model (Ohlsson 1980, Faxén, Odhner and Spånt 1988, pp. 54-6, and Hibbs and Locking 1996 and 2000).

The 1970s and, particularly, the 1980s are decades of a Swedish departure, although not an absolute one, from the R-M model. Fiscal and monetary policies were too expansionary, resulting in a strong reliance on incomes policy, and the governments did not give priority to public saving. Solidaristic wage policy was challenged by decentralized bargaining and profit booms in the 1980s, but wage differentials were still small by international standards at the end of the decade. The labour market policy is a salient explanation of why Sweden did not take the road to massive unemployment in the 1970s and early 1980s. Some Swedish economists accused labour market policy, especially relief work, of being inflationary and, therefore, for being harmful for employment as well – the policy leads to higher wage claims and lower job search intensity (Calmfors and Forslund 1990, Holmlund 1990, Calmfors 1993). But expenditure on relief work and 'defensive' demand-oriented measures directed to firms was only approximately half of total expenditure on active labour market policy in the 1970s and early 1980s. Matching and supply oriented measures and measures targeting problem groups in the labour market were probably less inflationary (Forslund 1994, Calmfors 1995). Besides, the avoidance of open unemployment in the mid-1970s and the early 1980s prevented hysteresis effects on Swedish labour markets.

The end of full employment

Under a Social Democratic regime in 1991, a period of exceptionally high economic activity and booming stock markets in Sweden turned into a deep recession. The recession deepened in 1992-93 under a Conservative-led coalition of non-socialist parties. Sweden experienced a more drastic decline in investments and GDP growth than all OECD countries except Finland in 1991-93. Swedish GDP growth was even negative for the three years. Total employment was reduced by more than 12 per cent from 1990 to 1994 (approximately 575,000 jobs disappeared) – only Finland suffered a larger decline. Employment in manufacturing fell by almost one fourth in the period. With only modest recovery until 1998, Sweden fell from ninth place in 1990 to nineteenth place in 1997 on the OECD ranking list of GDP per capita. By 1993, open unemployment had risen above 9 per cent and was only approximately 1.5 percentage points lower than the EU average according to standardized OECD data. Swedish unemployment remained at this high level until 1998 in spite of a Social Democratic government from autumn 1994, an international recovery and a Swedish export boom. Hence, Sweden, the very example of a full employment economy, had joined the group of countries with massive unemployment.

From the angle of the R-M model, the serious macroeconomic problems in Sweden in the early 1990s were grounded in the preceding boom. The model assumes that a state of full employment cannot be long-lived if achieved through high aggregate demand – serious overheating, as the one in the 1980s, will inevitably lead to cost and profitability crises. It seems that this view is confirmed by Swedish experience. In 1988-91, there was a significant increase in Swedish relative unit labour costs and decrease in the rate of return and profit shares in Swedish manufacturing. Further, the dramatic employment decline in manufacturing in 1991-93 largely reflected 'over-employment' tendencies and the low priority of rationalization for firms during the boom of the 1980s. The willingness and potential to raise labour productivity by lay-off was exceptionally high in Swedish industries in the recession of the early 1990s.

High domestic demand of the late 1980s, which had primarily benefited the construction industry and the private service sector, was reversed in the early 1990s. Real estate, construction and financial companies in particular were seriously hit by declining demand and asset prices, and by higher capital costs. There was an exceptional increase in firm bankruptcies in 1991-92, especially as an excessive number of new businesses had expanded with high debt ratios in the preceding decade. Liquidations, and financial problems of surviving firms, led to a deep Swedish bank crisis, at that time comparable only to the Finnish one. The financial crisis was soon resolved, but the rise in real rates of interest paved the way for an exceptional increase in Swedish household saving rates in the first half of the 1990s.

Social Democratic policy in the beginning of the crisis

In May 1991, the Social Democratic government tried to restore lost confidence in the SEK by linking it to the ECU. The government also pursued a more or less neutral fiscal policy despite a downturn in the economy and the effectiveness of fiscal policy at fixed exchange rates and perfect capital mobility according to macroeconomic theory. The cuts in public expenditure under this fiscal policy reflected efforts to appease the financial market, but were also in line with theories about public crowding out. Fiscal policy was expansionary but less so than in most other OECD countries.

A Keynesian policy for full employment was finally abandoned in Sweden in the early 1990s when the Social Democratic government accepted the criticism of an 'accommodating' economic policy. The new policy was meant not only to please international capital markets but also to reduce inflationary expectations in labour markets. The Social Democratic government wanted to reduce interest-rates, prices and wages by convincing capital and labour markets that an expansionary fiscal and exchange rate policy would not be undertaken. However, the government often painted a too dark picture of Sweden's relative rate of inflation in the past.

The Social Democrats could no longer devalue. The government looked to incomes policy to restrain prices and wages. Already, when overheating reached its peak, the so-called Rehnberg Commission was formed to persuade the employers' and employees' organisations to adopt wage restraint. The commission managed to bring into being comprehensive labour market agreements in 1991-92.

The non-accommodating policy of the Social Democrats in the early 1990s was not in itself a break with the R-M model. For example, it would have been possible to claim by reference to the model that Swedish growth and price stability was promoted by a hard-currency policy. But Swedish scholars maintained that the Social Democrats abandoned their priority goal of full employment in favour of policies to fight inflation. An argument about a downgrading of the priority of full employment is primarily based on programmatic statements in the Budget Bill of January 1991 (Lindbeck 1997, p. 1303, Jonung 1999, pp. 69-85 and 211, and Johansson, Lundborg and Zetterberg 1999, pp. 2-4) and also on the practice of employment policy (SOU 1993:43, pp. 38-9 and 47). Expenditure on active labour market policy increased in the final year of the Social Democratic government but in absolute numbers this increase was more modest than the increase in cash assistance and it was not sufficiently extensive to prevent a major increase in unemployment in 1991. However, the emphasis on price stability in official documents in the early 1990s mainly reflected the government still being occupied with the negative effects of overheating rather than with an approaching recession. Further, the modest size of the active labour market programmes in 1991 indicated that the government was not yet prepared to meet the tendencies towards massive unemployment.

The Rehn-Meidner model on the 'One Way'

The new Conservative-led coalition government adopted a non-accommodating strategy. The 'One Way' (the words of Carl Bildt, the new prime minister, who used to contrast his policy to the 'Third Way') was really an extension of the Social Democratic policy of the 1990s, which involved structural reforms (including deregulations and cuts in public transfers and taxes), a fixed exchange rate and a tight fiscal policy. But the non-socialist government created a new norm: harmonisation with the EU. The previous Social Democratic government had applied for EU membership, but the new government pursued a more deliberate policy aimed at, among other things, adjusting Sweden's tax burden to the European tax profile. The purpose of reducing VAT in 1992 was not primarily to counter the recession, but to better fit the tax profile in the EU countries. In addition, the rules on convergence to a monetary union in the Maastricht Treaty in 1991 reinforced government confidence in a restrictive fiscal policy and a fixed exchange rate.

It is paradoxical that the 'One Way' resembled an economic policy strategy considered antiquated by not only the economists and non-socialist politicians, but also Social Democratic politicians and trade unionists – namely the R-M model. A restrictive fiscal policy was part of both these strategies. The non-socialist parties also expressed a Rehn-Meidner style criticism of the Social Democrats' 'Third Way'. Anne Wibble, the Minister of Finance, referred explicitly in her rejection of devaluation policy, and in her arguments against reducing payroll taxes, to the need for transformation pressure to accelerate growth in Sweden.

Rehn-Meidner and the non-socialist coalition government shared suspicion of incomes policy. Besides, more than any earlier government, this one counted on an active labour market policy to combat growing unemployment. In budget year 1991/92, expenditure on active labour market policies as a ratio of GDP rose to 4.4

per cent, a larger proportion than ever before (SOU 1993:43, table 3.1). The largest increase was in labour supply and adjustment measures, especially labour market training, as advocated in the R-M model. Even the non-socialist politicians who thought that the R-M model was obsolete made an exception for labour market policy.

But there are differences between the 'One Way' and the R-M model. The tax relief for owners of property and for incomes from capital introduced to improve growth hardly followed the equity principles of the R-M model, as well as being an ineffective means of stimulating growth according to the model. Further, the non-socialists' employment policy was too passive to satisfy the objectives of the model. The objective of full employment appears to have been downgraded in priority somewhere along the 'One Way' (the Revised Budget Bill of 1992, p. 2). However, the serious obstacles encountered by economic policies must be taken into account.

The policy of the 'One Way' failed its main task: to create confidence in the SEK. There was a substantial increase in the public budget deficit in 1992, making it highest in relation to the GDP in the OECD (with the exception of Greece) in the following year. The Central Bank failed to prevent a major outflow of capital from Sweden during the currency crisis in November 1992 even though it introduced record increases in the marginal interest rate and a package of crisis measures agreed by the non-socialist coalition government and the Social Democratic opposition. The politicians attempted to reassure the capital market by bringing down payroll taxes and making cuts in the transfer systems. But the measures were ineffective with the result that Sweden had to abandon the fixed exchange rate system. In one year (1993) the SEK was depreciated by 25 per cent against the currencies of competing nations, similar to that at the beginning of the 1980s, when the SEK was devalued twice.

It is harder to point to a break with the R-M model in other aspects after the currency crises in 1992. The inflation targets defined by the Central Bank of Sweden as a means of creating stable macroeconomic conditions (2 per cent inflation with a permitted departure of 1 percentage point in both directions) are clearly in line with the R-M model, although perhaps too strict and connected with a too passive employment policy to be in keeping with the spirit of the model. The priority given to full employment in the model may presumably have justified a more expansive fiscal and monetary policy in the two final years of the non-socialist government. Fiscal policy was only cautiously counter-cyclical in 1993 and 1994 despite high rates of unemployment and a marked fall in both the absolute and relative rates of inflation. The combination of inflation targets, EMU convergence rules and the doubts about Sweden by financial actors served as effective brakes on fiscal policy.

But the absence of a tight fiscal policy is one explanation of why Sweden did not experience the high levels of unemployment of its neighbour country Finland in the mid-1990. Another explanation is the extensive use of selective employment programmes in Sweden. Labour market policy escalated further under the non-socialist government in 1993 and 1994. The proportion of the labour force in labour market programmes reached a record rate of 5.3 per cent in 1994. Without this policy, open unemployment would, in statistical terms, have been as high as 13-14 per cent instead of 8-9 per cent. Labour market training was given a smaller weight at the expense of demand-oriented job introduction projects (Ackum Agell 1995, pp. 70-3). But training was still the most important component of labour market policy with the possible exclusion of targeted demand-oriented measures for youth that had expanded in 1993 (The Budget Bill of 1995, table 5.4 and Forslund and Krueger 1997, fig. 6.2). Further, the government introduced a system of marginal employment subsidies in 1994 although the proposal was more limited than Rehn had envisaged, among other things, by being temporary and by offering too small subsidies. A Conservative-led government's practice of selective employment policy was the major victory for the designers of the R-M model in the decade of non-interventionist policies.

A new Social Democratic policy

As in the early 1980s, rising unemployment became a political burden for a non-socialist government. The left parties won the election in September 1994 and the Social Democrats formed a new government. Yet, the new government considered reductions in the public deficit and debt as its main task, pursuing an exceptionally tight fiscal policy during a period of record high unemployment and exceptionally low household demand. The contraction of fiscal policy in Sweden in 1994-98 was unmatched among OECD countries (OECD Economic Outlook, December 1999, table 31). Fiscal restraints were supported in Parliament either by the Centre party (the former Agrarian party) or by the Left party (the former Communist party).

Fiscal policy from 1994 definitely constituted a break with earlier economic policies pursued by the Social Democratic party even if leading representatives saw it as an exceptional response to massive unemployment. The Social Democrats' argument was that fiscal restraint, though exacerbating unemployment in the short run, would eliminate it in the long run. This argument is not rooted in the R-M model or in its underpinning Keynesian model. The removal of fiscal restraints in 1999 and 2000 indicates that Swedish fiscal policy has deliberately become pro-cyclical.

The new Social Democratic government feared in the mid-1990s that an expansionary fiscal policy would be a threat to the inflation targets of the Central Bank and thus lead to contractionary monetary policy. Further, the government had the same ambition as the former non-socialist one to reduce long-term interest rates by deflecting expectations that inflation in Sweden would increase. The difference between Swedish and German long-term interest rates rose in 1994-95, which induced the Central Bank to raise its short-term interest rates in 1994-95. The government saw the large public deficit as the main obstacle to higher confidence in

Sweden. It also wanted to convince a sceptical capital market that the Social Democrats, in spite of their traditional commitment to full employment, had no plans to slacken fiscal policy. The government probably assumed that large public deficits would result in expectations of a depreciation of the SEK since high rates of relative inflation would weaken Swedish competitiveness. The Social Democrat leadership was also particularly anxious to meet the requirements of the Maastricht treaty as the party had been engaged in the campaign for a membership in the EU in 1995.

The government did not argue, as did the OECD, that the rise in Swedish unemployment in the 1990s largely reflected a rise in 'equilibrium employment'. But the Social Democrats seemed yet to support a hypothesis that a significant part of unemployment was 'structural', caused by inefficient labour markets and wage bargaining systems. In 1995, the government decided to reduce unemployment benefits and planned for new labour market legislation. These proposals can be looked upon as parts of a strategy to shift the 'wage-setting' curve downward, by reducing reservation wages, and increase the flexibility of the labour market (the Revised Budget Bill of 1995, p. 31). In the election year of 1998, however, unemployment (and other social) benefits were raised to its earlier level (from 75 to 80 per cent) under the pressure from the LO and an increasingly popular Left Party. The government suggested rather modest modifications to the unemployment insurance system in 2000. It did not propose any restrictions on the duration of unemployment benefits but proposed some other measures to stimulate individual search efforts, including that the maximum compensation level should be raised but only for the first five months of unemployment (Swedish Government 2000).

Since the mid-1990s, the Social Democratic government has been worried about the pace of nominal wage increases in Sweden compared with competing countries. Therefore, the government has advocated a return to co-ordinated wage bargaining. The greater ambitions of incomes policy in the Social Democratic crisis strategy compared with the non-socialist 'One Way' is illustrated by the suggestion of tripartite wage negotiations in the mid-1990s. The plans were not realized but the Social Democrats did manage to set up a government wage mediation body in 2000. Further, trade unions made commitments to 'voluntary' incomes policy in the second half of the 1990s. For example, the aim of maintaining Swedish competitiveness by nominal wage moderation governed a joint wage agreement between trade unions and employer organisations in Swedish manufacturing for the 1998-2000 period (Industrins Ekonomiska Råd 2000).

The priority of full employment in the R-M model may probably have called for a more expansionary fiscal policy than the Social Democratic one. Moreover, selective employment policy was extensive but may yet be considered as too passive from the viewpoint of the R-M model. The percentage of the labour force in labour market programmes decreased from 5.3 per cent in 1994 to 4.4 per cent in 1995 and was then maintained at this lower rate in the following two years. The government introduced a form of marginal employment subsidies in 1995 – firms that recruited unemployed people were given financial assistance. Neither this nor the corresponding non-socialist proposal one year earlier seem to have had a significant impact on either the rate of inflation or the level of employment (Anxo and Dahlin 1996, and Johansson, Lundborg and Zetterberg 1999, pp. 111-27).

The R-M model is compatible with the Social Democratic view in the 1990s that Swedish unemployment to a certain extent reflected rigidities in labour markets caused by high unemployment benefits. The model does not deny the importance of push mechanisms for labour mobility. But intensified wage competition by reductions in unemployment benefits is hardly a preferable strategy due to its effect on income-distribution, growth and the position of organized labour. Besides, Rehn and Meidner were 'orthodox' Keynesians, or Post-Keynesians rather than Neo-Keynesians, in their scepticism of the possibility of preventing large macroeconomic imbalances by real wage flexibility.

According to the R-M model, relatively high nominal wage increases in Sweden in the second half of the 1990s did not reflect any failure of the wage bargaining system but an adjustment to exceptional macroeconomic events. Record high profitability levels in Swedish wage-leading sectors must lead to significant market-induced wage increases and compensatory wage claims from wage earners who had fallen behind. International capital markets seem to have accepted that the pace of wage increases in Sweden in the second half of the 1990s was a part of an adjustment process rather than a structural problem – the SEK appreciated dramatically against the currencies of competing countries in 1995-96 and the following depreciation tendencies have been weak.

The Social Democratic crisis strategy seems to have been successful. The public deficit disappeared in 1998 and even turned to a significant surplus in 1999. The stable SEK and the narrower gap between German and Swedish long-run rates of interest in the second half of the 1990s showed that the government managed to raise confidence in Sweden. The recovery in growth and employment in 1999-2000 may also indicate that the Social Democrats were right in claiming that production and employment would recover through a restrictive fiscal policy in the course of time. On the other hand, the current recovery may reflect the development of a 'new' dynamic economy or cyclical phenomena, unrelated to economic policy in the 1990s, and even the ease of fiscal policy in 1999 and 2000. It is definitely too early to make a reliable evaluation of Swedish economic policy in the 1990s.

It is possible to talk about a revival for the R-M model in the 1990s as far as the means of economic policy are concerned. The Social Democratic government applied an extreme version of the model in 1994-98, combining an ambitious labour market policy with an exceptionally tight fiscal policy. In addition, the government formulated in 1999 an explicit restriction on fiscal policy – the public deficit must show a surplus over the business cycle, namely 2 per cent of GDP. The restriction satisfies the goal of low inflation in the R-M model.

My account of the application of the Rehn-Meidner policy model in Sweden in the 1990s has deliberately given it an ambiguous and indeterminate profile. The ambiguity derives from the fact that governments have generally adopted the means but not the goals of the model. Tight fiscal policies, extensive labour market programmes, public saving and even marginal employment subsidies were all parts of the Social Democratic strategy in the latter half of the 1990s. Then, when revaluations were no longer possible, the government considered strengthening the SEK as an intermediate goal. On the other hand, full employment was a long run rather than a short run target of economic policy in the 1990s.[15]

The validity of the Rehn-Meidner model

A common conclusion in Sweden today is that the R-M model is obsolete. The art of social engineering that the R-M model undoubtedly represents came under increasing public suspicion already in the 1980s. More specifically, opponents of the model referred both to negative experiences of the model and to new economic and political circumstances. One objection is that the model is unable to cope with the current unemployment problems in the EU member countries.

Globalisation tendencies in the post-war period are the bases for the main 'structural' argument against the R-M model. The increased overseas production by multinational corporations and mobility of capital, it is argued, limits the scope for a national policy aimed at curbing profits. Such policy will result in capital outflows, especially if other countries try to attract capital by profit tax exemptions. Moreover, internationalisation of labour markets is said to have narrowed the scope for solidaristic wage policy. Wage earners in high demand have greater opportunities today of moving to countries with greater wage differentials. Further, there is no institutional or political support today for a co-ordinated policy of fair wages, particularly on the EU level. This argument is often linked to the effects of new technologies and work organisations: the trends towards more differentiated and flexible jobs have made it more difficult to define identical work and, therefore, uniform wage standards.

Globalisation and information technologies are the main driving forces behind 'the new economy'. A widespread opinion is that this economy is more productive, more resistant to inflation tendencies and also more associated with large wage and income differentials than 'the old economy'. The R-M model claims that 'unfair' wage differentials are inflationary and also possibly growth damaging since rationalizations, and even innovations, may be delayed by weak transformation pressure. The model seems to be repudiated by American experience in the second half of the 1990s. Large wage differentials did not prevent the United States from having low rates of inflation despite low unemployment and also higher GDP growth than in most other OECD countries.

Another, although related, structural argument against the R-M model is based on the growing importance of services and human capital. The OECD and the IMF have claimed that wage differentials between sectors must expand to create new jobs in countries like Sweden. The service sector has lower productivity than manufacturing and must hence pay lower wages. The EU Council made a similar recommendation for its member states in the mid-1990s – real wages should decrease in some sectors of the economy to create jobs (the Council of the European Union 1994). According to Swedish economists, Sweden lagged in developing a private service sector in the 1960s and 70s because of solidaristic wage policy; the service sector could only expand through an expansion of the public sector. Moreover, they claim, Swedish investment in human capital was inhibited, even in the 1980s, by the fact that individuals were offered a too small wage premium (Henrekson, Jonung and Stymne 1996, pp. 265-77 and Lindbeck 1997, pp. 1295 and 1311).

Some other components of the EU project are difficult to reconcile with the R-M model. Proclamations of social partnership and macroeconomic dialogues by the EU in the 'White Paper' (Commission of the European Communities 1993) and at the Cologne Summit in June 1999 have been based on the idea that overall wage moderation will boost European competitiveness and profitability. Rehn and Meidner thought that such incomes policy actions are either inefficient measures in the struggle against inflation or obstructive for the development of an advanced industrial sector.

The argument that the R-M model is less relevant in a situation of high unemployment has been made by a heterogeneous group of economists. The group consists of Keynesians, who favour co-ordinated actions among EU member states to raise effective demand, and also of economists who advocate reductions of real wages, either by structural reforms in labour markets or by reductions in corporation taxes. Both perspectives can be supported by studies showing that labour market policy programmes were both ineffective and insufficient measures to combat unemployment in Sweden in the 1990s (Ackum Agell 1995, and Forslund and Krueger 1997).

Internationalisation has undeniably limited the application of the R-M model, particularly in a single country. But tight economic policy to depress average profits need not exclude measures to increase marginal profits. Rehn's marginal employment subsidy proposal is a direct incentive for companies to expand in the country. The policy is non-inflationary if the 'Rehnian paradox' is absent, i.e. if wage inflation depends on average profits and profit margins rather than on marginal profitability. Of course, Rehn and Meidner did not deny that there are limits on the possibilities to hold down average profitability in a single country.

A further defence of the R-M model is that globalisation of financial markets challenge a pure Keynesian strategy, rather than a model which relies on supply oriented measures in product and labour markets. An expansionary fiscal policy to obtain full employment is possible in a single EMU country but the strategy demands significant public saving over the business cycle as advocated by the R-M model. Besides, co-ordinated expansionary fiscal policy actions by EMU countries might be needed to reduce unemployment but they can lead to monetary restraints by the ECB to preserve the value of the Euro.[16]

The Rehn-Meidner model is a macroeconomic project which aims to combine full employment with price stability. Other stabilization policy models have been discredited in the last three decades because they either gave priority to one of these objectives or they failed to achieve these objectives simultaneously. The R-M model is, in reality, one of the few economic policy visions that, therefore, have not lost its credibility. Recent declarations by the EU that full employment must be given priority without giving up the objective of price stability have put the model into the spotlight again.

Notes

* A longer version of this chapter is available as a working paper from the Department of Economics, Stockholm University (http://www.ne.su.se/research/workingpaper.htm).

1 However a common conclusion by Swedish economists is that the favourable economic development in Sweden in the 1930s is explained by depreciations of the krona, an expansionary monetary policy and German rearmament, not by an expansionary fiscal policy (Lindbeck 1975, p. 102).

2 The Swedish devaluation followed a devaluation of the pound sterling. As other countries followed the British example, the SEK was devalued with 13-15 per cent in relation to competing currencies.

3 Leading Social Democrats had different economic policy positions in the late 1940s (Appelqvist 2000), but all were Keynesian, as widely defined.

4 Wage drift accounts for about half the total increase in blue-collar workers' wages in Sweden in the post-war period (Calmfors and Forslund 1990, pp. 91-2; Holmlund and Zetterberg 1991, p. 102; Nilsson 1994, p. 9).

5 According to the 1938 Saltsjöbaden agreement, labour market conflicts in Sweden should be resolved through negotiated agreements and not by legislation. Statutory incomes policy is not compatible with the spirit of the Saltsjöbaden agreement.

6 Rehn and Meidner's priority of fiscal rather than monetary policy measures in stabilization policy in the 1951 LO Report can be explained by the low-interest policy in Sweden, and by the fixed exchange rates of the Bretton Wood system, at that time. Further, their emphasis on tight fiscal policies is explained by the priority given to public saving in their model. Finally, Rehn and Meidner were probably influenced not only by the *General Theory* but also by Gunnar Myrdal who had argued for a combination of low rates of interest and high profit taxes on income-distribution and industrial-policy grounds (Myrdal 1944).

7 A system of investment funds had already been introduced at the end of the 1930s, but was not used as a stabilization policy tool until the mid-1950s. Companies were allowed to make deposit deductions from their profits (up to 40 per cent) for placement in special investment reserves. Some of these deductions had to be placed in interest-free accounts in the Central Bank. These frozen reserves could only be regained following an assessment on stabilization policy grounds. The investment funds were primarily instruments in a Keynesian strategy to shift investments from boom periods to recession periods more than indications of a R-M model influence.

8 The adjustment of women's wages to men's wages was, however, as comprehensive in Denmark and the Netherlands.

9 The R-M model would not have been challenged, however, by the absence of a positive relationship between solidaristic wage policy and structural change. The model says only that this wage policy is an equally efficient instrument as large wage differentials to obtain structural change, but still a better alternative in terms of income distribution and price stability.

10 The reduction in effective profit taxes was primarily due to depreciation allowances and the investment funds. It seems however that the tendency to a slower profitability decline in the 1960s and early 1970s because of reductions in effective taxes also appeared in other OECD countries (Erixon 1997a, p. 52, Södersten and Lindberg 1983, pp. 30-2, and Hoeller et al. 1996, table 9).

11 Furthermore, the restrictions on the investment funds were lifted in the middle of the 1970s which, in conflict with the R-M model, meant there was a general profit subsidy.

12 The non-socialist coalition government gave extensive non-permanent assistance to individual companies in depressed industries, mainly mining, steel, and shipbuilding. Industrial grants totalled SEK 42 billion from 1975 to 1983, about 37 per cent of expenditure on labour market policy in that period (Johannesson, 1991, table 1). The massive industrial support in the 1970s and the early 1980s has been used as an argument against the R-M model by its detractors. But Rehn and Meidner did not argue in favour of a policy which preserved jobs, they argued for market conformist subsidies in a strategy for price stability and structural change. Subsidies to unprofitable industries had been rejected by Rehn and Meidner in the case of solidaristic wage policy.

13 The profit-oriented strategy along the 'Third Way' could also have dampened economic growth. There is scope in the R-M model for a hypothesis that the profit boom delayed structural change and weakened companies' motivation to rationalize and introduce new products, technologies and work organizations. Productivity growth in Swedish manufacturing was relatively low in the boom years of the 1980s. The transformation pressure was too weak according to the government Productivity Council (Produktivitetsdelegationen, 1992). In addition, the devaluations may be an important explanation for Sweden losing market shares in the 1980s, despite a favourable cost position. High profitability in the traditional export industries weakened companies' and the capital market's incentives to invest in dynamic sectors (Erixon, 1989 and 1991).

14 Keynesians at that time, at the LO as elsewhere, turned the R-M model upside down by

their rejection of contractionary fiscal policies and their support of selective measures to restrict activity levels in the most overheated sectors. Like the Brooking economists, the LO economists accepted in the late 1980s that Sweden, with the high priority it gives employment, must have a somewhat higher rate of inflation than other countries (Bosworth and Rivlin 1987). This kind of 'equilibrium inflation' strategy was already criticized by Rehn and Meidner in the 1951 LO report (Meidner, Rehn et al. 1953, pp. 80-2).

15 The theory behind the Social Democratic economic policy has never been explored in detail. One difficulty is that investments are primarily a function of real rates of interest; the effects of fiscal and monetary restraint on real interest rates are ambiguous. The theory of a natural rate of unemployment, supported by influential Swedish economists in the 1990s, denies that macroeconomic policies have long-run effects on production and employment.

16 It is also too early to declare the death of solidaristic wage policy. Labour market mobility across borders is still limited. Further, the reduction in the 'wage premium' for higher education in Sweden from the late 1960s to the early 1980s is mainly explained by market forces, especially by an increase in the supply of highly-educated labour, rather than by wage policies (Edin and Holmlund, 1995. See also Lindbeck 1997, p. 1281). And more important, the R-M model allows for wage differentials based on differences in job content, competence and education. But Rehn and Meidner would probably have claimed that the current wage levels for IT specialists and R&D personnel are distorted short run phenomena which must be met by extensive educational and labour-market programmes to eliminate excess labour demand.

References

Ackum Agell, Susanne (1995), 'Swedish labor market programs: efficiency and timing', *Swedish Economic Policy Review*, vol. 1, pp. 65-98.

Akerlof, George A. and Janet L. Yellen (1990), 'The fair wage-effort hypothesis and unemployment', *The Quarterly Journal of Economics*, vol. 105, pp. 255-83.

Andersson, Linda, Ola Gustafsson and Lars Lundberg (1998), 'Structural change, competition and job turnover in the Swedish manufacturing industry 1964-96', FIEF Working Paper no. 148, Trade Union Institute for Economic Research (FIEF), Stockholm.

Anxo, Dominique and Pernilla Dahlin (1996), *Utvärdering av det generella och det riktade anställningsstödet*, Ministry of Labour, Stockholm.

Appelqvist, Örjan (2000), *Bruten brygga – Gunnar Myrdal och Sveriges ekonomiska efterkrigspolitik 1943-1947*, Santhérus Förlag, Stockholm.

Arai, Mahmood (1994), 'An empirical analysis of wage dispersion and efficiency wages', *Scandinavian Journal of Economics,* vol. 96, pp. 31-50.

Bergström, Villy (1969), *Den ekonomiska politiken i Sverige och dess verkningar*, The Industrial Institute for Economic and Social Research (IUI), Stockholm.

Bishop, John and Robert Haveman (1981), 'Targeted wage subsidies: their rationale and effectiveness,' in Gunnar Eliasson and Jan Södersten (eds), *Business Taxation, Finance and Firm Behavior*, The Industrial Institute for Economic and Social Research (IUI), Stockholm, pp. 297-344.

Blanchflower, David G., Andrew J. Oswald and Peter Sanfey (1996), 'Wages, profits, and rent-sharing', *The Quarterly Journal of Economics*, vol. 111, pp. 227-51.

Bosworth, Barry P. and Alice M. Rivlin (1987), *The Swedish Economy*, The Brookings Institution, Washington D.C.

Calmfors, Lars and Anders Forslund (1990), 'Wage formation in Sweden', in Lars Calmfors (ed.), *Wage Formation and Macroeconomic Policy in the Nordic Countries*, SNS Förlag and Oxford University Press, Stockholm and Oxford, pp. 63-130.

Calmfors, Lars (1993), 'Lessons from the macroeconomic experience of Sweden', *European Journal of Political Economy*, vol. 9, pp. 25-72.

Calmfors, Lars (1995), 'Labour market policy and unemployment', *European Economic Review*, vol. 39, pp. 583-92.

Christofides, Louis N. and Andrew J. Oswald (1992), 'Real wage determination and rent-sharing in collective bargaining agreements', *The Quarterly Journal of Economics*, vol. 107, pp. 985-1002.

Commission of the European Communities (1993), 'Growth, competitiveness, employment. The challenges and ways forward into the 21st century. White Paper', *Bulletin of the European Communities, supplement 6/1993*, Office for Official Publications of the European Communities, Luxembourg.

Council of the European Union (1994), 'Council recommendation of 11 July 1994 on the broad guidelines of the economic policies of the member states and of the Community', *Official Journal of the European Communities, no. L 200/41*, Office for Official Publications of the European Communities, Luxembourg.

Edin, Per Anders and Bertil Holmlund (1995), 'The Swedish wage structure: the rise and fall of solidarity wage policy?' in Richard B. Freeman and Lawrence F. Katz (eds), *Differences and Changes in Wage Structures*, University of Chicago Press, Chicago, pp. 307-43.

Erixon, Lennart (1987), *Profitability in Swedish Manufacturing – Trends and Explanations*, Almqvist & Wiksell International, Stockholm.

Erixon, Lennart (1989), 'Den tredje vägen – inlåsning eller förnyelse?' *Ekonomisk Debatt*, vol. 17, pp. 181-95.

Erixon, Lennart (1991), 'Omvandlingstryck och produktivitet', in *Konkurrens, regleringar och produktivitet*, Expert report no. 7 to the Productivity Council (Produktivitetsdelegationen), Allmänna Förlaget, Stockholm.

Erixon, Lennart (1997a), 'The golden age of the Swedish model – the coherence between capital accumulation and economic policy in Sweden in the early postwar period', Report 97:9. Institute for Social Research, Oslo.

Erixon, Lennart (1997b), 'The father of the Swedish model – in memory of Gösta Rehn', *Journal of Economic and Industrial Democracy*, vol. 18, pp. 635-50.

Erixon, Lennart (2000), The 'Third Way' Revisited. A Revaluation of the Swedish Model in the Light of Modern Economics, *The Trade Union Institute for Economic Research,*

Stockholm.

Faxén, Karl-Olof, Clas-Erik Odhner and Roland Spånt (1988), *Lönebildningen i 90-talets samhällsekonomi*, Rabén & Sjögren, Stockholm.

Forslund, Anders (1994), 'Labour market policies and wage setting: a study of Swedish unemployment insurance funds', *Oxford Economic Papers*, vol. 46, pp. 245-61.

Forslund, Anders and Alan B. Krueger (1997), 'An evaluation of the Swedish active labour market policy: new and received wisdom', in Richard B. Freeman, Robert Topel and Birgitta Swedenborg (eds), *The Welfare State in Transition – Reforming the Swedish Model*, The University of Chicago Press, Chicago and London, pp. 267-98.

Fries, Harald (1983), 'Structural change and industry performance in four Western European countries', in Gunnar Eliasson, Mark Sharefkin and Bengt Christer Ysander (eds), *Policy Making in a Disorderly World Economy*, The Industrial Institute for Economic and Social Research (IUI), Stockholm, pp. 111-68.

Government Proposition 1995/96:25, *En politik för arbete, trygghet och utveckling.*

Hansen, Bent and Gösta Rehn (1956), 'On wage-drift. A problem of money-wage dynamics', in *25 Economic Essays in Honour of Erik Lindahl*, Ekonomisk Tidskrift, Stockholm, pp. 87-138.

Henrekson, Magnus, Lars Jonung and Joakim Stymne (1996), 'Economic growth and the Swedish model', in Nicholas Crafts and Gianni Toniolo (eds), *Economic Growth in Europe since 1945*, Cambridge University Press, Cambridge.

Hibbs, Douglas H. and Håkan Locking (1996), 'Wage compression, wage drift and wage inflation in Sweden', *Journal of Labor Economics,* vol. 14, pp. 109-41.

Hibbs, Douglas H. and Håkan Locking (2000), 'Wage dispersion and productive efficiency: evidence for Sweden', *Journal of Labor Economics*, vol. 18, pp. 755-82.

Hoeller, Peter, Marie-Odile Louppe and Patrice Vergriete (1996), 'Fiscal relations within the European Union', Working Papers no. 163, Economics Department, OECD, Paris.

Holmlund, Bertil (1990), 'Den svenska lönebildningens drivkrafter', in *Svensk lönebildning – teori, empiri, politik.* Appendix 24 to the Medium Term Survey. Allmänna Förlaget, Stockholm.

Holmlund, Bertil and Johnny Zetterberg (1991), 'Insider effects in wage determination – evidence from five countries', *European Economic Review*, vol. 35, pp. 1009-34.

Industrins Ekonomiska Råd (2000), 'Industriavtalet – utfall och framtidsutsikter', mimeo.

Johannesson, Jan (1991), *On the Outcome of Swedish Labour Market Policy*, The Expert Group for Labour Market Policy Evaluation Studies (EFA), Ministry of Labour, Stockholm.

Johansson, Sten, Per Lundborg and Johnny Zetterberg (1999), *Massarbetslöshetens karaktär och vägarna till full sysselsättning*, (Second revised edition), Trade Union Institute for Economic Research (FIEF), Stockholm.

Johnson, George E. and Richard Layard (1986), 'The natural rate of unemployment: explanation and policy', in Orley Ashenfelter and Richard Layard (eds), *Handbook of Labor Economics – Volume II*, North-Holland, Amsterdam, pp. 921-99.

Jonsson, Lennart and Claes-Henrik Siven (1984), 'Löneutjämningens mekanismer',

Ekonomisk Debatt, vol. 12, pp. 429-41.

Jonung, Lars (1993), 'Riksbankens politik 1945-1990', in Lars Werin (ed.), *Från räntereglering till inflationsnorm – det finansiella systemet och riksbankens politik 1945-1990*, SNS Förlag, Stockholm, pp. 288-419.

Jonung, Lars (1999), *Med backspegeln som kompass – om stabiliseringspolitiken som läroprocess*, Rapport till Expertgruppen för studier i offentlig ekonomi, Ds 1999:9.

Keynes, John Maynard (1936), *The General Theory of Employment, Interest and Money*, MacMillan St Martin's Press, London.

Layard, Richard and Stephen Nickell (1980), 'The case for subsidising extra jobs', *The Economic Journal*, vol. 90, pp. 51-73.

Lindbeck, Assar (1975), *Svensk ekonomisk politik*, Aldus, Stockholm.

Lindbeck, Assar (1997), 'The Swedish experiment', *Journal of Economic Literature*, vol. 35, pp. 1273-319.

Matthiessen, Lars (1971), 'Finanspolitiken som stabiliseringspolitiskt instrument', in *Svensk finanspolitik i teori och praktik*, Aldus/Bonniers, Stockholm.

Meidner, Rudolf (1969), 'The goals of labour market policy', in *On Incomes Policy – Papers and Proceedings from a Conference in Honour of Erik Lundberg*, SNS, Stockholm, pp. 189-200.

Meidner, Rudolf (1988), 'Gösta Rehn as an LO economist', *Journal of Economic and Industrial Democracy*, vol. 9, pp. 455-74.

Meidner, Rudolf, Gösta Rehn et al. (1953), *Trade Unions and Full Employment*. Report to the LO Congress in 1951, The Swedish Confederation of Trade Unions (LO), Stockholm.

Myrdal, Gunnar (1944), 'Höga skatter och låga räntor', in *Studier i ekonomi och historia tillägnade Eli F. Heckscher*, Almqvist och Wiksell, Stockholm, pp. 160-9.

Nilsson, Christian (1994), 'Negotiated wages and wage drift: a study of the Swedish pulp and paper industry', in Bertil Holmlund (ed.), *Pay, Productivity, and Policy*, Trade Union Institute for Economic Research (FIEF), Stockholm.

Nilsson, Christian and Zetterberg, Johnny (1987), *Lönestruktur och strukturella arbetsmarknadsproblem*, Appendix to the Medium Term Survey 1987, Allmänna Förlaget, Stockholm.

Ohlsson, Ingvar (1980), 'Den solidariska lönepolitikens resultat', in *Lönepolitik och solidaritet*, The Swedish Confederation of Trade Unions (LO), Stockholm.

Produktivitetsdelegationen (1992), *Forces of Productivity and Prosperity*, Summary of 1991:92.

Rehn, Gösta (1952), 'The problem of stability: an analysis and some policy proposals' and 'A reply to professor Lundberg, in Ralph Turvey (ed.), *Wages Policy Under Full Employment,* William Hodge and Company Ltd., London, pp. 30-54 and 72-9.

Rehn, Gösta (1977), 'Finansministrarna, LO-ekonomerna och arbetsmarknadspolitiken', in *Ekonomisk debatt och ekonomisk politik*. Nationalekonomiska föreningen 100 år, Norstedts, Stockholm.

Rehn, Gösta (1980), 'Idéutvecklingen', in *Lönepolitik och solidaritet*, The Swedish Confederation of Trade Unions (LO), Stockholm.

Rehn, Gösta (1982), 'Anti-inflationary expansion policies (with special reference to marginal employment premiums?', Report to the Commission of the European Communities, Occasional Papers No. 4, Commission of the European Communities, Brussels.

SOU 1993:43, *Politik mot arbetslöshet*. Report from the Expert Group for Labour Market Policy Evaluation Studies (EFA), Allmänna Förlaget, Stockholm.

Swedish Government (2000), *En arbetsmarknadspolitik för full sysselsättning och uthållig tillväxt*. En skrift om regeringens arbetsmarknadspolitik, June 2000.

Södersten, Jan (1971), 'Företagsbeskattning och resursfördelning' in Erik Lundberg et al., *Svensk finanspolitik i teori och praktik*, Aldus, Stockholm, pp. 322-59.

Södersten, Jan and Thomas Lindberg (1983), 'Skatt på bolagskapital – Sverige i jämförelse med Storbritannien, USA och Västtyskland', *Forskningsrapport nr 20*, The Swedish Institute for Economic and Social Research (IUI), Stockholm.

Söderström, Hans Tson (1990), 'Stabiliseringspolitiska lärdomar och framtidsperspektiv', in Bo Södersten (ed.), *Marknad och politik*, Dialogos, Lund, pp. 55-94.

PART 2
Swedish Perspectives

Chapter 3

Gösta Rehn and the Swedish Model: Did we follow the Rehn-Meidner Model too little rather than too much?

Klas Eklund

Introduction

To many social scientists, 'The Swedish Model' is synonymous with the 'Rehn-Meidner Model'. That is only half true. While Swedish economic and political development was strongly influenced by Gösta Rehn and his colleagues, the Rehn-Meidner strategy and the subsequent thinking of Gösta Rehn in particular were in important respects much more modern and original than the actual, real-life Swedish Model they are associated with.

To compare Gösta Rehn's recommendations on labour market policy, welfare and growth with the actual Swedish Model as it was implemented in Sweden in the 1970s – the heyday of the Swedish welfare state – is not unproblematic. While others will no doubt disagree, both with my interpretation and my conclusion, my central argument is that the Swedish Model in practice was in fact more rigid and less flexible in adapting to changes in the world economy and Swedish society than is often perceived, and that it would have fared better had it, in important respects, been shaped more like Gösta Rehn had wished. To make this argument, I will first compare the Rehn-Meidner Model and then Gösta Rehn's views on labour and society to the actual development of certain key aspects of the Swedish Model. Let me begin with a few notes about Gösta Rehn himself.

Gösta Rehn and his model

Gösta Rehn was born in 1913 and studied at the university and the 'Social Institute' in Stockholm. In the late 1930s he commenced his work for the Swedish trade union movement. After temporary writing and teaching jobs, interrupted by his service as a volunteer in the 1940 Finnish Winter War, he came to work as an economist at LO, the blue collar workers' trade union confederation in 1943. In the 1950s he worked for several government economic commissions on labour market-related issues, and in 1959 he joined the Ministry of Finance as 'head of planning,' in charge of the government's economic forecasts and analyses of effects of economic policy. In 1962 he moved to Paris to head the Department of Labour and Social Affairs at OECD. In 1973 he became professor of labour market policy at the Swedish Institute for Social Research at Stockholm University; a position which he held until he retired. He died in 1996.

These are the bare outlines: but they need to be filled in by the originality of Rehn's ideas and their impact. During the 1940s, while still a young man, he became very influential in the debate on wage-setting, and in the late 1940s and early 1950s he and his colleague Rudolf Meidner created their framework for full employment and low inflation – the so-called Rehn-Meidner Model. This model was far more ambitious than similar attempts in other countries. In the 1950s and 60s he occupied himself with labour market policy and the issues of flexibility of working life. In his later years, he returned to the eternal issue of how to attain low inflation and full employment simultaneously, calling for an economic policy strategy of stimulating 'marginal expansion'.

All in all, a very rich life, full of relevant economic thinking – as well as an extraordinary impact on the Swedish economy and Swedish day-to-day life. Gösta Rehn was a one-man crusade for rational and fair economic policy; persuasive, untiring and stubborn as hell. When it comes to practical economic policy in his home country, he was one of the most influential Swedish economists of the second half of the 20th century – although he was not at all as influential as he would have liked to have been and often grumbled that neither politicians nor fellow economists listened as much as they should have.

There are many interpretations of the Swedish Model as well as of the Rehn-Meidner Model. Gösta himself would probably have been scared witless if he had heard this scholastic debate about different 'models'. Gösta Rehn was always a modest person – well aware of his own importance, but never allowing himself to become self-righteous or pompous.

Nonetheless, when we talk about the 'Rehn Model' or the 'Rehn-Meidner Model' we mean the set of propositions first put forth by Gösta Rehn and Rudolf Meidner in the late 1940s and the 1950s. When, over ten years ago, I asked Gösta to summarise their views for a textbook that I was writing, he did it in these four main points:

- An overall tight fiscal policy to fight inflation. Total demand should be restrained in order to avoid over-heating and rapid cost increases.
- A selective labour market policy to fight unemployment should retrenchment cause problems in the labour market. The task was to ease problems for individuals and regions, which were too harshly squeezed by the tightness of the anti-inflationary policy.

- An active labour market policy to both pull and push labour to move to new job opportunities. This policy was to be a policy of transition, moving people *out of* unemployment – not to support them while being unemployed.
- A solidaristic wage policy, i.e. equal pay for equal work. The aim of this was not only egalitarian, but also a way to put pressure on firms, as it would be impossible for one firm to out-compete a similar firm simply by paying lower wages. Thus, weak firms would be pushed out of business, while high-productive companies would prosper. Structural transformation would be speeded up. Also, a fair wage structure would diminish wage competition, and hence inflation.

For me, this is the core of the Rehn-Meidner Model. There are other important issues taken up by either Gösta or Rudolf, individually or in tandem. But they are not part of the Rehn-Meidner Model itself, and Gösta and Rudolf did not necessarily agree about them. Thus, Rudolf Meidner's proposal for wage earners' funds was not part of the Rehn-Meidner Model, and neither were Gösta Rehn's proposals for a flexible working life and subsidies of marginal employment subsidies (Rehn actually opposed the wage earners' funds proposed by Meidner). I return to some of Rehn's own proposals as well as to the Rehn-Meidner Model itself below.

The Swedish Model

Let us, however, first turn to the Swedish Model. It became famous in the 1930s as the 'Middle way', but to Swedes the 'Model' actually means the much more elaborate set of institutions and policies developed during the 1950s and 60s, when the big expansion of the public sector occurred, and which reached its fullest expression in the 1970s.

Some people have jokingly referred to the Swedish Model in terms of 'Big business, Big government, Big unions'. Although these are certainly important characteristics of the Swedish economy, I prefer to say that in its more general form the actually existing Swedish Model, as built up during the post-war years, comprised the following main characteristics:

- A large public sector with high taxes, providing free public services in many areas
- Generous transfer systems, including pensions, parental leave, sick leave, unemployment and other safety nets
- Big unions and compressed wages
- Large private firms in the export sector, negotiating with big unions and big government
- Full employment through a big public sector and active labour market policies
- Social Democratic political hegemony.

Some elements – such as the active labour market policy – are similar to the Rehn-Meidner Model, but others are lacking or differ. The active labour market policy was developed in the late 1950s and vigorously pursued both by the Ministry of Finance and the newly created Labour Market Board (AMS). It was during these years – during the late 1950s and early 1960s – that the Rehn-Meidner model was most influential.

In the 1970s, however, its practical influence waned. The active labour market policy became more defensive, both because of slower growth and because of a growing popular resentment towards labour mobility. In particular, the emphasis placed by Gösta Rehn and Rudolf Meidner on keeping steady pressure on firms – by tight fiscal policies, equal pay for equal work, low inflation etc – was something that the actual Swedish Model did not adhere to. Rather, full employment was gradually allowed to result in high wage inflation, which was then accommodated by repeated devaluations. This in fact alleviated the transformation pressure, which was an integral part of the Rehn strategy.

In my view, this was a major factor underlying the increasing problems encountered by the Swedish model in the 1970s and 80s. These problems arose after many years of stellar Swedish performance. Therefore, to most Swedes the Swedish model seemed to work well long after its problems became clear to economists. Such a claim is of course difficult to assess, not least because of the long lags between cause and effect in historical growth processes.

The Swedish economy was extremely successful during the first half of the 20th century. Sweden catapulted to the ranks of the richest economies in the world. There are different views on why, but nobody contends the fact that Sweden managed the Great Depression of the 1930s better than most other countries, at the time when the first foundations of the Model were laid. However, in the 1950s and 60s, when the Model was built up and its legend grew, Sweden's economy actually grew somewhat slower than it main competitors, but the absolute accumulation of wealth was such that hardly anybody noticed any warning signals.

In the 1960s, most Swedes, including economists and conservatives, hailed the Swedish model. But success often creates the roots of its own destruction. Just at the time when Sweden's successes were challenged by new competitors, rapidly rebuilding themselves after WWII or just stepping onto the world market, and Rehn's and Meidner's Model actually recommended important changes in economic policy in Sweden, the feeling of national hubris led politicians to push the model – with the big public sector, high tax pressure etc – to its limits. That gradually created tensions as the actual Swedish Model in the 1970s changed its colours.

Why did the Model crack?

The functioning of the Swedish model deteriorated during the 1970s and 80s. The reasons are – in retrospect – not hard to discern. While the system became more rigid and centralised, the social preconditions moved in a totally different direction.

The background is the long-term change in the labour market and social structure that was taking place in most industrial countries. As the traditional labour class diminished and the 'middle' class white-collar worker groups grew, traditional collective large-scale solutions based on the shop floor experiences of manufacturing were no longer as successful. Instead the growing middle class craved more individualistic solutions and showed more sophisticated demand patterns, not least as regards services from the public sector. As the middle classes grew, they gradually became larger than the traditional hard-hat, industrial working class. And consequently, a model based on industrial labour and collective action started to seem outdated.

Thus, the political background of the economic policies changed. But more important were the economic changes that gradually wore down the model.

- As the labour market became more differentiated and the human capital element became more important, the wage compression strategy turned out to be more problematic. As 'Fordism' went out the door, individual approaches to wage-setting and related matters became necessary. At the same time, however, unions pressed even harder for egalitarian wage setting. 'Equal pay for equal work' was gradually superseded by more aggressive wage claims, aiming to sharply reduce wage differences even between different work. This was reflected in a sharp reduction of the wage differential between skilled and unskilled workers. I am convinced that in this manner the wage structure became more compressed than Rehn had originally intended.
- The effect of this compressed wage structure is a source of much debate among Swedish economists. I can see pros and cons. It definitely aided in creating a more egalitarian society, but it probably also dampened growth, not least by creating a shortage of skilled workers. There are different views among Swedish analysts on this growth effect; but it is quite safe to say that we all agree on another negative effect, namely that the wage setting structure and wage formation process did create inflation. This came about through several channels. Full employment pushed up wages: the compression of the wage structure to a large extent took place by lifting the lowest paid. Also, the wage negotiations themselves – with negotiations on several levels (local, branch, central) – added wage costs. Compensatory wage claims and wage drift were the markets' answer to the administrated wage setting process. And on top of that, repeated devaluations to restore competitiveness when wage inflation got out of hand added to the inflationary pressures.
- The actual Swedish model included a big – and growing – public sector. There were several reasons for this: First, egalitarian ambitions to provide the population with 'free' education and health care and an ambitious pension scheme. Second, the expansion of the public sector was one way to increase

employment, especially for women. For almost two generations of Social Democratic politicians, public expansion became the answer to most challenges, and taxes were gradually increased to pay for this expansion. Up until the late 1960s, the Swedish public sector was not much bigger than that of the average OECD country; but in the early 1970s the growth of the public sector accelerated, as the egalitarian ambitions expanded. However, the tax ceiling was eventually reached; exactly when is open to debate, but as far as I am concerned we saw strains emerging quite rapidly as the tax ratio approached 50 per cent of GDP. This happened in the early 1970s – at which time growing budget deficits started to show. Increasing problems in financing the growth of public expenditure gradually changed the outlook of politicians. From the mid-70s the momentum of public sector growth has not been allowed to play the central political role it did during the previous decades, when the Swedish Model was built up. Instead, gradually at first, and more intensively later on, the major concern came to be to use public resources more efficiently, rather than to expand them. The tax ratio has, albeit with some oscillations, remained at the same level since the mid-70s.

- Globalisation has, of course, been an important factor. Cheap housing and an expanding public sector relied on a regulated capital market with low interest rates. Repeated devaluations to uphold employment were made possible by currency controls. High taxes were paramount for financing the public sector and for high wages in the service sector. Increasing mobility of labour and capital – and tax bases – has during the past decade made it ever more difficult to keep capital regulated and taxes high. Gradually, Sweden has been forced to adapt, thus making it more difficult to preserve the peculiarities of the old model.

The demise was gradual. But oil crises, inflation and repeated devaluations during the 1970s created increasing problems. At first, they were greeted with incredulity. Quite a few people saw them as temporary, something which would pass and therefore ought not to affect – indeed, should not be allowed to influence – the Swedish Model. Instead, the first response to these external shocks was to hike taxes and wages even more, to engage in a strong public expansion to bridge the fall of demand, and to further enhance labour security through labour legislation. Nowadays, the major view among Swedish economists is that this refusal to adapt the model actually made things worse in the longer run – although that was not the view at that time.

In raw numbers, the problems are quite visible. During the 100 years from 1870 to 1970, Sweden enjoyed the fastest GDP per capita growth in the world after Japan. The golden decades were 1910-1950, when Swedish performance was outstanding. These were the years when the first characteristics of the Swedish Model were shown – but it was also a period when Sweden reaped the harvests from earlier investments and when our country stayed outside two devastating World Wars. From 1950 to 1970, the formative decades and heyday of the Swedish Model, Sweden experienced almost the same growth as the OECD average. But after 1970, when the Model was over-extended, economic growth contracted, both in absolute terms and compared to other countries. For the first time since industrialisation, Sweden clearly showed slower growth than comparable competitors. At the same time foreign debt as well as budget deficits exploded, despite frantic attempts to bolster competitiveness through devaluations.

The big U-turn

The defensive struggle continued through the 1970s and 80s. Gradually, however, strains increased, and today the traditional Model has indeed cracked. The early 1990s – after some 15 years of permanent problems – proved to be a watershed. During the late 1980s, growth was slow – only about 1 per cent, which in turn relied on an increase of labour supply, not on productivity growth – but inflation nevertheless ran wild at almost 10 per cent annually. Nominal wage increases were tenfold the level of productivity growth. Absenteeism was huge – in manufacturing almost one third of the labour force on average was absent for 'health' reasons – partly because of the very high labour participation rate (which meant people with a high degree of absenteeism were in the labour force), but also because of extremely high compensation levels for sick leave (almost 100 per cent). At the same time, a speculative bubble developed in the real estate market as domestic credit controls were lifted.

In this environment, with slow growth and increasing structural ailments but booming inflation and asset prices, another devaluation was obviously the wrong medicine. Increasing internationalisation of capital markets was beginning to push up Swedish interest rates, as a response to high inflation and a weak currency. The government became more and more desperate, searching for measures to stop inflation. Finally, in 1990, it even tried price and wage controls, but failed to obtain sufficient parliamentary support. The result was a governmental crisis, with the Minister of Finance leaving office, publicly saying this was the end of the 'third road' in economic policy-making. The SAP approval rates fell to an all-time low in the polls.

After that came the turn-around in economic strategy. The SAP government rapidly tightened fiscal policy, cut benefit levels (contrary to election promises), proclaimed a hard-currency policy (tying the krona to the ecu basket) and applied for Swedish membership in the European Union. A comprehensive tax reform sharply cut income tax rates, especially for high-income earners. Currency controls were abolished. The target of stamping out inflation was in the 1991 budget elevated to the highest priority, above full employment, despite that fact that the business cycle was turning downward. These sweeping changes signified the historic fact that the SAP government had openly abandoned Keynesianism, 50 years after it had been the first one to embrace it.

The impact of this turnaround was compounded by the collapse of communism, which occurred at exactly the same time. One might wonder why that event would affect Swedish policy-making; after all, Sweden had nothing in common with the Soviet Union. Still, on a psychological level it did affect the policy-makers. If the Swedish Model had been perceived as the 'Middle way' between planning and market, between communism and capitalism, and one of these alternatives collapsed – economically, politically, morally – why then make any compromises with it at all? Questions like these negatively affected the self-consciousness and the self-perception of the Swedish Model and its protagonists.

To sum up: 1990-91 was the big U-turn in Swedish politics. Instead of pushing forward, still trying to build a 'Model' of its own, Sweden has spent the last decade – albeit grudgingly – adapting to its neighbours. This has entailed budget reforms, making the budget process more stringent; making the Central bank independent giving it an inflation target free of direct political control; accession to the European unions and signing of the Maastricht treaty, i.e. accepting a much stricter institutional framework for economic policy. The result – after some years with huge swings in budget deficits and unemployment – was low inflation but high unemployment, just like most other European countries. We still differ in some respects from the average European country – we have higher taxes and stronger unions. But more and more, Sweden is adapting to Europe, for better or worse.

Many analysts – political scientists, historians, economists as well as politicians – have different views on what went wrong and why, which lessons could be drawn and in which respects the 'model' is still there, albeit in a new form. But, as should be clear by now, my view is that the model, the way it was actually shaped in the 1970s, became too rigid, unable to respond in a flexible way to the challenges of globalisation. Also, I believe that in certain respects it was carried too far. For instance, wage compression went too far as did centralisation and high taxation. This made the model less flexible and less capable of adapting to new circumstances, created by globalisation and new technologies. The history of the past decade has to a large extent been the history of – painfully! – cutting away the excesses of the 1970s.

Rehn was more modern than the Swedish Model

This rather critical view of the actual development of the Swedish model is not uncommon among Swedish economists – even among Social Democratic economists, sympathetic to the goal of combining egalitarianism with growth. However, in Sweden the debate on what to do and how to change the 'Model' for the future is strangely quiet.

It would be an exciting task to pick up that discussion. But my task here is more limited and I will only try to fit some pieces of that larger jigsaw puzzle. I want to draw some specific lessons as concerns Gösta Rehn's contributions. I will claim that in at least four important respects, Gösta Rehn was much more modern than the actual Swedish model as it developed in the 1970s and 80s. They pertain to the long-term growth strategy, wage formation and labour market policies, the cyclical economic policy and the view of working life flexibility. My thesis is that if the actual Swedish Model had looked more like Gösta Rehn's recommendations, the excesses of the 1970s would not have occurred and the subsequent crises might have been less difficult.

Long term growth

We can most assuredly debate – at length – how economic growth is created. As a former chairman of the Swedish government's Productivity Commission, I tend to answer in general terms in the following way: there has to be an incentive structure which contains both driving forces for growth – rewarding those who launch new innovations, work hard, save, invest, etc. – but also a strong transformation pressure that makes it impossible to reap windfall gains from not attempting to innovate, educate, work and save.

The point is that both carrot and stick are needed. The carrot part is well known and advertised; we have, all of us, heard the arguments for tax incentives, profitable investments, etc. But the other side of the equation must not be forgotten. Companies should not have a comfortable, well-paved road ahead. They must meet the risk of ruin as well as the chance of reward. They must face competition, challenges and pit-falls to avoid growing fat and lazy. The fact that external pressure is needed to increase efforts to increase productivity is well known in economic theory. Sometimes it is expressed in terms of stiff competition leading to more rapid growth; sometimes it is expressed in terms of 'X-efficiency' and 'principal-agent' theories, claiming that external pressure will strengthen efforts to reduce production slack. This is something that Gösta Rehn knew well, and in the Rehn-Meidner model the need for stiff transformation pressure is one of the cornerstones.

In Sweden, however, the incentives for growth weakened sharply in the 1970s – at the very time that oil crises and other external shocks challenged the Model and the Swedish economy. Just when they were needed the most, the driving forces for growth weakened. Here are just some examples:

- Marginal tax rates were hiked – the top bracket in some extreme cases could actually exceed 100 per cent (!), while the 'normal' marginal tax rate for high-income earners was 'only' 85 per cent. At the same time, deductions were very generous, which made it profitable to look for loop-holes – and the result was what you could expect. An increasing number of Swedes started to plan their lives, their work, their savings and investments not according to what was good for the social economy but to what benefited their personal tax situation. Gunnar Myrdal said aptly: 'The Swedes are turning into a nation of cheaters'.

- Wage compression accelerated. The wage premium for education fell drastically, which of course diminished the incentive to study. At the same time the thresholds of entrance to the labour market became higher as wages for young people were hiked sharply.
- Benefit levels were hiked to the level where absenteeism and early retirement skyrocketed.

A weakening of the 'transformation pressure' also compounded the effects on growth. In our investigation (published in 1991), the Productivity Commission put a lot of emphasis on the fact that repeated devaluations during the 1970s and 80s – the result of the government and the central bank accommodating excessively high wage increases – created windfall gains for many firms. In practice, companies were given profits 'for free' through monetary policy (i.e., a lower exchange rate). This had important, detrimental effects on growth.

- Firstly, the need to innovate and increase productivity diminished as firms could rely on government policy to keep up the level of profits.
- Secondly, the relative price of labour and capital changed. Repeated devaluations gradually pushed up real rates of interest while inflation lowered real wage costs. This created incentives to slow down the capital-for-labour substitution. Slower capital accumulation was in turn one of the main factors behind the slow growth of the 1970s and 80s.
- Thirdly, the devaluations, although they did give exports short-term boosts, gradually hurt the long-term growth potential, mainly because they were not followed by any tight anti-inflationary policy. On the contrary, domestic inflation soared. This became a drawback to the export industry, which had greater difficulties in pushing cost increases on to consumers than had the sheltered domestic sector. As a result, structural transformation slowed down, compared to other countries.

On top of this defensive currency policy, the government during the 1970s also engaged in an extremely defensive industrial policy. For some years, heavy subsidies were handed out to companies and whole sectors that were threatened by foreign competition and high cost increases. The most conspicuous case was the shipyard industry, where the value-added during the worst years was negative; i.e., taxpayers' money was used to destroy steel. Naturally, no jobs were saved; the industry was extinguished – but with a delay. And resources, which would have been better used in building up new production and new technologies, were spent defending old, doomed industries.

To summarise: One important factor causing a relative slow-down of Swedish growth in the 1970s was low transformation pressure, leading to a lower rate of capital accumulation and a slowing-down of structural adjustment.

Now, obviously this is as far from the Rehn-Meidner intentions as one could possibly come. Remember Gösta Rehn's recommendations: tight policy should fight inflation, while selective labour market policy was given the task of alleviating labour market problems should such arise due to the fight against inflation; a solidaristic wage policy should further tighten transformation pressure. This is almost the opposite of what was actually carried out. Instead of transformation pressure, we experienced a concerted effort by the Central Bank and the government to shower firms with easy profits from devaluation!

Wage setting and labour market policies

Wage formation was crucial to this development. It is obvious that wage formation during these years ran amok. 'Solidaristic wage policy' was admittedly a key phrase during this period, but it was practised in a way which was far from what Rehn himself had wanted. In the original Rehn-Meidner Model the solidaristic wage policy had three aims. First, it aimed at creating a more just wage structure, equating wages for similar jobs. Secondly, it aimed at diminishing wage competition. Thirdly, by preventing companies from surviving simply by paying low wages, the solidaristic wage policy was an instrument to kill off low productive companies and increase transformation pressure.

This was – in this respect – a good idea. But in practice many unions after some time interpreted this policy to mean equal wage not only for equal work but equal wage for just about every kind of work. This was one factor contributing to the rapid wage inflation: This administrated policy of compressed wages was counteracted by market forces which tried to re-establish wage differentials, not least via wage drift – which then triggered a new round of compensating wage claims.

Gösta Rehn strongly disliked this self-enforcing process of compensating wage claims. His aim was to search for a wage structure which would be seen as fair, and thus not cause this wage-wage-spiral characteristic of Sweden in the 1970s and 80s. However, here we encounter the eternal problem of the trade-off between employment and inflation. In Sweden there is clear evidence that the tightness of the labour market itself is the single most important factor creating wage inflation. Thus, would not full employment create inflation? Indeed, there are such risks, and we will return to this issue in the next section, but it should be recalled that Rehn was well aware of this conflict. The Rehn-Meidner solution was to make low inflation the permanent aim of a tight fiscal policy, counteracted by a selective labour market policy where and when needed.

Once again, we see the differences between the Rehn-Meidner strategy and the actual Swedish Model, as it developed in the 1970s. To Rehn, transformation pressure was to be kept up by tight policies and wages which refused to give away windfall gains to companies. Labour market policy was a way to fight unemployment while maintaining a high level of transformation pressure. In order for this strategy to function as intended, unemployment insurance and active labour market policies must be temporary means to ease the transition from unemployment to employment. They cannot be allowed to become permanent means of support for large groups of people.

However, this is exactly what occurred in Sweden. Easy fiscal and monetary policies – budget deficits and devaluations – accommodated all too rapid cost increases, and when labour market problems grew, authorities answered by increasing the level of labour market activities – not only as temporary measures, but rather as a permanent instrument to back up employment during a period when growth slackened and labour market flexibility decreased. Early retirement schemes consequently became a common way of reducing open unemployment and guarantee permanent support for many who could not make it in the regular labour market. And on top of this, a growing political resentment of urbanisation and industrialisation – a 'green' surge in politics – made the active labour market policy much less active in promoting mobility; instead it focussed more on defending the existing jobs even in declining regions and sectors.

Of course, these policies also eased the pressure on unions, as labour market problems and excessive nominal wage growth were not allowed to surface in open unemployment. This may have been understandable from a humanitarian and solidaristic point of view, but for some time it hid the real problems of the Swedish economy and created wrong incentives for both unions and companies, as it shifted the responsibility and the burden away from the unions and employers to the government and tax payers.

The conclusion: Even though the massive amount of resources spent on active labour market policies may, superficially, have looked to be well in line with the recommendations of Rehn-Meidner, I contend the opposite: the massive doses of labour market policy were a signal that something was fundamentally wrong – and in my view one important fault was that the long-term growth policy did not follow Gösta Rehn's views on the need to keep up transformation pressure.

Stabilisation policy

The distinction between long-term growth and short-term stabilisation may look simple in theory. The first concerns itself with increasing long-term, potential GDP, while the latter aims at reducing the gap between actual and potential GDP. In practice, however, we know that these two activities interact. For instance, a long period of unemployment and of economic growth below potential may have negative effects on (real as well as human) capital formation and consequently hurt long-term growth. Conversely, a high level of demand may have positive long-term effects. One important feature of the Rehn-Meidner Model is its claim that demand management is not sufficient to stabilise the economy; today, with our increased emphasis on supply-side measures, we realise that a policy that includes supply side stimulus may give better long-term effects.

The conventional wisdom of the 1950s – the time when the actual Swedish Model was built up and when the Rehn-Meidner Model was hotly debated – was dominated by rather simple Keynesianism. Economic policy in those days was all about stabilising the business cycle. Demand management was in vogue, and textbooks taught economic students and politicians how to calibrate fiscal policy in order to – through the almighty multiplier effect – reach full employment. Inflation or bottlenecks in the labour market had not yet become serious problems. The aggregate supply function was, thus, *de facto* seen as totally elastic – which, of course, was the opposite of what the Rehn-Meidner Model stated, with its emphasis on labour market policies.

In the late 1950s and early 1960s this simple version of Keynesianism was made more sophisticated by the Tobin analysis of asset prices and wealth effects, on the one hand, and the notion that there was a (stable) trade-off between inflation and unemployment, as expressed by the Phillips curve, on the other. Through expansionary policies it was, according to this expanded Keynesian model, still possible to reach full employment, but at a price – viz. inflation. A higher – but stable – rate of inflation had to be paid to reach lower unemployment. This was the economic policy-making core of what Samuelson dubbed the neo-classical synthesis of the 1950s.

The Phillips curve and the trade-off between unemployment and inflation could be regarded in different ways. One was not very ambitious. Here, the position of the Phillips curve was seen as more or less given and thus as some kind of economic-political smorgasbord, where policy-makers could pick the combination of unemployment and inflation suitable. From this starting point different governments could reach different positions on the curve. Republican governments in the USA and conservative governments in Europe were likely to choose low inflation and high unemployment, while Democratic and Social Democratic governments were likely to pick high inflation and low unemployment. Another, slightly more ambitious way to look at the Phillips curve was to regard it as an analytical starting-point for a counter-cyclical policy, where policy-makers through variations of expansion or retrenchment would be able to slide up or down along the curve, depending on the cyclical situation of the economy.

These views – not far apart – helped give economists and politicians of that era the impression that they could fine-tune the economy, picking exactly the combination of unemployment and inflation that would be optimal at any given time and for given circumstances. Today, we know that was too optimistic a view. Paradoxically, we can at the same time in retrospect see that it was strangely passive, accepting the position of the existing Phillips curve, accepting only demand management as the tool for economic policy.

Here Gösta Rehn and Rudolf Meidner were much more ambitious than the conventional Keynesian/neoclassical wisdom. The Rehn-Meidner Model was formulated several years before the break-through of the Phillips curve, but it is still quite possible to interpret it in Phillips terms. Gösta Rehn used the provocative title *'Hate inflation!'* for an article he published in 1957 to make his point. (Actually, he used that title for several articles during his entire career to emphasise that point, over and over.) The task was to make full employment possible at a low level of inflation, not to accept high inflation to reach low unemployment; such a policy would in the long run be self-defeating, Rehn asserted. The real objective of economic policy was to change – improve – the trade-off between inflation and unemployment. In Phillips curve terms this meant pushing the curve closer to the origin. Translated into aggregate supply and demand analysis it means pushing the supply curve outwards. A rightward move of the supply curve implies that the aggregate equilibrium level – and consequently the employment level – can be increased without higher inflation.

In this way, Rehn and Meidner in important respects actually were predecessors of what was later to be called 'Supply-side economics'. Before you rush to conclusions and start cursing Arthur Laffer, let me remind you of a very important fact. Gösta Rehn and Rudolf Meidner did not primarily see supply side improvements as tax reliefs (of course not – in those days, the tax ratio in Sweden was only half of what it is today!); they prescribed a much broader range of measures. Remember, Rehn and Meidner wanted fiscal policy to be tight, to combat inflation, but on the supply-side they wanted numerous actions, in particular a broad program of active labour market policies – education, training, labour market exchanges – to break up bottle-necks, subsidies to increase geographical mobility, and – as stated above – equal pay for equal work both to ease mobility and to squeeze out low-productivity firms. All these measures could – and should – be coined supply-side measures since they work on the supply side of the economy.

It is important to make this very clear. Today, the term 'supply-side economics' is all too often associated with narrow tax-cutting proposals, and in particular with the 'voodoo economics' of the Laffer curve. But of course, any well-functioning economic policy today must work both through demand and supply management. In this sense, we should all embrace supply-side measures – such as an active labour market policy – as necessary ingredients in economic policy.

In practice, however, not many governments – certainly not the Swedish – followed this advice back in the 1960s and 70s. The Rehn-Meidner model presumed governments would be brave enough to carry out a tight fiscal policy also in years with rather slow growth, as well as to use both carrot and stick to promote mobility. Most governments, however, chose the easier way, i.e. to try to 'buy' lower unemployment through fiscal expansion. Moreover, in Sweden quite a few policy actions made the supply-side of the economy deteriorate rather than improve. I've already mentioned some of them; in particular, the very sharp tax hikes of the early 1970s were bound to have a negative impact.

We know now, in retrospect, that this policy mix created perverse effects. As inflation rose, the allegedly stable trade-off between inflation and unemployment proved to be highly unstable. Instead of low unemployment at the price of somewhat higher inflation the result was both high inflation and high unemployment – the 'stagflation' trap of the 1970s.

This was pretty much in line with what Rehn had predicted. However, in the academic and political debate on stagflation during the 1970s, the monetarist approach dominated, not the Rehn-Meidner strategy. As the long-term Phillips curve was seen to be vertical, conventional wisdom turned. It became accepted that the main task of stabilisation policies was to simply stamp out inflation – the tougher the better, since shock therapy was regarded as the most efficient way to crush inflationary expectations. The result we all know: low inflation again, but only after a long and gruelling struggle, which also carried with it permanently high unemployment in Europe.

Looking back, this stands out as a tragic experience. Neo-classical and monetarist economists and many conservative politicians set up vulgar Keynesianism as a straw man – the enemy to beat down – which they did. The alternative – to search for solutions à la Rehn-Meidner with another mix of monetary and fiscal policy and a more sophisticated approach to supply and demand – was never tried. The goal of full employment *and* low inflation was never really discussed.

As was described earlier, Sweden was no exception to this rule, although the Swedish turn-around came much later – not until the early 1990s. What is noticeable is that in the meantime – the late 1970s and 80s – the Swedish government did not attempt the Rehn-Meidner strategy, but relied primarily on traditional demand management and devaluations. Let me underline this: the Swedish Model – i.e. Swedish economic policy in practice – did not follow the Rehn-Meidner prescriptions as regards stabilisation policies. As has already been pointed out, fiscal policy was not as tight as Rehn had wanted. On the contrary, from the mid-1970s, Sweden experienced rapidly growing budget deficits. Neither was monetary policy tight. There were five devaluations between 1976 and 1982 and a big another big depreciation of the currency in 1992-93. During both the 1970s and 80s, inflation was high – clearly higher than the OECD average. Labour market policies were used less and less in the supply-enhancing way that Rehn had prescribed, but rather as a means of giving permanent support to the unemployed.

The truth is that there was no clear economic-political strategy in Sweden during these crucial years; neither monetarist nor Rehn-Meidner. Rather it was a process of muddling-through, while – sometimes desperately – keeping up the rhetoric of the Swedish Model.

My own conclusion is clear. Had Sweden – and other countries – more actively pursued the stabilisation policies prescribed by Gösta Rehn, the shocks and swings of the 1970s and 80s might have been less violent. The mix between supply and demand side measures was in fact more balanced in the Rehn-Meidner world than it turned out to be in the more rigid, demand-side dominated world of the actual Swedish Model of the 1970s and 80s.

Lately, however, Sweden has also learned that supply-side actions are important. During the past decade we have – belatedly – seen several important measures aimed at improving the supply side of the Swedish economy. There has been a comprehensive tax reform, broadening the tax bases and lowering tax rates, deregulations in a number of sectors have caused competition to stiffen and productivity to increase. But several of these measures were introduced during a period of extremely low demand, and their short-term effects were sometimes problematic.

To me this just proves the point even more. Had the actual Swedish Model included more supply-side ingredients, the U-turn would not have had to become as brutal, and the ensuing effects on disposable income and employment would not have been as difficult. The conclusion is, once again, that Gösta Rehn in his broader outlook on economic policy was far more flexible and modern than the practical policy pursued in his home country.

Life-long flexibility

Another area where Gösta Rehn has proved to be more far-sighted and flexible than those shaping the real-world Swedish model is the issue of working time. Here he early on argued for a greater flexibility in the working week – a theme that gradually developed into a plea for flexibility also in the time spent for education and vacation, indeed for the entire working life. 'Life-long flexibility' was the aim and the slogan he tried to popularise.

Gösta Rehn already in the 1930s, as a very young man, strongly opposed all proposals to shorten the regular working week as a means to lower unemployment. Such measures were defeatist, he claimed, since they would entail lower production and income; they would only mean accepting unemployment, albeit sharing it in another fashion. This conviction Rehn carried with him all his life, and consequently his view was that a general reduction of the working week was to be seen as a welfare reform best carried out during good times, as an alternative way (i.e., to real wage increases) to reap the benefits of increased productivity.

Having said this, Gösta Rehn was all for individual flexibility and shortening of the workweek. Already in the 1940s – long before anybody else – he proposed that workers should have the possibility of taking a total of three extra months off during a six-year period. These extra 'vacations' could be used for studies, vocational training or just being free, and the timing was to be co-ordinated with periods of slack in the labour market. Thus, more freedom of choice for the individual could also be used as a device to smooth the cyclical swings of the labour market. Soon he made his proposal more sophisticated, introducing incentives to postpone or change the timing of this extra 'vacation' depending on the labour market situation.

In the 1950s, during a great domestic debate that for several years raged over the future pension system, Rehn took his analysis a step further, claiming that the individual should have greater freedom to allocate his earned pension points as well. For instance, should he wish to spend some of them working part-time or taking some time off before his retirement, that ought to be encouraged.

This view he later, especially during his OECD years, expanded even more, finally arriving at the conclusion that the individual ought to have great freedom in allocating his working time over his entire life. Old age pension, education, vacation, etc – all this should be financed through one comprehensive insurance system, giving the individual a total 'drawing right' on his time for individual use. The wage earner in question then himself decides how and when to take time off for education, vacation, part-time work, etc., up to a limit which is decided by a certain need for resources for old age. The net effect of the time spent then determines retirement age.

This idea was never popular with the centralised Swedish social welfare system. No doubt it would have introduced a whiff of anarchy in the strictly regulated Swedish system. The development during the 1970s, when the different systems were expanded, was rather the opposite of what Rehn recommended, since they were kept separate, with different financing systems and rules, not to mention separate bureaucracies. Even today, the different systems – unemployment, education, pension – have their own rules and it is not possible to exchange time between them the way Rehn envisaged, even though greater flexibility as regards the working week itself has been introduced. Although it is hard to prove, my personal view is that this - separation of different programs, each adding its own costs and financing to the budget, was one factor leading to the explosion of the budget deficits in the 1970s and 80s.

The actual development of the Swedish Model during the 1970s was at odds with Rehn's proposals for a flexible working life also from another – political – point of view. The expansion of union power through labour market legislation in Sweden during the 1970s often restricted the possibilities for the individual to decide for himself, as the collective was given higher priority than the individual. Rehn was highly critical of this development and often complained to the SAP leadership that the system was becoming too regulated and inflexible. Using Hirschman's terminology, Rehn wanted to make 'exit' a more viable option for the individual, not only 'voice' for the union.

Rehn's ideas are obviously more in line with modern working life and its requirements for the individual to upgrade and re-educate his human capital. Actually, they are also – contrary to what rigid Swedish administrators have claimed – to a large degree compatible with a comprehensive welfare state and collective financing. A 'sabbatical' can easily combine individual freedom with the security of common financing and thus be an important improvement in the welfare system, without threatening it.

So far this proposal has not been accepted in Sweden. But recently we have begun to see the first cracks in the monolithic system. Greater flexibility as regards pension age will be an important part of the future Swedish pension system, a decision taken by parliament two years after Gösta's death. A 'labour time bank' is being discussed in the negotiations in the manufacturing sector, where union members at a cost are to have the right to take some time-out from work for different reasons. The economist Stefan Fölster, the grandson of Gunnar Myrdal, has introduced a controversial idea of an all-encompassing 'citizen's account' including most of the social welfare systems. And even the government itself has from time to time been flirting with the idea of using the sabbatical as a way to ease the burden of unemployment.

Personally, I fear that Sweden – like France and other countries on the continent – may start to look at shortening the work week as a way to fight unemployment. Several government commissions explored this strategy. Nevertheless, I am convinced that here too Gösta Rehn will prove to have been more far-sighted than the politicians and the administrators.

The original thinker and the epigones

My conclusion is that in important respects – in this paper I have covered long term growth strategy, wage formation, stabilisation policy and working life – Gösta Rehn was more original and far-sighted than the politicians and administrators who were responsible for the actual 'Swedish Model'. Moreover, I see Gösta's later developments, particularly regarding the sabbatical and working life issue, as transcending the original Rehn-Meidner Model. Gösta Rehn was obviously himself a more flexible and pragmatic thinker than many of his followers.

This is not a new experience. We have often seen how original thinkers have come up with thoughts which followers have turned into 'models', whereupon some of the originality and freshness were lost. Instead, the model gets equipped with scholastic adornments and turns rigid – and as a result becomes less fit to grapple with ever-changing reality.

We have seen it among the world's greatest economists and philosophers. Marx is an obvious example; Keynes is another. As the 'General Theory' became mathematised it also lent itself more easily to over-simplification and vulgarised economic-political policy conclusions.

Rehn did not become vulgarised in the same way – partly because Gösta himself was around to eagerly fight any such attempts. But the real-life Swedish Model that was built up and often defended with arguments originally created by Rehn surely did not look like what Rehn himself had advocated. I sense that this is something that many foreign proponents of the Rehn-Meidner Model and the Swedish welfare state have not realised. My own experience from meeting foreign friends, sympathetic to Sweden and Gösta Rehn, indicate that they often see the Swedish Model and the Rehn-Meidner Model as synonymous. As has been stated in this paper, this is not the case. The similarities between the two were great in the early 1960s, but after that the actual Swedish model became more rigid than Rehn had ever wanted it to be. This is obvious if you analyse the developments of the actual Swedish economic policy of the 1970s and 80s. Another divergence, one which grew during the same period, was that between Rehn and Meidner – Rehn becoming the more 'liberal' of the two, stressing the need for flexibility and freedom of choice, becoming highly critical of Meidner's wage earners funds' proposal, while still remaining an ardent Social Democrat.

My conclusion is that it is quite possible to hail Gösta Rehn as an original thinker and still be critical of the way the Swedish Model functioned in reality.

Conclusion

Given this background, an inevitable – but untestable – hypothesis is that had the actual Swedish model been more like Gösta Rehn's program and proposals, it would have been more flexible and resistant to external shocks. Harder transformation pressure would have meant higher growth and thus less vulnerability of both employment and budgets. More supply-oriented stabilisation policies would have made Swedish economic development less inflationary and thus less prone to fall into the stop-go politics characterising the past 15 years. And a more flexible organisation of working time and working life would have been both more modern and less costly than the strict centralisation that dominated the actual policy-making.

Another hypothesis follows from this. If we want to reform the ill-functioning Swedish Model of the 1980s – which is something the Swedes have been struggling with during the last decade – there are good reasons to look for advice and inspiration to the original Rehn-Meidner Model and also to the subsequent ideas of Gösta Rehn.

Gösta Rehn worked and fought all his life for a society that could combine economic growth with a humane and dignified life for all citizens. Central to him was to try to reach for full employment and low inflation. In political terms he wanted individual freedom and a market economy, co-existing with strong unions and a safety net giving security to the unfortunate.

Those of us who want to build such a society would do well to search for inspiration in the ideas of Gösta Rehn. We can of course search among his own recipes, which – I claim – were indeed more original and modern than the more rigid realisation of them in the 'Swedish Model'. We should reject the view that we must choose between full employment and low inflation. But we should also look to Gösta Rehn for inspiration in attitude and in methods of working and thinking. If Gösta Rehn had been here today, to attack unemployment, injustice and inflation, he would not have started by looking for available theories, blueprints or 'models' to follow.

He would have asked: What are the problems? What do we want to achieve? Had the available theories proven inadequate, he would gladly have thrown them out the window, only to proceed to kill off a number of sacred cows and happily propose any sacrilegious idea he could think of!

Why? Because, to quote Gösta himself, 'intelligent people are superior to the theory they happen to have available'. This was a motto he tried to follow all his life – more successfully than most. Is there a better challenge for a social scientist today?

Chapter 4

New Conditions in the Labour Market

Anders Bäckström

This paper argues that, unlike what is often assumed, structural changes on the labour market during the last 50 years have made Gösta Rehn's ideas even more relevant than they were at the time when they were developed.

For a long time the political economy literature tended to treat labour as a homogeneous factor of production. From the perspective of the last half-century this seemed to be a reasonable assumption in most cases. What was it that led Gösta Rehn to be one of the first economists to challenge this idea? (When I refer to Gösta Rehn, the reader should be aware that in most instances the appropriate reference would include Rudolf Meidner, since they worked closely together). Part of the explanation is that Gösta Rehn, working as an economist for trade unions, was much closer to everyday realities of the labour market than most other economists.

The late 1940s and the 1950s, the period when Gösta Rehn's ideas began to find their way into policies, was in Sweden, though by no means everywhere else, a rather idyllic period. Manufacturing was flourishing and expanding rapidly, attracting labour from the shrinking agricultural sector. As a result, unemployment figures were usually in the vicinity of two per cent. At that time it was fairly easy to go from one job to another. Most workers had only a short, basic education. A minority of the workers were craftsmen with more specialised skills. But by far largest proportion was general labourers.

Educational differences were considerable. The average length of education of young workers was 7 years, less than half that of professionals, who averaged 17 years. Since then this 10-year difference has been considerably reduced. Today there is only a 4-year difference in educational attainments, with young blue-collar workers averaging 12 years, and the professionals averaging 16 years.

One might expect that the rising level of education should make it easier for people to find jobs, but we know that is not the case. If it were, unemployment rates would not have risen to 8 per cent in Sweden as they did during the early 1990s. The effects of a general rise in the level of education are difficult to judge; what does count in every individual case is a person's relative education compared to other job applicants.

It is easy to see that more years spend in school reduces the risk of becoming unemployed. Figure 4.1 shows how unemployment rates are reduced through longer education.

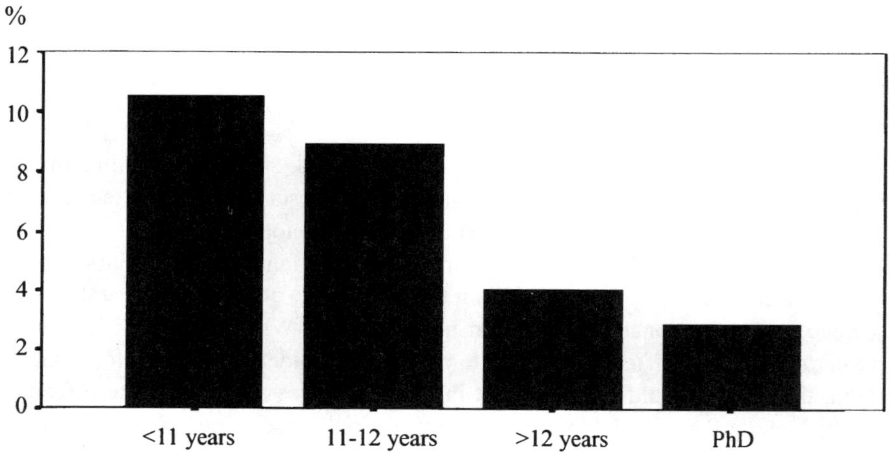

Source: Statistics Sweden, AKU.

Figure 4.1 Unemployment by education in 1996

These (1996) figures illustrate that staying in school longer significantly reduces the risk of becoming unemployed. This is due to a) the combination of a shortage of educated people and b) employers using education as a screening test in their hiring practices, reasoning that people have proved themselves capable through longer studies. Thus, even if educational differences are smaller than they used to be, they are more salient, nevertheless, when it comes getting to a job. When it comes to keeping a job, it is likely that, depending on the type of job, the frequency of on-the-job training is the salient factor.

As can be seen in Figure 4.2, on-the-job training has been increasing in Sweden in recent years. Presumably this trend has been prevalent for a much longer period of time, even though there are no statistics to prove it. But the distribution of the training is 'perverted' from the point of view of unemployment risk. People with less education receive much less on-the-job training than do people who have more education to begin with. This is not to say that there may not be rational explanations for this distribution of training, based on current or previous economic needs. Similarly, studies have found that, in general, people with more years of formal education are more prone to enrol in adult private or voluntary education in their leisure time.

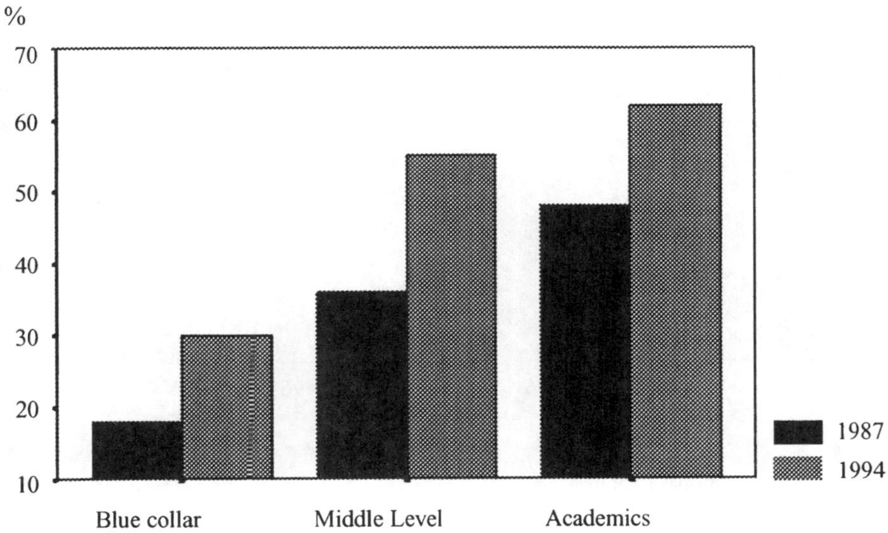

Source: Statistics Sweden.

Figure 4.2 In-firm-training 1987 and 1994

Statistics such as these show that there is room for corrective measures to promote better and more equal chances on the labour market. This is much easier to see nowadays than it was 50 years ago, when Gösta Rehn first drew his conclusions about the need for an active labour market policy in which labour market training and re-training was and still is an important part.

Increasing the labour market called for more specific skills for workers and by the late 1970s half of the new job offers were contingent on such skills having been acquired through either education or work experience. As can be seen from Figure 4.3, employers have since dramatically increased their expectations on new recruits. While twenty years ago a person without specific skills was eligible for half of the new jobs, since then opportunities have sharply decreased. In 1996, when this classification was abandoned, only 7 per cent of new jobs were available to unskilled persons.

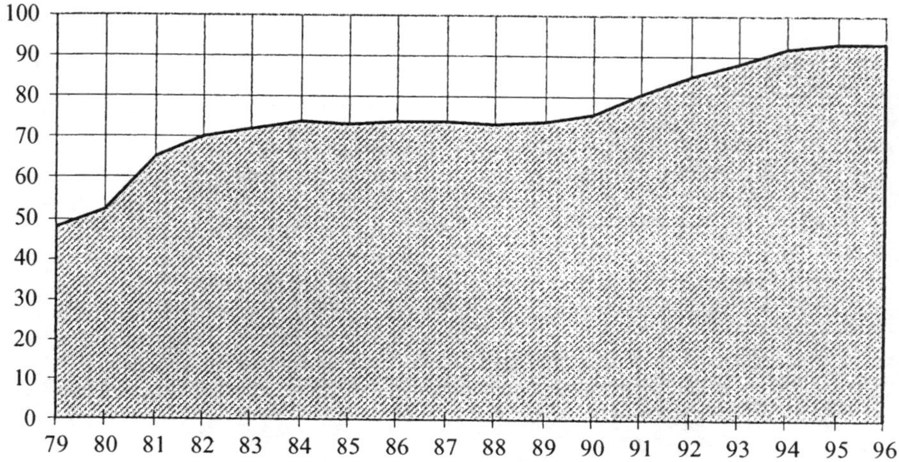

Source: AMS, National Labour Market Board.

Figure 4.3 Percentage of new vacancies with specific requirements 1979-96

This has made it overwhelmingly clear that it is necessary to raise the professional qualifications of most of the unemployed; many older people especially have weak educational backgrounds. If their specific skill becomes outdated they need retraining or upgrading. The situation is similar for young people with only a general education and no work experience. They need job-oriented training to improve their chances of getting a first job. Immigrants are of course in the absolutely worst position. They need both language training and job-specific training to have a chance of finding a job.

In this regard, there is much to be learned from the dual systems, of schooling and apprenticeships, practised in Austria, Germany and Switzerland, which for young people could constitute a good alternative or complement to labour market re-training programs.

What distinguished labour market training from other types of education and training? Firstly, it is automatically directed towards those who are most in need of training, namely those who are unemployed. In that way it can be said that the labour market training system corrects for mistakes earlier made in the chain of education and training. The second factor is its great volume. There are years when 5 per cent of the labour force in Sweden undergoes such training. The total number of participants every month corresponds to 1 to 2 per cent of labour force, but with a turnover time of 5 months, 2.5 sets of participants can be trained every year. That allows for a total of 2.5 to 5 per cent of the labour force.

Economic development requires a continuous structural change. This has brought and continues to bring rising standards of living. This positively affects most of us – but not those who lose their jobs. That is why there must be training programs that help the unemployed persons to strengthen their positions on the labour market and in new sectors of the economy. All of us benefit from this.

During the 1990s we saw the fastest structural change in the Swedish economy. Half a million jobs – in net terms – disappeared in a few years. The normal turnover of jobs is annually something between 500,000 and 800,000. The replacement jobs are often quite different from the jobs that were lost. Hundreds of thousands of persons must be re-trained or upgrade their qualifications.

The Swedish government has a strategy for overall increased competence on a broad basis through general education. That is a good long run strategy, but it has to be complemented by short-term activities, such as occupational training within labour market programs. It is a paradox that, even when we had over 10 per cent total unemployment (if we include those enrolled in labour market programs), we were able to observe increasing shortages of qualified workers. For some professions the shortage proved countrywide, such as the shortage of technicians, IT professionals, pipe welders, certified welders and machine operators.

Locally there are shortages of nurses, teachers, toolmakers, cooks, fast-food personnel, fitters, repair personnel, etc. The shortage of key persons in many cases prohibits companies from hiring other workers who are available. When unemployed persons receive appropriate training for these occupations, through labour market training, we have found that 70 to 100 per cent of them have found suitable jobs within 90 days.

Conclusions

Since the breakthrough associated with Gösta Rehn's ideas, there have been great changes in the labour market. But those changes have not in any way made his ideas obsolete. On the contrary, the need for an active labour market policy is more evident than ever. In many cases the level of labour market training needed nowadays is higher than that 50 years ago. But this is usually a specific manifestation of the overall developments in society. Let us cherish Gösta's heritage as he would have wished – by implementing what he suggested!

Chapter 5

Gösta Rehn, Civic Literacy, and the Swedish Model

Henry Milner

Introduction

In this article I seek to draw a link between the ideas of Gösta Rehn and what I term civic literacy, which I argue (Milner, forthcoming) to be a fundamental, though neglected, element of the Scandinavian social democratic welfare state. A society's level of civic literacy, simply put, corresponds to the proportion of its citizens able to competently exercise that citizenship. I contend that since informed individuals can better identify the effects alternative policy options have upon their own interests and those of others, high civic-literacy societies are more likely to attain relatively egalitarian social outcomes. And because those excluded from informed participation through lack of civic competence tend to be those at the bottom of the social ladder, the cost of low civic literacy is borne especially by the economically disadvantaged, while its economic benefits go mainly to the privileged.

In democratic societies, policy choices do not directly affect the values of adults; they do affect the incentives framing interests plus the information brought to bear in identifying one's interests and acting on them in accordance with one's values. My work describes how the policies and institutions of Scandinavian welfare states, popularly known as the 'Swedish Model', directly and indirectly foster a more civicly-literate population which uses that knowledge, in turn, to reinforce more egalitarian outcomes and institutions. In this paper, I make the case that this applies in particular to those aspects of the Swedish Model associated with the ideas of Gösta Rehn, foremost economic thinker of the postwar Swedish labour movement.

In the long term, successful redistributive welfare states are those able to maintain a high level of civic literacy by organizing institutions, as Olof Palme put it (referring to the handicapped), 'so that their demands and needs be as self-evident for social planning as the needs and interests of other more established citizens' (cited in Tilton 1994, p. 218). In this they take into account the fact that, as American economist Mancur Olson (1990, p. 58) stated: the costs of redistribution to the poor are lower, but – unlike their needs – more conspicuous than the costs of the combination of tariffs, quotas, subsidies, favourable regulations and similar 'implicit redistributions' to powerful interests.[1]

The above statement is found in a little-known monograph in which Olson offers some useful insights into Sweden's unexpectedly satisfactory economic performance from the 1950s to the 1980s. Sweden proved able to resist implicit redistributions, he argues, in part due to the high level of influence of its – extremely competent – professional economists.[2] Mancur Olson died prematurely in 1998, and never had the opportunity to pursue the matter further: what was it about Sweden that accounted for its economists' exceptional influence? He would have found the answer, in particular, in the distinct role of economists and economic ideas in the Swedish labour movement as it developed in the 20th century. And he would have found no better example than Gösta Rehn.

In the first part of this chapter I show how Rehn's ideas and approach were built on and contributed to the close link between the policies identified with the Swedish Model, on the one hand, and civic-literacy enhancing institutions and the policies that typified the traditional approach of the Swedish labour movement, on the other. I then argue that, in breaking this link in certain policies in the 1970s and 80s, leaders of the labour movement weakened the underpinnings of the Swedish Model. In the final part, I look at current indicators of civic literacy to assess the resilience of the Model at the start of the new century.

Gösta Rehn, the Rehn-Meidner Model and civic literacy in Sweden

Arriving in Stockholm in the summer of 1985, I discovered, to my pleasant surprise, that the man I knew of as father of the Swedish Model, Gösta Rehn, had an office in the same university building. I had come to Sweden to learn about social democracy in practice. In so doing, I was expressing misgivings about the presumption common among North American democratic socialists that socialism did not have to prove itself as practical and practicable in the real world (since the real world was a capitalist one in which the individual's 'true' human nature was repressed). Gösta put an end to any remaining vestiges of that notion at our first encounter. His very (Swedish) personality made him distinctly uncomfortable with ambiguity and fine theoretical distinctions distant from immediate practical choices: social democracy would succeed through the choices of real people in the real world or not at all.

Not that Gösta had abandoned his commitment to making a better, more equal society and world. But he would never let his – or my – ideals cloud our thinking about policies. Policies stand or fall by whether they can be implemented to meet concrete, measurable objectives under existing conditions. Hence his choices of where to expend his considerable intellectual energies – writing academic papers would never suffice, just as important was making the case before relevant decision makers, and the public, through op-ed pieces, letters to the editor, etc.[3] Note that this practicality had nothing to do with limits placed upon him by his long-time employer, the Swedish (blue-collar) union federation, LO. Gösta would never accept anything less than full intellectual freedom, and his attitude toward his American counterparts, whose job he understood as to provide economic arguments to support the union's line, was a mixture of sympathy and disdain.

Freedom of expression was a principle built into both his theoretical assumptions and policy objectives. Consider his attitude toward working time. He shared the preoccupation of the Swedish labour movement with redistribution through work rather than income; yet denounced as poor economics the programs of continental social-democrats that assumed that the amount of work was fixed so that unemployment could be fought by reducing the work week or forcing early retirement upon everyone. As recounted elsewhere in this volume, Gösta's alternative of 'life-long flexibility' proposed a sophisticated flexible approach, which maximized freedom of choice for individuals based on differing needs at different stages in their working lives.

As an economist, Gösta was skeptical of the scientific validity of the 'softer' social sciences, and pushed me to operationalize and concretize my own analysis, which emphasized the role of knowledge-disseminating institutions. Yet he did acknowledge that successful application of his own ideas presupposed informed workers and citizens, and that this was especially characteristic of Sweden and its Nordic cousins. These were matters that he simply took for granted, but they were achievements that could not but impress an outsider like myself (and led to my interest in identifying how this knowledge dimension found its way into the policies and assumptions of the Swedish labour movement, including in the postwar decades when Rehn's ideas had their greatest impact).

The components of the Rehn-Meidner Model are spelled out in other contributions to this book; here we are concerned primarily with those aspects linked to civic literacy, namely wage solidarity and active labour market programs. Both presuppose centralized bargaining; indeed, they rest on a corporatist relationship between labour, business and government. In a previous work (Milner 1994) I analyzed, from a corporatist theoretical framework, the particularities of the choices confronting a worker or employer under Swedish institutional arrangements. For Gösta, the matter was straightforward: trade unionists, whatever their values, were rational actors. In the context of centralized corporatist bargaining, leaders of encompassing trade unions in an export-oriented economy could not but be aware of the fact that increasing inflation slowed growth, and, thus, harmed the position of their members, such knowledge at the top was not enough. It was crucial, in effect, that the knowledge be disseminated to the shop floor – otherwise leaders could not be expected to keep the lid on their members' wage demands – whatever government was in power.

Hence part of the job of trade unionists and their advisors was to explain the facts and analyses underlying their policy positions in a manner understandable to the rank and file and consistent with their experience: Gösta wrote frequently in the trade union press and was always available to speak to any group. In words and actions he exemplified what was fundamental to the Swedish labour movement. In the terms of this analysis, application of the Rehn-Meidner Model was premised on a high level of civic literacy, that is, on the expectation that workers and citizens would (be able to) have the sophisticated historical, geographical and economic knowledge to place into context their wider and long-term interests. Implicit in the Model (and in many of Rehn's other proposals, as well as his choices as a social actor) was a legacy of labour-movement practices enhancing civic literacy which are described in the next section.

Today, these practices are taken for granted in Sweden. Yet, in fact, while choosing to build on aspects of inherited Scandinavian culture that were conducive to civic literacy, the Swedish labour movement could have done otherwise. Labour movements elsewhere placed less priority on enhancing civic literacy: on one side, 'business unions' explicitly limited concerns to bread and butter issues; on the other, rhetorically revolutionary unions dismissed individual interest – and therefore, implicitly, the knowledge to act upon it – as 'false consciousness.' It is in this sense that Sweden's course most merits the description of 'the middle way.'

The roots of civic literacy in the Swedish labour movement

Sweden entered the 20th century among the more – but not most – literate of societies.[4] The hierarchical structure of society – including and especially institutions disseminating knowledge – came under attack in the 19th century through the Free-Church and temperance movements. At the same time, the Folk High Schools movement spread out from Denmark to provide secondary-level education to talented and ambitious young workers and peasants. By the beginning of the 20th century, the mantle of adult education had been picked up by popular educational associations, the most important of which were linked to the labour movement. The ABF (the Workers' Educational Association) was founded in 1912 by Rickard Sandler, who later became Prime Minister. The ABF, which is affiliated with the LO, the Social Democratic Party (SAP), cooperatives and organizations representing women, retired persons and tenants, drew inspiration from the early study circles of the temperance lodges in developing the principles guiding its program: the equal value of all people and the ability of every person to take responsibility for his or her own life and share in the responsibility for the common concerns of society. Sandler 'had a strong belief in the workers' capability and their right to choose their own education,' which translated into ABF's refusal to accept the position of authoritarians of the right or left who assumed that workers need guidance as to how to think (Blid 1989, p. 9).

A valuable insight into the approach developed in this period is found in the work of social historian Ronny Ambjörnsson, whose 1987 paper entitled 'The Honest and Diligent Worker' evocatively recreates the experiences in the coastal town of Holmsund in the Northern region of Västerbotten around the turn of the century.

> The debates become successively more lively... What shall society that allows good people to live a good life look like? From reading aloud, the step is not long to a more regular, educational activity and already by the middle of the 1890s the ground has been laid for a library that not only comprises temperance literature but also books of a more general, culture-historical interest... The diligence that the lodges cultivated finds its expression even in the early enthusiasm of the trade union movement... Joint parties and trips were often arranged.... for education is also high within the union. One reads aloud articles from the papers *Socialdemokraten* and *Västerbottenskuriren* and also recommends the studying of different books. Ignorance is seen to be as great an enemy as drunkenness.... The discussions... can be seen as exercises in looking at reality from different angles.... Reading has a similar function.... Within the study-circle ... is developed ... the idea that it is a person's duty as an individual to take part in the discussions that, alone, lead to a better world... Parallel to the courses in... culture and literature, [are] courses ... in local-government.... Knowledge – or more correctly education – shall guarantee democracy.

ABF's program commits it 'to educate the members of its affiliated organizations for positions in associations, working life and society; and to create conditions for everyone to participate in freely chosen education and cultural life.' Study circles 'seek to stimulate a critical attitude, to help clarify the difference between facts and opinions on crucial issues of the day.' Courses concerned with civic education are thus given priority.[5] For example, the current (fall 1999) program of the ABF in Umeå (Holmsund is now a suburb of Umeå) offers the usual range of courses in languages, computers, art, music, and nature appreciation, but also courses in organizing groups and co-operatives, in public speaking, writing and understanding media, as well as study circles on social and civil rights, the United Nations, war and peace, the future of democracy, feminism, various aspects of history, and important contemporary books. Such courses supplement more specific courses given by the trade unions themselves to enable members to improve organizational skills, interpret financial documents, and understand economic and social policies. Local trade unions also appoint 'book ombudsmen' (see Milner 1989, 1994).

The ABF is the largest of 11 adult education associations organizing study circles and related activities.[6] Moreover, adult education neither begins nor ends with the study circles but extends to the municipally-run Komvux courses for completing compulsory and upper secondary education,[7] the various programs offered annually to some 200,000 Swedish adults in the Folk High Schools,[8] and the labour-market training courses run in close collaboration with employers' organizations and trade unions. These latter constitute a direct application of the 'active labour market policies' at the core of the Rehn-Meidner Model. But, as understood here, they are but the tip of the iceberg of informed workers and citizens on which the model is based.[9]

The concern with continuing education extended beyond the education sector. The charter of SR, the Swedish public broadcasting system, mandated it to promote adult education in cooperation with the adult education societies.[10] It took the lead in producing radio programs for use by 'listening circles' whose 'foremost common denominator was their role as a school for citizenship' (Nordberg 1998, p. 377). The content of radio and, later, television programming continued to be influenced by this relationship, even after the formal link had been cut.

The SAP entered government in the 1920s, and the 1930s marked the beginning of a period of close-to hegemony for the party. The dominant image, articulated in the favourite metaphor of Per-Albin Hansson, Prime Minister in the 1930s and 40s, was of Sweden as (building) the 'People's Home,' in which one acts toward others as toward family members, the weakest to be helped, not exploited. Such help, it was clearly understood, was designed to foster intellectual at least as much as material advancement. This theme pervaded the work of Gunnar and Alva Myrdal, who significantly influenced the Swedish welfare state in its formative years. The Myrdals' approach seems manipulative by today's standards, but their position is sometimes exaggerated because of a tendency to treat programs they designed to protect children as if they were meant to be applied to adults (see Milner 1997a). This misses a fundamental distinction: unlike children, adults can become what Gunnar Myrdal termed 'propaganda safe.'

> Except in Sweden, a person's wealth and income is not a matter for public record, but is supposed to be entirely his own private affair – with the provision only that they must be disclosed in confidence, to the tax-assessing authorities.... In this undemocratic and protective social system a major role is played by the formidable power of the communications industry to influence people's attitudes and choices.... Under the influence of propaganda for private consumption of all kinds, which is not matched by any equally powerful campaign for the consumption of services provided by organized society, the voters tend to keep the public spending below the level that would be rational.... Reforms in the interest of the effective implementation of the voters' true inclinations ... have everywhere to overcome tremendous inhibitions, created by the services of the communications industry (Myrdal 1958, pp. 80-1). Progress has to rely on education.... I am quite aware that this prescription is nothing less and nothing more than the age-old liberal faith that 'knowledge will make us free' (Myrdal 1958, pp. 80-1).

For Gunnar Myrdal, economists and other intellectuals had a key role to play in helping individuals make sense of their world.[11] But Myrdal's domestic political involvement ended abruptly after the War, shortened by his failure as a member of the government to see that the Keynesian policies he and other 'Stockholm-School' economists had successfully promoted in the 1930s would not suffice in the post-war boom of high profits and little unemployment.

The underlying premises of the Rehn-Meidner model

After the war, a new generation of economists emerged, among the most influential of which was Gösta Rehn. The Rehn-Meidner Model, in effect, sought to (re)build the people's home in the context of the conditions prevailing after the war. Like his predecessors in the Stockholm School, Rehn was clear-minded about the real choices economic actors made and, thus, the importance of appropriate incentives. Rehn saw that Keynesian non-selective macroeconomic stimulation, because it depended on the unions restraining wage demands, was a long-term prescription for job-destroying inflation. Only under conditions corresponding to the Model could trade unionists be expected to take the principle of wage solidarity – equal pay for equal work – into contract negotiations, and thus promote efficient industries and enterprises.

Active labour market policies would move trained workers from declining to expanding industries, promoting optimal labour-market choices on the part of workers and consumers (well-informed through the network of adult-education oriented activities noted above). Moreover, non-inflationary growth could be attained by enlisting the support of labour as well as employers for tight fiscal and monetary policies to enhance the demand for, and supply of, appropriately trained workers – their mobility underpinned by universalistic welfare-state guarantees. The workings of the Model thus required that welfare-state entitlements be tied to one's status as citizen rather than employee so as not to inhibit the requisite mobility. But note that it was a means to an end, not an end itself. It was Rehn's flexible approach to social and labour market policies, an approach reflected in a number of innovative policy contributions later in his career, including tax-supported wage subsidies and voluntary early retirement and sabbatical schemes, that, as we shall see, distinguished Rehn from certain of his successors. For Rehn, it was outcomes that mattered, and different means of achieving those outcomes could be envisaged for different circumstances.

Effective adaptation is thus the key: Rehn understood the paradox that only by adapting to changing economic circumstances could the dual social-democratic objectives of high employment and egalitarian outcomes be maintained. This is even truer today under the constraints that globalized markets place on the policy choices. The Rehn-Meidner Model was an optimal formula for attaining this under the conditions of the 1950s and 60s; but it was only a formula. Rehn understood as well as anyone that new elements needed to be introduced if it were to serve the requisite purposes under the conditions of 'stagflation' in the 1970s, and the new international economic environment that followed the oil shocks. Key Swedish social democratic policy makers sometimes did not, however, with – as Eklund argues forcefully elsewhere in this volume – unfortunate consequences.

In terms of the argument presented here, it is an informed citizenry that is a crucial, though seldom acknowledged, prerequisite to the effectiveness of this process of adaptation. And it is because they operated from a theoretical framework, which neglected this dimension, that Rehn's successors at key moments failed to adopt policies that served the needed purposes. This is not to suggest that the commitment to civic literacy was repudiated; on the contrary, it has been regularly reaffirmed. For example, the opening section of the SAP's official position paper on EU membership proclaimed as its starting principle: 'that everybody is both desirous and capable of playing a part in the running of society… of acquiring knowledge and insights which will enable him to play a part in the life of the community' (SAP 1993, p. 6).

Civic literacy also found its way into certain policy choices of the 1970s, notably in keeping with certain recommendations of the Report of the SAP working group on equality, chaired by Alva Myrdal (1971). One was to allow older Swedes to return to school to catch up on opportunities missed and thus enter the 'educational society for all', a recommendation taken up in the 1974 Education Act, which explicitly established 'recurrent education' as a core objective. Another was to attempt to counteract the potentially adverse effects of commercialism on civic literacy, taken up that same year in the comprehensive bill on cultural policy, one of the four objectives of which was to counteract the adverse effects of commercialization.

Decommodification and the Rehn-Meidner model

Nevertheless, the radical rhetoric of the Myrdal Report, which became a powerful statement of Swedish social-democratic policy goals for the next decade, paved the way for policies which did not live up to the commitment to informed free individual choice in the labour market. Influenced by New Left ideas, a new generation of labour intellectuals had come to question the old corporatist 'historical compromise' with business. It sought to use the state to impose on business a number of regulations, which violated that compromise. Ironically, this approach came to be associated with Rudolf Meidner, who headed an LO task force to rethink the relationship between labour and management within enterprises. While a case can be made that the union dominated wage-earner funds called for in the Meidner Report constituted a trade-off for wage restraint on the part of workers in the high-profit manufacturing sectors, this was not the way it was originally presented or at least and – more importantly – perceived.

The wage-earner funds, as claimed in certain public statements at the time,[12] were intended to rupture rather than reinforce the old historical compromise between business and labour by leading to a gradual take over of key segments of industry by the funds.[13] As such, the Meidner Plan in effect sought to put into action the 'power-resource' theorists' (e.g. Esping-Andersen 1985) call for a class coalition around the public control of investment capital as the next stage in the struggle of 'politics against markets'. Meidner did not necessarily share Esping-Andersen's view of the 'decommodification of labour' as the unalterable defining criterion of the social-democratic welfare state; Rehn certainly did not. But it nevertheless came to be seen as the dominant intellectual position of the Labour movement.

At least rhetorically, the labour movement of the 1970s came to view decommodification as an end in itself, and not a means – as under the Rehn model. The transformative pressure central to the Rehn model, which was based on workers acting on their informed interest to move to productive sectors, industries and firms, fits very poorly with decommodification which seeks to shelter workers from such pressure. Moreover, casting decommodification policies in the language of workers' interests is misleading. In reality, such policies sooner or later set informed workers' individual interests against those of others since an informed worker understands that though she benefits by being freed of market-driven imperatives inhibiting her from staying home when capable of working, she loses if (many) others draw the same benefit.

This is just what happened. To decommodify workers, sick-leave and long-term disability replacement rates were raised to 90 and even 100 per cent of pay, while measures to monitor employees' actions were minimized, and financial incentives for employers doing so removed. In the tight Swedish labour market of the latter 1980s, this drove absenteeism and the relative cost of labour up to worrisome levels. High absenteeism showed what practical economists like Gösta Rehn always knew, that support for welfare-state institutions and outcomes (which polls showed had not declined) was no safeguard against such free riding. As long as one can assume that one's own choices do not affect the overall outcome (and thus the plight of the weakest), even good social democrats can free ride on the bus to the people's home.

The SAP was defeated in 1976, and when it returned to power in 1982, it removed the confiscatory elements from the watered down version of the wage-earner funds that was implemented. But the damage could not be undone. LO's adoption of the Meidner Plan symbolized the end of the traditional corporatist relationship. Business leaders opposed to that relationship had mobilized to fight the wage-earner funds and, in so doing, gained ascendancy in the employers' organization (SAF). Centralized bargaining was undermined, and, by the end of the 1980s, SAF representatives had been withdrawn from central corporatist bodies. The overall effects have been well summarized by Rothstein.

> The Swedish Model rested on a limited role for government. It left the parties in the labour market to sort out their problems by themselves. This limited role for the political sphere in the labour market was abandoned during the 1970s. The LO and the Social Democratic party gave the electorate the impression that the political system would be able to increase social equality through the expansion of the welfare state, introduce

> economic democracy through the wage-earner funds, establish industrial democracy through the new system of labour laws, secure full employment through an active labour market policy and Keynesian economics, and so forth. The result in every one of these areas has been retreat or outright defeat... The SAF abandoned the central wage negotiations, began a vigorous and rather successful campaign supporting neo-liberal economic principles and withdrew from all corporatist boards and agencies. The situation between the parties today can best be described as endemic distrust... According to the chairman of the SAF, 'there is too little confidence in the Swedish labour market. And when there is no confidence, distrust will grow' (Rothstein 1998, p. 60).

SAF remains opposed to centralized bargaining and its representatives have not returned to the peak corporatist labour market and related bodies. The Swedish labour movement has renewed its commitment to centralized bargaining and corporatist structures, but its organizational and political strength – compared to its counterpart in the other Nordic countries – give it little incentive to accept corporatist compromises that could win employer support. As Jochem describes elsewhere in this volume, foundations were laid in the 1980s in the other Nordic countries for remodeling the wage bargaining systems to accommodate the new conditions – but not in Sweden. Hence, Swedish corporatism cut a poor figure in the last quarter of the 20th Century. Corporatism in Denmark is on relatively solid footing; the same is true of Norway[14] – and, especially, of Finland.[15] As a result of the diminution of its capacity to adapt to external shocks through corporatist compromises combined with a slowdown in the international economy and greater capital mobility, Sweden's economy performed dismally through most of the 1990s.

The current situation: Civic literacy in Sweden in comparative context

Yet Sweden's poor showing did not entail, despite the affirmations of certain critics, the demise of the Swedish Model. This is because corporatist relationships and expectations go deeper than developments in the more visible central institutions. For example, Agell and Lundborg (1993, p. 18) concluded from their research[16] that Swedish 'firms are much less convinced about the advantages of decentralized bargaining than the organization that speaks in their name.' And in the 1990s there were somewhat successful efforts to contain inflation through pattern bargaining, even though agreement on adapting labour laws to the globalizing economy proved elusive.

Sweden recovered impressively late in the decade, on the heels of cuts in entitlements. Their overall effect does not appear to have undermined the redistributiveness of outcomes.[17] In the last two sections of this paper, I argue that this ability to rebound from even serious mistakes at the top is due to the resiliency of the underpinnings of corporatism in civil society. Drawing upon comparative indicators of civic literacy (see Milner forthcoming), I contend that in Sweden, as in its Nordic neighbours, the civic-literacy enhancing institutions and policies continue to foster the capacity of relevant actors to make informed choices to adapt ever more rapidly to changing conditions.

A good place to start is the OECD International Adult Literacy Survey test of functional literacy (IALS), in which Sweden scored highest among the participating countries (OECD 1997, 2000). Figure 5.1 below reveals that the main reason for Sweden's ranking lies in the high levels of functional literacy among Swedes who haven't finished high school.[18]

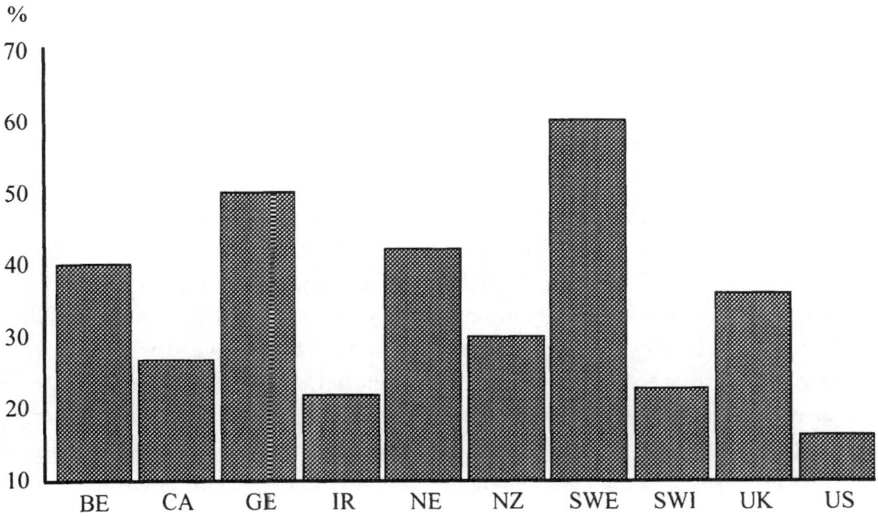

Source: OECD 1997, p. 29.

Figure 5.1 Functional literacy without high school completion

How has this been achieved? Adult education is clearly part of it. A 1998 Royal Commission Report investigating adult education services found that study circles and related activities still play a prominent role in the lives of citizens. There were a total of 336,037 study circles in 1997, lasting an average of 35 to 40 hours, with a total of 2,844,356 participants. While it was down from the decade's high of 343,732 in 1990-91, it was higher than most years since.[19] In addition, adult education societies in that year organized 165,000 miscellaneous popular cultural events (a number that has been rising steadily), as well as 38,000 non-course pedagogical activities, such as conferences and lectures.

Another area, also noted above, consists of policies that reduce dependence on commercial media – especially television – and promote the development and use of alternate sources of public-affairs knowledge. This entails reducing the comparative cost of newspapers and other printed sources of information as well as encouraging public-service television and radio. Norway, Finland and Sweden subsidize daily newspapers that are not leaders in their markets (Sanchez-Tabernero 1993, p. 229),[20] which benefit to an amount between 5 and 35 percent (averaging around 11 per cent) of revenues, while the subsidies traditionally account for 3 to 4 per cent of all newspaper revenues (Hadenius and Weibull 1999, Salokangas 1999).[21] Not surprisingly, then, among European countries, Norway, Sweden and Finland rank first, second and fourth in daily newspaper titles (Sanchez-Tabernero 1993, p. 40). Despite cutbacks in several but not all of the Nordic countries in the 1990s[22] there is still an unambiguous relationship between such government efforts at encouraging newspaper reading and national circulation figures.[23] Scandinavia stands out as that corner of the world where reading daily newspapers remains an unquestioned part of everyday life. Except for Denmark,[24] 80 to 90 per cent of people over 16 read at least one reasonably good daily newspaper,[25] with little variation by gender or even educational background (Hadenius and Weibull 1999, p. 149).[26]

A direct parallel is to be drawn between an approach emphasizing newspaper reading and one that regards radio and television primarily as media of public service information. Despite the recent inroads of commercial broadcasting, it is still fair to say that in all four Nordic countries public-service channels remain dominant, if not always in audience share, certainly in setting the standard in news and public affairs.

Newspaper subsidies were established not simply to foster diversity in the media, but also to facilitate the political parties publicly presenting their views.[27] Conversely, but for the same civic-literacy related reason, the Scandinavian countries are among the strictest when it comes to equal access to television. Sweden and Norway have, by and large, eliminated political party television commercials, while Denmark restricts campaign television commercials to the public-service channels with equal time allotted to all parties. Hence written information remains a significant feature of Nordic politics.[28] So do study circles. Each of the Swedish parties is associated with one of the adult educational associations, which, especially during election years, arrange study circles to familiarize party members and sympathizers with party programs and strategies. Parliament also gets into the act: for example, in the latter half of 1995, the all-party commission[29] to look into changes in the structure of European institutions (that became the Amsterdam Treaty) was mandated to inform the population by stimulating discussion in study groups, schools, etc to ensure that by the date the Intergovernmental Conference began, at least half the population had adequate knowledge about the issue.

Civic literacy is also enhanced by regulations governing the availability and accessibility of information related to the public interest. There are two key guarantees related to civic literacy: first, the requirement (noted in the quote from Gunnar Myrdal) that tax-return information be public,[30] and, second, the obligation of all public institutions to open their books to interested citizens, with ombudspersons appointed to ensure that this is done (Axberger 1996).[31]

In these and other ways civic literacy is enhanced. Citizens have (ready access to) the knowledge to exercise their citizenship competently, and thus better attain their policy objectives. A very graphic illustration of the relationship between civic literacy and the outcomes sought by Gösta Rehn and his colleagues is provided by a Figure 5.2, a chart taken from the latest IALS survey, which included Denmark and Norway.[32]

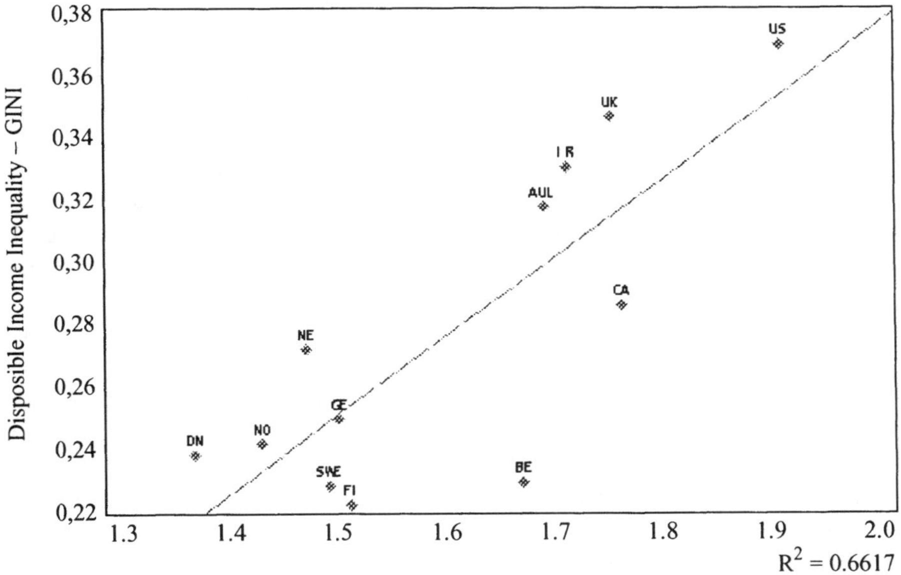

Sources: OECD (2000) and Luxembourg Income Study (www.lis.ceps.lu/ineqtable.htm)

Figure 5.2 Inequality in the distribution of literacy (9th to 1st decile)

Prospects for the future

Gösta Rehn would have rejected any attempt to treat the prescriptions of his model as absolute. His concern was flexible adjustment to existing conditions in order to attain the desired outcomes of close to full employment and fair income distribution. I contend that as long as it can count on an informed population, the Swedish or Scandinavian model should be able to find appropriate means of adapting to the exigencies of the day. Just as the Rehn-Meidner Model served in the 1950s and 60s, so contemporary versions will be developed, consisting of appropriately tailored policies making it possible to fairly distribute both the benefits and costs of globalization. In Sweden, practically all students (98 per cent) now continue beyond compulsory school at age 16, and 80 per cent graduate from upper secondary schools within four years (Skolverket 1998), compared to only 75 per cent in 1971. Recent trends in media consumption are, on balance, fairly encouraging. Swedish newspapers showed signs of (re)gaining readers at the end of the 1990s. The proportion of Swedes watching at least one of the public television news broadcasts has remained steady, even among young people.[33] A recent study conducted at Gothenburg University[34] shows further that even with the increase in private station viewership, the feared 'race to the bottom' has not materialized.[35]

Unlike elsewhere, the development of information technology does not appear to be creating greater inequality of intellectual resources in the form of a widening 'digital divide.' A March 1999 Eurobarometer study (#50.1) entitled 'Measuring Information Society' found that among Europeans, the proportion that used a PC in their own home and were connected to the Internet was highest in Sweden, as was the level of interest in, and willingness to pay for, on line/interactive training. The attitude toward IT training is paralleled by that toward electronic access to local or national government information about local or national policy initiatives and decisions, local services, etc, with Denmark, Finland and Sweden, among the seven EU member states above average in both interest in and willingness to pay for them.

Related to civic literacy is the Scandinavian attitude toward Europe. On one side, they display 'Europeaness' in their attitudes toward people from other European countries, fluency in European languages, and propensity, when young, to travel and live outside their national boundaries.[36] Yet they evince a high level of awareness of the possible dangers presented by continental integration to the institutions that have secured traditional welfare outcomes. Norway remains outside the EU; Denmark and Sweden are members, but have so far eschewed monetary union. Only Finland, which joined along with Sweden, is part of EMU, but due to history and geography is very much aware of its quite distinct identity.[37] They all strongly insist on transparent relations with the EU[38] and oppose political union.[39]

The danger of political union lies in its effect on civic literacy. To remain informed, citizens must understand not merely the relationship between the institutions of her own state and those of the supranational bodies, but also the cultural-ideological-institutional context of representatives of other member states. Political union is thus in contradiction with the institutional transparency underlying civic literacy. This need not be the case with further European economic integration. While monetary union will deprive the Swedish State of an important macroeconomic tool for attaining desired policy outcomes – and is strongly opposed for that reason by a minority among whose spokespersons is Rudolf Meidner – the mainstream position is more nuanced, one privately expressed by Gösta Rehn as his health was failing. In principle, it welcomes rather than fears economic integration, even monetary union, remembering that Sweden had benefited from earlier phases of economic integration by responding with appropriate policies to pressure it placed on Swedish firms and employees. In the 1950s and 1960s, the main component of these policies was the Rehn-Meidner Model, and they brought out the best in Sweden: a high-employment, highly technological industrial economy and a generous efficient welfare state.

But, as we have seen, things changed after the 1970s when inappropriate choices turned the mechanisms themselves into absolute principles, rather than adapting mechanisms and policies to attain desired outcomes under changing circumstances, resulting in poor economic performance. In the latter 1980s and especially the 1990s, Sweden fell behind its Nordic neighbours, and its vaunted middle way served as model no more. Out of this experience, it appears, came an uncertainty in Sweden's institutional capacity to adapt to external changes, and thus a profound ambivalence about the role of Sweden in an integrating Europe. If the analysis presented here – that the capacity of the social democratic welfare state to adapt is linked to civic literacy – is accurate, then Sweden need not fear economic integration (see Milner forthcoming). The high civic literacy characteristic of the Swedish Model does not seem to have been eroded, and can expect to be maintained as long as political union is avoided.

The overall success of the Model in Scandinavia in the latter half of the last century was based on – and has perpetuated – a kind of virtuous circle. An informed population chooses institutions and policies that reinforce egalitarian outputs and outcomes but also, indirectly, contribute to keeping the population informed. As we enter the 21st Century, we have reason to expect that the Scandinavian countries will continue to constitute an alternative 'model' to low civic literacy societies which reduce a large segment of their population to ill-informed consumers. Those societies, of which the US is at the leading edge, can be expected to become more and more a reflection of the globalized world economy: a minority of 'winners,' indeed 'big winners,' and a majority of 'losers.' They will be losers not so much due to economic deprivation, but in lacking the capacity to take informed action to make their society better for themselves and others. The most important legacy of Gösta Rehn, and those who came before and after, remains: to show that we can do better.

Notes

1 These narrow special-interest organizations, he adds elsewhere, represent only a tiny minority of the population and can be outvoted, except that 'most of the society doesn't notice or understand what is happening [and that understanding depends] on the quality of economic thought and the extent of economic literacy' (Olson 1996, p. 78).

2 In particular, Olson attributes Sweden's performance to its embracing free trade and thus inhibiting implicit redistributions to powerful interest groups through tariffs and other forms of protectionism. The economic gain to be realized from trade liberalization is probably the most important shared policy principle of professional economists.

3 This was the norm, not the exception, for leading Swedish economists like Myrdal, Ohlin, etc. Of course, Rehn frequently complained that his advice went unheeded. But it was seldom ignored. A good example is the commission set up by the Ministry of Finance in the early 1980s to assess his proposal of marginal employment subsidies. Rehn was himself made a member and, ultimately in vain, did his best to sell it as practicable: He was put on the committee in part, it has been suggested, to dampen his public criticism of the government's failure to act.

4 Crafts (1997, p. 306) cites statistics from 1870, indicating literacy in Sweden to be 75 per cent, placing it even with the US, and behind Switzerland, Denmark, Germany, the Netherlands, Canada and the UK, though well ahead of Norway, at 55 per cent, with Finland, at only 10 per cent.

5 Over 50,000 people participated in ABF study circles on EU membership in the period preceding the 1994 referendum.

6 The ABF annually organizes about 100,000 study circles for over a million participants (roughly 30 per cent of all study circles in Sweden).

7 In 1999, more than 200,000 adults took such Komvux courses at the upper-secondary level (Swedish Budget Statement 1999, p. 18).

8 These are approximately 140 popular institutes of adult education that provide specialized courses in many areas of knowledge usually tailored to the needs of the economy in the regions where they are situated – including distance education in the remote regions.

9 Rehn's interest in the relationship between work and education is manifested by the fact that his only monograph (Rehn 1980) is on Education and Youth Employment, undertaken for the Carnegie Council on higher education policy.

10 In 1931 Yngve Hugo of the ABF was appointed head of the educational division of SR.

11 Myrdal described his own work as that of an 'economic technician... grouping problems even before they reach actuality and formulating them in a way that is intelligible to the general public ... [to] lead public opinion and by his initiative give a realistic setting and a rational shape to political questions as they arise' (cited in Olsson 1994, pp. 48-9).

12 For example, according to the LO newspaper Fack in 1975, the funds 'deprive capital owners of their ownership' without which 'we can never fundamentally alter society and carry through economic democracy' (cited in Heclo and Madsen 1987, p. 298).

13 Rehn, in Paris at the OECD when the idea was put forth, privately expressed his displeasure, and reluctantly acquiesced to the wage-earner funds only in a watered-down form (see Milner 1989, pp. 131-7).

14 According to Wallerstein and Golden (1997, pp. 724-5) bargaining in Norway has been recentralized. (See also the article by Høgsnes and Longva in this volume, as well as Dølvik and Stokke 1998).

15 In Finland, 'continuity is still the strongest feature.... Contacts and implicit understandings ... can be used as the social 'infrastructure' for consensual policy making at the national level' (Lilya 1998, p. 187, Bobacka 1999). See also the article by Ervasti in this collection.

16 The research consisted of a survey of personnel directors of 180 Swedish manufacturing firms, employing 40 per cent of the sector's employees.

17 Evidence from a recent study on income distribution in Sweden suggests that: 'Sweden has been able to retain its position... as one of the four or five countries with the most equal distributions of annual income... [with no less] long run equality and... equality of opportunity' (Björklund 1998, pp. 75-6).

18 A related IALS question asked subjects about their parents' educational attainment, income and occupation. For each of these categories, differentials in IALS scores were smaller for the Nordic participant, Sweden, than for all other countries.

19 Music appreciation was the most popular subject, followed by international affairs and media studies. Overall, about one-third of study circles centered on political-social issues, the number rising and declining according to the proximity of elections and referenda, and the salience of issues in public debate at the national or local levels.

20 The only other country known to this writer with direct subsidy programs is Austria.

21 In 1990 there were roughly 275 daily newspapers in the three countries plus Denmark (Høst 1991), which have a combined population slightly lower than that of Canada – where, by way of comparison, there were 106 dailies in 1995. To this should be added the large number of weekly newspapers and magazines – in the early 1990s in Sweden there were 85 and 46 respectively.

22 The most significant decline was in Finland, where the total subsidy was drastically reduced from a high of 478 million FIM in 1991 to 150 million FIM in 1993, and since reduced even further, and where overall circulation declined almost 15 per cent between 1989 and 1996 (Salokangas 1999, p. 100). In Sweden, circulation also declined, at more than 1 per cent per year in the early 1990s (Hadenius and Weibull 1999), though subsidies amounting to 435 million SEK were only slightly reduced (Carlsson and Bucht 1997). Norwegian subsidies remained more or less steady at 250-300 million NRK (Høst 1999, p. 119) in the early 1990s (though the subsidy declined to 188m NRK in 1998); Norway has also seen the smallest reduction in circulation.

23 I have written on the importance of such policies in earlier books on the development of the contemporary welfare state in the Nordic countries (Milner 1989, 1994).

24 In Denmark in 1993, only 78 per cent of men and 71 per cent of women read daily newspapers. Denmark has never directly subsidized newspapers (Søllinge 1999).

25 Overall, a daily morning paper is read by 72 per cent of Swedes (aged 9-79) but only 60 per cent of those aged 15-24 (Mediebarometer 1997, p. 54). (This does not include the very popular free daily Metro in Stockholm and Gothenburg.) Those not reading at least one morning or (less weighty) afternoon paper in Sweden make up 19 per cent of those aged 9-79 (Mediebarometer 1997, p. 52). (In 1995, for Norway it was 16 per cent, for Finland 3 per cent (aged 12+), and for Denmark (age 13+) 28 per cent (Carlsson and Bucht 1997, p. 156).

26 Concerted efforts are also made to encourage the reading of books, through both subsidies to publishing and distribution, and programs offered by local public libraries. Libraries in Sweden, for example, provide free home delivery for shut-ins and services to hospitals and homes for the elderly. One other policy with a very pronounced positive effect on reading bears mentioning: all foreign language television programs as well as films and

videos are subtitled. This is due to the fact that the populations speaking the Nordic languages are small, making dubbing very expensive; but it is also a matter of a conscious policy choice to promote reading.

27 While not as partisan as they used to be, Scandinavian newspapers generally still identify with a party.

28 One manifestation is to be found in the political information kiosks set up during campaigns. The visitor to a Swedish city or town square will encounter wooden huts reminiscent of the summer cottage (stuga) where parties distribute their programs and campaign literature and where candidates and party leaders meet electors.

29 The Nordic EU members, following the Danish example, have special parliamentary committees where proposals to be brought before the European Council are discussed, in the full view of the media and the public.

30 The principle is that paying taxes is a public and not a private act. All aspects of personal life are sheltered from public view; but tax revenues make social services possible. Hence keeping its sources secret would contribute to public ignorance over policy alternatives and arouse suspicions that others are not paying their share. The public thus knows, for example, how much of the King's income goes toward taxes. When journalists write about public (or even not so public) figures, they usually include annual income in the profile (along with age, marital status).

31 The facts and figures on spending by governments and public institutions, and the results of comprehensive and detailed research into the effects of that expenditure, is widely disseminated.

32 While we have no single comparative indicator of civic literacy, the accumulated evidence from different partial indicators leaves little room for doubt as to continuing high level of civic literacy in the Nordic countries.

33 This information comes from personal communications from Hans Bergström, editor of Dagens Nyheter, and Bengt Nordström, who is responsible for monitoring audience magnitude for SVT.

34 The study was summarized in an article by Kent Asp in Dagens Nyheter on October 13, 1999, p. A4.

35 Dramatic differences were found between the public (SVT1 and SVT2) and private channels in the proportion of information versus entertainment oriented programs, and in the variety of sources. Though, as a rule, the private (cable) channels offered largely 'top ten' music shows and American sitcoms and films, the most popular (and terrestrial) channel, TV4, fell halfway between them and the high-variety, high-information public channels. In fact, programming trends since 1993 (when commercial TV became readily available in Sweden) show SVT1 and SVT2 – and TV4 – to have actually increased the information program content.

36 Eurobarometer #51 (p. B12) found 31 per cent of both Swedish and Danish respondents to be 'very attached' to Europe (second only to the Luxembourgeois).

37 The Eurobarometer has regularly found 'two distinct groups of member states. The first group includes Ireland, Italy, Luxembourg and the Netherlands, where the citizens

questioned were in each instance more numerous in declaring their support for European integration. The second group consists of Austria, Sweden, Denmark, the UK and Finland where the people asked expressed a lack of support for Europe more often than elsewhere' (#46, October–November 1995). More or less the same division appeared over the question of whether the respondents identified primarily or exclusively with their nation or with the EU in Eurobarometer #50 in the fall of 1998. The Swedes were second highest (60 per cent compared to 62 for Britain), followed fairly closely by the Danes and Finns (with 53 and 52 per cent), to identify only with their country.

38 Real democratization, the Scandinavian members insist, is really a matter of public access to EU operations and documentation. For the Danes, it was only when transparency in Council activities was guaranteed that they were willing to reconsider the Maastricht treaty they had previously rejected by referendum. Sweden waited only three months after entering the EU to join in the Danish-led push for removing the veil of secrecy from EU institutions. The Finns took a similar position, stressing access to documents. Both new entrants insisted that this aspect of transparency be included in the treaty – a reflection of their own constitutional guarantees of citizen access to all documents, unless specifically excepted for reasons of security.

39 A solid majority of Danes continues to insist that 'member states retain full sovereignty and the right of veto' (Worre 1994, p. 2). And in their official statements to the EU Intergovernmental Commission which drafted the Amsterdam declaration, the two new Nordic EU members made their position clear: 'The Finnish government's ... point of departure is that the Union's character as an association of states should be preserved' (Government of Finland 1996, p. 24). 'The Swedish government's starting point is that the EU would continue to develop a community of independent states to which some decision-making power may be transferred, so that common goals may be more easily achieved' (Government of Sweden 1996, p. 13).

References

Agell, Jonas and Per Lundborg (1993), 'Theories of Unemployment: Survey Evidence from Swedish Manufacturing Firms', IUI, Stockholm.

Ambjörnsson, Ronny (1987), *The Honest and Diligent Worker*, HLS Förlag, Stockholm.

Axberger, Hans Gunnar (1996), 'Public Access to Official Documents.' *Current Sweden* #414, Swedish Institute, Stockholm.

Björklund, Tor (1988), 'The Norwegian Local Elections: A Protest Election with a Swing to the Right', *Scandinavian Political Studies*, vol. 13, pp. 211-34.

Blid, Henry (1989), *Education by the People – Study Circles*, ABF, Stockholm.

Bobacka, Roger (1999), 'The Development of Working Hours Legislation in Finland in the 1990s – Concertation as Principle vs. Concertation in Practice', presented at the ECPR joint sessions. Mannheim, April.

Carlsson, Ulla, and Catharina Bucht (1997), *MedieSverige; Statistik och analys*, Nordicom,

Göteborg.

Crafts, Nicholas F. R. (1997), 'The Human Development Index and Changes in Standards of Living: Some Historical Conditions', *European Review of Economic History*, vol. 1, pp. 299-322.

Dølvik, Jan-Erik and Torgeir Aarvaag Stokke (1998), 'Norway: The Revival of Centralized Concertation', in Anthony Ferner and Richard Hyman (eds), *Changing industrial relations in Europe.* Blackwell, Malden, MA.

Elvander, Nils and Bertil Holmlund (1998), *The Swedish Bargaining System in the Melting Pot: Institution, Norms and Outcomes*, Arbetslivsinstitutet, Stockholm.

Esping-Andersen, Gösta (1985), *Politics against Markets*, Princeton University Press, Princeton.

Government of Finland (1996), 'Finland's Points of Departure and Objectives at the 1996 Intergovernmental Conference', Report to the Parliament by the Council of State, 27.2.1996.

Government of Sweden (1996), 'The EU Intergovernmental Conference 1996', Government Report to the Parliament, 1995/96.

Hadenius, Stig and Lennart Weibull (1999), 'The Swedish Newspaper System in the Late 1990s. Tradition and Transition', *Nordicom Review*, no. 1.

Heclo, Hugh and Henrik Madsen (1987), *Policy and Politics in Sweden: Principled Pragmatism*, Temple University Press, Philadelphia.

Høst, Sigurd (1991), 'The Norwegian Newspaper System, Structure and Development', in Helge Rønning and Knut Lundby (eds) *Media and Communication.* ISAF, Oslo.

Lilya, Kari (1998), 'Finland: Continuity and Modest Moves toward Company Level Corporatism', in Anthony Ferner and Richard Hyman (eds), *Changing industrial relations in Europe,* Blackwell, Malden, MA.

Mediebarometer (1997), *Medienotiser.* Nordicom, Gothenburg.

Milner, Henry (1989), *Sweden: Social Democracy in Practice*, Oxford University Press, Oxford.

Milner, Henry (1994), *Social Democracy and Rational Choice: The Scandinavian Experience and Beyond*, Routledge, London.

Milner, Henry (1997a), 'Institutions, Information and Values: Collective versus Individual Interest in the Swedish Welfare State', in Pauli Kettunen and Hanna Eskola (eds), *Models, Modernity and the Myrdals*, Renvall Institute, University of Helsinki.

Milner, Henry (forthcoming), *Civic literacy in Today's World: How to Make Democracy Work.*

Myrdal, Alva, et al. (1971), *Towards Equality: The Alva Myrdal Report to the Swedish Social Democratic Party*, Prisma, Stockholm.

Myrdal, Gunnar (1958), *Beyond the Welfare State,* Duckworth, London.

Nordberg, Karin (1998), *Folkhemmets röst: Radion som folkbildare 1925-50,* Brutus Östlings Bokförlag Symposium, Stockholm.

OECD (1997), *Literacy Skills for the Knowledge Society: Further Results from the International Adult Literacy Survey*, OECD, Paris.

OECD (2000), *Literacy in the Information Age: Final Report of the International Adult*

Literacy Survey, OECD, Paris.

Olson, Mancur (1990), *How Bright are the Northern Lights? Some Questions about Sweden*, Lund University Press, Lund.

Olsson, Ulf (1994), 'Planning in the Swedish Welfare State', in Wallace Clement and Rignie Mahon (eds), *Swedish Social Democracy: A Model in Transition*, Scholar's Press, Toronto.

Rehn, Gösta (1980), 'Sweden', in Gösta Rehn and K. Helveg Petersen (1980), *Education and Youth Employment in Sweden and Denmark*, The Carnegie Foundation, New York.

Rothstein, Bo (1998), 'Social Capital in the Social Democratic State: The Swedish Model and Civil Society', presented at the 1998 Conference of Europeanists, Baltimore, March.

Salokangas, Raimo (1999), 'From Political to National, Regional and Local. The Newspaper Structure in Finland', *Nordicom Review*, vol. 6, pp. 77-106.

Sanchez-Tabernero, A. (1993), *Media Concentration in Europe*, European Institute for the Media, Manchester.

SAP (1993), 'Social Democracy on the Eve of the EC Membership Negotiations.' Official translation of position adopted by the Parliamentary Group, January 19, 1993.

Skolverket (1998), *Gymnasieskola för alla – andra. En studie om marginalisering och utslagning i gymnasieskolan*, Skolverket, Stockholm.

Søllinge, Jette (1999), 'Danish Newspapers. Structure and Developments', *Nordicom Review*, vol. 6, pp. 31-76.

Tilton, Tim (1994), *The Political Theory of Social Democracy*, Clarendon, Oxford.

Wallerstein, Michael and Miriam Golden (1997), 'The Fragmentation of the Bargaining Society: Wage Setting in the Nordic Countries, 1950 to 1992', *Comparative Political Studies*, vol. 30, pp. 699-731.

Worre, Torben (1994), 'European Integration, Legitimacy and Democratic Representation: Danish Perspectives', presented at the ECPR Joint Session of Workshops, April, Madrid, Spain.

Chapter 6

Can Security *Enhance* Efficiency? Testing a Little-Noted Assumption of the Rehn-Meidner Model[1]

Axel van den Berg

Introduction: the assumption in question

One thing should be abundantly clear from the various contributions to this volume: Gösta Rehn was no ordinary labour economist. But then, the Swedish labour movement itself has had a certain unconventional streak, by the standards of traditional labour and social democracy. In particular, many of its theoreticians and leaders have, to a far greater extent than their comrades elsewhere, been concerned almost as much with the pursuit of efficiency as with equity. Moreover, they have insisted that there need not be a painful trade-off between the two.[2] Gösta Rehn stood at the very pinnacle of this trend in Swedish social democratic thinking; indeed, he arguably was that pinnacle.

Outside of Sweden, this tough-minded insistence on economic efficiency and productivity[3] as an indispensable basis for the long-term social democratic project of constructing a more equitable 'people's home' (*folkhem*) never did sit very well either with the anti-capitalist instincts of more traditional social democrats or with the image of 'featherbedding' trade unions advanced by their political opponents. This is no doubt one reason why it has not come in for much sustained scrutiny in either the celebrations or denunciations of the so-called 'Swedish Model' – as opposed to the praise or scorn heaped upon the Swedish welfare state, the ultimately ill-fated wage earner funds, or the co-determination legislation of the 1970s.

Yet it is this unflinching commitment to getting the economics right in order to produce the resources necessary to be able to set other matters right that is characteristic of Gösta Rehn's thinking throughout his long career. And it certainly is at the very core of the much-admired but not always well-understood Rehn-Meidner plan. This core consisted of two policy recommendations: 1) a 'solidaristic wage policy' which aimed at forcing employers to observe the principle of 'equal pay for equal work', irrespective of differences in profitability, that is, ability to pay, between firms; and 2) a policy of strict fiscal restraint on the part of the (Social Democratic, naturally) government. The result of this would be a double squeeze on relatively inefficient firms, which would face both higher labour costs and less access to easy liquidity. In this way it was the plan's explicit intention to accelerate the rate of structural change in industry above and beyond what would have been generated by the 'free market' itself. In addition, the solidaristic wage policy was expected to reduce the dangers of a wage-wage inflationary spiral caused by inter-union rivalry, thus meeting another of Rehn's rather unorthodox – for a social democrat – policy goals.[4]

On the face of it, this sounds more like the sort of thing proposed by right-wing think tanks than by LO, the world's most powerful blue-collar labour movement. How did Rehn and Meidner expect the union's rank-and-file, who also happen to be the Social Democrats' core constituency, to agree to such a policy package which would, after all, impose the heaviest burden of adjustment on them? Their answer is deceptively simple: by transferring that burden to the community at large. For the Rehn-Meidner plan contained two additional central planks intended not only to smooth the overall restructuring process but also to help reconcile workers whose jobs were at risk to the overall strategy of accelerated change and growth. First, it recommended that a vast system of 'active' labour market programmes be implemented, providing workers who had lost their jobs or were at risk of doing so with an array of placement services, (re-)training opportunities and mobility support rather than mere 'passive' cash benefits. Second, the government was to put the highest possible priority on achieving and maintaining full employment, without resorting to 'crude' Keynesianism and its inflationary tendencies, a job made somewhat easier by the selective effects of the active labour market programmes. As a result, and in combination with the citizenship-based social guarantees provided by the welfare state programmes implemented by the Social Democratic government, 'the costs of structural change would be shifted from the workers involved to the society as a whole' (Martin 1984, p. 205). The individual worker could rest assured that whatever happened to the previous job the worker would receive all the support necessary to find another one at comparable wages.

This is not the place to discuss what became of this ingenious plan.[5] What matters here is that it was clearly and explicitly predicated on a major assumption that flies in the face of the more familiar 'adversarial' assumption to be found in much neoclassical as well as radical economic thinking.[6] The assumption is that worker security and labour market flexibility need not only not be mutually inimical but can actually strengthen each other. Rather than facing a trade-off of flexibility *versus* security, the Rehn-Meidner plan argued that flexibility could be had in exchange for security. That is, if properly designed and institutionalised, a generous system of employment and earnings security would enhance rather than undermine workers' acceptance of rapid structural and technological change. It is important to stress once again that the security was emphatically not intended to refer to any existing job or employer but to the assurance of finding a roughly equivalent job should one lose one's present job. As Rehn used to say, the security not of the turtle but of the wings (*vingarnas trygghet*).

Gösta Rehn himself was fully aware of the important assumption upon which his recommendations necessarily rested. As he himself later put it, '[an] important element in this policy development was the fact that on the basis of this active labour market policy the trade unions could moderate any tendencies towards 'Luddite' reluctance to technical progress or a protectionist resistance to structural change among their members' (Rehn 1984, p. 9). One of his successors in the job of top LO economist – and a contributor to this volume – explained his organization's favourable view of industrial change thus:

> The basis for this very favourable attitude towards technology has been that unemployment was low and that people have had work. With the relative security, which characterises the Swedish labour market, no one need fear a development, which necessitates changes... Thus it is not strange that Swedish trade unions can have a very positive attitude to technological development. We share the fruits of the developments. ...
>
> It is equally natural that trade unions in certain other countries have a less positive attitude to technological progress. If full employment is not a priority political goal and trade unions also lack the opportunity to influence developments, then it is nigh on inevitable that trade unions will oppose all changes in a desperate attempt to protect the existing jobs (Bäckström 1986, pp. 134, 144).

The research that I shall briefly describe in the following pages was designed specifically to address this crucial, but little-noted assumption underlying the Rehn-Meidner plan. Formulated as a hypothesis, it sought to test whether Swedish workers are, by virtue of their relatively greater degree of employment and earnings security, indeed less fearful of, and more favourably disposed towards various forms of technical and structural change affecting their present jobs than comparable workers elsewhere who do not enjoy the same degree of security.

Some confusing findings from a comparative test

As the case against which to measure Swedish workers' responses to pressures for change we chose Canada. For several reasons Canada and Sweden are particularly appropriate comparative cases for our purposes. On one hand, Canada is considerably closer to the laissez-faire end of the political spectrum where labour market policies, welfare state programmes and employment policy are concerned. As a result, the degree of labour market and earnings insecurity faced by Canadian workers is considerably higher than is the case for Swedish workers. On the other hand, partly as a result of geography and trade linkages, the two countries' industrial structures are remarkably alike. These structural similarities should minimize the effect of possible confounding factors due to differences between industrial sectors and also enable us to compare industries that are likely to require similar levels of change and flexibility in the two countries.

Several types of data were gathered and analysed in order to assess the differences in responses to various forms of industrial change between Canadian and Swedish workers, and the role of labour market (in)security in accounting for what differences were found. These included available statistics on mobility and change in the two countries' economies and labour markets, attitudinal surveys of representative samples of the employed labour force specifically designed for this study, and the results of about 150 semi-structured interviews conducted by the researchers with representatives of three industries in the two countries (pulp and paper, steel, and telecommunications equipment). The attitudinal surveys included questions about recent experience with workplace change, concerns about one's own earnings and employment prospects, and attitudes toward various forms of workplace change. The factory interviews dealt with recent major changes at the plant in question (new technology and/or equipment, redundancies, reorganizations) and sought to identify sources of resistance, if any, to them.

The results of these interlocking research efforts have been published in a book and a number of more specialized journal articles.[7] Here I will have to limit myself to a brief summary of the main findings and their implications for Gösta Rehn's belief in the possibility of enhancing the adaptability of labour by means of raising the level of labour market security. For more detailed reports of our findings the reader is referred to the publications mentioned. I begin by reviewing the main findings by the type of data used.

Labour market (mobility) statistics

While there has been much debate in recent years about labour market flexibility, there is a surprising dearth of good indices of such flexibility that permit direct international comparison. We were able to collect some comparable statistics on job gains, losses and turnover by industrial sector, unemployment and its average duration, and average job tenure. There are some data on vacancies and labour market mobility as well, but their cross-national comparability is severely circumscribed.

Our main finding is, simply, that there is surprisingly little difference between Canada and Sweden on any of these measures. The finding is surprising because there are so many reasons for expecting there to be considerable differences. First, following the reasoning underlying the Rehn-Meidner model, one might expect Swedish workers to be less inclined to resist redundancies and factory closures than their Canadian counterparts. This would lead one to expect higher job turnover rates in Sweden. On the other hand, in some respects Sweden has gone farther than most European countries in implementing policies and creating institutions – including the job security legislation of the 1970s that in some respects represented a significant retreat from the initial change-accelerating intent of the original Rehn-Meidner plan – that have been blamed by critics of 'Eurosclerosis' for the alleged rigidity of Europe's labour markets.[8] Seen from this perspective, one might expect job turnover rates in Sweden to be lower than in Canada.

Yet if anything, the figures for both countries are strikingly similar (see van den Berg, Furåker and Johansson 1997, pp. 101-10). Overall turnover rates appear to be slightly higher in Sweden than in Canada, but there are also some hints that Canadian firms find it easier to hire and fire (see also Smith et al. 1995; Smucker et al. 1998). Certainly, our findings do not suggest any clear and systematic differences in terms of degree of labour market flexibility. The difference in overall unemployment rates between Canada and Sweden has, at least until Sweden was hit by a severe recession in the early 1990s, historically been considerable, with Swedish rates rarely rising above one third of Canadian rates. Yet average unemployment durations and long-term unemployment (6 months and over or 12 months and over) as a percentage of total unemployment are similarly low in both countries by international standards. Given that, on the one hand, unemployment is itself a sign of some form of labour market inflexibility while, on the other hand, average unemployment spells are usually closely related to overall levels (the more overall unemployment there is, the harder it is to keep average duration down), these findings, too, suggest a split decision as to which country's labour market appears to be more flexible.

In short, at this global level the differences between Sweden and Canada do not appear to be such as to suggest any systematically higher levels of flexibility in either country. One intriguing possibility, though not one we are able to test directly, is that the two forces pushing in opposite directions that I mentioned above (Rehn-Meidner flexibility versus other rigidity-enhancing institutions) work to counteract each other in Sweden, thus producing similar figures to those in Canada but by quite different mechanisms. For instance, whereas the generous Swedish unemployment and sickness benefits may push up reservation wage levels and hence increase the length of job searches and, thereby, unemployment spells, this effect may be counteracted by those of active labour market policies and the solidaristic wage policy.

Attitudinal survey data

We were able to commission three surveys of sub-samples of the regularly conducted Labour Force Surveys from the Swedish and Canadian official statistics bureaus, one in Canada (conducted in November 1992) and two in Sweden (October-November 1991 and February-March 1993). The sub-samples we have primarily used for our analysis consisted of representative samples of employed blue-collar workers in manufacturing industries only (sample sizes: 779, 1293 and 1205, respectively). These are among the segments of the labour force most directly affected by technological change and industrial restructuring in recent decades. They are also the most directly comparable since there are major, potentially confounding differences between other occupational categories and economic sectors. In particular, a far larger proportion of services is provided by the public sector in Sweden than in Canada. Moreover, this sector is much more heavily feminised in Sweden. For a study addressing the relation between labour market (in)security and responses to market-driven workplace change, such differences could seriously compromise the results.

Between 1991 and 1993 Sweden suffered the most serious economic downturn since the Great Depression. The Swedish rate of unemployment rose from less than 2 per cent in 1991 to over 8 per cent two years later. The fall in total employment was even more dramatic, dropping by around 15 per cent – with the manufacturing and construction industries hit hardest by far. As government budget deficits soared, the newly elected 'bourgeois' government set out to reduce the benefit levels of the various earnings support programs, including unemployment insurance. In short, in the span of only a few years, a number of the central pillars upholding the whole system of labour market and earnings security came under severe strain. One would expect such dramatic developments to have had a considerable negative impact on the *sense* of labour market security experienced by the average Swedish manufacturing worker. The fact that we were able to have surveys conducted at the onset of the crisis and at a time when it was reaching its nadir permits us to capture whatever effects this sudden deterioration might have on workers' responses to industrial change.

Of course, one cannot measure such responses directly, in the act as it were, by means of this kind of survey. All one can do is measure attitudes towards change and their connection, if any, with perceived employment and earnings (in)security, on the assumption that there is likely to be at least some congruence between attitudes and action. Consequently, we asked respondents questions about their recent experience with workplace change, their concerns about their own earnings and employment prospects, and their attitudes toward various forms of change in working life and, finally, their opinions about certain forms of defensive protectionism. If the hypothesis underlying the Rehn-Meidner plan is valid, Swedish workers should be significantly less worried about their labour market prospects than their Canadian counterparts, they should be significantly more favourably (or less unfavourably) disposed towards various forms of change and less favourably (or more *un*favourably) disposed towards protective measures, and these latter attitudinal differences should be largely explicable as a result of the differences in the former, the degree of worry.

Our findings did, to some extent, confirm the first two of these predictions. Limiting ourselves in the first instance to the Canadian and the Swedish 'pre-crisis' samples, we found that considerably fewer Swedish than Canadian blue-collar manufacturing workers reported having been laid off in recent years, considered it likely that they would become unemployed at some time in the next two years or worried about the possibility of losing their jobs in the near future.[9] Thus, in terms of relative (in)security with respect to their employment and earnings prospects, the main independent variable in our hypothesis, our two samples differed in the ways we would have expected.

In getting at attitudes toward changes in employment conditions, two of our questions were of a hypothetical behavioural nature. We asked, first, whether respondents would be willing to move to another town or prefer to remain unemployed for a year if they were to lose their present jobs and, second, whether they would be willing to take a pay cut if it were necessary to keep their present job and if so, by how much. Here Canadians were clearly more inclined to be 'flexible' than the Swedes. More than half of the Canadian workers said they would move for a job, as opposed to only 29 per cent of the Swedes, and close to 80 per cent of Canadians, as opposed to 59 per cent of the Swedes, would take a pay cut to save their job, with the likelihood of the latter being willing to take a cut in excess of 10 per cent being about one third of the Canadians' willingness to do so.

The second finding is not necessarily as much at odds with our hypothesis as it might appear at first glance. It is worth recalling here that from the perspective of the Rehn-Meidner plan, wage cuts are viewed as an undesirable form of flexibility that may actually inhibit more important forms of flexibility (i.e. accelerated restructuring in favour of the most efficient firms). So a refusal to accept a pay cut to save a job could well be taken as an endorsement of a certain kind of flexibility.[10]

The finding that Swedes are less willing to move for a job is another matter, however. It would seem to indicate that the Swedish policies intended to increase the mobility of labour have not been entirely effective – or that their effect has been counteracted by the opposite effect of others. This has been well recognized as long ago as the early 1970s when, in response to what was widely perceived as growing protest against the 'moving van' policies of the Labour Market Authority (Arbetsmarknadsstyrelsen, or AMS), regional support policies were significantly strengthened and a flurry of job protection and codetermination legislation was passed. In some respects, that legislation may be seen as a significant retreat from the intentions of the original Rehn-Meidner plan. We should, however, keep in mind that a host of other factors, including population density, housing markets, the prevalence of two-earner families and so on, affect geographic mobility and thus complicate a direct comparison between our two country samples in this respect.

But with respect to more general attitudes towards industrial change the Swedes appear to be the more flexible. Swedish workers were considerably less willing to endorse a statement to the effect that 'employees are justified in resisting technical change because such changes often mean job losses in the long run', and more inclined to endorse the principle that workers should be willing to 'switch employers from time to time' in order to maintain standards of living for all, than the Canadians were. Swedes also appeared to be significantly less favourably disposed towards protectionism than the Canadians. On the other hand, almost three quarters of Swedish workers thought it a good idea for the government to 'try to save jobs by temporarily subsidizing companies that are having economic difficulties' as compared to 59 per cent of the Canadian workers. This finding would appear to be a little troubling from the Rehn-Meidner perspective, as it flies in the face of just the kind of resolute pursuit of efficiency that Gösta Rehn favoured, 'removing the need to subsidize weak firms in the interest of maintaining jobs' (Esping-Andersen 1985, p. 230; cf. Tilton 1990, pp. 200-1).[11]

But if these findings appear somewhat inconclusive with respect to the basic 'flexibility-for-security' hypothesis, when we tried to link the differences in attitudes to differences in the degree of concern with one's labour market prospects it fared far worse. Recall that the crucial prediction was that, to the extent that Swedes appear to be more favourably disposed to change than Canadians, this difference should at least in part be explicable by the already documented difference in the amount of perceived labour market (in)security. In other words, if one controls for recent lay-off experience, perceived chances of becoming unemployed and extent of worry about that prospect, at least *some* of the difference between Canadian and Swedish attitudes to change ought to be 'explained away.'

I do not mind admitting here that we were rather stunned ourselves by the spectacular way in which our data refute this prediction. As it turned out, *for* none of the six attitudinal variables for which we had found statistically significant differences between the two countries' samples did the introduction of the (in)security variables *reduce* the level of statistical significance. Moreover, it hardly affected the magnitude of the effect, and in some of the cases where it did, it did so in the 'wrong' direction (i.e., increasing the magnitude of the difference)! In other words, whatever the reasons behind the differences in attitudes toward various forms of industrial change between Swedish and Canadian manufacturing workers may be, they seem to have nothing whatsoever to do with differences in perceived labour market (in)security.

Our comparison of Swedish workers' responses before and after the onset of the recent economic crisis further confirms this general conclusion. We found that the degree of perceived insecurity certainly did rise in tandem with the dramatic increases in 'objective' insecurity. The numbers of respondents reporting that there had been recent personnel reductions at their workplace, that they themselves had been laid off, that they considered their own unemployment 'likely', and so on, rose substantially between Fall 1991 and Spring 1993. Yet these rising worries had no effect whatsoever on attitudes towards various forms of change. These attitudes remained eerily stable in fact during this turbulent period, the greatest shift being a three percentage points (from 73 to 76!) increase in the proportion willing to endorse temporary government subsidies for ailing companies. While one may argue over the exact operationalization of the variables used, a refutation as categorical and clear as this is indeed rare in the social sciences.

Factory interviews

As noted, between 1991 and 1993 we conducted almost 150 interviews with management and labour (usually union) representatives in three industries: steel, pulp and paper, and telecommunications equipment. These particular industries were chosen because they are major, internationally competing industries in both countries and because they represent a range of technologies and production processes as well as recent employment and production trajectories. We constructed more or less matching (in terms of size, product line, technology and so on) samples of each industry in each country. In Canada interviews were conducted with plant representatives in 17 pulp and paper plants, 11 steel plants and 16 telecommunications equipment plants. In Sweden the numbers were 10 (pulp and paper), 10 (steel) and 9 (telecommunications equipment), respectively. The interviews were semi-structured in character and centred specifically on three kinds of change: investment in new equipment and technology, relatively recent layoffs, and work organization reform. Where applicable, we asked about the extent to which the change in question had occurred at the plant; what major obstacles had been encountered on the way, and how employees and unions had responded.[12]

The main aim of the interviews was, as before, to find out whether there were any systematic differences in how Canadian and Swedish workers responded to such major changes in their work environment. Again, our findings were somewhat unexpected, at least from the perspective of the basic hypothesis we sought to test. Overall, we were most struck by how little difference we found in the reported shop-floor reactions to change between the two countries and the three industries, and how little evidence of any active resistance of any kind. In fact, and contrary to a long tradition of more or less Marxist-inspired literature spawned by the work of Marglin (1974) and Braverman (1974), our respondents were almost unanimous in insisting that workers' responses to change, especially technical change, were generally quite favourable.

To the extent that we did encounter differences in this respect, they were rather subtle. There are some hints that in all three industries slightly more Swedish than Canadian workers reacted positively to the changes discussed, and the Swedes' positive responses tended to be phrased in slightly stronger terms. Canadian managers and employee representatives were noticeably more prone to mention at least initial reticence on the part of the workers and this was often directly attributed to these workers' apparent fears of possible job loss. The steel industry seems to be a bit of an exception; there were more answers suggesting worker resistance here, but again more so in Canada than in Sweden. In Sweden these mostly had to do with organizational restructuring, while in Canada there were some references to general resistance to technological change – virtually the only ones we encountered anywhere. Thus, the differences are not dramatic, but, according to our respondents, Canadian workers do seem to be a little more averse to workplace change than

Swedish workers, and this does seem to have something to do with the Canadian apprehensions about their employment prospects. But given the small number of cases, the non-random samples and the probable sensitivity of these results to contextual factors of various kinds, I would hesitate to view this as strong evidence that Swedish workers are more positively disposed toward change due to their greater sense of labour market security.

Rather than the differences between *workers'* responses that we were initially looking for, the most striking difference that emerged from our interviews was in fact the difference between the unions' responses in the two countries. By almost all accounts, including those given by the managers among our respondents, the Swedish local unions had been extremely supportive of the changes discussed, particularly production organization reform and especially so in the steel and telecommunications equipment industries. In fact, not infrequently the union was said to have been the 'driving force' behind the changes. The local union leaders in our Swedish plants appeared to be rather *more* favourably inclined toward change than their rank-and-file, in some cases even to the point of coming into conflict over it with them.

In Canada, by contrast, where any complaints were heard at all they were almost all from managers complaining about the unions' resistance to change and frequently suggesting that the unions were more obstructionist than their constituents in this respect. A fair number of the Canadian unionists themselves sounded rather suspicious of whatever changes managers might contemplate. While the majority of Canadian unionists appears to have taken a fairly constructive position with respect to most technical change, such support was rarely reported to be more than passive acceptance and a sizable minority was said to be rather negatively disposed to any changes. We heard a number of complaints along these lines from managers, and recorded a number of answers from the union representatives that seemed to confirm them.

The fact that the apparently most enthusiastic union promoters of change were to be found in the telecommunications equipment and steel industries rather than in pulp and paper suggests a possible explanation as well. Both these industries are organized by the powerful 'Metall' union, known for its 'progressive' ideas about new management techniques and technology. In several cases we were told by the unionists themselves that, in fact, many of the changes they had been pushing for at the local level had been inspired by 'Metall' in its regular conferences, union-distributed literature, and so on. Thus, we got the distinct impression of something of a top-down 'neocorporatist' arrangement in which the central union organization pursues policies that are somewhat 'ahead of' the preferences of the rank-and-file. This was often justified with claims to the effect that the union central was better able to see 'the general picture' and hence the workers' long-term interests, and with explicit references to the whole 'security-for-flexibility' bargain underlying the unions' conception of the Swedish Model.

They appear to thus confirm the 'neocorporatist' theory (Cawson 1986; Schmitter 1974; Lehmbruch and Schmitter 1982; Williamson 1989), which focuses on organizations and their elites, especially unions, and their interrelations, rather than on individuals, to explain the relative flexibility and competitiveness of economies. It argues that in certain countries with exceptionally powerful union movements, of which Sweden is a prime example, the union leadership has, by its very success, been drawn into a system of highly centralized bargaining with similarly organized employers and the state. Such a neocorporatist arrangement permits the striking of peak-level bargains in which union leaders can commit themselves and, more importantly, their constituencies, to 'constructive' behaviour in exchange for a negotiated and secure share of the long-term economic benefits of that behaviour for their members.[13]

The kinds of differences between Swedish and Canadian unionists that appear in our factory interviews fit rather well with this neocorporatist interpretation. Swedish unionists did seem to be rather well integrated in a system of fairly constant consultation at several levels. There were some signs, however muted, of the occasional tensions between them and their rank-and-file that one would expect from such a system of 'co-optation.' As well, while conflict was by no means absent from Swedish industrial relations, it did seem relatively less bitter and entrenched than what we encountered in the Canadian plants. While there was a fair amount of conflict in Sweden over such general issues as wage differentials, in Canada most of the local conflicts were over legalistic 'job control' issues typical of a more adversarial system of industrial relations (cf. Perlman 1928 and Thompson 1993).

Conclusion: Rehn vindicated after all?

How, then, do we make sense of these disparate and sometimes apparently contradictory findings? At the very least, our results suggest that neither the attitudes nor the behaviour that we have tried to gauge are much affected by how worried workers are with respect to their employment and earnings prospects. Rather, the responses to our 'quasi-behavioural' survey questions (willingness to move for a job; willingness to take a pay cut to save one's present job) suggest that actual behaviour may well be inspired primarily by immediate self-interest, responding mostly to the constraints and opportunities available. Workers will move or accept pay cuts when they feel they do not have much of a choice. This is perhaps not all that surprising, but it does have some important implications which may not, perhaps, have been entirely absorbed yet by social democrats of a less hard-nosed variety than the likes of Gösta Rehn who object, for instance, to any kind of work requirement attached to the right to receive work-related social benefits – a policy long taken for granted as part-and-parcel of the 'Swedish Model' but not often noted by its outside admirers.

On the other hand, the sort of general attitudes toward change that we have sought to elicit may, if anything, be a reflection of the general political culture and institutional set-up of each country. Resisting technical change and resorting to protectionism against foreign competition are just not quite so respectable in the Swedish public discourse which is much influenced, of course, by the thinkers, debaters, publicists and, especially, economists of the labour movement. And these general attitudes appear to be quite robust even in the face of fairly dramatic changes in the economic environment.

To be sure, this must remain speculation at best, since we have no way of knowing what Swedish workers' attitudes were before the launching of the Rehn-Meidner model and therefore can only guess how much influence it and the labour movement have really had. Moreover, one may wonder whether such abstract attitudes matter much in practice. Our evidence from the factory interviews suggests that they might matter a bit in actual in-plant behaviour. There is at least some tentative evidence here that Swedish workers are slightly more disposed to act according to the lofty general principles they endorse when it comes to dealing with the implementation of new technology, organizational change and perhaps even redundancies than their Canadian counterparts. But our evidence is still fairly skimpy on this point, and further shop-floor studies should throw interesting and much-needed light on this question.

But in addition to influencing, however marginally, shop-floor behaviour, such general attitudes are, of course, supportive of the entire system of neocorporatist negotiation of industrial change in the context of relative employment and earnings security for the rank-and-file. It may express a certain degree of rank-and-file acceptance for the often-heard position taken by union officials to the effect that given the assurance that the cost of change will be borne in large part by the community, one may reasonably demand that the rank-and-file accept those changes that do in the end increase overall efficiency. Thus, Rehn's model may not have succeeded in affecting Swedish workers' behaviour directly by means of a flexibility-for-security trade-off, but it may have helped to achieve something similar indirectly by providing the infrastructure and justification for an institutional set-up permitting relatively close cooperation between unions and employers in matters of innovation while retaining the general support of the rank-and-file.

But in fact Gösta Rehn was even more right than this. Hard-nosed economist that he was, he was actually rather sceptical of the likelihood of effecting deep changes in the attitudes and behaviour of the rank-and-file. Consequently, he was an advocate of fairly forceful incentives and policies to keep workers in the labour force and to prevent them from 'abusing' the generous income, retraining and employment support programs, such as the strict application of the willingness to work requirement just mentioned, strong emphasis on mobility support, and so on, and as little use of subsidies as possible.

Instead of counting on a change in the mentality of the rank-and-file, Rehn tended to emphasize the role of union organizations. In fact, he anticipated, by some decades, the later theory of 'encompassing organizations'. In an early article entitled 'Organizations and Freedom', he argued that unlike the relatively small trade unions in the United States that 'were instruments of egoistical group monopolies which operated without regard to the working class and the interests of society', large organizations like the LO 'had a broader perspective, interesting themselves more in the rise of productivity [because]... LO was so large that a part (LO) did not stand in manifest opposition to the whole (society) [creating]... an identity between special interests and the public interest' (cited by Öhman 1974, p. 47). Judging by our findings, he may have had it right from the start. So here's to Gösta Rehn and to the continuing quest for a world of efficiency and equity.

Notes

1 The research on which this chapter reports was supported by the *Swedish Humanistiska och Samhällsvetenskapliga Forskningsrådet* (HSFR), the Quebec *Fonds pour la formation de Chercheurs et l'Aide à la Recherche* (FCAR), the Social Sciences and Humanities Research Council of Canada (SSHRCC) and Statistics Canada. It was conducted by a Swedish-Canadian research team including Bengt Furåker (University of Gothenburg) and Leif Johansson (University of Umeå), Joseph Smucker (Concordia University), and Michael R. Smith and Anthony C. Masi (McGill University). I am greatly indebted to all of them.

2 For some cross-country evidence suggesting that, if anything, equality may raise efficiency, see Kenworthy (1995). The mechanisms by which Kenworthy assumes this to occur, however, are rather different from those posited by Gösta Rehn, which will be spelled out below.

3 Tilton (1990, ch.9) captures this characteristically hard-nosed, 'economistic' streak in Rehn's thinking quite well.

4 Note that even the much-celebrated 'solidaristic wage policy' was originally conceived as a way to ensure that wage levels that should, by the orthodox economic textbook, result from perfectly competitive markets actually did come about. Only with time did this policy acquire the pronounced egalitarian character it later became known for, possibly simply because of the difficulty of assessing what exactly constitutes equal work (see Heclo and Madsen 1987, p. 117, Tilton 1990, pp. 200 and 201, fn.3).

5 For a highly persuasive insider's discussion see Klas Eklund's chapter in this volume.

6 For some examples of the latter see Shapiro and Stiglitz (1985), Green (1988) and Green and Weisskopf (1990).

7 See Smith et al. (1995, 1997), Smucker et al. (1998), Smucker and van den Berg (1991), van den Berg and Smucker (1992), van den Berg et al. (1998) and van den Berg, Furåker and Johansson (1997).

8 Although Sweden's labour markets are still far from Europe's most regulated. See e.g. OECD 1999.

9 For the detailed report of these and the other survey results discussed here, see van den Berg, Furåker and Johansson (1997, Ch. 7 and 8).

10 See also van den Berg, Furåker and Johansson (1997, pp. 174-5) and van den Berg et al. (1998).

11 In fact, Gösta Rehn did support various temporary support measures for ailing companies as long as these did not help to prop up 'obsolete' jobs or industries. Nevertheless, his strongest emphasis was always on supply-side measures.

12 For more details on the nature of the samples, industries and our data, see Smith et al. (1995, pp. 691-7) and Johansson (1990).

13 Often some variant of 'encompassing organizations' theory is used to explain why large, powerful unions would want to collaborate in such an institutional bargain (see Olson 1982, Hollingsworth 1982, and Hollingsworth and Hanneman 1982).

References

Bäckström, Anders (1986), 'New Technology, Economic Progress and Employment: A Trade Union View', paper presented at the International Conference on Industrial Change and Labour Adjustment in Sweden and Canada, York University, December 10-12, 1986.

Braverman, Harry (1974), *Labour and Monopoly Capitalism*, Monthly Review Press, New York.

Cawson, Alan (1986), *Corporatism and Political Theory*, Basil Blackwell, Oxford.

Esping-Andersen, Gösta (1985), *Politics Against Markets*, Princeton University Press, Princeton.

Green, Francis (1988), 'Neoclassical and Marxian conceptions of production', *Cambridge Journal of Economics*, vol. 12, pp. 299-312.

Green, Francis and Thomas E. Weisskopf (1990), 'The Worker Discipline Effect: A Disaggregative Analysis', *The Review of Economics and Statistics*, vol. 72, pp. 241-9.

Heclo, Hugh and Madsen, Henrik (1987), *Policy and Politics in Sweden: Principled Pragmatis*, Temple University Press, Philadelphia.

Hollingsworth, Rogers J. and Robert A. Hanneman (1982), 'Working-Class Power and the Political Economy of Western Capitalist Societies', *Comparative Social Research*, vol. 5, pp. 61-80.

Hollingsworth, Rogers J. (1982), 'The Political-Structural Basis for Economic Performance', *Annals of the American Academy of Political and Social Science*, vol. 459, pp. 28-45.

Johansson, Leif (1990), 'Structural Change in Canada and Sweden. A Look at the Evolution in Three Industries', Department of Sociology, University of Umeå.

Lehmbruch, Gerhard and Phillipe C. Schmitter (eds) (1982), *Patterns of Corporatist Policy Making*, Sage, London.

Kenworthy, Lane (1995), 'Equality and Efficiency: The Illusory Tradeoff', *European Journal of Political Research*, vol. 27, pp. 225-54.

Marglin, Stephen A. (1974), 'What Do Bosses Do? The Origins and Functions of Hierarchy in Capitalist Production', *Review of Radical Political Economy*, vol. 6, pp. 33-60.

Martin, Andrew (1984), 'The Shaping of the Swedish Model', in Peter Gourevitch (ed.), *Union and Economic Crisis: Britain, West Germany and Sweden*. Allen and Unwin, London, pp. 190-359.

OECD (1999), *Employment Outlook 1999*. OECD, Paris.

Öhman, Berndt (1974), *LO and Labour Market Policy since the Second World War*, Prisma, Stockholm.

Olson, Mancur (1982), *The Rise and Decline of Nations: Economic Growth, Stagflation, and Social Rigidities*, Yale University Press, New Haven.

Perlman, Selig (1928), *A Theory of the Labor Movement*, Macmillan, New York.

Rehn, Gösta (1984), 'Cooperation between the Government and Workers' and Employers' Organisations on Labour Market Policy in Sweden', The Swedish Institute for Social Research, Stockholm.

Rehn, Gösta (1985), 'Swedish Active Labor Market Policy: Retrospect and Prospect', *Industrial Relations,* vol. 24, pp. 62-89.

Schmitter, Phillippe C. (1974), 'Still the Century of Corporatism?' *Review of Politics*, vol. 36, pp. 85-131.

Shapiro, Carl and Joseph E. Stiglitz, (1985), 'Equilibrium Unemployment as a Worker Discipline Device', *American Economic Review,* vol. 74, pp. 433-44.

Smith, Michael R., Anthony C. Masi, Joseph Smucker and Axel van den Berg (1995), 'External Flexibility in Sweden and Canada: A Three Industry Comparison,' *Work, Employment and Society*, vol. 9, pp. 689-718.

Smith, Michael R., Anthony C. Masi, Joseph Smucker and Axel van den Berg (1997), 'Insecurity, Labour Relations, and Flexibility in Two Process Industries: A Canada/Sweden Comparison', *Canadian Journal of Sociology*, vol. 22, pp. 31-64.

Smucker, Joseph, Anthony C. Masi, Michael R. Smith and Axel van den Berg (1998), 'Labour Deployment in Plants in Canada and Sweden: A Three-Industry Comparison', *Relations Industrielles/Industrial Relations*, vol. 53, pp. 430-57.

Smucker, Joseph and Axel van den Berg (1991), 'Some Evidence of the Effects of Labour Market Policies on Workers Attitudes toward Change in Canada and Sweden', *Canadian Journal of Sociology*, vol. 16, pp. 51-74.

Thompson, Mark (1993), 'Industrial Relations in Canada', in Greg J. Bamber and Russell D. Lansbury (eds). *International and Comparative Industrial Relations: A Study of Industrialised Market Economies* (second ed.), Routledge, London, pp. 83-99.

Tilton, Tim (1990), *The Political Theory of Swedish Social Democracy: Through the Welfare State to Socialism*, Oxford University Press, Oxford.

van den Berg, Axel and Joseph Smucker (1992), 'Labour Markets and Government Interventions: A Comparison of Canadian and Swedish Labour Markets Policies,' *International Journal of Contemporary Sociology*, vol. 29, pp. 9-46.

van den Berg, Axel, Bengt Furåker and Leif Johansson (1997), *Labour market Regimes and Patterns of Flexibility: A Sweden-Canada Comparison*, Arkiv, Lund.

van den Berg, Axel, Anthony C. Masi, Michael R. Smith and Joseph Smucker (1998), 'To Cut or Not to Cut: A Cross-National Comparison of Attitudes toward Wage Flexibility', *Work and Occupations*, vol. 25, pp. 49-73.

Williamson, Peter J. (1989), *Varieties of Corporatism: A Conceptual Discussion*, Cambridge University Press, Cambridge.

PART 3
Nordic Perspectives

Chapter 7

Fragmentation and Individualization? The Legitimacy of Corporatism among the Finnish Labour Force

Heikki Ervasti

Introduction

The core idea of the Rehn-Meidner model was the coordination and integration of fiscal, monetary, wage and labour market policies. According to the model, economic goals such as a high level of employment, a fair distribution of income, low inflation, steady economic growth and even a rapid structural change of the economy could be attained through active cooperation of government, employers and trade unions. Employers were expected to observe the principle of solidaristic wage policy and government was supposed to simultaneously pursue strict fiscal policies and active labour market policy measures. The unions were assumed to accept this policy package because the labour market and social policies clearly shift the heaviest burden of adjustment to the society as a whole, not to individual wage earners.

This type of an integrated model of policy-making was based on certain unusual characteristics of the labour markets of the Scandinavian countries. Consensual co-operation and corporatist[1] arrangements such as a highly centralised collective bargaining system have been a condition *sine qua non* for the implementation of the policy suggestions of the Rehn-Meidner model. Furthermore, powerful labour market organisations and a high rate of unionisation and employer organisation have been important prerequisites of the model (see Ahlén 1989, Delsen and van Veen 1991).

In Finland these conditions were met in the late 1960s when labour market organisations developed on a substantial scale and firm relationships emerged between them and the government. Since then, wages and salaries, labour legislation, and, to a notable degree, all economic, social and employment policies have been guided by tripartite negotiations between labour market organisations and the government (see Arter 1987, Helander 1983, Kauppinen 1994, Mansner 1990).

However, the Finnish model of economic and social policies is clearly distinctive from the other Scandinavian models. First of all, the transition from an agrarian to an industrial society, together with the advent of modern industrial relations did not take place in Finland until after World War II. Until the 1950s Finland was still predominantly an agrarian country. Thus, in Finnish politics, agrarian interest has been more powerful than in the other Scandinavian countries. On the other hand, the labour movement has been less influential in Finland than in the other Scandinavian countries. A special feature in Finnish politics has been the split between the far left (communists) and the Social Democrats (e.g. Elvander 1990, p. 8, Andersson et al. 1993).

In a Scandinavian comparison, the distinctiveness of the Finnish economic policies can be seen in the structure of Finnish politics and interest mediation and in the central status of export competitiveness. The principal aims have been to assure the competitiveness of the dominating export sector, i.e. the forest industry, economic growth and high investment. These priorities have implied that it may have been necessary to ignore such aims as full employment and stability of economic development, especially in the short run. Since the world market demand for forest products is subject to powerful cyclical shocks, and Finnish economic policy tends to accentuate these disturbances, business fluctuations have been large. When the profitability of the exports sector has weakened and the economy has entered a recession, policies have reacted in a contractive fashion. Fiscal and monetary policies have been tightened, the currency has often been devalued and wages have been frozen in order to restore profitability. As a result, unemployment rates have been relatively high in Finland. In good years, wages grow again and unemployment rates decrease (Andersson et al. 1993, Kosonen 1998).

The Finnish state has traditionally been quite interventionist. Especially, it has given a high level of protection to agriculture. On the other hand, the state has strongly promoted industrialization both indirectly and directly through the establishment and expansion of state companies. Also in forming labour market agreements, the state has played an important role (Andersson 1989, pp. 274-375).

For a small open economy like Finland, this type of integrated and corporatist model of economic policies has been a success. In a political sense, as Korpi (1983) emphasises, the working class has managed to diminish its disadvantage in power resources in relation to capital through its union organizations, not only through parliamentary politics. In an economic sense, wage earners have achieved moderately but continuously rising wages, a more even redistribution of income and several improvements in social security (e.g. Kauppinen 1994). For employers, centralized collective bargaining has offered a hope of industrial peace and fewer disputes[2] and a means to restrain the development of wages. From the point of view of the government, corporatism has offered a means to attain several economic goals like high employment, low inflation rate and steady economic growth. All in all, there is clear evidence that corporatism has benefited the whole economy (see Katzenstein 1985, Pekkarinen et al. 1992). Adjustments to economic turbulence have gone smoothly, and the concessions required have been attained flexibly, by consensus (Pekkarinen et al. 1992).

Recently, however, corporatist arrangements have been strongly questioned. Centralised bargaining, the central role of the labour market organisations, and the whole corporatist power structures have become the subjects of a critical debate. Several factors like structural changes in the economy, the emergence of the service economy and the decline of traditional industrial production, technical development and changes in the labour process, and increasing globalisation and international competition, put new pressures on corporatism and trade unionism. Especially the employers, supported by several right-wing politicians, strongly criticise corporatism, campaigning for deregulated and decentralised industrial relations. In brief, they accuse corporatism of creating inflexibilities in the labour market, thus making the whole economy less efficient. As they emphasize, despite the centralised labour market, unemployment rose dramatically during the recession of the 90s, the growth of GDP was negative for a couple of years and the balance of payments deteriorated. In the employers' view, corporatism has failed. On a broader level, corporatist power structures are considered undemocratic. According to these claims, the great influence of the trade unions in the society distorts democracy. Parliamentary democracy has been superseded by corporatist power structures (see Kauppinen 1994 for an overview).

The reluctance of the employers and certain right-wing politicians to maintain centralised industrial relations has been well-reported in Finland (e.g. Ilmonen and Kevätsalo 1995 and Kauppinen 1994), as well as in several other countries[3] (Gallie et al. 1996, Pestoff 1991 and Ferner and Hyman 1992), but far less is known about the wage-earners' stances toward industrial relations. However, serious doubts have been cast on the legitimacy of corporatism among the labour force. Several authors argue that there is an ongoing structural change in which the 'fordist' society characterised by well-established societal institutions and firm and inflexible relations between them, is being transformed into a 'postfordist' society in which the old institutional settings are no longer sustainable. In the new 'risk society' (Beck 1986) or 'post-traditional' and 'reflective' society (Beck, Giddens and Lash 1994), old institutions like trade unions and centralised industrial relations lose their legitimating basis, and thus, have to be replaced by more flexible and less centralised institutions.

Working life, the labour market and the labour process are changing rapidly. Allegedly, an inevitable consequence of the postfordist structural change is that the wage-earners no longer share common interests, they are no longer willing to enhance their interest collectively, nor do they trust old institutions like trade unions and centralised industrial relations. Also the traditional collectivist and egalitarian values and ideologies are said to be vanishing. The category of wage earners becomes ever more fragmented and individualised, thus unable and unwilling to act as a unitary class. Under these conditions, trade unions will most likely have difficulty in articulating a definite organisational policy and thus, the members move even further away from them (see also Micheletti 1990).

Indeed, the unions have faced problems in maintaining their present membership. Union density has declined in several European countries (Visser 1992, Ben-Israel and Fisher 1992). In Finland, like in other Scandinavian countries, union density has remained high, but previous research reports that there has been some decline in ideological commitment to unions (Helin and Erkkilä 1991). The main reason for belonging to a trade union appears to be mere economic interests and, most importantly, access to earnings-related unemployment benefit. So it seems that the unions have to justify if not their existence, at least their central role in the society even to their own members.

This article reports on a Finnish survey that investigated wage-earners' attitudes towards industrial relations and trade unions. There are two main questions to be answered. 1) Are there signs of fragmentation and ideological individualisation among wage-earners and are these possible phenomena causing a decline in the legitimacy of trade unions and corporatist institutions such as centralised industrial relations? 2) Are certain parts of the labour force abandoning collective organisation and willing to move to a more decentralised system of industrial relations?

The structure of this article is as follows. First, I review the earlier discussion about the possible fragmentation and individualisation of the labour force in more detail. Then I discuss the consequences these phenomena are expected to have on the popularity of trade unionism and corporatism. After that, I present the empirical data used in the analysis and test the hypotheses raised on the grounds of the previous discussion. Finally, I conclude with a summary and discussion of the obtained results.

Fragmentation and individualisation of the labour force: Hypotheses

Since the early days of corporatism, remarkable changes have taken place in the Finnish society, in the labour market and in the labour force. Compared to the monolithic working class of the heyday of trade unionism, the present labour force falls into different segments with supposedly divergent interests and varying cultural and ideological emphases. In particular, it has been claimed that the growth of the middle class and service occupations, and the changes in the way employers organise work and employ wage-earners, fragment the labour force and thus decrease the legitimisation of trade unions and corporatism. On the other hand, however, there are also two trends that may have had an opposite effect on the legitimacy of corporatism. These trends are the growth of the public sector and the feminisation of the labour force.

Moreover, these inter-linked structural changes have been said to intensify certain cultural and ideological changes. For some, like Fukuyama (1992) and Inglehart (1990), there has been a fundamental and permanent change in the dominant world ideology. In this view, the traditional leftist ideologies have been gradually superseded by rightist political orientation and free-market ideologies.

Especially Hirch and Roth (1986), among others, have argued that the structural changes in the labour force have intensified the ideological changes. As the labour force becomes increasingly fragmented, the traditional collectivist values, which once underpinned trade unionism, have been replaced by values emphasising individual choice and personal achievement. As a more even redistribution of income has been one of the main targets of incomes policy agreements (see Delsen and van Veen 1992, p. 87), and as corporatism has provided the prerequisites for many welfare state policies (see Cawson 1982), increasing economic individualism and support for free market ideologies should contribute to declining support for trade unions and corporatism.

All in all, on the grounds of previous discussion it can be hypothesised that the structural and ideological changes affect directly the legitimacy of corporatism. Moreover, as it has been suggested that the structural changes also have stimulated the ideological changes, it is reasonable to hypothesise that there are also indirect relations between structural variables and variables measuring attitudes on unions and industrial relations. I discuss each hypothesis in detail.

Growth of the middle class and service occupations. First of all, the occupational structures of Western societies have changed remarkably since the early days of corporatism. The driving force in this change has been the introduction of sophisticated technology and the passage from labour-intensive manufacture to know-how intensive industries. Traditional working-class occupations, once the bastion of trade union strength, have been declining and correspondingly, the traditionally less unionised service sector occupations have become increasingly important (see Alestalo 1986). An often-heard argument is that all class-based collectivities fade as traditional industrial production declines and the service sector expands (see Crouch 1990). Previous research reports that collectivism and trade unionism are far less common ideologies among the middle classes than among the working class[4] (e.g. Bain and Elias 1985, and Hundley 1988). In this view, the growth of the middle classes contributes to the decline of the traditional working class culture and ideology. The middle classes adopt economically individualist values and are more likely to support the political right than the left. On these grounds the first hypothesis can be formulated as follows:

> H_1: *Middle class characteristics (a high occupational status, employment in a service occupation, a higher level of educational attainment, a high income and a 'non-workerist' subjective class identification) stimulate anti-union attitudes and negative stances toward collective bargaining and centralised industrial relations directly and indirectly by generating individualistic ideologies and economic anti-egalitarianism.*

Growth of the public sector and feminisation of the labour force. Especially in the Scandinavian countries, the public sector has been growing as the welfare state has been developed. To a certain degree, the public sector employees may have ambivalent attitudes toward trade unions and centralised industrial relations. In centralised agreements the public sector employees have often had lower wage increases compared to private sector employees (see Uusitalo 1983). This may stimulate negative stances toward centralised bargaining. But, on the other hand, in incomes policy agreements, the public sector employees have been guaranteed at least a certain level of wage increases. Without centralised agreements, the wage increases in the public sector might have been even smaller. Furthermore, there is also evidence that the employees of the public sector have a less individualised orientation (e.g. Madsen 1997) and hold more economically egalitarian and welfarist values (Knutsen 1986) than those working for private firms. These effects can be summed up as follows:

> H_2: *Employees of the public sector have both economic interests in and ideological commitment to centralised bargaining.*

The growth of the public sector has in particular created jobs for women. Rising female labour force participation has been a general trend in most Western countries. In Finland, however, it was comparatively high even before the period of corporatism, but only recently have female interests in the labour market been brought into daylight. Often, in earlier discussion, it has been emphasised that women's economic dependency on the welfare state contributes to a notable degree towards economic egalitarianism and support for redistributive policies among women (see Hobson 1990). Especially, it has been noted, female wage earners have benefited from solidaristic wage policy. Although feminist analysts (e.g. Martikainen 1996) have shown that the centralised agreements have clearly favoured male-dominated occupations more than female-dominated occupations, it is clear that solidaristic wage policy has lowered income differentials between the two genders within occupational groups. On these grounds I hypothesize that:

> H_3: *As female wage earners hold economically egalitarian values, and a special interest in solidaristic wage policy, women support centralised industrial relations more often than men do.*

Changes in employers' strategies. Changes in employers' strategies have formed an important part of the post-industrial structural change. Production processes have become less standardised and uniform. The old fordist modes of production have been replaced with new ones. Under fordism, rationalised work rules and taylorist forms of labour control were used in a mass-production system. In contrast, postfordism heralds the eclipse of mass production. Production now becomes characterised not by taylorism and rationalised workplace rules, but by 'flexibility' and 'self-coordination'. These changes have had several consequences.

First of all, the labour force may well be divided more clearly into those who gain from the structural change and those who do not. New forms of work rules increase the autonomy of the work of some wage earners. Flexible systems of production demand greater independence of workers from direct management control and increased participation in production teams. Instead of the earlier fordist work rules, a part of the labour force may influence the way they do their own work, and thus they find it more challenging and pleasant. Others fall into less challenging and less autonomous jobs (like 'McDonalds jobs'). Work autonomy may well increase individualist orientation among wage earners. Workers no longer shape a collective identity separate from management as planning and managing their own work becomes a part of their daily practices. Thus:

> H_4: *Having autonomous, challenging and pleasant work generates less favourable stances toward unions and collective industrial relations.*

Secondly, and closely connected to the changes in the labour process, the size of enterprises has been declining, and this may also decrease the power of trade unions. During the 1970s, enterprises aimed at centralised production and scale production. Since the 1980s, a contrary strategy has been emerging. Enterprises have decentralised their organisational structures and they have started to use subcontractors instead of carrying out certain phases of production themselves. Whereas previously the trend toward larger-sized establishments favoured trade unionism, this has been reversed to the benefit of small establishments. In fact, encouraging people to establish small firms has become a central theme in the policies of most Western governments. As Rainnie puts it, a small enterprise 'is supposed to be not only beautiful, but also dynamic, efficient, competitive and perhaps most important, a source of new jobs' (Rainnie 1989, p. 1) Often, larger establishments are held to be conducive to higher levels of unionisation and commitment to trade unionism (see Bain and Elsheikh 1979, Elsheikh and Bain 1980; see also Bain and Elias 1985). Employees in large establishments are likely to have a more distant and impersonal relationship with their employers, leading to more strained authority relations. Furthermore, unionisation in larger establishments is more likely to be attractive to both union organisers (because of lower per capita costs of recruitment) and employers (because of more effective communication with the workforce and the possibility of enhancing the legitimacy of work arrangements). (Gallie 1996, pp. 150-1). All in all, I hypothesize that,

> H_5: *Employees working in small establishments are critical of unions, and support decentralisation more often than employees of large firms.*

Thirdly, the changes in the labour process have affected the way enterprises employ workers. Not much seems to be left of the ideal type of a typical fordist worker who worked permanently in a full-time job for a single employer. An increasing number of wage earners fall into the category of atypical workers in which at least one of the above-mentioned characteristics is missing. Notable part-time working and temporary employment have become more common during the last decades (Sutela 1998; c.f. Nurmi 1998).

Both part-time working and temporary employment can be expected to reduce the legitimacy of corporatism. Previous research (Bain and Elias 1985) indicates that commitment to unionism is lower among part-time workers than among full-timers. The fact that a person knows or fears that his/her job will end in the near future may also stimulate negative attitudes toward unions. At least the unions themselves have expressed their concern about the increase of temporary workers, fearing that temporary workers have less commitment to collective organisation. In a short employment relationship, workers do not get attached to the work collective. If a person suspects that he/she will be out of work and will probably have to change his/her employer or even occupation, he/she will probably be less committed to protecting the collective interests of his/her current occupational group. So, I hypothesize that,

> H_6: *Part-time working, as well as knowing or fearing that one's job will end in the near future stimulates anti-collectivist views.*

Partly because of the changes in the strategies of the employers, partly because of technological development and a rapid increase in the productivity of labour, and partly due to the economic recession and the policies adopted to fight it in the early part of the 1990s, the level of unemployment has risen dramatically. Furthermore, during the 1990s unemployment became a problem of all occupational groups, not only of the traditional blue-collar workers. In the beginning of 1994, the unemployment rate in Finland was more than 18 per cent. Since then, the Finnish economy has recovered but the unemployment rate has decreased only moderately. The current unemployment rate is around 9 per cent. The dramatic levels of unemployment in Finland may make the legitimacy of trade unions questionable. It has been suggested that the unemployed are often alienated and estranged from most social institutions. But even more importantly, in public discussion, trade unions are often accused of creating obstacles to employment. This kind of bad publicity may well enforce negative reactions toward unions especially among those who have personally experienced unemployment. Thus,

> H_7: *Those with several experiences of unemployment and/or having atypical employment become estranged from unions.*

Control for Age. Finally, there is a good reason to expect that wage earners of different age hold diverging attitudes on unions and labour markets. In an ideological sense, the youngest age groups are said to hold economically individualist values (Inglehart 1990). Many have argued (e.g. Jokivuori et al. 1996) that one of the main problems of trade unions is to find a way to make themselves more appealing to the youngest wage earners. Thus, the last hypothesis is formulated as follows:

> H_8: *The youngest wage earners hold economically individualist and anti-egalitarian values and, thus, they also hold negative views on unions and collective bargaining.*

Data and methods

Data. The data for this study were selected from a data set gathered in a mail survey conducted in Finland in autumn 1994 as a part of the International Survey of Economic Attitudes (ISEA). The original sample is a representative sample of the Finnish population aged 18 to 70. From this sample, those currently working were selected for this analysis. Originally, the questionnaire was sent to 3,100 individuals of whom 1,737 returned the completed questionnaire. Thus, the final response rate was 56 per cent. Although the response rate compares well with recent experiences on mail surveys on the general public in Western countries, a non-response of 44 per cent naturally may cause some bias in the results. During the time the questionnaire was in the field the number of those who were employed was 914, which is the size of the sample used in this analysis.

Exogenous variables. Definitions, scoring and the factor loadings of the variables used as exogenous variables in the model are depicted in Appendix A. I measured objective stratification hierarchies conventionally by occupational status, income and educational attainment. For occupational status, I used the Erikson-Goldthorpe class scheme (Erikson and Goldthorpe 1992), which distinguishes between skilled and unskilled manual workers, routine non-manual workers, service classes I and II and self-employed. Those not falling into any of these categories were categorised as 'other occupation'. Income was measured by thousands of Finnmarks per month and educational attainment by years in education.

Consistently with the hypotheses described above, I included certain variables measuring workplace characteristics in the model. These are dummies for sector of employment (public vs. private) and labour market position (full-time vs. part-time), and an ordinal variable measuring the size of the workplace. In addition, I used a latent construct as a measure of subjective perception of the continuity of the work. This latent variable was measured with three observed variables. Regrettably, there is no direct measure of work autonomy in these data. A latent construct with two observed variables, measuring how challenging the respondent's work is, therefore, was used as a proxy for the quality of work (see Appendix A).

Endogenous variables. As the endogenous variables I used class identification, political orientation, economic egalitarianism, support for trade unions, attitudes toward centralised bargaining, and attitudes toward decentralisation of industrial relations. Definitions, scoring and the factor loadings of these variables are shown in Appendix B. Class identification and political orientation were measured with two observed variables. Class identification may not be seen as an important or even a suitable variable in an analysis like this because most people think of themselves as members of the middle class (see Evans et al. 1992). In this context, however, it is reasonable to expect that class identification plays an important role in people's attitudes. If collectivism, support for unions, industrial action and centralised bargaining are identified as a 'workerist' thinking, a higher self-placement in stratification hierarchies should produce negative stances toward them. If people think that they belong to the middle-classes, it is reasonable that they also disregard equality and do not support unions and centralised industrial relations. Political orientation was measured by two items in which the respondents were asked what party they voted for in the two preceding parliamentary elections.

As a measure of egalitarianism, only items measuring attitudes toward economic equality are available in the data used in this analysis. However, it is reasonable to expect that instead of more abstract items on egalitarianism, items on economic equality are essential for attitudes on unions and industrial relations. Above all, it is economic equality that forms the basis of all kinds of equality and traditionally the unions have emphasised economic equality. Two variables were used as measures of union attitudes (see Appendix B).

Method. All in all, the discussion reviewed above suggests that there are both direct and indirect effects of objective and subjective class variables, work characteristics, gender and age in regards to attitudes toward trade unions and industrial relations. The hypotheses above suggest that the indirect effects are mediated by ideological factors like political orientation and economic egalitarianism. To estimate these direct and indirect effects I employ a structural equation model with latent variables (e.g. Bollen 1989). In the model, background variables like stratification hierarchies affect class identification, which in turn affects party political affiliation and more general political attitudes, most importantly economic egalitarianism. These variables in turn affect more practical political attitudes like support for trade unions and attitudes toward centralised industrial relations and decentralisation of the labour market. More specifically, the structural model was formed as follows (see also Appendix C for a graphic description of the model):

Support for trade unions =
f(Economic egalitarianism, Political orientation, Class identification, Objective position in stratification hierarchies, Labour market characteristics, Gender, Age, ε_1*);* (1)

Attitudes toward centralised industrial relations =
f(*Support for trade unions, Political orientation, Class identification, Objective position in stratification hierarchies, Labour market characteristics, Gender, Age,* ε_2); (2)

Attitudes toward centralised industrial relations =
f(*Support for trade unions, Political orientation, Class identification, Objective position in stratification hierarchies, Labour market characteristics, Gender, Age,* ε_3); (3)

where objective position in stratification hierarchies is:

Objective position in stratification hierarchies =
f(*Occupational status, Educational attainment, Income*); (4)

and labour market characteristics, class identification, political orientation and economic egalitarianism are:

Labour market characteristics =
f(*Sector of employment, Labour market status, Size of the workplace, Perceptions of continuity of work, Experiences of unemployment,* ε_4); (5)

Class identification =
f(*Objective position in stratification hierarchies, Labour market characteristics, Gender, Age,* ε_5); (6)

Political orientation =
f(*Class identification, Objective position in stratification hierarchies, Labour market characteristics, Gender, Age,* ε_6); (7)

Economic egalitarianism =
f(*Political orientation, Class identification, Objective position in stratification hierarchies, Labour market characteristics, Gender, Age,* ε_7). (8)

I estimated the structural equations simultaneously in a single maximum-likelihood solution. Since most of the variables in the model are ordinal, I used polychoric and polyserial correlations to estimate standardised parameters. I estimated the full structural model and then pruned out (i.e. fixed to zero) the effects that were not significant at the 5 per cent level and that lacked a strong theoretical basis.

'Goodness of fit' is not a crucial aspect in the analysis, because the main purpose of the analysis is to test hypotheses. However, it is prudent to pay some attention to it. The Root Mean Square Error of Approximation (RMSEA) of the model was satisfactorily low (.034) and the Goodness of Fit Index (GFI) reasonably high (.96). Chi-square with 292 d.f. was 817.79. A careful examination of modification indices revealed no theoretically plausible flaws in the model. No correlations between error terms were allowed to reduce the chi-square, because often ad hoc error correlations seriously bias the parameter estimates.

Results

Basic findings. However strong the theoretical arguments about the declining trade unionism are, empirical evidence shows that the unions are still rather popular in Finland. As shown in Table 7.1, a majority of 56 per cent of the sample thinks that the trade unions are doing a fairly good or excellent job for the country. Furthermore, it seems that most Finnish wage earners do not think that the unions have too much power, either. Clearly a minority, less than 40 per cent of the respondents, thinks that the unions have too much power. Paradoxically, both centralised industrial relations and decentralisation gain support among the Finnish labour force. It is quite possible that some people support decentralisation in certain circumstances although, in principle, they support centralisation or vice versa. However, I think it is more likely that some people simply have not given any thought to the matter and thus, they have inconsistent attitudes.[5]

Multivariate analysis (Table 7.2) shows that attitudes toward unions depend mainly on class identification and political orientation. Support for centralised bargaining, for its part, is mainly a function of class identification, political orientation, economic egalitarianism and more general perceptions of trade unions.

Hypothesis 1: Middle class characteristics. Many have argued that as the traditional working class gradually vanishes, the unions will lose their public appeal and most wage earners will come to support a decentralised system of industrial relations. Basically, the results give some support to this argument. In essence, the results suggest that attitudes toward unions and industrial relations depend on subjective class identification and the level of education rather than on occupational status.

Nevertheless, the results show a slightly more complicated pattern of attitudes. Perhaps surprisingly, a high subjective class has a positive direct effect on attitudes toward centralised bargaining and a negative effect on attitudes toward decentralisation. However, as a higher level of class identification stimulates a more rightist political persuasion and less favourable stances toward economic egalitarianism and trade unions, the indirect effects of subjective class undermine the direct effects. Thus, after all, those with a higher subjective class do not support centralised

Table 7.1 Attitudes toward trade unions, centralised bargaining and decentralisation of the industrial relations. Percentage distributions (N=914)

Item				
ATTITUDES TOWARD TRADE UNIONS	Excellent or very good %	Fairly good %	Not very good %	No good at all or terrible %
In general, how good a job would you say the trade unions are doing for the country as a whole?	13.9	42.0	23.5	20.7
	Far too much or too much %	About right %	Too little or far too little %	
Do you think that trade unions in this country have too much power or too little power?	39.2	47.9	12.9	
ATTITUDES TOWARD CENTRALIZED BARGAINING	Strongly agree or agree %	Neither agree nor disagree %	Disagree or strongly disagree %	
Wages and salaries should be set nationally in negotiations between the government, trade union confederations, and employer groups.	59.7	11.3	29.0	
All important economic decisions should be made jointly by the government, trade unions and employers' groups.	61.2	9.5	29.3	
ATTITUDES TOWARD DECENTRALIZATION	Strongly agree or agree %	Neither agree nor disagree %	Disagree or strongly disagree %	
Wages should be negotiated in each individual company, rather than for the industry as a whole	53.3	13.6	33.1	
Employers should have the right to negotiate earnings with each individual worker	54.1	8.0	37.9	

Table 7.2 Predictors of attitudes toward trade unions and industrial relations. Maximum likelihood estimates. Direct (D) and indirect (I) effects

	Class Identi-fication	Political Orientation		Economic Egalitaria-nism		Attitudes toward unions		Attitudes toward centralised bargaining		Attitudes toward decentra-lisation	
	D	D	I	D	I	D	I	D	I	D	I
Occupational Status											
Manual Worker	ref.	ref.	Ref.	ref.	Ref.	ref.	Ref.	Ref.	Ref.	Ref.	Ref.
Routine Non-manual	-(a)	-(a)	-	-(a)	-	-(a)	-	-(a)	-	-(a)	-
Service I	-(a)	-(a)	-	-(a)	-	-(a)	-	-(a)	-	-(a)	-
Service II	-(a)	-(a)	-	-(a)	-	-(a)	-	.07	-	-(a)	-
Self-employed	.13	.09	.05	-(a)	-.09	-.09	-.10	.09	-.08	-(a)	.11
Other Occupation	.10	-(a)	.04	-(a)	-.06	-(a)	-.05	-(a)	-(a)	-(a)	-(a)
Educational Attainment	.59	-(a)	.24	-(a)	-.34	-(a)	-.31	-.21	-.07	-(a)	.13
Income	.13	-(a)	.05	-(a)	-.07	-(a)	-.06	-(a)	-(a)	-(a)	-(a)
Age	.15	-(a)	.06	-(a)	-.09	-.11	-.08	-(a)	-.07	-(a)	.11
Gender											
Male	ref.	ref.	ref.	ref.	Ref.	ref.	ref.	ref.	ref.	Ref.	Ref.
Female	-(a)	-(a)	-	.08	-	-(a)	.01	-(a)	.03	-(a)	-.01

Sector of employment											
Private	ref.	ref.	ref.	ref.	Ref.	ref.	ref.	ref.	ref.	Ref.	Ref.
Public	-(a)	-(a)	-	.12	-	.11	-(a)	.10	.09	-.11	-.08
Labour Market Status											
Full-time	ref.	ref.	ref.	ref.	Ref.	ref.	ref.	ref.	ref.	Ref.	Ref.
Part-time	-(a)	-(a)	-	-(a)	-	-(a)	-	-(a)	-	-(a)	-
Size of the workplace	-(a)	-.11	-	-.08	(a)	.13	.03	-(a)	.06	-(a)	-.11
Perceptions of Continuity of work	-.11	-(a)	-.04	-(a)	.06	.11	.06	-(a)	.07	-.14	-.10
Experiences of Unemployment	.10	-(a)	.04	-(a)	-.06	-(a)	-.05	-(a)	-(a)	-.11	-(a)
Having a Challenging Job	.22	-(a)	.09	-(a)	-.13	-(a)	-.12	-(a)	-(a)	-(a)	.05
Class Identification		.41	-	-.53	-.05	-.31	-.14	.30	-.42	-.15	.36
Political Orientation				-.11	-	-.34	-.42	-(a)	-.20	-(a)	.24
Economic Egalitarianism						.12	-	.31	.06	-(a)	-.08
Support for Unions								.47	-	-.69	-
R^2	.53	.18	.36	.47	.35	.45					

(a) Not significantly different from 0.

bargaining but instead they are in favour of decentralisation of labour markets. The strong indirect effects, mediated by political orientation and economic anti-egalitarianism, suggest that the support for decentralisation among those with a high subjective class is of ideological origin rather than a consequence of mere economic interests.

The effects of income and especially of educational attainment give further support to the hypothesis about the critical middle classes. A high level of education decreases support for centralised bargaining both directly and indirectly. A high level of income stimulates a higher-class identification and, thus, it also contributes to a more rightist political orientation and less favourable stances toward economic egalitarianism and trade unions.

Hypotheses 2 and 3: Gender and sector of employment. The next two hypotheses suggested that women and those working in the public sector are more in favour of trade unions, support centralised bargaining and disfavour decentralisation. Again, the hypothesis gets some support. The differences between men and women are very small but they show that women do hold more egalitarian values than men and, thus, they are also indirectly slightly more in favour of unions and centralised industrial relations.

The employment sector generates slightly larger differences than does gender. The effects of the employment sector are consistent with expectations. Compared to those working in the private sector, the public sector employees are more egalitarian, more in favour of unions and support centralised industrial relations rather than decentralisation.

Hypotheses 4-7: Work characteristics. The results show that, again, the differences are not very large and not all of the hypothesised effects can be found. For example, there are no statistically significant differences between those working full-time and those having a part-time job. Also, having an interesting and challenging job correlates with a high subjective class and rightist political views. Thus, those with a challenging job hold moderately anti-egalitarian economic values and negative views on trade unions. Despite this, having a challenging job has only small effects on attitudes on bargaining systems. However, having a job in a small firm or having the feeling that the job may soon prove to be temporary are factors which correlate both with negative attitudes toward unions and positive attitudes toward decentralisation.

The effects of experiences of unemployment are somewhat surprising. On the one hand, recent experiences of unemployment generate a higher subjective class and, thus, these experiences also indirectly contribute to a slightly more rightist political orientation and a slightly lower level of economic egalitarianism. These findings are not easy to interpret. On the other hand, experiences of unemployment directly stimulate less favourable attitudes toward decentralisation of the labour market.

Hypothesis 8: Age. Contrary to expectations, the youngest age groups are not estranged from the unions. Increasing age correlates negatively with support for unions and positive attitudes on centralised bargaining and positively with attitudes toward decentralisation.

Summary and conclusions

For several decades, Finnish policy-making has been clearly influenced by the Rehn-Meidner model. An integrated model of policy making, particularly the corporatist cooperation of the labour market parties and the coordination of fiscal, monetary, wage and labour market policies have been peculiar to Finland. To a marked degree, economic decisions have been based on tripartite negotiations between labour market parties and government. Recently, however, the integrated model of policy-making has been put under pressure. Especially employers have started to strongly criticise the centralised system decision-making, particularly demanding more flexibility to the labour market. Moreover, it has been argued that in the current structural change, the labour force becomes ever more fragmented and individualised, thus unable and unwilling to act as a unitary class in societal decision-making. As a consequence, it has been claimed, the overall legitimacy of centralised industrial relations and the corporatist power structures has declined as wage earners hold increasingly conflicting views on trade unions and the system of industrial relations.

The purpose of this article has been to analyse what the Finnish labour force thinks about trade unions and their role in society as well as corporatist arrangements like centralised bargaining. As a basic finding, the analysis indicated that, despite all the theoretical and political speculation about the decline of trade unionism and the collapse of the legitimacy of corporatism, most Finnish wage-earners still support trade unions and want to maintain their central role in the society. Also a majority of Finnish wage earners is still in favour of centralised industrial relations. However, the analysis also showed that there are certain signs of opposition to corporatist arrangements. Although a majority supports centralised industrial relations, a majority also seems to be in favour of decentralisation. Nevertheless, these results suggest that people do not categorically reject decentralisation although they may hold inconsistent labour market attitudes.

According to previous discussion, attitudes toward unions and their role in society, as well as attitudes toward industrial relations, depend on one's position in stratification hierarchies, gender and sector of employment, certain work characteristics and age, both directly and indirectly, by generating ideologies less favourable to traditional corporatism. The effects of these factors were tested in a multivariate analysis. The multivariate analysis showed that in several cases differences were smaller than expected. For example, attitudes depend very little on occupational status, gender or part-time working. However, some of the hypotheses based on recent discussion about the fragmentation and individualisation of the labour force did receive some support. For example, the well educated are clearly critical of corporatism. Likewise, a high subjective class does, indeed, generate anti-corporatist ideologies. But even more importantly, a perception of the discontinuity of one's work, employment in a small establishment, and, to a lesser degree, experiences of unemployment stimulates anti-unionist and pro-decentralisation attitudes. From the point of view of the unions, these findings may be worrying. Atypical employments, especially temporary employment relations with shorter or longer periods of unemployment between the temporary jobs, as well as the declining size of workplaces, are apparently irreversible trends. Therefore, if the unions do not find new strategies to appeal to the atypical workers, they may face persisting problems.

Since the days Gösta Rehn and Rudolf Meidner designed their famous model, economic and ideological climate has changed remarkably. Certain structural changes, increasing international competition, and the changing strategies of employers, as well as perhaps the rising support of individualist ideologies, may put pressures to the traditional model of policy-making. However, in the light of this analysis, the consequences of the fragmentation and individualisation of the labour force should not be over-emphasised. The majority of wage earners still support the unions and consider the corporatist power structures justified. The traditional model of policy making will not fail because of declining support for it among the labour force.

Notes

1 The term 'corporatism' is ambiguously defined in the literature (e.g. Hernes and Selvik 1981, pp. 103-5). I follow the definition suggested by Lehmbruch (1977) according to which corporatism is an institutionalized mode for policy design, within the framework of which large interest groups collaborate with each other and with public authorities in order to mediate and allocate interests and to implement policy.

2 It is commonly thought that usually collective agreements are the price employers pay for industrial peace. However, during the 1970s Finland was far more conflict-prone than other Scandinavian and European countries.

3 British researchers (Gallie et al. 1996, p. 6) actually talk about a determined 'Employers Offensive' in which the employers have moved against unions taking every advantage of a friendly government, the growing body of employment legislation and the possible union hostility among the public. In Finland, there are also clear signs of such an 'Offensive'.

4 More precisely, Hundley (1988) shows that in occupations requiring a higher level of education the inclination to organize is lower. However, when the occupational level is controlled, membership rises with education. In other words, at the same occupational level, the better educated are more inclined to organize.

5 Further analyses revealed that although this inconsistency was rather evenly spread among the sample, the self-employed, those voting for the Rightist parties and those with a low level of educational attainment were over-represented among those with inconsistent labor market attitudes.

References

Ahlén, Kristina (1989), 'Swedish Collective Bargaining Under Pressure: Inter-union Rivalry and Incomes Policies', *British Journal of Industrial Relations*, vol. 27, pp. 330-46.

Alestalo, Matti (1986), 'Structural Change, Classes and the State', Research Group for Comparative Sociology, Research Reports no. 33, University of Helsinki.

Andersson, Jan Otto (1989), 'Controlled Restructuring in Finland?', *Scandinavian Political Studies*, vol. 12, pp. 373-89.

Andersson, Jan Otto, Pekka Kosonen and Juhana Vartiainen (1993), 'The Finnish Model of Economic and Social Policy – From Emulation to Crash', Nationalekonomiska institutionen Ser. A:401, Åbo Akademi.

Arter, David (1987), *Politics and Policy-Making in Finland*, Wheatsheaf, Sussex.

Bain, George S. and Farouk Elsheikh (1979), 'An Inter-industry Analysis of Unionisation in Britain', *British Journal of Industrial Relations*, vol. 17, pp. 137-57.

Bain George S. and Peter Elias (1985), 'Trade Union Membership in Great Britain: An individual level analysis', *British Journal of Industrial Relations*, vol. 23, pp. 71-92.

Beck, Ulrich (1986), *Risikogesellschaft. Auf dem Weg in eine andere Moderne*, Suhrkamp, Frankfurt.

Beck, Ulrich, Anthony Giddens and Scott Lash (1994), *Reflexive Modernization: Politics, Tradition and Aesthetics in the Modern Social Order*, Polity Press, Cambridge.

Ben-Israel, Gideon and Hanna Fisher (1992), 'Trade Unions in The Future: Organizational Strategies in a Changing Environment.' in *Trade Unionism in the Future.* International Industrial Relations Association. 9th World Congress. Proceedings, vol. 2, pp. 85-97.

Bollen, Kenneth (1989), *Structural Equations with Latent Variables*, Wiley, New York.

Cawson, Alan (1982), *Corporatism and Welfare,* Heinemann, London.

Crouch, Colin (1990), 'Generalised Political Exchange in Industrial Relations in Europe during the Twentieth Century', in Bernd Marin (ed.), *Governance and Generalized Exchange*, Campus and Westview, Frankfurt and Denver, pp. 171-87.

Delsen, Lei and Tom van Veen (1992), 'The Swedish Model: Relevant for Other European Countries?', *British Journal of Industrial Relations*, vol. 30, pp. 83-105.

Elsheikh, Farouk and George Bain (1980), 'Unionisation in Britain: An Inter-Establishment Analysis Based on Survey Data', *British Journal of Industrial Relations*, vol. 18, pp.169-78.

Elvander, Nils (1990), 'Incomes policies in the Nordic countries', *International Labour Review*, vol. 1, pp. 1-21.

Erikson, Robert and John Goldthorpe (1992), *The Constant Flux. A Study of Class Mobility in Industrial Societies*, Clarendon, Oxford.

Evans, M.D.R., Jonathan Kelley and Tamas Kolosi (1992), 'Images of Class: Public Perceptions in Hungary and Australia', *American Sociological Review*, vol. 57, pp. 461-82.

Ferner, Anthony and Richard Hyman (1992), 'Industrial Relations in the New Europe: Seventeen Types of Ambiguity', in Anthony Ferner and Richard Hyman (eds), *Industrial Relations in the New Europe*, Blackwell, Oxford, pp. xvi-xlix.

Fukuyama, Francis (1992), *The End of History and the Last Man*, Hamilton, London.

Gallie, Duncan (1996), 'Trade Union Allegiance and Decline in British Urban Labour Markets', in Duncan Gallie, Roger Penn and Michael Rose (eds), *Trade Unionism in Recession*, Oxford University Press, Oxford, pp. 140-74.

Gallie, Duncan, Roger Penn and Michael Rose (1996), 'British Debate on Trade Unionism', in Duncan Gallie, Roger Penn and Michael Rose (eds), *Trade Unionism in Recession*. Oxford University Press, Oxford, pp. 1-32.

Helander, Voitto (1983) 'Self-Sustaining Corporatism? The Finnish Incomes Policy System 1968-1982', in Voitto Helander and Dag Anckar (eds), *Consultation and Political Culture: Essays on the Case of Finland*. Commentationes Scientiarum Socialium no. 19, University of Turku, Turku, pp. 81-120.

Helin, Jukka and Mika Erkkilä (1991), '90-luvun palkkatyöläinen. SAK:n järjestötutkimus', SAK, Helsinki.

Hernes, Gudmund and Arne Selvik (1981), 'Local corporatism', in Suzanne Berger (ed.), *Organizing Interests in Western Europe*, Cambridge University Press, Cambridge, pp. 103-19.

Hirch, Joachim and Roland Roth (1986), *Das neue Gesicht des Kapitalismus. Vom Fordismus zum Post-Fordismus*, VSA, Hamburg.

Hobson, Barbara (1990), 'No Exit, No Voice: Women's Economic Dependency and the Welfare State', *Acta Sociologica*, vol. 33, pp. 235-50.

Hundley, Greg (1988), 'Education and Union Membership', *British Journal of Industrial Relations*, vol. 26, pp. 195-200.

Ilmonen, Kai and Kimmo Kevätsalo (1995), *Ay-liikkeen vaikeat valinnat*, Palkansaajien tutkimuslaitos, Helsinki.

Inglehart, Ronald (1990), *Culture Shift in Advanced Industrial Society*, Princeton University Press, Princeton.

Jokivuori, Pertti, Kimmo Kevätsalo and Kaj Ilmonen (1996), 'Ay-jäsenen monet kasvot' Jyväskylän yliopisto, Sosiologian julkaisuja 60.

Kauppinen, Timo (1994), *The Transformation of Labour Relations in Finland*, Ministry of Labour, Helsinki.

Katzenstein, Peter J. (1985), *Small States in World Markets. Industrial Policy in Europe*, Cornell University Press, Ithaca.

Knutsen, Oddbjørn (1986), 'Sosiale klasser og politiske verdier i Norge': Middelklassen i den offentlige sektor som den "nye klasse"', *Tidsskrift for samfunnsforskning*, vol. 27, pp. 263-87.

Korpi, Walter (1983), *The Democratic Class Struggle*. Routledge and Kegan Paul, London.

Kosonen, Pekka (1998), *Pohjoismaiset mallit murrohsessa*,Vastapaino, Tampere.

Lehmbruch, Gerhard (1977), 'Liberal Corporatism and Party Government', *Comparative Political Studies*, vol. 10, pp. 91-126.

Madsen, Morten (1997), 'The Relationship between Working Life and Individualisation: A Study among Danish Trade Union Members', *Work, Employment and Society*, vol. 11, pp. 197-217.

Mansner, Markku (1990), *Suomalaista yhteiskuntaa rakentamassa*, Gummerus, Jyväskylä.

Martikainen, Riitta (1996), 'Työehtosopimusten sukupuolet', in Merja Kinnunen and Päivi Korvajärvi (eds), *Työelämän sukupuolistavat käytännöt*, Gummerus, Jyväskylä, pp. 51-69.

Micheletti, Michele (1990), 'Toward Interest Inarticulation: A Major Consequence of Corporatism for Interest Organizations', *Scandinavian Political Studies*, vol. 13, pp. 255-76.

Nurmi, Kaarina (1988), '"Se pieni ero" hyvinvointivaltioiden koulutus- ja työmarkkinoilla', Turun yliopiston julkaisuja C:140.

Pekkarinen, Jukka, Matti Pohjola and Bob Rowthorn (1992), *Social Corporatism – A Superior Economic System?* Oxford University Press, Oxford.

Pestoff, Victor A. (1991), 'Den Svenska modellens nedgång och det organiserade näringslivets uppgång som en betydande politisk aktör', in Timo Kauppinen and Virpi Köykkä (eds), *Arbetsmarknadssystem och det politiska systemet 2000*, Arbetsministeriet, Helsingfors, pp. 89-122.

Rainnie, Al (1989), *Industrial Relations in Small Firms. Small Isn't Beautiful*, Routledge, London.

Sutela, Hanna (1998), 'Muutoksia määräaikaisuudessa', *Hyvinvointikatsaus*, no. 2/1998, pp. 24-7.

Uusitalo, Hannu (1983), 'Incomes Policy in Finland: Economic and Social Effects in a Comparative Perspective', *Scandinavian Political Studies*, vol. 6, pp. 1-25.

Visser, Jelle (1992), 'Union Organisation: Why countries Differ?' in *Trade Unionism in the Future*, International Industrial Relations Association. 9th World Congress. Proceedings, vol. 2, pp. 158-76.

Appendix A. Definitions, scoring and factor loadings (*) of the exogenous variables used in the analysis

Latent Variable	Observed Variable	Measurement	Factor Loading λ
Occupational Status	Manual worker	Ref.	
	Routine Non-manual	Dummy	1
	Service I	Dummy	1
	Service II	Dummy	1
	Self-employed	Dummy	1
	Other Occupation	Dummy	1
Educational Attainment	Years in Education		1
Income	10,000 per month		1
Age	Full years		1
Gender	Male	Dummy	
	Female	Female = 1	1
Sector of employment	Private	Dummy	
	Public	Public = 1	1
Labour Market Status	Full-time	Dummy	
	Part-time	Part-time = 1	1

Size of the workplace	'About how many other people usually work for the company as full-time paid employees not counting yourself?' Answering options were 0 - 'none'; 1 - 'one'; 2 - ' 'two'; 3 - '3 to 10'; 4 - '11 to 25'; 5 - '26 to 100'; 6 - '101 to 500'; 7 - '501 to 1000'; 8 - '1000 to 5000'; and 9 - 'More than 5000'.	Ordinal in equal sequences between 0 and 100	1
Perceptions of Continuity of work	1.'Is your future in this company secure?' Answering options: 1- 'No, definitely not' to 5 - 'Yes'	Same as above	.69
	2. 'Do you think your company will still be in business 5 years from now?' Answering options as in the previous item.	Same as above	.77
	3. 'How satisfied or dissatisfied are you with... The security and predictability of your future?' Answering options: 1 - 'Terrible' to 8 - 'Delighted'	Same as above	.62
Experiences of Unemployment	Weeks unemployed during the last 12 months	Ordinal	1
Having a Challenging Job	'How would you describe your job... 1. Does it require special talents and abilities that most people do not have?	Ordinal in equal sequences between 0 and 100	.60
	2. Does it require a lot of thinking?' Answering options: 1- 'No, definitely not' to 5 - 'Yes'		.95

Appendix B. Definitions, scoring and factor loadings (*) of the endogenous variables used in the analysis

Latent Variable	Observed Variable	Measurement	λ
Class Identification	1. 'Thinking about your education, work, income, and standard of living, are you and your family near to the top of society, near the bottom, or somewhere in between?' Answering options: 1 - 'Bottom of society' to 10 - 'Top of society'	Ordinal in equal sequences between 0 and 100	.59
	2. 'If you were asked to use one of four names for your social class, which would you say you belong to?' Answering options: 1 - 'Lower class'; 2 - 'Working class; 3 - 'Middle class'; 4 - 'Upper class'	Same as above	.86
Political Orientation	1. 'Thinking back to the Parliamentary election in 1987, who got your vote?'	Leftist parties = 0; Rightist parties = 100 (a)	.95
	2. 'And the election in 1991, who did you vote for?'	Leftist parties = 0; Rightist parties = 100 (a)	.82
Economic Egalitarianism	1. 'Differences in income in Finland are too large' Answering options: 1 - 'Strongly disagree' to 5 - 'Strongly agree'.	Ordinal in equal sequences between 0 and 100	.81
	2. 'It is the responsibility of the government to reduce the differences in income between people with high incomes and those with low incomes' Answering options as above.	As above	.79
	3. 'There is too much of a difference between rich and poor in this country' Answering options as above.	As above	.86
	4. 'Income and wealth should be redistributed toward ordinary working people' Answering options as above.	As above	.77
	5. 'One of the most important aims in this country over the next ten years should be to reduce differences between rich and poor' Answering options as above.	As above	.87

Support for Unions	1. 'In general, how good a job would you say the trade unions are doing for this country as a whole?' Answering options: 1 - 'Terrible' to 6 -'Excellent'.	As above	.68
	2. 'Do you think that trade unions in this country have too much power or too little power?' Answering options: 1 - 'Far too little power' to 5 - 'Far too much power'.	As above	.78
Attitudes toward Centralised Bargaining	1. 'Wages and salaries should be set nationally in negotiations between the government, trade unions and employers' organisations.' Answering options as above	As above	.71
	2. 'All important decisions should be made jointly by the government, trade unions and employers' organisations.' Answering options as above.	As above	.87
Attitudes toward Decentralisation	1. 'Wages should be negotiated in each individual company, rather than for the industry as whole.' Answering options as above.	As above	.75
	2. 'Employers should have the right to negotiate earnings with each individual worker.'	As above	.80

APPENDIX C. A heuristic description of the structural equation model used in the analysis

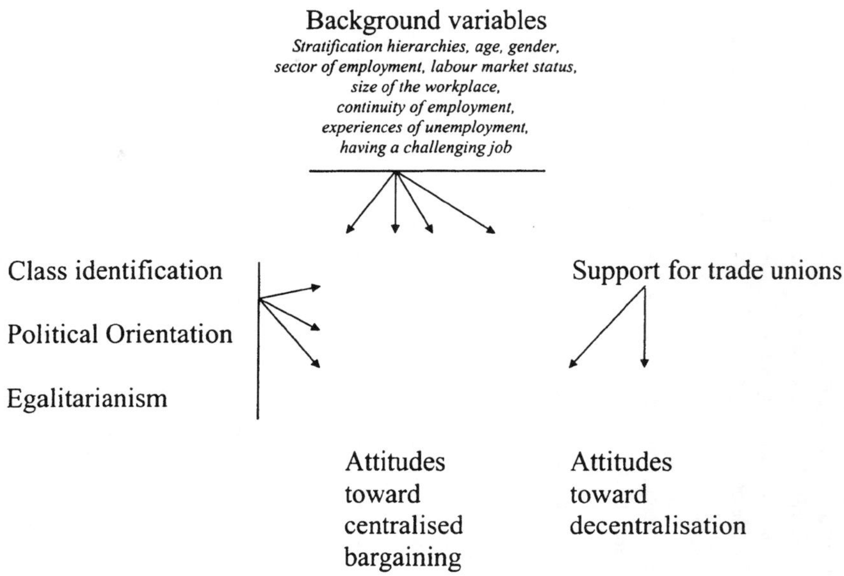

Chapter 8

Decentralized Wage Bargaining: A Threat to Incomes Policy Goals or an Instrument of Flexibility?[1]

Geir Høgsnes and Frode Longva

Introduction

As described elsewhere in this collection, two Swedish union economists, Gösta Rehn and Rudolf Meidner, in articles published in the late 1940s made the original arguments in favour of central and solidaristic bargaining concerning macroeconomic stability and efficiency (Moene and Wallerstein 1995). However, in this article we focus on the role of more decentralized forms of wage determination in relation to national incomes and labour market policy goals in the case of Norway. Decentralized components have mainly consisted of local or firm level wage bargaining and agreements. Other forms of non-centralized bargaining, however, are also of relevance in this connection and have to be included in a broader analysis of the efficiency of Norwegian wage determination in relation to macroeconomic performance.

We start with a discussion of the Norwegian system of wage determination in relation to the more general Nordic model. Then, in order to situate the Norwegian development in a broader context, we proceed to a description of major actors and then to how wage formation has been conducted during the last decades. Our next section presents various views on the role of decentralized components in relation to broader incomes and labour market policy goals. Finally, we discuss recent trends in wage bargaining in relation to the future prospects of the Norwegian model.

In the international literature, Norway is characterized as having a highly centralized form of wage determination representing a variant of the broader 'Nordic labour market model'. Though somewhat contested (Mjøset 1992), the concept of a distinct Nordic model refers to the broad common traits and features of post-war Nordic labour market organization. It is associated with strong and relatively unitary organizations of labour and capital, a centralized system of solidaristic collective bargaining, extensive welfare state provision, and macroeconomic policy aimed at full employment.

The original arguments of Rehn-Meidner regarded solidaristic wage policy as a means towards greater labour market efficiency, and centralized bargaining was a prerequisite for a successful combination of effective labour allocation and a solidaristic distribution of wages. Indeed, probably the most common explanation for the success of the Nordic countries during the post-war period is the effective operation of these mechanisms (Dølvik et al. 1997).

However, during the last two decades developments have weakened this description, particularly with regard to labour market developments, and important distinctions have evolved between the Nordic countries. Both Sweden and Finland faced increasing unemployment and soaring budget deficits in the beginning of the 1990s, and Denmark had to cope with persistently high unemployment since the oil crisis in 1973. Furthermore, Sweden, for decades symbolizing the virtues of the Nordic model, has gradually - though unevenly - decentralized its bargaining system since the 1983 withdrawal of the metal working industry from centralized bargaining (see Elvander 1988). The Swedish employers' organization finally decided to abandon the system of centralized co-ordination in 1992. Such evidence has led many observers to declare the death of the Nordic model of full employment, suggesting that wage equality and centralization per se creates severe problems for the allocation of labour and workers' productivity. From this perspective, adoption of the flexibility of the decentralized 'American-style' labour market is the only route to full employment.

However, Norway, presents a contrast to this decentralized picture with its low unemployment, narrow wage differences and centralized system of wage bargaining. This appears to be an interesting paradox in view of the widespread international predictions of corporatism's demise, resulting from globalization and technological, structural and social transformation (Streeck 1993, Teague and Grahl 1992). Moreover, the common definition of corporatism as a system of wage determination takes as its point of departure that the state is, indirectly or directly, an active partner in the bargaining game. Furthermore, a corporatist system presupposes interest organizations having a monopoly within their respective fields, especially on the labour and employer sides.

Norway, as we will see, deviates in important ways from such an ideal type of corporatism. The most important factor is that the Norwegian system, contrary to the Swedish (and Danish) system, is characterized both by competing unions and by competing confederations. As such, the Norwegian variant of the Nordic model has in many respects traditionally been a lighter version of the Swedish system (Dølvik et al. 1997).[2] The survival and success of the Norwegian system must therefore partly be explained with reference to these deviations. We will argue that the decentralized features of the Norwegian system of wage bargaining should be viewed as a way of coping with these deviations, and as such they are an important part of the explanation of the survival of the Norwegian system. Therefore, in analysing the foundations of the present Norwegian system we pose the question of whether an abandonment of the traditional centralized system is the only answer to problems inherent in the original Nordic or Rehn-Meidner model. Is there a path other than that taken in Sweden in the early 1990s that is open to those systems that were previously highly centralized?

A notable relevant characteristic of the Norwegian system is the attitudes and priorities of the main actors that have dominated the wage determination process. The government and the leadership of the Norwegian Confederation of Trade Unions (LO) and the Confederation of Norwegian Business and Industry (NHO) have assumed that the main target for unions and union members is real wage developments and not the relative wage positions between various groups of employees. In our view, this assumption is not always appropriate, and we will explain our doubt with reference to wage determination in Norway during the last twenty years, concentrating on more recent developments during the 1990s.

The solidarity alternative

A key issue in connection with wage negotiations and settlements during recent years has been how outcomes may affect the persistence of the kind of incomes and labour market policy which have characterized and dominated Norway from 1992/93 onwards. This policy, known as the 'Solidarity Alternative', is based on three foundations: (1) a solidaristic wage policy, (2) an active labour market policy, and (3) an active macroeconomic policy. While the first two foundations conform to the Rehn-Meidner model, the third is in contrast to the more cautious or restrained macroeconomic policy associated with the Rehn-Meidner model. In this article we deal mainly with the first of these foundations. A key question is how solidaristic wages maintained as a basic foundation of present Norwegian economic policy, in spite of disagreements concerning wage distribution issues in Norway.

The background of the 'Solidarity Alternative' policy was that Norway, after several years of high growth rates, suddenly found itself in 1986 in a deep economic crisis. This crisis was mainly caused by the over-heated Norwegian economy following the liberalisation of the credit system in the early 1980s, combined with continued control of interest rates by state authorities. A sharp drop in oil revenues during winter 1985/86 followed this. The fall of the Willoch government in May 1986 and the return of the Social Democrats to power marked the peak of the crisis.

As Gro Harlem Bruntland returned to power with her new Labour government, a tight economic policy was launched. This policy aimed at re-establishing and improving the competitiveness of the Norwegian economy and went through various phases. A very restrictive economic policy and especially a restrictive incomes policy characterized the first years following 1986. Within the sphere of wage determination, these years were characterized as 'exception years' (1987) or by 'exception laws' (1988 and 1989). In 1987 this meant zero wage increases in connection with national-level wage bargaining. In 1988 and 1989 wage increases agreed in the national-level negotiations between the main actors in the Norwegian labour market were given the status of law by the parliament, Stortinget. Thereby, in close co-operation with the government, the Norwegian Confederation of Trade Unions, LO, and the Norwegian Employers' Association, NAF (from 1989 re-organized as the Confederation of Norwegian Business and Industry, NHO) completely controlled the rate of wage growth.

After this period of re-organization of the Norwegian political economy, a new economic policy was launched in 1992/93 based on the recommendations of a governmental committee appointed in late 1991 (published in the Government Report NOU 1992:26). The head of this committee was Per Kleppe, during the 1970s and early 80s minister of finance. In that position he became known as the architect behind the most ambitious incomes policy experiment in Norway in the post-war area, the 'Combined Settlements' and 'Kleppe Packages'.

The new economic policy, the 'Solidarity Alternative', recommended by Kleppe in the early 1990s, was aimed at securing the positive results obtained in wage and price development during the previous period. This policy was based on a continuation of the strategy of wage moderation that characterized the late 1980s, combined with rather ambitious goals involving growth rates and reduction of unemployment, which had increased dramatically during the late 1980s and early 1990s. (Norwegian unemployment was below 3 per cent during the 1970s and the early 1980s; it peaked at about 9 per cent, including those on active labour market schemes in 1993; Rødseth 1997.) This alternative has dominated wage settlements from 1992/93 up to the present, and it is given credit for the prosperity of the Norwegian economy and a sharp growth in employment. From 1993 to 1997 employment grew by about 10 per cent, leaving Norway at the top of the employment/population rankings of the OECD.

In the years since the introduction of the 'Solidarity Alternative', those responsible for the Norwegian economic policy have been engaged in propagating the 'line of moderation'. The fact that much energy is put into such a campaign indicates that not everyone is convinced. Indeed, those opposing the moderation strategy seem to be more successful in spreading their message than are the government and LO/NHO.

Until 1997, when the initial period for the 'Solidarity Alternative' ended, there seemed to be a general willingness to continue according to the main principles of the incomes policy. However, a change in government led to uncertainty on the labour side regarding the new government's future support for the pact. Although the new Christian-led government soon signalled such support, it was not enough to prevent the 1998 wage settlement producing record high wage increases and loss of competitiveness for Norwegian firms. In 1999, however, we saw a revitalization of the co-operative venture of incomes policy, leading the main partners to join efforts toward a revitalization of the positive elements of the 'Solidarity Alternative.'[3] This revitalization may signal that the massive nominal wage increment of 1998 in fact served as an adjustment mechanism to maintain legitimacy for continuing wage moderation both among union members and among unorganized workers. This is, however, yet to be seen.

To sum up so far: the idea behind the 'Solidarity Alternative' is based on traditional incomes policy reasoning, where the major labour market conflict is the one between labour and capital. Within a corporatist framework the goal of such a policy is to improve economic performance through a strategy of consensus building, which means achieving compromises between conflicting interests of these two parties. But there is another dimension to the conflict with increasing impact on developments, namely the conflict between competing actors on labour's side of the bargaining table. The most urgent question today, in our opinion, is to what extent and how is the Norwegian framework for wage bargaining and determination able to handle this kind of conflict.

Since 1997 those responsible for Norwegian economic policy in general and incomes policy more specifically, have feared that the final outcome of wage negotiations would undermine the 'Solidarity Alternative'. During this period demands of key actors in the bargaining game went far beyond what was considered to be within the framework of 'solidaristic solutions'. Even worse, the demands from the various unions tended to point in completely opposite directions. Conflicting demands have made it very difficult to reach agreements with which all parties can live. However, in spite of this fact, the system has worked better than feared. To see how this is possible, we need to look closer at various components of total wage growth in Norway during recent decades. First of all we shall give a brief presentation of the major actors on the union side and their strategies.

The composition of the Norwegian labour market parties

There are in Norway today four union associations organizing workers. First is the Norwegian Confederation of Trade Unions (LO), established in 1899, which organizes more than 600,000 workers, the majority from the private-industry sector (55 per cent). Second is the Federation of Norwegian Professional Associations (AF), established in 1976, which organized more than 200,000 highly educated workers by 1997. The third main association is the Confederation of Vocational Unions (YS), established in 1977, which organizes about 170,000 workers, roughly evenly distributed between the private and public sector. The fourth association, the Academics, was established in 1997 as a result of a split in AF, leaving AF with mainly semi-professional occupations within the public sector. Today the Academics organizes approximately 100,000 professional workers with university degrees, both in private and public industries (for all figures see Nergaard 1999). In addition there are some independent unions, for example, the Norwegian Police Federation and the Norwegian Union of Teachers.

To some extent, all union confederations are in direct competition with each other. That is, in contrast to both Sweden and Denmark, there has been no general agreement between the trade union federations as to which workers they are to represent. In addition, their existence as separate actors reflects disagreements concerning the internal distribution of wage incomes among various categories of wage earners. That is, LO, AF, YS and The Academics have different opinions as to what are reasonable wage inequalities and, thus, differ on the distribution principles or social norms which should govern Norwegian wage distribution policy (Høgsnes 1990, 1994).

During the entire post-World War II era, LO has given priority to a so-called 'solidaristic wage policy'. During the 1950s and 1960s this meant that LO acted in favour of the principle of 'equal wage for equal work'. That is, types of work with similar training and skill requirements should be paid the same wage, without regard to *who* the worker was, and *where* employed. This meant that during the first two decades after World War II the phrase 'solidaristic wage policy' only peripherally concerned wage inequalities between workers employed in jobs requiring different skills and formal qualifications. Where it did, it was limited to unionized workers (Frøland 1992, pp. 48-9), among whom LO opposed having large wage inequalities between skilled, semi-skilled and unskilled workers.

In the beginning of the 1970s a major shift took place within LO concerning its strategy of wage distribution. The substance of the concept 'solidaristic wage policy' changed. From 1974/75 onwards LO decided that 'solidarity' meant giving priority to the goal of *reduced wage inequalities between different strata of wage earners* (Hanisch and Høgsnes 1988). It is this pivotal point that we have interpreted as a switch to a new social norm, namely a modified version of the principle of 'equal wage regardless of type of work'. This switch was contrary to the core ideas of the Rehn-Meidner view of wage solidarity.

This strategic turn had important consequences for employees in various parts of the labour market, especially the state sector. For employees in that sector a new era began, characterized by reduced wage inequalities between low, medium and high wage groups. A similar development took place in the Swedish labour market somewhat earlier (Elvander 1988, p. 35). Høgsnes and Hanisch (1988) argue that in the Norwegian case the two other newly established union associations, AF (1975) and YS (1977), appeared partly in response to LO's new redistribution strategy in the 1970s. The new LO strategy clearly threatened the interests of numerically important groups of employees.

It is clear today that the four main union confederations have different goals concerning the distribution of wages. This is most pronounced in the case of AF and The Academics, which from their very beginnings have argued and acted in favour of a wage distribution that more strongly reflects variations in length of education (formal qualifications) and responsibility. This strategy clearly contradicts LO's wage equalization goal and, in part, YS's strategy of closing the wage gaps between male and female dominated occupations.

In addition, from AF's and The Academics' point of view, the demand for wage differentials based on education and responsibility transcends preservation of existing wage inequalities; it entails re-establishment of wage inequalities from earlier times. The present strategy of both unions is to demand higher wage increases for their relatively well paid members, compared to what low- and middle-waged workers are to receive in both absolute and relative terms. In particular, such demands clearly sharpen the conflict with the traditional labour movement, LO, and its conception of 'solidaristic wage policy'.

Why then was a separate union created for those with many years of education, i.e. The Academics? Here we arrive at the core question concerning union strategy and the dilemma between maximizing the number of members and promoting the interests of existing members. Though AF and the Academics share principles of wage distribution, they find themselves representing different wage strata in Norwegian society. It is obvious that the numerical strength of, for example, the female-dominated Norwegian Association of Nurses (NSF) within AF was seen as an obstacle to male dominated unions with highly educated members such as medical doctors, lawyers, chartered engineers, architects and psychologists. Arguments in favour of wage equalization between occupations dominated by men and women were thus not compatible with arguments in favour of increased wage differentiation based on length of education.

The establishment of YS was initially founded on a desire to have an alternative union association which, contrary to LO, would act 'party politically neutrally' (Pettersen 1990, p. 10). As well YS, may be characterized as having conflicts with LO over social norms, similar to those of AF and The Academics. Today YS may be said to represent an alternative to the assumed male dominance within LO. Certainly YS and its concern for wages of female occupations is reflected in its wage distribution policy. Especially since the early 1980s, YS has given priority to wage demands which have been aimed at improving pay conditions of workers in female dominated positions, primarily in the public sector. Equal pay for public and private sector workers engaged in 'work of similar value' has been an important YS demand.[4]

YS today might thus be viewed as the union association which most openly and strongly opposes wage inequalities that are not in conformity with the principle of 'equal wage for equal work'. In that way, YS has remained faithful to LO's old tradition of fighting against pay differentials based on firm, industry or sector of employment. Within LO this concern, as described above, became less important after the mid-70s.

In sum, the conflicting principles of the four major actors on the labour side clearly indicate that struggles over internal wage inequalities among groups of employees have become a central element in Norwegian wage determination. We now turn to questions of how this is handled within the current mode of co-ordination, and how it might affect the prolongation of the co-operative venture of incomes policy.

Central elements in the Norwegian system of wage bargaining

In Norway, wage bargaining mainly takes place on two levels, at the central (national) level and the local (firm) level. Central negotiations usually take place between national unions or federations of trade unions and employers' associations, with the state as a more or less active partner. Local bargaining takes place on the company level or firm level. A key characteristic of the Norwegian system is that more decentralized forms of bargaining play a significant role when it comes to total wage growth during a year. In private industries this has been the case for several decades. Wage growth at the local level in excess of the central agreements (so-called wage drift) has made up on average more than half of total wage growth during the last three decades. Drift is the outcome either of local bargaining or of individual employers' attempts to adjust to market conditions or to set efficiency wages. This means that employer and employee representatives encounter each other in two different contexts, in which very different kinds of logic prevail.

During recent years a similar trend has come to characterize the public sector, on both the state and the municipal government levels. The wage determination system in the public sector is even more complicated than in the private sector. Wage bargaining in the public sector takes place in three different arenas. First, we have the central main negotiations, which usually follow the settlements in private industries. In the second arena there is a component known as 'central adjustment negotiations' in the public sector. These negotiations focus on which occupations deserve extra wage increments given the results of the central settlement and wage developments in the past period. They take place after the central agreement has been settled. There is a long tradition of these kinds of extra wage increments in the public sector. In fact, the amounts of money set aside for this kind of negotiation, as well as other more decentralized negotiations, are agreed upon in connection with the main central negotiations, which take place in late spring.

Though the distribution of money set aside for such adjustments are bargained at the central level, we prefer to classify these negotiations as a non-centralized element. We do so because the distribution of money takes place in a much more secret atmosphere with less attention from the media compared to the central main negotiations. Added to this more decentralized component of public sector negotiations is the third arena: local bargaining and local agreements. Unlike adjustment negotiations, local bargaining is a more recent element in the public sector.

A major difference between the role of more decentralized negotiations in the public and private sectors is that in private industries the parties are relatively free to determine the level of local wage growth, based mainly on productivity changes and the 'pay ability' of the firms. In contrast, in the public sector it is the central actors who make decisions about the economic framework for these more decentralized negotiations. Wage drift per se is thus of minor importance in the public sector.

The guiding principles in connection with wage negotiations in these different arenas are certainly related. For example, norms referred to in the central negotiations to a large extent affect norms used in the local level negotiations. However, the same norms do not give direction to the outcomes in both contexts. It is rather the opposite: arguments based on norms which did not win at the central level are now more likely to direct the distribution of money set aside at the local level. That is, in decentralized settings, norms and forces counteracting those guiding central settlements prevail.

The difference between the two sectors also means that struggles over wage distribution principles are more acute in the public sector compared to private industry. This is reinforced by the fact that union competition is much more important and direct in the public sector. In part this is due to the absence of any 'objective' criteria for 'ability to pay' or for productivity differences among various groups of employees, but also because the four main union associations act on more equal terms. As a consequence, a more open struggle over distribution principles emerges at all bargaining levels in the public sector. Even though LO still dominates the public sector (with just below 50 per cent of unionized workers) it is equalled by the combined share of AF/Academics (with about 25 per cent), plus YS and independent unions. In the private sector, however, LO represents more than 60 per cent of organized workers (Nergaard 1999).

An empirical overview of components of total wage growth

Two perspectives on the impact of decentralized or local settlements on total wage growth may be outlined. One is that decentralized bargaining threatens the strategy of wage moderation by undermining wage growth rates agreed to at the central national level. The other perspective is that local bargaining and local agreements represent a necessary and flexible correction to the rigidity that characterizes central wage agreements. It should be noted, however, that these perspectives are not necessarily mutually contradictory but can be present in different aspects of the process of co-ordination. In the next two sections we will discuss arguments in support of both these perspectives.

Underlying this discussion is the fact that in the last quarter of the 20th century local wage increments in private industries, on average, have made up more than half of total wage growth. And unlike earlier when this only characterized private industries, from the early 1990s onwards a new wage system has made the impact of local bargaining and local wage growth more important in the public sector.

Tables 1-3 summarize the main indicators of the relationship between various components of wage growth during the last two decades. The tables refer to the three main sectors of the Norwegian labour market, the private industries (the so-called LO/NHO area), and the state and the municipal government sector.

Table 8.1 Contributions of various components to total wage growth in Norway from 1976 to 1997 (percentages). Figures in brackets refer to the due date of increments. Workers employed in the LO/NHO area

Year	Cent.	Local[1]	Total	Loc./Tot.
1976	9.5	5.5	15.0	36
1977	2.9	7.3	10.2	72
1978	2.1	3.8	5.9	64
1979	0.3	2.4	2.6	92
1980	5.2	8.3	13.5	61
1981	1.8	6.6	8.3	80
1982	5.5	6.3	11.8	53
1983	1.0	5.2	6.1	85
1984	3.0	5.9	8.9	66
1985	0.5	6.9	7.4	93
1986	3.6	6.9	18.3[2]	66[3]
			10.5[3]	
1987	0.2	8.3	8.5	98
1988	1.7	0,7	2,4	29
1989	4.1	-0.2	3.9	0
1990	3.3	3.0	6.3	48
1991	1.6	2.5	4.1	61
1992	0.5	2.4	2.9	83
1993	0.8	1.8	2.6	69
1994	1.3	1.1	2.4	46
1995	1.1	2.7	3.8	71
1996	2.6	1.7	4.2	41
1997	1.0	3.0	4.1	73

1 The figures refer to changes from the first quarter one year to the first quarter the next year. That is, the 1985 figure marks changes from the end of first quarter 1985 to first quarter 1986.
2 Actual increases in hourly earnings.
3 Corrected for reductions in agreed working time.
Source: NHO: Wage and Sick Leave Statistics.

Table 8.1 shows that the impact of local wage drift on total wage growth in the NHO/LO area has been significant every year since 1975. In fifteen of twenty-one years, local wage growth has been larger than the centrally agreed wage increment, which seems to indicate that the outcome of local bargaining undermines incomes policy targets. However, analyses made by Rødseth and Holden (1990) suggest this to be too hasty an interpretation. In the period prior to 1990, local increments seem to have been successfully anticipated by the central partners. Hence, local wage-drift was not simply added to the centrally agreed wage-level (Rødseth and Holden 1990, p. 272).

If we concentrate on the period dominated by the 'Solidarity Alternative', i.e., from 1992 onwards, local wage increases as a proportion of total wage growth has been as low as 41 per cent (1996) and as high as 83 per cent (1993). Hence, while central level agreements in connection with the 'Solidarity Alternative' are kept within reasonable frames from the point of view of macro-economic performance, there is still space for significant local adjustments.

A similar feature may be extracted from Tables 8.2 and 8.3, which contain information about centralized and more decentralized components of wage growth in the two main parts of the public sector. For the municipal government sector there are no figures available prior to 1985. The far right column contains information about both local wage growth and wage growth due to central adjustment negotiations as a proportion of total wage growth, whereas in Table 1, it is only local wage growth as a percentage of the total. It is to be noted that figures in Tables 2 and 3 are not directly comparable with those of Table 1, as the figure for total wage growth in this table (and the following one) refers to annual wage growth from one year to the other including so-called 'overhang' due to wage increments late in a calendar year.

Within the municipal government sector (see Table 8.2) the proportion of decentralized wage increases is less than in the private industries and the state sector. It varies between 0 per cent (1988) and 26 per cent (1990), and for almost half of the years it is below 10 per cent. Further, there is no sign that the impact of decentralized bargaining has increased during the 1990s compared to the 1980s. Thus, in spite of the formally increasing flexibility of the wage determination system, the reality still mimics a centralized system.

A somewhat different trend may be extracted from Table 8.3 concerning the state sector. Here the wage system went through a major change in 1991 when it was opened for local wage negotiations. Until then the decentralized component was represented by money set-aside for adjustment negotiations. From the table we see no signs that money reserved for local bargaining has been extracted from the adjustment pot. There is a weak tendency toward decreased significance of central wage growth during the 1990s, indicating a trend toward more decentralization. Local or decentralized wage growth as a proportion of total wage growth is on average above the level of one third after 1992, far above what we observed in the municipal government sector.

The question posed in the introduction was the following: does decentralization of the wage determination process represent a problem? These trends and figures, however, do not say anything about the effects of decentralized forms of wage negotiations.

Table 8.2 Contributions of various components to total wage growth in Norway from 1985 to 1998 (percentages). Figures in brackets refer to the due date of increments. Workers employed in the municipal government sector

Year	Cent.	Adjust.	Local[3]	Total	Decent./Tot
1985	4.35		0.80	6.70	12
1986	5.95		0.3	8.35	4
1987	1.43 (1/1)		0.75 (1/1)	7.18	10
1988	1.70 (1/1)			3.51	0
	1.0 (1/4)				
	0.10[1] (1/7)				
	0.50[2] (1/7)				
1989	3.7		0.2	4.8	4
1990	1.92	0.74	0.38	4.24	26
1991	0.31 (1/9)		0.1	4.81	2
1992	1.34		0.3 (1/1)	3.041	20
			0.3		
1993	0.77	0.28 (1/10)	0.15	2.35	18
1994	0.77		0.18	2.32	13
			0.12 (1/10)		
1995	1.27	0.01 (1/1)	0.28	2.95	10
	0.53				
1996	2.06	0.05 (1/8)	0.125 (1/10)	4.28	4
	0.75 (1/8)				
1997	0.78		0.12 (1/11)	3.81	3
1998	3.07	0.9 (1/9)	0.13	6.04	17

[1] Parental leave increment.

[2] Low-wage increment.

[3] The total represents the total wage growth over the year. This also reflects changes in wages due to changed composition of the labour force, wage drift, and so-called 'overhang', i.e. annual wage growth due to wage increments granted at various stages the previous year.

Source: The Norwegian Association of Local Authorities: Wage and Employee Statistics (The 'PAI' register).

Table 8.3 Contributions of various components to total wage growth in Norway from 1976 to 1998 (percentages). Figures in brackets refer to the due date of increments. Workers employed in the state sector

Year	Cent.	Adj.	Local	Total[3]	Decent./Tot.
1976	7.20			14.48	0
1977	7.7	0.8		8.97	9
1978	6.3	0.5		7.57	7
1979	Wage stop			-0.69	
1980	11.3	2.3		13.87	17
1981	7.2, 0.5[1]	4.0 (1/10)		9.37	43
1982	8.3, 0.1			13.93	0
1983	5.60	1.20 (1/8)		6.05	20
1984[2]	4.21, 0.29, 0.16 (1/10)	1.05 (1/8)		8.02	13
1985	4.5	0.7		6.04	12
1986	4.85 4.20 (1/7)	0.53, 0.50 (1/9), 1.20 (1/10)		12.94	17
1987	0	1.0 (1/1)		1.88	53
1988	1.5 (1/1) 1.2 (1/4)	0.5		3.96	13
1989	4.2	0.13		6.15	2
1990	3.0	1.27		5.76	22
1991	0.79, 3.58 (1/9)	0.15, 0.3 (1/9)	0.25 (1/10)	6.41	11
1992	0.01	0	0.1 (1/10)	1.17	9
1993	1.0	0.2 (1/1), 0.7	0.1 (1/1), 0.40	2.99	47
1994	1.0	0.2 (1/7)	0.35 (1/9)	1.96	28
1995	1.70	1.0 (1/7)	0.35 (1/9)	2.78	49
1996	2.7	1.30 (1/8)	0.45 (1/9)	5.02	35
1997	1.1	1.2 (1/8)	0.55 (1/8)	4.2	44
1998	4.25	2.0 (1/8)	0.55 (1/9)	6.0	43

[1] Low-wage increment.

[2] Decision by the National Wage Board.

[3] The total represents the total wage growth over the year, i.e. annual wage growth. This also reflects changes in wages due to changed composition of the labour force, wage drift, and so-called 'overhang', i.e., annual wage growth due to wage increments granted at various stages the previous year.

Sources: Ministry of Planning and Co-ordination, and NOU 1998:2 and NOU 1999:12 for 1997 and 1998, respectively.

A negative view on decentralized wage negotiations

The increasing significance of local agreements means that the targets and success of Norwegian incomes policy are highly influenced by what takes place at the local firm level. This concerns both the level of local wage drift and the internal wage distribution profile of local agreements compared to central agreements.

In Norway, the former head of the National Bank, Hermod Skånland, has been a key spokesman for the view that free local bargaining represents a threat to incomes policy targets and stability. This is his main message in a book from the early 1980s (Skånland 1981), where he puts forth the famous concept of the 'uneven triangle'. This triangle identifies internal contradictions between three supreme goals of the economic policy of central government: full employment, fair distribution of wage income, and free collective bargaining.

According to Skånland, while the two first goals have been subject to political debate, the third one is less frequently articulated. Contrary to Sweden, there is no general formal law in Norway that guarantees the right to free bargaining. But the principle is no less important as it underpins the Norwegian Labour Dispute Act that dates back to 1927. Skånland in the early 1980s considered the application of this basic principle as the greatest threat to the capacity to reach incomes policy targets. According to Skånland, decentralized settlements are much more difficult to control and, as a consequence, make macroeconomic planning impossible. Local wage growth is thus seen as an add-on to what the parties have agreed to be a reasonable wage growth from the point of view of the whole economy. As such, it undermines macroeconomic wage and price growth targets.

By stressing the effects of free collective bargaining, Skånland's argument diverges somewhat from most comparative explanations of Norwegian success. Even so, his argument coincides with mainstream explanations by focusing on the centralized Norwegian system. Centralized wage bargaining features most prominently in explanations of real wage flexibility and low unemployment in Norway. Some comparative research even claims that the incentives for wage restraint under centralization are so strong as to produce continuous full employment (Jackman 1990, Layard et al. 1991). According to this view, centralized bargaining mimics a perfectly competitive labour market (Moene and Wallerstein 1995). Hence shifts of labour-demand should only affect real wages, not employment.

Calmfors and Driffill's (1988) classic article further elaborated this line of argument, suggesting a hump-shaped relation between real wages and centralization. In their view, wage flexibility and economic adjustment capacity is best in countries with either a highly decentralized (USA) or a highly centralized bargaining system. They consider Norway to be a highly centralized system, thus, explaining its ability to contain wage-price inflation and keep unemployment low. Cast in this way, the hypothesis leads to the following conclusion: by prompting high inflation, increasing local wage growth will undermine Norwegian incomes policy goals.[5]

The main weakness in this kind of classification is the tendency to focus purely on the system's formal characteristics. In the previous section we showed that the bargaining system in Norway actually produced severe local wage drift in the 1970s and 80s, despite the formal centralization of the system. In the 1990s, on the other hand, local wage growth as a proportion of total wage growth has not been increasing as much as we could expect given the ongoing formal decentralization of the Norwegian bargaining system. Thus, while commentators earlier tended to overestimate the degree of centralization, they tend to do the opposite today. The deficiency in both cases is that it overlooks the strength of informal features inherent in the bargaining system.

The Calmfors-Driffill argument prescribes greater centralization to attain real wage flexibility and low unemployment in Norway. On the contrary, we argue that it is exactly the decentralized features of the Norwegian system that represent the necessary flexibility of the system to survive. The Calmfors-Driffil hump-shaped hypothesis, which is based on pure economic reasoning, has to make room for different forms of formal decentralization and various informal social mechanisms of control, power and norms of fairness – not least insofar as conflict resolution is concerned.

Skånland's perspective and his 'centralization' perspective apply better to private industry than to the public sector. In private industries it is evident that NHO often has problems limiting local wage growth, especially with a tight labour market at present (Summer 2000). But in the public sector the money set-aside for adjustments and local bargaining is decided in connection with the main negotiations in both the state and municipal government sectors, giving the parties involved full control over total wage growth.

An alternative view

The alternative view to this negative conception of local bargaining is that wage bargaining at different levels and at different points in time creates the necessary flexibility that allows the Norwegian system to survive. That is, there are several distributional tensions baked into the present system, and these tensions can only be handled if there is more than one arena for settling wages. What we have in mind is that most central settlements are dominated by a so-called social profile, which means that special attention is paid to the low-wage employees and the goal of wage equalization. Examples of wage negotiations and settlements during recent years may shed light over this view.

The fact that an agreement was reached in 1997 without strikes may partly be explained by the voting procedures surrounding 'main' and 'intermediary' negotiations. There is no demand for referenda among rank and file union members in connection with intermediary settlements. The outcome is either accepted or rejected at the table by the bargaining delegations.

However, a peaceful solution probably also has to do with the flexibility contained in the Norwegian system of wage bargaining, with the 'two steps' procedure which every round of wage bargaining follows. In such a context it is also important to note that the options concerning use of conflict measures are limited in the second step.

The first step of this procedure is the central national level bargaining and settlement. The use of open conflict measures is limited to this first step. This central level bargaining is followed up by plant level negotiations (second step), where the Norwegian Labour Law, however, prescribes 'peace obligation'. This means that regular conflict measures such as strikes and lockouts are forbidden. The flexibility following such a procedure is related to the fact that everything does not have to be settled at the central level. That is, dissatisfaction with central agreements does not necessary lead to a majority of 'no' votes, or that the members of the delegations who would have liked a more favourable agreement for their members will turn it down. They know that there is still room for upward adjustments for the majority of workers within the private industries.

Something similar developed in the public sector during the 1990s. The impact of local bargaining has increased as the public-sector pay system was loosened in the early 1990s. Much effort, however, has been put into keeping wage settlements in the public sector in line with private sector agreements. A precondition for doing this is that the frames of less centralized wage increments are settled in connection with the main negotiations. A key question, however, still remains to be answered. Does the system with different levels of negotiation support or undermine the present incomes policy regime? To give a complete answer to such a question one has to make detailed investigations, in line with Elster's (1989, p. vii) recommendation of thick phenomenological descriptions. We are not able to do anything close to that here, but limit ourselves to a brief overview of what took place in the 1996-98 rounds of wage negotiations.

A brief overview of the 1996-1998 settlements

It is a fact that both in the 1996 main settlement and in the following year (see EIRR 284, pp. 17-19), the parties in the public sector managed to reach agreements without open conflicts and within frames of what is considered to be moderate and, thereby, in line with the 'Solidarity Alternative'. Both in 1996 and 1997 the public sector employers agreed on general wage increases roughly in line with the profile of LO's demands. This also largely satisfied what YS (the Confederation of Vocational Unions) asked for. Without any possibilities for further wage adjustments these settlements would have meant strikes among members of AF unions.

AF has long experienced difficulties in having its demands met during central negotiations. As a consequence, it has chosen an alternative strategy: to put more effort into reaching central agreements where part of the total wage increase within the public sector is set aside for so-called 'central adjustment negotiations' and for local bargaining. The reason why both the 1996 and 1997 public sector negotiations resulted in peaceful solutions was that these demands where satisfied. Both 1996 and 1997 the amount of money retained for adjustment and local negotiations in the state sector was larger than what was distributed through the main central negotiations (for more details see EIRR 282, p. 10).

When the results of the adjustment negotiations within the state sector in 1997 were published they showed that, as usual, members of AF unions had become the clear winners. For example, teachers at all levels of the education system and most others with academic education at the university level were granted an extra wage increase. This extra increment was at least at the level of one step up on the state pay scale (approximately NOK 4000) and many groups received twice this.

What we may learn from this is that the famous so-called 'uneven triangle', i.e., the combination of the goals of (1) full employment, (2) fair wage distribution, and (3) free bargaining, is not as bad as is usually claimed. This triangle points at internal contradictions between these three supreme goals of the economic policy of central government, and that in order to reach the two first goals one ought to skip the third. The experience from Norway during recent years shows rather that without the third pillar in this triangle, incomes policy based on the 'Solidarity Alternative' would have broken down in the country. In other words, it is the flexibility represented by wage bargaining at different levels that actually still makes the ideas behind the Solidarity Alternative the basic foundation of Norwegian economic policy.

This has become even clearer in the 1998 main round of negotiations and in the new compromise reached in the so-called Arntsen committee in early 1999 (see EIRR 303, p. 11 for more on the Arntsen committee). This committee followed the 1998 settlement, which was considered far in excess of the 'Solidarity Alternative' (EIRR 303, pp. 32-4). In our opinion it would have been impossible to reach an agreement on wage moderation in the following years without having different arenas of wage bargaining. Taking into account all the different views represented in the Arntsen committee (which comprised all major labour market actors in Norway) it would not have been possible to reach a compromise with only central national level wage bargaining. That is, bargaining at different levels of co-ordination makes it possible to reach compromises between competing legitimate norms of distribution.

Future prospects

In this article we have described developments in various components of total wage growth during the last two decades. While local wage growth in private industries as a proportion of total wage growth has remained significant over the whole period, there has been a tendency toward more emphasis on decentralized settlements in the public sector, and especially the state sector during recent years. The question proposed here is what consequences do these developments have upon macroeconomic performance and the capacity to maintain the moderate line that is the key element of the Solidarity Alternative.

The threat of an excessively expansive wage growth at the local level obviously increases with a tight labour market situation. Most private industries are experiencing a labour shortage and, as a result, a pressure toward increased wage growth. The wage settlement in the private sector in 1998 indicated that wages might increase significantly in the near future. This can be expected even if labour demand declines in the years to follow, since bargained minimum wages in 1998 were raised especially in industries such as the building and construction industry where wages are highly exposed to variations in labour demand.

Also the preparations for the year 2000 main round of negotiations suggest heavy obstacles to wage moderation. In spite of widespread agreement among central actors in sustained wage moderation, distributional conflicts traced back to highly skilled occupations within the public sector threaten to counteract such targets. Dissatisfaction with wages within semi- and highly skilled occupations in the public sector has caused a campaign for realignment of relative wages. The outcome of this struggle, however, is yet to be seen.

The key question at this time is whether such an increase has contagious effects upon the remaining parts of the labour market, and especially the public sector. Moreover, parts of the public sector face a labour shortage at a level similar to that in the building and construction industry, indicating wage levels below what is called for by the market. However, employers in the public sector cannot appeal to highly visible market signals to legitimate wage deferential. For example, there is no legitimate argument in favour of differentiating according to market signals among teachers and nurses. In addition, unlike in the private industry, the formal legal framework limits wage flexibility. Consequently, a labour shortage in parts of the public sector labour market tends to increase wage growth all across the board. Can anything be done to avoid such a situation?

There is no simple answer to this question, but the fact that there are several arenas where wage determination mechanisms exist opens up some possibilities. There are clear indications that the wage policy of the LO leadership, that is, advocating moderate wage increases, is easier today to implement at the local level than what was the case in the 1970s and first half of the 80s. And, as underlined above, the control of local wage growth is greater in the public sector. The key issue will be to create legitimacy for a more flexible distribution policy in the public sector.

The following scenario may prove to be the probable future outcome. LO, partly in co-operation with YS, will dominate wage settlements at national level negotiations. Redistribution of wage incomes between high and low-waged employees and between male and female dominated occupations will, at this level, seek to give legitimacy to moderate overall wage demands. AF, which currently organizes the numerically large groups of employees in the public sector, such as teachers, nurses and engineers, will concentrate on central adjustment negotiations. It will not be able to exploit money set aside for local bargaining for the large member groups if, like the teachers, it sticks to the principle of 'equal wage for equal work'. (This could hinder the necessary differentiation incorporated in local agreements and adjustments.) But such differentiation is central to the strategy of the recently established new peak union association, the Academics which is likely to concentrate on bargaining at the local level to achieve its strategic goals in the wage struggle.

Certainly, whether this scenario becomes reality will depend mainly on which legitimate criteria for distribution come to dominate local bargaining in the private sector. At the local level we will need to pay close attention to an important distinction between collective and individual agreements. There is a clear tendency toward relatively high-wage employees being covered by individual agreements, while rank-and-file workers are remunerated according to collective agreements. As a consequence, the internal distribution of local increments between groups with different agreements at the firm level will prove important.

Whether or not specific groups do benefit more from firms' profits can effect not only the local incentives stemming from such surpluses, but also the legitimacy of wage moderation in national level bargaining. Empirical evidence suggests that workers in the highest wage-strata have the highest incidence of individual agreements and also gain most from efficiency or outcome based rewards. If workers with individual agreements are granted a higher amount of the firm's surplus than is regarded as fair by those covered by collective agreements, local wage increments may have negative consequences both for the incentives for increasing local efficiency and efforts, and the prospects for continuing central-level moderation. Hence, the disproportionate distribution of types of local agreements among wage strata may contradict important symbolic values, which in turn may make unattainable key goals of national level wage settlements.

This prospect may prove especially compelling in a booming economy such as Norway's where private firms have to distribute their surpluses according to certain criteria. In an economic downturn, the firms' surpluses will be smaller and central level moderation will be easier to defend. What is regarded as fair distribution at the local level, therefore, has important consequences for the functioning of the Norwegian wage determination system as a whole. In addition, what is considered a fair principle of distribution of burdens during a downswing may not apply during economic upswings.

Whatever the future may bring, the existing system of wage determination that presently characterizes Norway clearly demonstrates that there is more than one alternative to the traditional highly centralized Nordic model. The Swedish way of abandoning the Rehn-Meidner model decentralizing the system of wage determination is not the only option. The Norwegian development during the last decade suggests that it is possible to have a highly centralized system for dealing with macroeconomic performance combined with decentralized elements to satisfy demands for flexibility, demands that are increasing in open economies including the Nordic ones.

Notes

1 Thanks to Bjørn Andersen, Arvid Fennfoss, Anders Todal Jenssen, Arne Kalleberg, Elin Kvande, Henry Milner, Terje Osmundsen, Jon Rogstad, Torgeir Stokke and Eskil Wadensjö for fruitful comments on earlier versions.

2 This is also true when comparing Norway and Sweden in relation to the size of the public sector, child care facilities, unemployment insurance, and the range of the welfare state in general prior to deterioration of the centralized Swedish model (Freeman 1997).

3 In contrast to the initial 'Solidarity Alternative', however, all the competing actors on the labour side of the bargaining table are part of the joint committee of today (see EIRR vol. 303, no.11 for further details).

4 The so-called 'female profile' within YS was strengthened as the Norwegian Union of Auxiliary Nurses (NHS), strongly dominated by female members, decided to join the confederation in 1988.

5 The whole argument is based on the classification of the Norwegian system as highly centralized. This is not necessarily true any more, even though it earlier was a frequently held view (Cameron 1984, Newell and Symons 1987, Jackman 1990, Layard et al. 1991). In later years, this classification has been questioned in several comparative studies, emphasizing differences in degree of centralization in the Nordic countries (Calmfors and Nymoen 1990, Dølvik et al. 1997).

References

Calmfors, Lars and John Driffil (1988), 'Bargaining Structure, Corporatism and Macroeconomic Performance', *Economic Policy*, vol. 6, pp. 13-61.

Calmfors, Lars and Ragnar Nymoen (1990), 'Real Wage Adjustments and Employment Policies in the Nordic Countries', *Economic Policy*, vol. 1, pp. 398-448.

Cameron, David R. (1984), 'Social Democracy, Corporatism, Labour Quiescence, and the Representation of Economic Interest in Advanced Capitalist Society', in John H. Goldthorpe (ed.), *Order and Conflict in Contemporary Capitalism*, Oxford University Press, New York, pp. 143-78.

Dølvik, Jon Erik and Arild Steen (eds) (1997), *Making Solidarity Work? The Norwegian Labour Market in Transition*, Scandinavian University Press, Oslo.

Dølvik, Jon Erik, Mona Bråten, Frode Longva and Arild Steen (1997), 'Norwegian Labour

Market Institutions and Regulations', in Jon Erik Dølvik and Arild Steen (eds), *Making Solidarity Work? The Norwegian Labour Market in Transition*, Scandinavian University Press, Oslo.

EIRR 282, 284 and 303, *European Industrial Relation Review*, July and September issues 1997, April issue 1999, Eclipse, London.

Elster, Jon (1989), *The Cement of Society. A Study of Social Order*, Cambridge University Press, Cambridge.

Elvander, Nils (1988), *Den svenska modellen. Löneförhandlingar och inkomstpolitik 1982-1986*, Allmänna Förlaget, Stockholm.

Freeman, Richard B. (1997), 'Are Norway's Solidaristic and Welfare State Policies Viable in the Modern Global Economy?' in Jon E. Dølvik and Arild H. Steen, *Making Solidarity Work? The Norwegian Labour Market Model in Transition*, Scandinavian University Press, Oslo, pp. 17-50.

Frøland, Hans Otto (1992), *Korporativt kompromiss gjennom korporativ konsert. Tariff- og inntektspolitikk i LO/N.A.F.-området 1950-1965*, Historisk institutt, Universitetet i Trondheim-AVH.

Hanisch, Ted and Geir Høgsnes (1988), *Problemer og motsetninger i norsk inntektspolitikk 1973 til 1985*, Report 88, no. 9, Institute for Social Research, Oslo.

Høgsnes, Geir (1990), 'Tillitsvalgtes strategivalg og holdninger til fordelingsnormer', in Hege Torp and Kåre Skollerud (eds) *Organisasjon, arbeidsmiljø og mobilitet – Resultater fra Arbeids- og Bedriftsundersøkelsen*, Report 90, no. 9, pp. 49-59, Institute for Social Research, Oslo.

Høgsnes, Geir (1994), *Collective Wage Bargaining and the Impact of Norms of Fairness – an Analysis Based on the Norwegian Experience*, Report 94, no. 8, vol. I and II, Institute for Social Research, Oslo.

Høgsnes, Geir and Ted Hanisch (1988), 'Incomes Policy and Union Structure – the Norwegian Experience from the mid seventies to the mid eighties', Working Paper no. 11, Institute for Social Research, Oslo.

Jackman, Richard (1990), 'Wage Formation and the Nordic Countries Viewed from an International Perspective', in Lars Calmfors (ed.), *Wage Formation and Macro-Economic Policy in the Nordic Countries*, SNS Förlag, Stockholm, pp. 289-322.

Layard, Richard, Stephen Nickel and Richard Jackman (1991), *Unemployment: Macro-Economic Performance and the Labour Market*, Cambridge University Press, Cambridge.

Mjøset, Lars (1992), 'The Nordic model never existed, but does it have a future?', *Scandinavian Studies*, vol. 64, pp. 652-71.

Moene, Karl Ove and Michael Wallerstein (1995), 'How Social Democracy Worked: Labour Market Institutions', *Politics and Society*, vol. 23, pp. 185-211.

Nergaard, Kristine (1999), 'Organisasjonsgrad og tariffavtaledekning målt ved AKU, andre kvartal 1998'. FAFO paper 1999, no. 5, Oslo.

Newell, A. and J. S. V. Symons (1987), 'Corporatism, Laissez-faire and the Rise in Unemployment', *European Economic Review*, vol. 31, pp. 567-605.

NOU 1992:26, *En nasjonal strategi for økt sysselsetting i 1990-årene*, Ministry of Finance,

Oslo.

NOU 1996:14, *Prinsipper for ny arbeidstvistlov*, Ministry of Local Government and Labour, Oslo.

NOU 1998:2, *Om grunnlaget for inntektsoppgjørene 1998*, Ministry of Labour and Administration, Oslo.

NOU 1999:12, *Om grunnlaget for inntektsoppgjørene 1999*, Ministry of Labour and Administration. Oslo.

Pettersen, Stig Petter (1990), 'Norges faglige hovedsammenslutninger – Ideologi og politikk', unpublished paper, Institute for Social Research, Oslo.

Rødseth, Asbjørn and Steinar Holden (1990), 'Wage Formation in Norway', in Lars Calmfors (ed.), *Wage Formation and Macro-Economic Policy in the Nordic Countries*, SNS Förlag, Stockholm, pp. 237-80.

Rødseth, Asbjørn (1997), 'Why has unemployment been so low in Norway?', in Jon Erik Dølvik and Arild H. Steen (eds), *Making Solidarity Work? The Norwegian Labour Market Model in Transition*, Scandinavian University Press, pp. 155-88.

Skånland, Hermod (1981), *Inntektspolitikkens dilemma. Kan det løses?* Cappelen Forlag, Oslo.

Streeck, Wolfgang (1993), 'The rise and decline of neocorporatism', in Lloyd Ulman et al. (eds), *Labour and an Integrated Europe*, The Brookings Institution, Washington, DC.

Teague, Paul and John Grahl (1992), *Industrial Relations and European Integration*, Lawrence & Wishard, London.

Chapter 9

Equality, Solidarity and the Welfare State. The Nordic Employment Performance in Comparative Perspective

Sven Jochem

Introduction

In the Nordic countries[1] powerful social democratic parties, together with encompassing trade unions, realised step-by-step a 'Social Democratic Image of Society' (Castles 1978) thereby combining – by and large – full employment, income equality and highly institutionalised and comparatively generous welfare states. The first two steps can be seen as the cornerstones of the Rehn-Meidner model, and as Gösta Rehn repeatedly mentioned (see Eklund this volume), full employment *and* price stability were major goals, and these should be reached by the following means: solidaristic wage policies, restrictive fiscal policies and active labour market policies. This policy mix enabled and enforced structural change as well as an impressive employment performance in Sweden. But, as it will be shown in detail below, the superior employment performance was to a certain extent dependent on two developments that were not part of the Rehn-Meidner model: 1) the growth of the public sector, i.e. the welfare state, and 2) the leeway to devalue the national currency in order to enhance economic competitiveness.

In the early 1990s, Sweden and other Nordic countries were challenged by economic crises, rising unemployment and rather dramatically shrinking employment. However, by the end of the millennium, in all four countries open unemployment was gradually reduced, inflation contained and the budgets were to a very great extent consolidated. In Denmark for example, open unemployment was reduced from 10.7 per cent in 1993 (the peak) to 5.1 per cent in 1998. Even more impressive was the development in Norway, where unemployment dropped from 6 per cent in 1993 to 3.2 per cent (1998), achieving one of the lowest unemployment rates at that time in the OECD world. And despite the severe economic crisis in Finland at the turn of the decade, even Finnish unemployment was significantly reduced after 1993 (17.7 per cent), as 1998 open unemployment was down to 11.5 per cent. However, in Sweden unemployment remained at approximately 10 per cent until 1997, thereafter shrinking modestly. Taken together, this may be interpreted as an impressive success story of the Nordic countries and their capacity to adapt to changing internal and external challenges, and this leads us to seek an explanation for these ups and downs of labour market performance.

According to Torben Iversen and Anne Wren, globalisation may not be the major challenge for advanced political economies at the beginning of the new millennium, but rather the 'transition from an economy dominated by (exposed) manufacturing production to one dominated by (sheltered) service production' (1998, p. 508). Indeed, manufacturing employment dropped everywhere in the OECD throughout the past decades, and employment growth is located primarily in the domestic service sector. But here, the logic of employment growth may differ considerably from the logic ruling in the manufacturing segment of the labour market. In short, Iversen and Wren argue that a 'trilemma of the service economy' is governing the OECD world, i.e. political actors may reach two goals simultaneously, thereby making a sacrifice of the third goal – i.e. it seems possible to combine budgetary constraint and earnings equality, but then, (service) employment is low. The Christian-Democratic model in Europe represents this constellation – and Germany may be seen as the paradigmatic case. The liberal model in contrast, combines fiscal discipline with impressive service employment growth, but there, market generated inequality seems to be the price to pay – the Anglo-Saxon countries represent this cluster. Finally, in Scandinavia, which represents the social democratic model, earnings equality was combined with high employment growth, mainly delivered in the public sector, even though this strategy sacrifices budgetary restraint.[2] Additionally, in a world of globalised capital flows, expansive fiscal policies – supposedly they induce budget deficits – are *de facto,* and under the constraints of the European Growth and Stability Pact, *de jure* blocked. Hence, as Torben Iversen has put it, 'the question for Scandinavian social democracy is whether it wants to deepen class divisions by accepting greater inequalities, or whether it wants to create a marginalized group of people, excluded from full participation in the economy' (Iversen 1998b, p. 73).

If this is true, not only does it hold out poor prospects for the Nordic economies, it also suggests the Rehn-Meidner model's objective of combining full employment and low inflation with greater earnings equality and solidaristic wage policies is ultimately unattainable. It remains to be seen, however, if rising inequality is the only viable way to promote employment under the constraints of the service economy. However, at least the Danish and Norwegian labour market performance might be seen as 'miraculous' in this context, which needs further explanation. As it is shown in detail below, the argument put forward by Iversen and Wren (1998) needs to be amended: the development of social security contributions has an overwhelming impact on employment performance, especially in the service sector – a fact not foreseen by Gösta Rehn nor by the mainstream research until today. Hence, equality may not be the major hindrance to (service) employment. Rather we should include in the analysis the incentives from the welfare state, and I argue that a reduction of social security contributions may mediate the trade-off between employment creation and equality.

Hence, this contribution is organised around the following points. First, an explanation for the partly dramatic breakdown of labour market performance in the early 1990s is presented. Second, the ways Nordic labour market policies reacted to the employment crises and choices which enabled the already mentioned reduction of open unemployment in some countries is described. Finally, the leeway to combine full employment and equality under the constraints of the service economy is discussed, putting the Nordic countries in a comparative perspective.

Explaining ups and downs of employment performance

Employment – measured in absolute terms as well as in employment rates – declined in all four countries during the late 1980s and early 1990s, and from a comparative perspective this decline has been exceptional.[3] Figure 9.1 reveals the developments in employment and labour force participation from 1970 until 1998. Until the end of the 1980s, employment increased gradually in all four countries. Then, employment in Finland and Sweden collapsed, whereas in Denmark and Norway the decline was – from a Nordic perspective – rather modest.

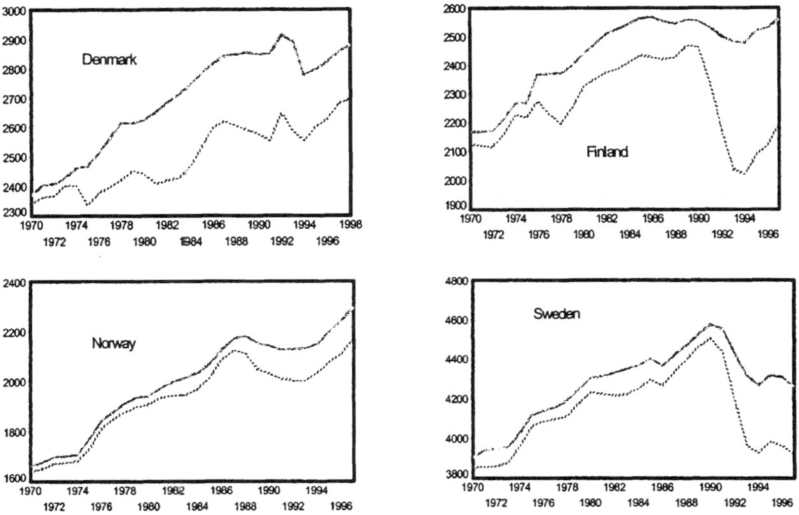

Key: —— = labour force participation in absolute figures; ---- = employment in absolute figures.
Sources: OECD 1997 and updates from OECD *Economic Surveys* for Denmark, Finland, Norway and Sweden (OECD various years).

Figure 9.1 Development of labour force participation and employment 1970-97/98

After 1993, declining employment could be reversed in Denmark, Finland and Norway, whereas the Swedish employment performance remains rather volatile. The point to be stressed here is that all four countries experienced a reduction of labour force supply in the early 1990s. Whereas this development was rather modest in Finland and Norway, it was very pronounced in Sweden, leaving Denmark in a middle position. At the end of the 1990s, the overall labour force participation rate in Sweden for example is down at a level lower than that in the mid-1970s. Indeed, the extensive reduction of the labour force supply cushioned the overall increase in unemployment significantly.[4] Hence, the use of the unemployment rate is questionable if we want to analyse employment performance. Therefore, in the following, I rely mainly on employment rates, only referring occasionally to the unemployment rate and how labour supply gradually emerged as a policy instrument to counteract unemployment (for a more detailed analysis see Jochem 2000).[5]

But, before I try to explain if and how the Nordic countries could reverse shrinking employment in the 1990s, it is useful to explain the collapse of employment first.[6] In this respect, we can distinguish three hypotheses. The first one states that economic crises in the early 1990s were so severe that there was no leeway to counteract them by political means. The second stresses the role globalisation has played for adjustments in labour markets; and the third, finally, focuses on domestic factors, particularly the effect of wage bargaining outcomes and the incentives of the welfare states.

Economic crises do not imply doom...

Low economic growth or shrinking growth rates do not imply doom to full employment: this is at least one central thesis of comparative labour market research (see Schmidt 1988; Scharpf 1987). The Nordic countries, however, underwent huge economic turmoil in the early 1990s, and this – it is argued – was the main reason for the breakdown of employment (Elmeskov 1994, Therborn 1995). However, from a comparative point of view, this argument does not hold very well. Certainly, in Sweden and Finland, economic growth deteriorated in the early 1990s, but this was not the case in Denmark, where growth was in line with the OECD average, and in Norway, where growth has been clearly above the OECD average throughout the 1980s and 1990s. Hence, the four countries show a significant variation in economic growth despite the common employment decline.

... but does globalisation?

Globalisation is the new growth industry in social sciences. However, there is some confusion about what globalisation is, and what consequences this development may have for labour markets. Here, globalisation may cover two dimensions: first, the increase in flows of investment capital; and second, the constitution of the financial markets. The internationalisation of capital markets, it is argued, forces the convergence of interest rates, fiscal, monetary and currency policies – a global process that is further enforced by European integration. Defaulting from the main trend in these areas is immediately punished by capital flight. As a consequence, the leeway for different 'Sonderwege' to stabilise employment is diminished.

All four Scandinavian countries experienced – with respect to the aspects mentioned above – a sharp increase in globalisation in the 1980s. To begin with, foreign direct investment outflows increased during the 1980s in all four countries, whereas the inflow remained on a rather low level (see Swank 1999). However, from a comparative point of view, high outflows of investment capital have not been unique to the Nordic countries. Even in the Netherlands, huge multinational firms have used the increased leeway to invest abroad. And as we see in the Dutch case, high outflows of investment capital are no hindrance for stimulating employment.[7] Hence, even this new development in the Nordic countries may not explain why these countries were hit by such extensive employment crises.

On the other hand, all four countries changed their economic policy stance: the defence of price stability became the main policy goal.[8] In Norway and Denmark, this policy shift had already occurred in 1981 and 1982 under the newly elected bourgeois governments. The other Nordic governments followed suit with a short delay. Not surprisingly, the relationship between the development of the consumer price index and the employment rate is negative for the OECD countries. And this argument holds relatively well for Denmark and Finland in a longitudinal perspective. In Norway and Sweden, however, the development in the employment rate reveals no clear relationship to the development of the consumer price index.[9] Hence, though we can argue that in the Nordic countries the fight against inflation became the major policy goal since the 1980s, this policy change *alone* can hardly explain the dramatic decline of employment in these countries. The politics of price stability may be rather seen as a reduction in the leeway available for governments to counteract shrinking employment rates, but not the cause of it.

Additionally, the diminished leeway in the currency policy may have induced the Scandinavian employment crises. The Nordic countries had relied for decades on a strategy that included strategic devaluations in order to regain competitiveness for domestic export industries (see Korkman 1992, Freitag 1999). By 1982, however, the Danish social democratic government could no longer use this policy instrument to the extent it wished. Instead of the desired devaluation of the Danish krone by 7 per cent, the partners in the European Union accepted only a devaluation of 3 per cent. In Sweden (1982), Finland (1982 and 1986), and Norway (1986), a devaluation strategy was still a viable policy option in the 1980s, but at the end of this decade, even in those countries, the currency policy had become more restricted. In Sweden, for example, the main trade union federation (LO) forcefully requested a major devaluation at the end of the 1980s in order to restore profitability to the export industries. However, the Carlsson Government rejected the claim: currency stability had become a major policy goal in Sweden at the end of the 1980s (see Mjøset 1996, p. 23). This, as a consequence, diminished the room to manoeuvre for governments (and central banks) to counteract negative developments with regard to competitiveness, i.e. the possibility to devalue itself out of domestic problems was no longer viable.[10]

The last hypothesis refers to domestic developments and the way the political actors adapted their strategies to external challenges. The Nordic wage bargaining systems were – at least until the 1980s – stylised by comparative researchers as being highly consensual and co-ordinated, but in the 1980s, the Nordic model of labour relations withered away (Wallerstein and Golden 1997; Huber and Stephens 1998; Iversen 1996, 1998b). As I will show in the following section, the erosion of the hitherto consensual wage bargaining systems, and the – partly – negative consequences resulting from the funding systems of the Nordic welfare states, did indeed contribute to the sharp decline of employment. Both dimensions influenced the capability of the Nordic countries to recover from the employment crises of the early 1990s.

Changing wage bargaining patterns

The Danish pattern

In Denmark, the turnover of government in 1982 was the starting point for the transition of the wage bargaining system. The newly elected centre-right coalition cancelled the price indexation of wages – and most social transfers – and implemented far reaching stabilisation policies (see Green-Pedersen 1999, Andersen 2000). Trade unions vehemently opposed this policy and, as a consequence, conflicts in the labour market escalated in 1985. The new government formulated annual wage ceilings of around 2 per cent; in fact, wages grew between 4 and 9 per cent annually in the years 1984-87.[11] Local wage drift accounted for the major part of the wage rise. Partly as a consequence, the Danish employers' organisation reformed its internal structure. Employers in the exposed sectors centralised their organisation and restored their dominance within the central employers' organisation (DA). At the same time, those employers were successful in decentralising wage bargaining. Since the late 1980s, bargaining rounds on the central level have only fixed minimum wages, whereas the effective wage is regulated at the sectoral level. Because of intense internal co-ordination in the employers' organisation, wage drift declined and, as a result, wage growth after 1987 gradually decreased. The process of 'centralised decentralisation' (Due et al. 1994) was accepted by the trade unions in the late 1980s. Furthermore, the labour market parties agreed in 1987 to hold wage increases below the wage development in Germany, the major trading partner.

In the mid-1990s, however, tensions in the wage bargaining process occurred again. Though there was moderate wage growth until 1994, later wage demands started to accelerate, as did tensions. The 1998 major strike is an example of the conflict potential of Danish labour relations. Then and afterwards, the government intervened frequently to ensure peace in the labour market and to hold down wage developments. In the spring of 1999, the government delivered a crisis package, in order to cool down public spending and consumption that was regarded as fuelling wage growth. As a consequence of the 1998 strike, DA and LO agreed to participate in a new tripartite forum, suggested by the government, that is aimed at playing a decisive role in future collective bargaining rounds as well as in the political process. Somewhat surprisingly, DA and LO immediately agreed to the first proposal: to reduce unemployment benefit entitlements from five to four years and this agreement was put unchanged into legislation. This agreement – despite major resistance from within the LO – paved the way for the climate agreement in 1999, where DA and LO reaffirmed the 1987 joint declaration, which put support for pay restraint in line with the principle of competitiveness in return for joint social partner input into larger political reforms. Whether this 'agreement on the framework for the arrangement of decentralised collective bargaining rounds', as it is called officially, will be conducive for moderate wage growth, however, remains to be seen during the current wage round 2000.

The Finnish pattern

In Finland, wage bargaining was highly centralised until 1987. This had been backed by the various governments through highly formalised tripartite package deals. Even in Finland, local wage drift accounted for up to 50 per cent of total wage growth (see Tyrväinen 1995, p. 170) and annual growth rates were between 6 and 10 per cent in the period 1984-89. The conservative-social democratic coalition government, however, initiated a deregulation of the wage bargaining system. The conservative party claimed that wage formation should follow the incentives of the market and, therefore, should be handled on a local, i.e. firm level. As a consequence, wage drift increased even more. In the aftermath of the economic crisis,[12] the employers in the export oriented manufacturing industries started to decentralise wage bargaining. And in the mid-1990s, wage bargaining in Finland was located at the local and sectoral level. But, as in the Danish case, there is much co-ordination amongst employers, leading to low wage drift. Since 1995, wage growth accelerated modestly, and the government enacted two incomes-policy agreements by 1999, mainly trading moderate wage growth for tax reductions and social policies. Therefore, wage growth could be kept within boundaries through the instrument of concertation, contributing to the impressive recovery of the Finnish economy after 1990.[13] At the end of 1999, however, a third incomes-policy agreement is being highly contested, as several affiliates of the Finnish trade union confederation (SAK) reject economy-wide concertation and request sectoral bargaining in order to solve sector-specific problems and this is opposed by the employers.

The Norwegian pattern

In Norway,[14] upon election the centre-right coalition of 1981 stopped the hitherto active role of the government in wage bargaining. As a consequence, wage drift skyrocketed in the 1980s, and amounted to up to 66 per cent of the total wage sum (see Elvander 1990, p. 9). The total wage growth was extreme, reaching its highest level in 1986 of an annual wage increase of 16 per cent. In contrast, the new social democratic party launched an emergency incomes policy, starting with moral persuasion in 1987 and progressing to a wage law in 1988, which determined wage agreements for the whole economy. As a consequence, wage growth began to decline. This was backed by several attempts of the new government to rebuild the consensual policy formation process. In 1992, agreement on a tripartite programme, the so-called 'Solidarity Alternative' (NOU 1992:26), was achieved in which an active incomes policy and further spending on education and training was promised by the government in order to promote consensual labour relations and moderate wage growth, i.e. a wage development below the growth rates of the major trading partners. However, since 1995 rank-and-file protests have contested this centralised wage bargaining strategy, and, thus, the main trade union confederation (LO) was unable to hold back calls for higher wage increases at branch level negotiations. In the 1999 wage bargaining round, the Norwegian economy is faced with severe challenges, as the tripartite wage bargaining system is contested by local wage pressures.

The Swedish pattern

Finally, in Sweden, the social democratic government launched the policy of the third way in 1982 (see Pontusson 1992, Feldt 1991), which started with a huge devaluation and relied on moderate wage growth in the future. Centralised wage bargaining, however, had already collapsed in 1983, as the employers in the manufacturing industry broke away and conducted a sectoral collective agreement. In 1985, the government stepped back from attempting to co-ordinate wage bargaining, thereby additionally opening the gate to accelerating conflicts and a further fragmentation of the bargaining process. In the remaining 1980s, wage competition between the private and the public sector accelerated, wage drift accounted for up to 50 per cent and the total wage development rose from 7 per cent up to 10 per cent annual wage growth between 1986 and 1989. In the early 1990s, decentralisation continued; the Swedish Employers Federation (SAF) dissolved its wage bargaining unit and implemented its withdrawal from the national corporatist institutions (see Pontusson and Swenson 1996). Because of these tendencies and the impact of the economic crisis, the government intervened and imposed a de facto centralised wage mediation, the Rehnberg Agreement (*Rehnberg-avtalen*) which lasted from 1991 until 1993. Since then, wage bargaining in Sweden has been in flux. The mix between centralised, branch-level and local bargaining changed several times during the years thereafter and opened the road for different bargaining patterns across the economy. A situation, complicated by the various guarantee and fallback clauses, which can set local bargaining, and result in wage bargaining outcomes at a higher level. However, wage drift was still a problem, as it counted for up to 50 per cent of the total wage growth in 1994 and 1995 (OECD 1999b, p. 68). Thus, despite the most serious economic crisis since the 1930s, despite relatively low inflation, and despite the changing wage bargaining pattern, total wage growth has remained comparatively high, and wage competition between the public and private sector is still very pronounced.

After the election in 1998, the governing social democratic party stopped collaborating with the centre party and was backed by the greens and the left-socialist party.[15] Partly as a consequence – and to circumvent public intervention into labour relations – the main trade union confederations and the employers' organisations agreed upon an 'alliance for growth'. The press information concerning the goal of this initiative was rather vague, but essentially SAF claimed that this concertation would lead to ways to reach four goals: first, to aid Sweden's mid-term membership in the European Economic and Monetary Union; second, to reduce the overall cost burden of capital; third, to deregulate labour law; and, finally, to upgrade and further expand education and training. However, in December 1998, the alliance crashed and the government announced a proposal for new parts of the labour law – especially regarding the power of the public mediator and the ways industrial conflicts are regulated – until the end of 1999 (see Pestoff 1999). Hence, a clear tendency in the Swedish bargaining pattern is not discernible.

As has been shown in the preceding paragraphs, the Nordic countries followed different pathways. In the 1980s, wage bargaining was a highly contested issue in all four countries, resulting in high wage growth and intense conflicts in the labour market. But in the 1990s, Denmark, Finland and Norway could rebuild a concerted wage bargaining strategy – albeit with diverging degrees of centralisation and public intervention – where wage restraint is traded for tax-deductions and social policies. Concertation does not necessarily imply a formally centralised pattern, but a mainly employer-driven co-ordination does take place, supported by tripartite bodies that support wage bargaining and provide statistical information.[16] In Sweden, on the other hand, wage bargaining shows no clear pattern especially after 1993. The conflict between the employers and the trade union confederations about the level of wage bargaining prevails, contributing to comparatively high wage growth.

Explaining the Nordic employment crises...

From this overview of wage bargaining developments in the 1980s and 90s the following question arises: what consequences has wage growth had on employment? Göran Therborn (1987) as well as Walter Korpi (1991) argue that the influence of wage growth upon the development of employment is not straightforward, and, even in the best case, holds true for only a few countries and only from time to time. However, in the 1980s and early 1990s, wage growth seems to have had a significant reverse relationship with employment (see Figure 9.2) – if one accepts the distorting impact from the outlier cases New Zealand and, to a lesser extent, Australia and Ireland.[17]

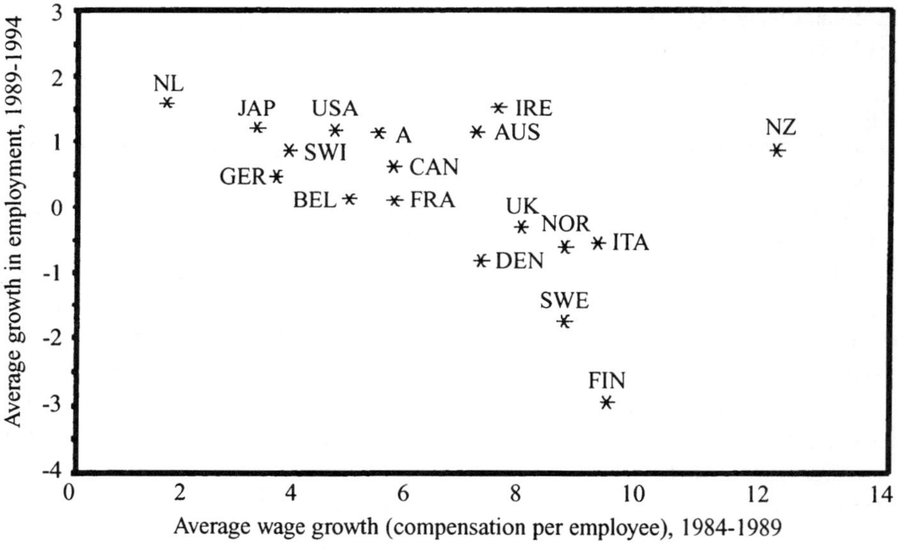

Sources: OECD (1997, 1999c, 1999d).

Figure 9.2 Wage growth and employment performance, 1984-1994

As can be seen from Figure 9.2, wage increases in the mid-1980s were exceptionally high in Finland, Sweden, Norway and Denmark. And in the covered time period, wage growth, indeed, has an inverse relationship with employment. Therefore, we can argue that the erosion of the Nordic wage bargaining systems in the 1980s, described above, has been one central cause of the employment crises in the early 1990s – given that other instruments to correct a decline in competitiveness, i.e. devaluing the national currency or accepting high inflation rates induced by expansive fiscal policies, are no longer viable solutions for the Nordic countries.

... and what determined the diverging recovery pathways?

But how can we explain the improved employment performance in Norway, Denmark and Finland after 1994? The way the Nordic countries reacted to the employment crises differed to a certain extent.[18] Average wage growth (1989-93) is still inversely related to employment growth in the following period (1994-98). However, the relationship is not as strong as in the 1980s. Unlike the 1980s, in the early 1990s the development of the unit labour costs does make a difference for the overall employment growth occurring at the end of the 1990s. Indeed, during the economic crises of the early 1990s, unit labour costs were pushed by wage growth, but more so by rising social security contributions, which in turn were driven by rising social expenditures as a consequence of rising unemployment.[19] As can be shown in Figure 9.3 an inverse relationship between unit labour costs and employment performance is obvious. However, the Irish case is a clear outlier, but if one accepts again that there may be special circumstances in this country that make it possible to explain the tremendous employment performance despite high growth in unit labour costs, then, for the rest of the OECD world, the relationship is clear cut.[20]

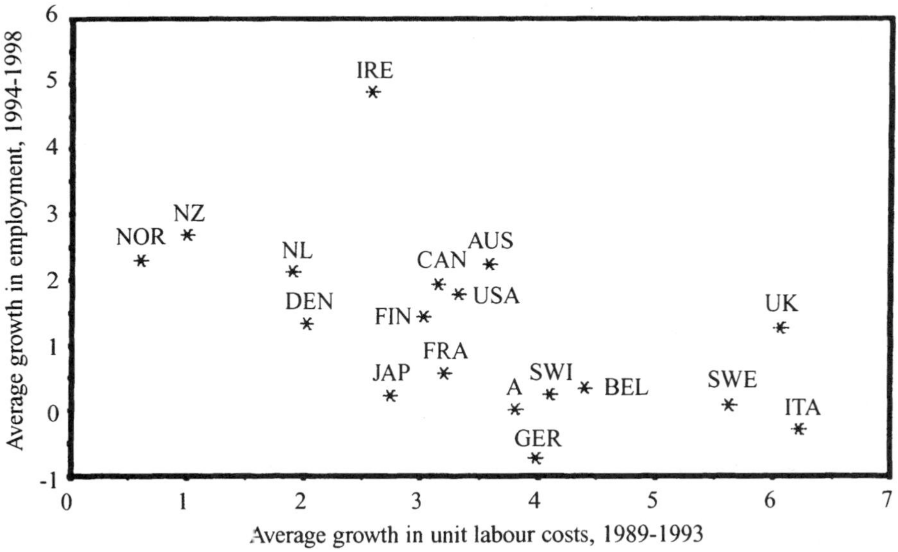

Sources: OECD (1997, 1999c, 1999d).

Figure 9.3 Unit labour costs and employment performance, 1989-1998

Hence, the way the welfare state is financed does influence the employment performance. In this respect it is noteworthy that Norway, Denmark and even Finland were able to change their funding systems to a certain extent. In Denmark, traditionally the largest part of the social policy bill was financed via taxation, but in the 1990s, the public share was reduced from 80 per cent in 1990 to 68 per cent in 1997, while the employee's share increased respectively from 5 to 18 per cent, and the employer's share was kept fairly constant at its low level.[21] This was partly accomplished through an expansion of means-tested co-payments in social security during the last decade. In Finland, a shift occurred between the employer's and employee's shares, lowering the burden for the former significantly from 44 per cent in 1990 to 35 per cent in 1997. Since 1986, the social democratic government in Norway gradually reduced the employer's part from 35 per cent (1985) to 24 per cent in 1997, but here the public share rose respectively.[22] Sweden followed the Finnish experience somewhat, but the shift was not as large as in Finland – still, from a Nordic perspective, the Swedish employers contribute the largest part of the welfare state's finances. However, the financing mix was significantly altered through the pension reform finally implemented in 1999 (see Anderson 1999), dividing contributions evenly between employers and employees.

In conclusion it should be emphasised that the Nordic employment performance in the 1990s was to a certain extent caused by wage growth in the 1980s. Thus, wage growth was triggered by the moving wage-bargaining patterns that went from centralised forms to decentralised ones, with the exception being Norway that was, and continues to be, highly dependent on public interventions. We can see that in Denmark, and to a certain extent in Finland, social partners gradually were able to agree on new bargaining forms, whereas in Sweden the conflict about the modus vivendi between labour and capital is still not mediated. Additionally, we see that the funding system of the welfare state influences employment dynamics. High social security contributions tend to block employment creation. In the following section this argument is further explicated and put in perspective regarding the imperatives of the service economy.

Promoting employment in the service economy

Considering the imperatives of the service economy and the consequences for the Nordic countries, I try to connect the arguments put forward by Iversen and Wren (1998) with my own empirical analyses (see Jochem and Siegel 2000; see also Scharpf 1999). If we examine the employment performance from the viewpoint of the service economy, we can – not surprisingly – state that in all four countries services are largely supplied in the public sector.[23] Additionally, overall wage dispersion in the Nordic countries is comparatively low and only slightly increasing – if at all – at the end of the 1990s.[24] In the private sector, employment was mainly created in the finance and business services in Denmark and Sweden, and as a Nordic exception, in Denmark in the wholesale and retail trade, restaurants and hotels segment of the labour market.[25] Thus, except for Denmark, service employment expansion was still mainly in the public sector, whereas, expansion in the private sector was only in segments with high wages. Given the budgetary constraints and the influence of the European Growth and Stability Pact, it seems questionable if employment creation in the public sector is a viable option in the future. And if we follow Iversen and Wren (1998), the road to enhanced employment performance in the Nordic countries seems to be blocked – as long as the trade unions in alliance with social democratic parties defend the goal of income equality and solidaristic wage policies, i.e. one prominent corner stone of the Rehn-Meidner model.

However, the trade-off between egalitarian wages and employment dynamics, as Iversen and Wren observe it, may be deferred by intervening welfare state effects. Indeed, as it is shown elsewhere in depth (Jochem and Siegel 2000), the way the welfare state is financed may make a difference for employment growth – especially for employment creation in the low wage segment of the service economy. As can be seen from Table 9.1, a generous welfare state as such does not constrain overall employment growth (Model 1). However, if the welfare state is financed mainly by social contributions (Model 2), a trade-off between employment performance and the welfare state has to be stated – a situation which is dominant in the Christian-democratic welfare states in Europe, but this holds true even for the Nordic countries, except Denmark.[26] Additionally, it has to emphasised that wage inequality may not be the only or most dominant factor explaining employment growth between 1980 and 1996. The coefficient is significant, but not as clear-cut as the change in social security contributions. Finally, as it is shown in Model 3, the employers' part of financing the welfare state makes a difference in employment performance, as it explains the larger part of the variance, outscoring the impact of wage inequality.

Hence, overall employment performance may be negatively affected by solidaristic wage policies in the time period observed – but it can be shown that the welfare state, i.e. the way the welfare state is funded, may have a much greater impact on employment dynamics. Accepting the reservations connected with the statistical approach applied here, we have nevertheless some good reasons to suggest that the argument put forward by Iversen and Wren (1998) should be amended, taking the welfare state – or, more precisely, the way it is financed –into consideration, too. This is even more compelling if we examine its impact on employment growth in one service sector which is one of the most dynamic sectors in many OECD countries: the low productivity, low wage segment of the service economy (see Table 9.2).[27]

As in Table 9.1 some potentially explanatory variables are included and *cum grano salis* the results for overall employment performance are confirmed for the low wage, low productivity segment of the labour market. Again, it can be shown (Model 1) that the level of welfare state expenditure does not make a difference for the

Table 9.1 Ordinary least squares estimates of overall employment performance, 1980-1996

y = change of employment rate 1980-1996					
Model 1		Model 2		Model 3	
Constant	15.26 (0.58)	Constant	-8.02 (-0.56)	Constant	0.71 (0.06)
Employment level, 1980	-0.11 (-0.46)	Employment level, 1980	-0.05 (-0.34)	Employment level, 1980	-0.09 (-0.74)
Social security *expenditure* (% GDP), 1980	-0.12 (-0.43)	Social security *contributions* (% GDP), 1980	-0.32 (-1.65)	Employers' social security contributions (% GDP), 1980	-0.64** (-2.87)
Change social security *expenditure* (% GDP), 1980-96	-0.75 (-1.35)	Change social security *contributions* (% GDP), 1980-96	-2.78*** (-5.43)	Change employers' social security contributions (% GDP), 1980-96	-2.44*** (-5.32)
Labour market protectionism index late 1990s	-0.78 (-0.55)	Labour market protectionism index late 1990s	0.95 (1.06)	Labour market protectionism index late 1990s	0.00 (0.01)
Earnings dispersion D5/D1 early 1990s	0.36 (0.05)	Earnings dispersion D5/D1 early 1990s	8.81** (2.45)	Earnings dispersion D5/D1 early 1990s	6.25* (1.86)
R^2	0.32	R^2	0.78	R^2	0.81
adj. R^2	0.01	adj. R^2	0.69	adj. R^2	0.73
F	1.02	F	7.95	F	9.45

Ordinary least squares regression; * significant at a 0.10 level, ** significant at a 0.05 level, *** significant at a 0.01 level (two-sided tests).
Source: MPI (1998), OECD (1997, 1999c, 1999e).

Table 9.2 Ordinary least squares estimates of employment performance in ISIC 6, 1980-1996

y = change of employment rate (ISIC 6), 1980-1996					
Model 1		Model 2		Model 3	
Constant	10.21 (1.40)	Constant	-2.05 (-1.09)	Constant	-1.02 (-0.44)
Employment level ISIC 6, 1980	-0.41 (-1.62)	Employment level ISIC 6, 1980	-0.27** (-2.62)	Employment level ISIC 6, 1980	-0.23* (-1.92)
Social security *expenditure* (% GDP), 1980	-0.19* (-2.02)	Social security *contributions* (% GDP), 1980	-0.23*** (-5.31)	Employers' social security contributions (% GDP), 1980	-0.30 (-0.44)
Change social security *expenditure* (% GDP), 1980-96	-0.29* (-2.21)	Change social security *contributions* (% GDP), 1980-96	-0.76*** (-6.80)	Change employers' social security contributions (% GDP), 1980-96	-0.51*** (-4.05)
Labour market protectionism index late 1990s	0.23 (0.49)	Labour market protectionism index late 1990s	1.16*** (5.28)	Labour market protectionism index late 1990s	0.85*** (3.35)
Earnings dispersion D5/D1 early 1990s	0.40 (0.23)	Earnings dispersion D5/D1 early 1990s(5.63)	4.07***	Earnings dispersion D5/D1 early 1990s	3.10*** (3.58)
R^2	0.55	R^2	0.88	R^2	0.83
adj. R^2	0.34	adj. R^2	0.83	adj. R^2	0.76
F	2.64	F	16.42	F	10.69

Ordinary least squares regression; * significant at a 0.10 level, ** significant at a 0.05 level, *** significant at a .01 level (two-sided tests).

Source: MPI (1998), OECD (1997, 1999c, 1999e).

employment dynamics in the ISIC 6 segment of the labour force, rather the way the welfare state is funded (Model 2). Additionally, again the employers' share of overall social contributions (Model 3) is highly significant, however, the explanatory power of this model is not as convincing as Model 2. Hence we can argue – given the reservations concerning the statistical methods – that it seems to be necessary to bring the welfare state back in if we want to explain the dynamics of service employment at the beginning of the new millennium. Iversen and Wren (1998) are right if they argue that one prominent goal of the Rehn-Meidner model – income equality – is blocking employment growth in the service economy. But they overestimate this finding and it is argued here that the way the welfare state is funded may explain a greater share of service sector dynamics observable in OECD countries.

Conclusion

The Nordic countries were challenged by the somewhat dramatic employment crises in the early 1990s. In this discussion we have shown that wage growth and the funding system of the welfare state – i.e. a welfare state financed mainly by social contributions – fuelled the Nordic employment crises. In the 1990s, Denmark, Norway and Finland could by-and-large rebuild wage co-ordinated bargaining patterns that resulted in moderate wage growth. At the same time, the social security contributions were reduced in Norway and Finland, and they remained at a very low level in Denmark. In contrast, in Sweden wage bargaining was still highly contested and wage growth was high, despite the economic turmoil and relatively high open unemployment – at least at the time of this writing. Furthermore, social security contributions – especially the employers' share – were the main source of financing the welfare state bill. This changed, however, with the pension reform finally implemented in 1999. Thus, it is argued that it is conducive to bring the welfare state and especially its funding pattern (back) into studies of employment performance.

Furthermore, the findings presented here cast at least some doubts on the argument put forward by Iversen and Wren (1998) that equality is the main hindrance for employment creation in the era of the service economy. I argue that this thesis has to be amended. Social security contributions do explain a greater part of the employment performance – overall employment performance as well as service sector employment performance in the ISIC 6 segment of the labour market – than earnings dispersions or regulations of the labour market. I therefore conclude that attributing employment problems in the Nordic countries to the solidaristic wage policies and greater economic equality sought by the Rehn-Meidner model alone is not justified. Instead, focus should be placed on an aspect not foreseen by Gösta Rehn and still widely neglected in comparative labour market analyses – the way the welfare state funds its programs.

Notes

1 'Nordic countries' or 'Scandinavia' includes Denmark, Finland, Norway and Sweden. Because of size, unique economic conditions, and data unavailability, Iceland is excluded from this analysis.

2 It should be noted that Iversen and Wren (1998, p. 522) define budgetary restraint as the 'inverse of the change in total public outlays for wages and salaries as a proportion of GDP'. However, taking budget deficits as a proxy for fiscal discipline, the Nordic countries reveal rather policies of 'sound public finances' at least until the late 1980s, as budget deficits were comparatively rather low and even declining through the 1980s (see Jochem and Siegel 2000)

3 Between 1988 and 1994, the employment rate dropped in Finland by 13.4 percentage points, in Sweden by 10.8, in Denmark by 5.6, and in Norway by 4.9, whereas in the other OECD countries employment dropped in this period on average by only 1.2 percentage points.

4 If we assume that labour force participation since 1990, the peak, had been constant, the hypothetical unemployment rate in 1998 would have risen further by approximately 4 percentage points. Hence, labour supply developments are crucial if one tries to explain the Swedish unemployment rate – a fact not considered by Iversen (1998a, p. 49).

5 In this respect it is important to keep in mind that employment rates delivered by the OECD are not controlled for part time employment. Therefore, countries with high and rising part time employment do have a comparative advantage in the following analyses.

6 This part of the paper rests mainly on the contributions in Wadensjö (1996) and my own research (Jochem 1998).

7 Of course, the development in the Netherlands is no example for an overall expansion of employment, rather the distribution of employment has changed, as the rate of part-time employment was expanded significantly in the last years – and this may explain a great deal of the 'Dutch miracle', beyond the emphasis on moderate wage growth after 1982.

8 Indeed, price stability was a prominent goal of the Rehn-Meidner model, and Gösta Rehn often emphasised that full employment and price stability should be ensured simultaneously. But at least in the 1980s, the Nordic countries could not contain inflation to such a degree as the other OECD countries – as price stability was undermined by inflationary wage leap-frogging. In this sense, the defence of price stability was a new goal (see for Norway and Sweden Notermans 1999).

9 The correlation between the consumer price index and the change of employment rates is for Denmark between 1984 and 1994: r = .54, for Finland: r = .55. In contrast, there is only a moderate correlation in Norway: r = .34 and Sweden: r = .39.

10 An argument put forward in accordance with Notermans (1999). However, for him EU membership is interpreted as a watershed for the Nordic countries. As I would argue, the stable currency goal dominated the Nordic economies already in the 1980s, hence, the watershed in the Nordic political economies occurred earlier – this may be interpreted as the dominant influence of the German model respectively the German monetary policy in

Europe and its appeal for countries even outside the European Union to follow the guiding lines drafted in Frankfurt by the German Bundesbank.

11 Wage growth data ('compensation per employee') here, and in the following parts are taken from OECD (1999d).

12 It is rather common sense that the Finnish recession can be explained with the breakdown of the trade with the former USSR, as indeed Finish trade into this region dropped from 15 to 5 per cent of total trade in 1990 (see Andersson, Kosonen and Vartiainen 1993). However, it should be noted that a very huge drain in investment capital was additionally caused by the retreat of Swedish investors from Finland in 1991 (see OECD 1995, p. 22).

13 In fact, Finland is behind Ireland, one of the most expansive economies in the late 1990s. Moderate wage growth helped to maintain the cost competitiveness, which was improved by the enforced depreciation of the national currency in 1991-1993 (see OECD 1999a, pp. 30-2).

14 See for the development in Norway the contributions in Dølvik and Steen (1997).

15 It should be noted that Göran Persson, the Swedish Prime Minister, announced in a newspaper article in January 2000 that the governing social democratic party will in the future even collaborate with the centre parties – how far this will succeed, however, remains to be seen (see *Dagens Nyheter* 18 January 2000, online version).

16 The Scandinavian experience confirms the argument put forward by Soskice (1990, 1999) that the employers' strategies are crucial for the development of bargaining patterns and the fortune of co-ordinated market economies.

17 In Figure 2 the independent and dependent variables are average values for two periods. The first roughly covers the period before the employment crisis (1984-1988), the second the period of the employment crisis (1989-1994). Hence, the dependent variable is lagged. One could question if such an extensive lag conforms to reality. Besides the argument that there is no rule for how long such a lag should be, I argue that in reality investment decisions do have effects over a large time span, and it is investment, which is the link between cost calculations of employers and employment developments. As can be seen from Figure 2, the correlation is highly dependent on critical cases as New Zealand, Australia and Ireland. If one accepts that in these countries specific circumstances enabled employment growth *despite* high wage growth, the correlation for the remaining 15 OECD countries would be: $r = -.86$, $R^2 = .73$.

18 It should be emphasised that labour force supply was extensively reduced in the early 1990s, which dampened the rise in open unemployment in all four countries. Especially in Sweden, this policy choice enabled the reduction of open unemployment at the end of the millennium, not employment growth (see Jochem 2000).

19 In the 1980s, wage growth and growth of unit labour costs were highly correlated ($r = .97$, $N = 18$). However, in the 1990s correlation is lower ($r = .79$, $N = 18$). A further analysis revealed that in some countries (Germany for example) the rise in unit labour costs was much more pronounced than the rise in wages. In contrast, in some other countries (Norway, and, to a lesser extent, Denmark and Finland for example) the unit labour costs were decoupled from wage growth, indicating that in these countries a reduction of social

security contributions dampened the cost rising effects of the welfare state on unit labour costs.

20 The correlation for 17 OECD countries, i.e. without Ireland, is: r = -.64, R^2 = .41.

21 These and the following data are taken from Nordic Social Statistical Committee (NOSOSCO 1999, p. 159).

22 Richard B. Freeman (1997, p. 35) emphasises that social security contributions in Norway are – despite the encompassing and expensive welfare state – very low, and 'the proportion of compensation due to the supplementary cost of hiring an employee does not differ much from that in the USA'. However, the large public part in funding the welfare state may be seen as a Norwegian peculiarity, as there the capacity to tax might depend on welfare generating oil revenues.

23 It should be noted that in Sweden and Finland public social services were reduced to consolidate public budgets in the early 1990s, a development not observable in the other Nordic countries (see Lehto, Moss and Rostgaard 1999).

24 This observation is based on the data reported in OECD (1996, pp. 61-2). For a sophisticated study of total income developments see Gustafsson et al. (1999).

25 These observations are based on data presented in MPI (1998) and OECD (1997).

26 As already mentioned above, social security contributions have been significantly reduced in Norway and Finland since the end of the 1980s. Only in Sweden social security contributions – especially for employers – remained very high until the end of the 1990s, but the pension reform may change the financing mix in Sweden. This may be a further piece of evidence that the principle of the social insurance state is on retreat (see the contributions in Clasen 1997).

27 The ISIC 6 segment of the labour force is chosen for the following analysis, and it should be added that I do not want to argue that only low wage and low productivity jobs occur there. But it is obvious that, in the wholesale and retail trade and in the restaurants and hotels industry, these jobs cover the majority of total employment contracts.

References

Andersen, Jørgen Goul (2000), 'Welfare Crisis and Beyond: Danish Welfare Policies in the 1980s and 1990s', in Stein Kuhnle (ed.), *Survival of the European Welfare State*, Routledge, London.

Anderson, Karen (1999), 'The Politics of Retrenchment in a Social Democratic Welfare State. Reform of Swedish Pension and Unemployment Insurance' (unpublished paper).

Andersson, Jan Otto, Pekka Kosonen and Juhana Vartiainen (1993), 'The Finnish Model of Economic and Social Policy - From Emulation to Crash', Åbo Akademi, Åbo.

Castles, Francis G. (1978), *The Social Democratic Image of Society. A Study of the Achievements and Origins of Scandinavian Social Democracy in Comparative Perspective*, Routledge, London.

Clasen, Jochen (1997), *Social Insurance in Europe*, The Polity Press, Bristol.

Due, Jesper, Jørgen Stehen Madsen, Carsten Strøby Jensen and Lars Kjerulf Petersen (1994), *The Survival of the Danish Model. A Historical Sociological Analysis of the Danish System of Collective Bargaining*, Jurist og Økonomforbundets Forlag, Copenhagen.

Dølvik, Jon Erik and Arild H. Steen (eds) (1997), *Making Solidarity Work? The Norwegian Labour Market Model in Transition*, Scandinavian University Press, Oslo.

Elmeskov, Jørgen (1994), 'Nordic Unemployment in a European Perspective', *Swedish Economic Policy Review*, vol. 1, pp. 27-70.

Elvander, Nils (1990), 'Incomes Policies in the Nordic Countries', *International Labour Review*, vol. 129, pp. 1-21.

Feldt, Kjell-Olof (1991), *Alla dessa dagar...*, Norstedts, Stockholm.

Freeman, Richard B. (1997), 'Are Norway's Solidaristic and Welfare State Policies Viable in the Modern Global Economy?', in Jon Erik Dølvik and Arild H Steen. (eds), *Making Solidarity Work? The Norwegian Labour Market Model in Transition*, Scandinavian University Press, Oslo, pp. 17- 50.

Freitag, Markus (1999), *Politik und Währung. Ein internationaler Vergleich*, Haupt, Bern.

Green-Pedersen, Christoffer (1999), 'The Danish Welfare State under Bourgeois Reign. The Dilemma of Popular Entrenchment and Economic Constraints,' *Scandinavian Political Studies*, vol. 22, pp. 243-60.

Gustafsson, Björn, Rolf Aaberge, Ådne Cappelen, Peder J. Pedersen, Nina Smith and Hanno Uusitalo (1999), 'The Distribution of Income in the Nordic Countries; Changes and Causes', in Mikko Kautto et al. (eds), *Nordic Social Policy. Changing Welfare States*, Routledge, London, pp. 215-34.

Huber, Evelyne and John D. Stephens (1998), 'Internationalization and the Social Democratic Model. Crisis and Future Prospects', *Comparative Political Studies*, vol. 31, pp. 353-97.

Iversen, Torben (1996), 'Power, Flexibility, and the Breakdown of Centralised Wage Bargaining. Denmark and Sweden in Comparative Perspective', *Comparative Politics*, vol. 28, pp. 399-436.

Iversen, Torben (1998a), 'Wage Bargaining, Hard Money and Economic Performance: Theory and Evidence for Organized Market Economies', *British Journal of Political Science*, vol. 28, pp. 31-61.

Iversen, Torben (1998b), 'The Choices for Scandinavian Social Democracy in Comparative Perspective', *Oxford Review of Economic Policy*, vol. 14, pp. 59-75.

Iversen, Torben and Anne Wren (1998), 'Equality, Employment, and Budgetary Restraint. The Trilemma of the Service Economy ', *World Politics*, vol. 50, pp. 507-46.

Jochem, Sven (1998), *Die skandinavischen Wege in die Arbeitslosigkeit. Kontinuität und Wandel der nordischen Beschäftigungspolitik*, 1984-1994, Leske + Budrich, Opladen.

Jochem, Sven (2000), 'Nordic Labour Market Policies in Transition', *West European Politics*, vol. 23, pp. 115-38.

Jochem, Sven and Nico A. Siegel (2000), 'Wohlfahrtskapitalismen und Beschäftigungsperformanz – Das 'Modell Deutschland' im Vergleich', *Zeitschrift für Sozialreform*, vol. 46, pp. 38-64.

Korkman, Sixten (1992), 'Exchange Rate Policy and Employment in Small Open Economies', in Jukka Pekkarinen, Matti Pohjola and Bob Rowthorn (eds), *Social Corporatism: A Superior Economic System?*, Clarendon Press, Oxford, pp. 280-97.

Korpi, Walter, (1991), 'Political and Economic Explanations for Unemployment: A Cross-National and Long-Term Analysis', *British Journal of Political Science*, vol. 21, pp. 315-48.

Lehto, Juhani, Nina Moss and Tine Rostgaard (1999), 'Universal Public Social Care and Health Services?', in Mikko Kautto et al. (eds), *Nordic Social Policy. Changing Welfare States*, Routledge, London, pp. 104-32.

Mjøset, Lars (1996), 'Nordic Economic Policies in the 1980s and 1990s', paper presented to the Tenth International Conference of Europeanists, Chicago, March 14-16.

MPI Adjustment Data Base (1998), Max Planck Institut für Gesellschaftsforschung, Köln.

NOSOSCO (Nordic Social Statistical Committee) (1999), *Social Security in the Nordic Countries. Scope, Expenditure and Financing 1997*, NOSOSCO, Copenhagen.

Notermans, Ton (1999), 'Europeanization and the Crisis of Scandinavian Social Democracy,' in Robert Geyer, Christine Ingebritsen and Jonathon Moses (eds), *Globalization, Europeanization, and the End of Scandinavian Social Democracy?*, Macmillan, London, pp. 23-44.

NOU (1992), *En nasjonal strategi for økt sysselsetting i 1990-årene*, (NOU 1992: 26), Oslo.

OECD (1995), *Economic Survey Finland*, OECD, Paris.

OECD (1996), *Employment Outlook*, OECD, Paris.

OECD (1997), *Labour Force Statistics*, OECD, Paris.

OECD (1999a), *Economic Survey Finland*, OECD, Paris.

OECD (1999b), *Economic Survey Sweden*, OECD, Paris.

OECD (1999c), *Employment Outlook*, OECD, Paris.

OECD (1999d), *Economic Outlook* (Spring), OECD, Paris.

OECD (1999e), *Social Expenditure Database*, OECD, Paris.

Pestoff, Victor A. (1999), 'The Disappearance of Social Partnership in Sweden during the 90s & its Sudden Reappearance in late 1998', paper presented at the 1999 ECPR Joint Sessions, Mannheim, Germany.

Pontusson, Jonas, (1992), 'At the End of the Third Road: Swedish Social Democracy in Crisis', *Politics & Society*, vol. 20, pp. 305-32.

Pontusson, Jonas and Peter Swenson (1996), 'Labor Markets, Production Strategies, and Wage Bargaining Institutions. The Swedish Employer Offensive in Comparative Perspective', *Comparative Political Studies*, vol. 29, pp. 223-50.

Scharpf, Fritz W. (1987), *Sozialdemokratische Krisenpolitik in Europa*, Campus, Frankfurt a. M./New York.

Scharpf, Fritz W. (1999), 'The Viability of Advanced Welfare States in the International Economy. Vulnerabilities and Options', MPIfG Working Paper 99/9. Max-Planck-Institut für Gesellschaftsforschung, Köln.

Schmidt, Manfred G. (1988), 'The Politics of Labour Market Policy', in Francis Castles, Franz Lehner and Manfred G. Schmidt (eds), *Managing Mixed Economies*, de Gruyter, Berlin, pp. 4-53.

Soskice, David (1990), 'Wage Determination: The Changing Role of Institutions in Advanced Industrialized Countries', *Oxford Review of Economic Policy*, vol. 6, pp. 36-61.

Soskice, David (1999), 'Divergent Production Regimes: Coordinated and Uncoordinated Market Economies in the 1980s and 1990s', in Herbert Kitschelt, Peter Lange, Gary Marks and John D. Stephens (eds), *Continuity and Change in Contemporary Capitalism*, Cambridge University Press, Cambridge, pp. 101-34.

Swank, Duane (1999), 'Social Democratic Welfare States in a Global Economy: Scandinavia in Comparative Perspective', in Robert Geyer, Christine Ingebritsen and Jonathon Moses (eds), *Globalization, Europeanization, and the End of Scandinavian Social Democracy?*, Macmillan, London, pp. 85-138.

Therborn, Göran (1987), 'Does Corporatism Really Matter? The Economic Crisis and Issues of Political Theory', *Journal of Public Policy*, vol. 7, pp. 259-84.

Therborn, Göran (1995), 'Patterns and Meaning of Unemployment', *Scandinavian Journal of Social Welfare*, vol. 4, pp. 122-30.

Tyrväinen, Timo (1995), 'Wage Determination, Taxes, and Employment: Evidence from Finland', Bank of Finland, Helsinki.

Wadensjö, Eskil (ed.) (1996), *The Nordic Labour Markets in the 1990's*, Elsevier, Amsterdam.

Wallerstein, Michael and Miriam Golden (1997), 'The Fragmentation of the Bargaining Society: Wage Setting in the Nordic Countries, 1950 - 1992', *Comparative Political Studies*, vol. 30, pp. 699-731.

Chapter 10

The Making of the Danish Employment Service, 1960-72.

Central and local policy choices, employer demand, and trade union resistance

Christian Toft

Introduction

A central part of the thinking of Gösta Rehn and also of the labour market policy recommendations of the ILO and the OECD during the period from the 1940s to the early 1970s centred on the role of the employment service in public policy. It was thought that a strong and efficient employment service and related active labour market policy measures would help improve efficiency in labour markets and thus facility economic growth. This paper examines how this strategy was debated and implemented in Denmark during the period from around 1960 to 1972.

Some admirers claim that Gösta Rehn invented active labour market policy with Rudolf Meidner at the LO research department in the early 1950s (see e.g. Esping-Andersen 1990, p. 168, Scharpf 1987, p. 119, Janoski 1996, p. 698). In reality all principles of active labour market policy were laid down in the 'Employment Service Recommendation' and related recommendations which were passed at the twenty-sixth session of the ILO in Philadelphia in 1944 (Toft 2000).[1] Hence instead of talking about the Rehn model - or the Rehn/Meidner model - of active labour market policy it would be more accurate and appropriate to talk about the Philadelphia model of active labour market policy. In the ILO legal system a recommendation needs only to be taken into consideration by Member States whilst a convention is communicated to all Members for ratification. During the war-time sessions no convention could be passed. Later, in San Francisco in 1948, the war-time employment service recommendation was polished and given the higher status of a convention.

Building on labour market policy discussions in the international policy community during the inter-war years, the new policy ideas had gained momentum from a concern about the socio-economic dislocation which was anticipated to follow from the imminent transition from war to peace. An active employment policy, based on centralised planning principles, should facilitate the efficient re-allocation of labour from a contracting military to an expanding civil industrial production, help establish the conditions for balanced growth, and prevent the emergence of unemployment. It was feared that unemployment, if left unattended, would lead to the kind of civil unrest amongst returning soldiers which had marred the aftermath of the first world war. In the post-war period and during Rehn's tenure at the OECD, the new policy was justified as an investment in labour market adaptation to economic growth (Toft 2000).

Whilst it is always difficult and disputable to determine qualitative differences, changes and breaks in public policy, it makes sense to view the ILO conventions and recommendations making up the Philadelphia ALMP model as prescribing a transition from a pre-war 'placement service' to a post-war 'employment service'. This involved a new and broader definition of the responsibilities, functions and methods of operation than provided by past placement services. As part of a nationally co-ordinated programme of full employment and optimal resource utilisation, the service would be responsible for the allocation of labour. In addition to the traditional placement provision, the employment service and related authorities would provide training and mobility measures as well as assist in infrastructure developments. A tripartite consultation mechanism would be established involving labour, employers and government.

Most industrialised countries had no difficulties in living up to the new political and institutional requirements of the Philadelphia model. By the early 1950s almost all had ratified the 1948 ILO Employment Service Convention. One of few exceptions was Denmark, which did not ratify the convention until two decades later in 1972. It was only two years prior to that ratification that a Danish employment service, living up to the requirements of the Philadelphia model, was actually established.

ILO member states are under no obligation to accept conventions. However, a comprehensive machinery does exist to monitor the compliance of states once they choose to ratify. Furthermore, member states, at least the European ones, hardly ever change domestic legislation in order to accommodate ILO conventions and recommendations. On the other hand, they also hardly ever abstain from ratification without good cause. Hence ratification behaviour tends to be fairly conservative, providing more of an indication of the degree to which the country's existing practices are already consistent with ILO norms than an indication of a commitment towards future policy changes.

The fact that countries as diverse as the Netherlands, Germany, the UK and Sweden experienced no difficulties in ratifying the convention demonstrates the widespread acceptance which its overall policy prescriptions and the full employment aim enjoyed. Even though many later came to view the particular Swedish adaptations as the 'ideal type', not least because of its promotion by Rehn during his tenure at the OECD, the policy requirements of the original Philadelphia model were not particularly stringent and thus allowed for a diversity of approaches. Danish exceptionalism was not motivated by a rejection of the aim of promoting full employment through a nationally co-ordinated policy programme nor was Denmark opposed towards the utilization of active labour market policy instruments. Instead its primary concern was about the central role delegated to the employment service in the implementation of this policy.

In the 1950s and 60s Denmark had a public placement service but it could not be characterized as living up to the Philadelphia ideal of a public employment service. Institutionalised placement provision was divided into a public system provided by a central government agency and a trade union controlled system provided by the unemployment insurance funds. Since 1907 unemployment insurance has been by provided by trade union insurance funds supported by central and local government subsidies (see Toft 1995). Insurance fund placement provisions developed firstly as a result of the legal obligations of the funds controlling unemployed members and secondly as a result of employers finding insurance fund unemployment and membership registers a useful source of information. Finally, until 1962 a local government placement system also existed but its share of placements was small.

From an organisational viewpoint the public system lived up to the prescriptions of the Philadelphia model but its penetration of the industrial labour market with which the model was concerned was minimal. For most of the period the share of placements of the two systems (government and trade union) were pretty similar but they operated in very different labour market segments. While the public system dominated the female market (domestic servants) segment, the trade union system dominated the male market (industrial labour) segment. Although employers' organisations had since the system's pre-WWI establishment repeatedly demanded the abolition of the trade union system, nothing had come of it. Abolition was only achieved in the late 1950s and then only within the context of a wider reform of labour market and social services.

The absence of reform initiatives in the 1950s was due partly to trade union resistance but more importantly to the lack of interest by all actors concerned. The dominant policy view was that extending public placement services would be costly and that the unemployment insurance fund placement service which had more than three thousand local offices was doing a sufficiently good job in placing unemployed workers. In any case, most job changes took place outside institutionalised arrangements.

Existing active labour market policy measures, notably the 1937/38-employment creation scheme, could be administered within the existing public administration structures. New measures were added on a piecemeal basis. In 1960 a new training scheme for unskilled workers and a rehabilitation scheme, uniting efforts with respect to handicapped workers in 12 regional centres, were set up. However, the poorly developed public labour market policy administration had only loosely connected the various old and new measures. For example, rehabilitation was given its own structure in the ministry of social affairs with only limited connections to the placement service. Since then, in contrast to rehabilitation policy in most other countries, in Denmark it has been viewed as a social policy issue rather than as a labour market policy measure.

It was in the early 1960s that public administration reform entered the Danish political agenda. The socio-economic context was the transition from an agricultural dominated economy to an industrial and service dominated economy and from a 'low-growth-cum-high-unemployment' to a 'high-growth-cum-low-unemployment' economy. The reform debate was not only influenced by the international debate concerning the appropriate status of the employment service, but also by the even wider international debate about social security and social services.

The provisions of the Beveridge Report that shaped the post-war welfare state in Britain proved to be a strong source of inspiration in Denmark. The Danish reformers argued, as did Beveridge, that administrative responsibility for social security should be unified and placed in the hands of one administrative body. But unlike Beveridge and the post-war British labour government, the Danish reformers argued that local government should be the appropriate provider of a unified system rather than a central government agency. Additionally, the mandate of the unified system differed from that of the Beveridge Report. The Danish term 'det sociale tryghedssystem', which is translated either as 'the social safety system' or as 'the social security system', always includes not only cash benefits (i.e. the British concept of 'social security') but also what the British term 'personal social services'. A unified social safety system does not only unify social security in one scheme (the Beveridge administrative principle) but also unifies social security and social services (cash and in-kind benefits). In post-war Britain social security became exclusively a central government responsibility while social services were provided by local government, thus, producing fundamental splits and divisions in the 'social safety system' (Toft 1993). By creating a unified social safety system with a base in local government, Danish reformers hoped it would be possible to pursue an active social policy that was designed to prevent rather than cure social ills.

Finally, as in the Beveridge scheme, the Danish reformers of the 1960s argued that social security benefits should be standardised and provided on the same basis regardless of the reason of claims. Unemployment, sickness, maternity and a number of other benefits should be given at the same rate and, as far as possible, according to the same principles. Disagreements emerged relating to the design of the benefit schedule. Bourgeois reformers wanted to maintain the original Beveridge principle of a flat-rated national minimum (social grundsikring). Danish socialist reformers argued for the institution of a Bismarckian style earnings-related benefit system which was in line with the thinking and policies of the Swedish Social Democrats and the British Labour Party in the late 1950s and 60s.

With the entrance into the debate of a unified social safety system, we see the crystallisation of two competing models for a Danish employment service. First, there is a conservative model based on a piecemeal expansion and rationalisation of the existing central government placement service. Second, a radical model emerges which integrates employment service provisions in a new local government social safety system. Eventually the conservative model prevailed. Even though the Social Democrats tended to favour the conservative model and the bourgeois favoured the radical model, it would be wrong to interpret the victory of conservatism as simply the result of Social Democratic strength.

In establishing the employment service, Danish policy actors never claimed to develop an equivalent to the so-called Swedish Social Democratic 'Folkhemsmodell' as it is described by Hedborg and Meidner (1984a, 1984b). No particular actor can possibly claim ownership to the Danish employment service and it would not be obvious why anyone would wish to. However, in contrast to the received wisdom regarding the Swedish model, which presents the making of this model as a result of trade union enterprise, Danish employers played a pivotal role in the making of social reform. While Gösta Rehn and the Swedish trade unions embraced the Philadelphia ALMP model to the extent that they asserted ownership of the whole idea of active labour market policy, Danish trade unions and policy makers initially rejected core features of the model. It was only due to pressures by employers and central government bureaucrats that a reform process could be initiated which eventually led to the establishment of an employment service that lived up to the Philadelphia model.

The creation of the Danish employment service was the outcome of a 10-year reform process in which all major political parties, bureaucrats, academics and interest groups played significant roles. All actors changed strategy at least once during the process. In the remainder of this chapter this policy process is examined. I begin by providing an overview of the process whereupon its separate stages are investigated. The findings of the chapter are summarised in a concluding section.

Overview of the policy process

From the war to the December 1973 election, the Danish party system might, somewhat simplified, be described as a five-party system consisting of the Social Democratic Party, the Socialist Peoples Party,[2] the Radical Centre Party, the Liberal (agrarian) Party, and the Conservative Party. (The Justice Party had a brief spell of influence when it participated in the Social Democratic led government from 1957 to 1960, but then failed to regain its seats in parliament in the 1960 election.) For most of the period there was a minority government. A majority government was only in power on two occasions, from 1957 to 1960 and from 1968 to 1971.

It was in 1960 under a Social Democratic and Radical Centre minority government that the reform process began, and the process was concluded in 1970 under a bourgeois majority government. The table below provides an overview of the process. Points in time when legislation relating to unemployment insurance and placement service reform was passed are indicated with a star (*).

Overview of the labour market policy reform process

1.	1960	Appointment of expert investigative committee on the administration of central government departments and institutions (known as A60). Two reports: 1962
2.	1962	Minister for Social Affairs and Labour Kaj Bundvad (Social Democrat) appoints the Kirstein Committee on the structure, functions and measures of the Danish placement service. Committee Report: December 6th 1963
3.	1963	Establishment of separate 'Labour Department'
4.	1963	Labour Minister Erling Dinesen (Social Democrat) announces December 12th the setting up of the Wechselmann Committee on unemployment insurance and placement service reform. Committee established: April 1964
5.	1964	Social Reform Commission: Liberals and Conservatives propose in March the setting up of a social reform commission to investigate and propose reforms of the entire social sector – social security, sickness, social services and labour market policy. Commission established: May
6.	1966	Preliminary report from the Wechselmann Committee containing a bill for a reform of unemployment insurance: October
7.	1966*	Wechselmann Bill passed by parliament with full unanimity: February
8.	1967	Establishment of a working group related to the Wechselmann Committee with the Labour Director, Borreschmidt, as chair to consider a reform of the placement service: March. Report containing a bill for a reform of the placement service: October
9.	1967	Borreschmidt Bill presented in parliament by the Social Democratic minority government: November/December. Bill not passed before the January 1968 election
10.	1968*	Borreschmidt Bill presented once again in parliament by the new bourgeois majority government: March. Bill passed, Social Democrats abstain, (11 left-wing MPs against)
11.	1969	Final report of the Wechselmann Committee containing bill stipulating a reform of unemployment insurance. The establishment of an 'Employment Service' is discussed in an ad hoc tri-partite 'contact group'
12.	1970*	Bill reforming unemployment insurance and establishing an 'Employment Service' passed by parliament with near unanimity: March (3 left-wing MPs abstain)
13.	1970	Social Reform Commission: Bill on the governance of social security, certain health matters, and social services: Passed May with near unanimity. The Social Democratic social affairs spokesman and Social Reform Commission member, Niels Mørk, as well as a number of other Social Democratic MPs abstain
14.	1972*	Unemployment insurance benefits increased by Social Democratic minority government: March. Cash Benefit Bill equalising and raising short term cash benefits (based on considerations of the Social Reform Commission): June. Bourgeois parties against both bills because of their costs

Since the establishment of the service was part of a wider social reform process a large number of interest groups were directly and indirectly involved in the process. The chief interest groups were the main organisation of the employers (Dansk Arbejdsgiverforening, DA), the main organisation of the unions (Landsorganisationen i Danmark, LO), skilled and unskilled workers trade unions, the Association of Sickness Insurance Funds, the three Local Government Associations, the County Association, and the Old Age and Invalidity Pensioners Associations.

In Danish politics investigative commissions and committees are important tools in the policy process. The very establishment of a commission or a committee can shape the agenda and hence the outcome of a reform process. Three types of bodies exist: 1) expert and civil servant investigative committees (used to bear to clarify a particular issue), 2) investigative committees (similar to expert committees but with a broader composition – political parties and interest groups are usually represented), and 3) investigative commissions (very broad and large bodies dominated by representatives from the political parties and the involved interest groups). While committees investigate a more restricted reform issue and are expected to report within a shorter period of time, commissions investigate larger issues and work for a longer period of time.

The Danish employment service was shaped by work done in such bodies. Three committees and one commission were instrumental in its establishment: 1) the expert committee on central government administrative reform, known as A60 (established 1960), 2) the Kirstein Committee on the structure, functions and measures of the placement service, 3) the Wechselmann Committee on unemployment insurance reform and a related sub-committee headed by Borreschmidt on placement service reform, and 4) the Social Reform Commission which was set up to investigate most aspects of benefit provision and social services.[3]

In the wider background the Local Government Reform Commission (established 1958) was at work. Its efforts led to a complete overhaul of the existing local government system, including governance, finance, functions, and size. Up until 1970 Denmark had some 1400 local government units, whereupon the number was drastically reduced to 275. In the absence of a local government reform it would have been impossible to implement the administrative and possibly also many of the substantive proposals of the Social Reform Commission. On the other hand, without the legislation which followed from the Social Reform Commission, much of the point of local government reform would have been lost as the social reforms provided the new local governments with many of their core functions.

Though the A60 Reform Committee, having produced five reports, ceased to exist after 1965, its administrative philosophy continued to exercise influence into the 1970s and beyond (Grønnegård Christensen 1993). The two first reports of the committee contained detailed examinations of the labour market policy administration as well as proposals for its future status within central government. The setting up of the Kirstein committee, which reported in December 1963, was at least in part a constituent element of the central government administrative reform process, which had been initiated by the A60 committee. Its report was of an academic nature, providing a view of what the experts saw as the most appropriate structure and functions of a Danish employment service. It is in the Kirstein report where we find the greatest influence of Rehnist thinking on Danish academic thought.

The reform process *per se* began in spring 1964 with the establishment of the Wechselmann Committee and the Social Reform Commission. Both bodies had strong interest group representation; in fact the Wechselmann Committee had no party political representation. In setting up two investigative bodies, the Social Democratic government aimed at separating reform of unemployment insurance and placement provision from the wider issue of universalist social reform. Yet this was not a once-and-for-all decision. The most urgent tasks of the Wechselmann Committee and the related Borreschmidt Committee were completed in spring 1968 when the work in the Social Reform Commission was only beginning to gather pace and its proposal for universalist social reform was beginning to take shape. At that stage a bourgeois government was in power.

Throughout the reform process and until legislation was passed in 1970, a central issue on the policy agenda was the uniting of a reform of unemployment insurance and placement provisions with the universalist reform concerns of the Social Reform Commission. As it turned out, the two reforms were kept separate and two very diverse social administration models were implemented: a) a universalist social security and social services model with a base in local government; and b) a particularist unemployment insurance and employment service model with bases in trade unionism and central government.

The Kirstein Committee, Gösta Rehn and the extended directorate model

The Kirstein Committee, together with the A60 Committee, developed the underlying conceptions of the central government bureaucracy with regard to the future of labour market policy and its position within central government administration. The tradition of Danish central government administration involves a dual structure distinguishing between departments, headed by a minister, and directorates, which are sub-departmental agencies. Departments are the backbone of Danish administration. In contrast to the famous Swedish boards, Danish directorates are smaller and have more limited and targeted functions. Directorates are agencies of delivery; they do not have the policy making and executive functions of Swedish boards. Not all departments have directorates. A minister may be responsible for more than one independent department and the ministerial title may be used even though no department exists.

The significance of the A60 Committee lay first of all in its delineation of an administrative philosophy and its promotion of an agenda for central government administrative reform. It argued for the implementation of a more rational and comprehensive division of government into departmental sectors by gathering together into one department various related functions and policy schemes which had heretofore been scattered across different parts of the government machinery. Furthermore, it argued for a more widespread application of the department-directorate distinction within central government administration.

We see the impact on labour market policy as the considerations of this committee led in 1963 to the establishment of a separate 'labour department' with its own departmental structure. The title of minister for labour had been invented during the war but divisions under the ministry for social affairs had conducted its functions. A60 made only a few recommendations with respect to the status of the labour directorate (established in 1921/22 to administer placements and unemployment insurance), and no recommendations with respect to the field organisation of labour market policy.

These issues became the subject matters of the Kirstein Committee which was established in 1962 by Kaj Bundvad, minister for social affairs and labour, to investigate the structure, functions and measures of the Danish placement service. Committee members – two professors and two senior civil servants – were drawn from public administration rather than labour market policy circles. Its most prominent member, Professor Bent Christensen, was one of the leading post-war experts on central government administration. However, more important than the actual committee members was the appointment of Per Kirstein, head of division in the ministry for social affairs and labour, to lead a three-person academic secretariat. Hornemann Møller (1981, p. 162) suggests that it was actually leading civil servants in the ministry, which had taken the initiative for the setting up of the committee, and that they also proposed its mission and composition.[4] It is likely that it was Kirstein who took the initiative of establishing the committee.

Kirstein had in the 1950s criticised heavily the unemployment insurance system, accusing it of being at least one major reason for Denmark's poor post-war employment performance (Kirstein 1958). A known admirer of so-called modern labour market policy, he belonged to the international labour market policy circles associated with Gösta Rehn and the OECD; co-authoring the 1963 OECD report on the Swedish employment service. The Committee report (Danish Government 1964a) appears to have been largely written by Kirstein. In what follows I refer to it as the Kirstein report.

From reading the report it is evident that the secretariat had been granted considerable intellectual freedom and felt there was an important message to convey. The concern was not so much to please the various interest groups – in particular the trade unions – but rather to present what was regarded as a systematic academic treatment of the subject matter. The report surveys the wider international context, including Denmark's attitude to various OECD policy statements and its failure to ratify relevant ILO conventions. Much emphasis was given on the implications of

Denmark's possible entry into the European common market. The report also contains a survey of the employment services of a number of countries, but it was the Swedish system the committee found reason to highlight, and went to Stockholm to investigate first-hand the functioning of the Swedish employment service.

The report outlined a detailed proposal (see chapter eight of the report) for a rational, unitary state employment service with clear divisions of functions between central, regional and local offices. This implied the abolition of the placement services provided by the unemployment insurance funds. No detailed analysis or proposals concerning the arrangement of the central level was given. However, it is clear that the committee had a Swedish-style devolved employment service in mind: 'Since the committee expects, on the one hand, a not insignificant decentralisation of powers to the labour directorate and, on the other, an extension of the labour market policy functions of the placement service, the committee's proposals would presumably have implications for the organisational construction of the central administration and its related advisory boards (råd) and tribunals (nævn)' (Danish Government 1964a, p. 61). The report had attached to it a draft-proposal for a bill for an employment service.

In developing a justification for the committee's demand for the establishment of an employment service, we find the clearest – and to my knowledge the only – evidence of Danish academic thought being influenced by Rehnist thinking as regards the relationship between macro-economic stabilisation policy and labour market policy. Rehn was not directly cited in the report but on pages 47-8 a lengthy quote from a 1962 OECD statement on labour market policy was printed. Mainstream Danish thought acknowledged that labour market policy could play a role in promoting labour market adjustment. However, it did not insist that this would have a significant effect on macro-economic balances and implications for the use of macro-economic fiscal, monetary, and incomes policy instruments.[5]

More precisely, four points of justification were given in the Kirstein report. The language of justification is interesting and peculiar in that it was not considered sufficient to simply state the case for a service. A more colourful underlining of each argument by way of a number of loaded adjectives and adverbs were felt to be needed. It was argued that 1) the aim of full employment and price stability 'can not *at any rate* be achieved without a more efficient placement service'; 2) a subefficient placement system would imply the emergence of an 'unsatisfactorily *large* number of bottlenecks in production'; 3) the internationalisation of the labour market and international collaboration, e.g. in the European common market, means that increasing and new demands will *inevitably* be put on the existing system; 4) the realisation of the aims of economic policy demands '*really* effective' information about the state of the labour market and its development (Danish Government 1964a, p. 54, my italics). An efficiency target, for example the share of job changes which the new state system was expected to mediate, was not set in the report, though it was admitted that any placement service would only be able to step in and supplement individual market clearing efforts (Danish Government 1964a, p. 52).

In line with Danish tradition, the relevant interest groups were invited to air their views on a draft report. According to the final report the trade union organisation (LO) did not comment on the overall issues but only on some of the measures, e.g. housing allowances relating to labour mobility. The employers (DA) stated that they 'support a unitary state system of the kind which is described in the report', while the representative from the Association of Unemployment Insurance Funds thought that 'the existing system ought to be preserved'. Employers and the union presented similar views in articles published in a special April-March issue of the journal *Socialt Tidsskrift*. Apparently, the Association of Unemployment Insurance Funds was not invited to present its views on that occasion.

On publication, the report did not receive the sort of joyous reception from the labour movement, which apparently had greeted the various writings of Gösta Rehn and Rudolf Meidner in Sweden in the 1950s. Unions were not only concerned about the proposal for a unitary state employment service but also with the whole tone of the report which contained statements such as that optimal socio-economic savings would 'only be achievable if also the (unemployment) insurance scheme would be transferred to the state placement service' (p. 67). The report's whole line of argument was unconvincing. For example, as has already been mentioned, it failed to specify any efficiency targets. A similar issue was raised by the Association of Unemployment Insurance Funds at one of the meetings with the committee. The Association pointed out that the draft report contained no proof that the present system had not been able to solve the existing labour market problems and no proof that it would not be capable of solving future problems. On this charge the committee in its final report could only counter by stating 'in this respect the committee wishes to state that literally taken this is perhaps correct, but a strong 'proof' would by nature be impossible but also unnecessary. There is on this issue – as in respect to great many social problems – room for diverging opinions. The committee's unanimous view is that a new organisational form is needed, as is already stated above and as is specified in more detail below' (pp. 57-58). Such a view might be acceptable amongst academic gentlemen in a local pub. But to ask a powerful interest group to give up vital interests and, at the same time admit that there was no proof whatsoever that it would lead to any gains as compared with the existing arrangements, appeared like academic arrogance and patronising overconfidence.

In August 1963, when findings of the committee were beginning to be known, the social affairs and labour administrations were split. Erling Dinesen, a former chairman of the Clerical and Office Workers Union, became labour minister while Bundvad continued as social affairs minister. We do not know for sure if there was a link between the work and findings of the Kirstein Committee and this move.[6] But, whatever the reason for his departure from the labour department, unions were pleased at Bundvad's departure and eager to have one of their own as his replacement.

Aware of its controversial content, Dinesen kept the Kirstein report under wraps for several months before it was released. According to Thomsen (1987, p. 9) and Jørgensen (1997, p. 9), during this period Dinesen was in close contact with the trade unions (LO) and the Association of Unemployment Insurance Funds who urged him to seize the initiative on the issue of unemployment insurance and the placement services.[7]

The unions and the Association were not only concerned about the impact of the Kirstein report and proposal on the policy agenda but also about the growing demand from the Liberals and the Conservatives for the establishment of a social reform commission to investigate the entire social administration framework, including unemployment insurance and the placement service. The bourgeois parties argued that the social administration framework was highly irrational and fragmented and therefore needed to be reformed. Instead of the existing system, a unitary system under local government administration ought to be implemented.

To make matters more precarious, people and interest groups within and around the Social Democratic party were beginning to air similar demands for fundamental reform.[8] For example in 1963 Bent Rold Andersen, then a young ambitious social scientist, published an article in the Social Democratic magazine *Verdens Gang* arguing for the need for fundamental social reform. At the 1963 annual meeting of the Association of Social Workers its chair, Eva Gredal, likewise produced a penetrating critique of the social administration system and demanded reform. For the unions and the Association of Unemployment Insurance Funds it was of vital importance that unemployment insurance and the placement system was not caught up in the reform zeal of all these groups.

Social reform and the Social Democratic dilemma

The social administrative reform presented the Social Democratic leadership and government with a delicate dilemma, which threatened the party and eventually led to splits within it. On the one hand, social reform was in general regarded as a Social Democratic prerogative. An outright rejection of Liberal and Conservative demands for a social reform commission was not considered possible in that it would have made the party look like a backward looking party which set up obstacles to reasonable reform demands in an area of central importance to the party. It did not help that similar demands had been raised within and around the party. On the other hand, any reform of social administration structures posed internal difficulties in that it put on the reform agenda vital institutions, which were controlled by the party. As stated by Rold Andersen in an interview with Hornemann Møller: 'Why was the Social Democratic Party uncertain with respect to it (the bourgeois social reform proposal)? It ought to be pretty obvious. The party was associated ideologically, emotionally and perhaps also with respect to its interests with some of the organs which became the focus of attention and which caused the system to be fragmented' (Hornemann Møller 1986, p. 85).

This applied not only to trade union unemployment insurance but also to sickness insurance. Similar to unemployment insurance, sickness insurance was arranged on a mutual benefit basis and had its own organisational structure. Unlike unemployment insurance, which was arranged according to trade and crafts, sickness insurance funds had their basis mainly in the local community. There was a separate fund for each local government area, a feature that assured that there was no competition between funds and that each fund could secure a certain degree of risk pooling. People had a choice between membership of the local fund or making private arrangements. Similar to unemployment insurance, the sickness insurance organisations were important Social Democratic power bases, which the party wished to preserve and if possible strengthen. Yet the case for the preservation of sickness insurance was much weaker than the preservation of unemployment insurance. While the latter was still very much restricted to workers, 98 per cent of the population in the mid-1960s were members of the sickness insurance schemes (Westergård 1971, p. 42). Hence the dual structure of local government and local sickness organisations was difficult to defend and it was impossible to keep sickness insurance separate from the overall issue of universal social reform.

The solution to the Social Democratic dilemma regarding unemployment insurance was to establish two investigative bodies. Less than a week after the publication of the Kirstein report at the beginning of December 1963, Dinesen announced his intention of setting up a broad tri-partite investigative committee on the reform of unemployment insurance under the chairmanship of Sigurd Wechselmann. This announcement killed off any real political discussion of the Kirstein report and the committee's Bill never received an earnest treatment in parliament. The Wechselmann Committee was established in April 1964 and a month later the government set up the Social Reform Commission. In contrast to the A60 and the Kirstein Committees, both had strong interest group representation. However, they differed substantially in their compositions and missions.

The Social Reform Commission had 23 members consisting of a representative from each of the main parliamentary parties, the three local government associations, the county association, employers (DA), trade unions (LO), two from the Sickness Insurance Funds Association, two from the Old Age and Invalidity Pensioners Associations as well as representatives from a number of other bodies. Its chairman, Hans Cai Seierup, came from the Invalidity Pensioners Association and was a committed Social Democrat.[9] The vice-chairman, Niels Mørk, was the official representative of the Social Democratic party but he was also chairman of the Sickness Insurance Funds Association. Hence, pensioners and sickness insurance had three members each. The commission was given a large secretariat of civil servants. Vocal members of the reformist wing in the Social Democratic party – notably Bent Rold Andersen and Eva Gredal – were not invited to sit on the commission, though Rold Andersen received access through the back door in that he became a member of a 'working group to support the chair' which Seierup established early on in the commission's work. Another member of this group was Ernst Andersen, one of the architects of the Liberal's social policy strategy in the early 1960s and a strong proponent of social reform.

The mission statement kept the tasks of the commission wide open. Almost any area of social security and services administration could be reviewed; only the hospital sector and education were explicitly excluded.[10] Bill proposals were not considered to be part of the commission's mission. Its aim was to develop a set of principles, which would be translated into bills in the ministry for social affairs. Additionally, it commissioned major research projects on social service structure and benefit structure. Here again Bent Rold Andersen came to play an important role, being appointed as leader of the research projects, which were conducted in the Copenhagen Institute for Social Research.[11]

The Wechselmann Committee was much narrower in composition and mission. It had 14 members, including the chairman, with three members each appointed by the Association of Unemployment Insurance Funds, the unions, employers, the civil service, and one economics professor. Political parties had no seats. Sigurd Wechselmann, the chairman, was a county prefect and a member of the labour market conciliation board (Forligsinstitutionen). He also had a long career in the ministry of labour and social affairs behind him; during the war he had been involved in complex reforms of unemployment insurance. A small secretariat of civil servants from the ministry of labour was attached. Per Kirstein was not invited to be a member of this. The mission of the committee was to consider the appropriate level, structure and finance of unemployment insurance benefits. Later, consideration of placement service reform was added. Research was not part of the mission but the drafting of reform bills was.

By establishing in Spring 1964 two separate investigative bodies the Social Democrats had managed to separate the unemployment insurance and placement service issue from the overall issue of universal social reform. Nevertheless, the situation was not stable. There could be no guarantee that unemployment insurance and placement service reform would not at a later date become an issue of the Social Reform Commission, the main body for social reform enquiry. Inspired by Beveridge, its basic philosophy was that all social security and social services should be unified in one scheme provided by local government. Benefit provision should be standardised, so that instead of the existing highly diverse rules, conditions and rates, one structure should provide all short-term benefits.

This reform philosophy implied of course the abolition of the existing unemployment insurance and placement services structures and their integration into a universal local government scheme. It would also have implied the creation of an employment service with a base in local government rather than a central government service. Final decisions on this issue were only made in Spring 1970 when a bill on the governance of social security, certain health matters and social services were passed by parliament. This and subsequent follow-up legislation unified all social security and service provision under local government control but refrained from making delivery of unemployment benefit and labour market policy part of that structure. Later, in 1972, unemployment benefit rates were integrated into a unified benefit structure so that administration and finance was kept outside and benefits inside the main framework of social security and service provision.

As it turned out, of the two main Social Democratic strongholds, only sickness insurance was abolished and this could only be achieved following a lengthy and painful conflict both within the Social Reform Commission and within the Social Democratic party in parliament. Within the commission, lines of conflicts developed between the representatives from the Sickness Insurance Funds Association, who were all Social Democratic party members, and the others, including Social Democrats from local government, the pensioners association, and the civil service as well as the bourgeois parties. Initially, sickness insurance proposal was able to count on some solidarity from the trade unions (LO) but that solidarity disappeared when it became clear at the beginning of 1970 that abolition of unemployment insurance would not be an issue (Hornemann Møller 1986, p. 91).

In this conflict the dual position of Niels Mørk as the official representative of the Social Democratic Party and chairman of the Sickness Insurance Funds Association increasingly became a liability to the party. To prevent abolition and preserve existing positions, Mørk and the Association went as far as to try to mobilise the medical profession, one of the most bourgeois of all professions, against the abolition proposal. The tactic also included the launch of a strong press campaign, which included personal attacks on the Social Democratic commission chairman who was labelled 'a great man in the art of distortions' (Christensen 1998, p. 142).

Within the Social Democratic Party in parliament the tactics of Mørk constituted a problem. He could not be removed from the commission and his status made it difficult to change party political strategy from a position of being wary with respect to the bourgeois universalist reform to a position of embracing reform. The preservation of the sickness insurance organisations was under no circumstances possible in a parliament with a bourgeois majority; and to vote against a social reform which abolished what most people regarded as defunct and obsolete institutional structures was considered a non-option.[12] It was after all the Social Democratic dominated Social Reform Commission that had proposed the abolition of the organisations.

In the end it proved impossible to control Mørk. Against strong pressures from the party leadership, who wanted a unanimous party vote in favour of reform, Mørk and a number of other Social Democratic MPs insisted on signalling their disagreement by abstaining from voting. Shortly thereafter the organisation he had chaired ceased to exist and within the party he no longer held any position of importance. Instead, the reformist outcasts who in 1964 had not been invited to be part of the reform process were brought in from the cold. Both Eva Gredal and Bent Rold Andersen later became Social Democratic social affairs ministers.

The Wechselmann Committee and the reform of unemployment insurance and placement provision

The actual reform of unemployment insurance and the establishment of a Danish employment service were negotiated in and around the Wechselmann Committee, which, as we have seen, was a tri-partite body without party political representation. Whilst the Kirstein Committee presented a broad 'vision' of the rationale of labour market policy and the Social Reform Commission aimed at a 'total' review, the Wechselmann Committee was highly focused and pragmatic. Instead of integrating all reform issues, as in the Social Reform Commission, the Wechselmann approach separated the issues as far as possible.

The reform process was conducted in three steps. First, in 1966-67 improvements in benefits and a reform of the financing of insurance were negotiated and implemented. The measure was preliminary and should be integrated into a wider reform, which was to follow. Second, in 1967-68 the transfer of control of the unemployed to the state placement system and prohibition of placements by insurance funds were implemented. This had not been an explicit issue in the original mission statement of the Wechselmann Committee, which had only included a vague reference to the Kirstein report on placement service reform. However, employers introduced the issue during the first stage of the negotiations, insisting that a reform of placements was a precondition for their acceptance of any rise in benefit generosity. Finally, in 1969-70 the entire legislation was revised, putting the structures of benefit provision on a new footing. At the same time, further improvements in benefits were implemented and an Employment Service was established. The latter was not negotiated in the Wechselmann Committee but in an *ad hoc* 'contact group' which had been set up by the labour minister for this particular purpose (see Folketingsårbog 1969-70, p. 138). Looking at the process as a whole we find that the wider comprehensive reform concluded the process but the most radical changes were conducted on a piecemeal basis during steps one and two.

The reform process did not go smoothly. Employers took a tough line at the outset stating that they felt that the Social Reform Commission was the appropriate place to discuss the ultimate situation regarding short-term benefits and the future of the unemployment insurance funds. This, of course, went against what the Social Democrats and the unions regarded as the main purpose of the committee, which was to keep unemployment insurance reform separated from the wider issue of social reform. Basically, trade unions felt safer in the company of the employers than in the company of their Social Democratic friends from the pensions and invalidity associations, local government and the civil service. Transferring the issue to the commission entailed the danger of having a sweeping rather than a pragmatic piecemeal reform.

For almost two years little happened until trade unions in Spring 1966 put pressure on Labour Minister Dinesen, urging him to try to speed up the work in the committee. We do not know if Dinesen took any action, but in October the committee presented a brief preliminary report and a bill for a reform of insurance benefits. However, the essential and most decisive compromise came into existence outside the committee meetings at a time when the negotiations had become totally stuck. 'Representatives from the two peak organisations (employers and unions) then met in private, and the compromise concerning the level of benefits, the replacement ratio, and the transfer of the placement service to the public sector was entered' (Hornemann Møller 1986, p. 107).

The Wechselmann Bill was put before parliament without any changes being made by the government and was passed with full unanimity. However, the bourgeois parties emphasised the preliminary nature of the measure and that they considered it to be just a matter of time before the unemployment insurance organisations would be nationalised, and thereby integrated into a general, universal social security system (Elm Larsen and von Nordheim Nielsen 1985, p. 52). Outside of parliament communist-dominated craft unions launched a heavy campaign against what they called the 'deportation law', by which they meant that the institution of a public placement monopoly could lead to workers being forced to take jobs in other parts of the country (Hornemann Møller 1981, p. 169). There is no evidence that this campaign had any tangible effect, but it illustrates the difficulties the Social Democrats and the unions and, in particular, the craft unions were facing on the issue.[13]

The next step, which implied the abolition of unemployment insurance fund placement provisions, went faster. It appears that following the negotiations of step one, unions and the Association of Unemployment Insurance Funds had come to terms with the fact that loosing control over placements was inevitable. Disagreements within the union movement helped smooth the process. Unskilled workers unions did not wish to jeopardise long fought for improvements in insurance benefits on the placement issue. The government had pledged to implement such improvements during the final step of the reform process. Though smaller than what had been achieved in 1967, they were still worth aiming for. Craft unions, on the other hand, had been better equipped in using placements to control the supply of labour to firms and were therefore more reluctant to hand over this weapon. However, they had become isolated as a result of the defection of the unskilled unions and could not on their own launch a realistic campaign against reform (Hornemann Møller 1986, pp 108 and 114).

Although not formally part of the Wechselmann Committee, the Borreschmidt working group, which had been set up by the labour minister to negotiate the practical details concerning the placement issue, was largely drawn from amongst the members of the Wechselmann Committee. The major category of new people who were drawn into the policy process was staff from the existing public placement offices whose expertise were demanded when developing the practical administrative details to be implemented as a result of the new system. Similar to the Kirstein Committee, the Borreschmidt group looked abroad for inspiration but again the main inspiration was derived from the Swedish example.[14] Also like the Kirstein Committee, the main inspiration the group derived from Sweden was the high degree of integration of labour market policy in that country.[15] A new point in comparison to the Kirstein report was that the Borreschmidt group looked more carefully into the wider use of mobility enhancing benefits in Sweden than in Denmark. As a direct result of this comparison, the group proposed that in future in Denmark all mobility enhancing benefits should be delivered by the new public placement offices and that the existing mobility benefits delivered by some of the unemployment insurance funds therefore should be abolished.

Like the Wechselmann Committee, the Borreschmidt working group produced a unanimous report and a bill, which was put before parliament without any changes being made by the government. However, the legislative process could not be completed before the election in January 1968, which returned a bourgeois majority leading to a bourgeois government. In early spring 1968 the bourgeois Minister for Labour put the same bill before parliament. Now suddenly the Social Democrats decided to abstain from voting, with the justification being that the political situation had now changed and that it was uncertain that the bourgeois government had any genuine intentions of honouring the pledge of improving benefit generosity during the final stage of the reform process (Folketingsårbog 1967-68, p. 230).[16]

Trade unions did not join in this confrontational strategy, partly because they themselves had negotiated the bill in the Borreschmidt working group and partly because a conflict with the bourgeois government could have endangered the survival of the unemployment insurance funds. Openly questioning bourgeois intentions regarding benefit generosity could of course also turn into a self-fulfilling prophecy in that it would place the government in a no-win situation. In this case, if the government actually went ahead and improved benefits, it could be construed as the government giving in to trade union pressures rather than implementing its own policy, whence it would be tactically more advantageous to stubbornly reject improvements.

During the third and final step new difficulties emerged within the Wechselmann Committee. At this stage, the major task of the committee was to undertake a technical revision of the entire unemployment insurance legislation, a task that was carried out by legal experts in the ministry for labour. On this matter, the committee had a largely supervisory role. More important for the members of the committee was the determination of the appropriate level of benefits. Further improvement to the ones implemented under step one had been pledged by the politicians but it was left to the committee to decide the details.

Unions demanded full compensation for loss of earnings during unemployment, a demand which employers could not accept. Negotiations had reached a stalemate when the bourgeois labour minister stepped in and called a meeting with the chairmen of the unions (LO) and the employers' organisation (DA) urging them to bring their members in the Wechselmann Committee to their senses. This involved spelling out a threatening alternative. According to Buksti and Sørensen, the minister explained at the meeting that 'if the committee did not come up with a unanimous proposal, there would not be a Bill proposal, and if there was no Bill proposal, the whole issue would be transferred to the Social Reform Commission' (Buksti and Sørensen 1971, p. 25).

We have already indicated union fears and employers affection of the Social Democratic dominated Social Reform Commission. However, it appears that at this stage employers' views had changed so that they were no longer particularly interested in letting unemployment insurance and the related issue of labour market policy become an issue of local government politics, which would have been the result of a transfer of the issue to the Social Reform Commission.

Furthermore, in the Social Reform Commission the employer representative had suggested that employers pay the first period of sickness instead of paying contributions to a public scheme (Christensen 1998, p. 134). Not all employers had welcomed that proposal. Given the commission's 'obsession' with universal principles, it could be predicted that if treated in the commission, unemployment would be subjected to the same financing principles as sickness. Yet, the introduction of an employer paid unemployment period – often called 'experience rating' – was something that would have provoked almost unanimous objections from employers. At this stage it was therefore better for the employers to keep unemployment as far away from the Social Reform Commission as possible.

In the end the Wechselmann Committee also reached a unanimous agreement on the benefit levels. The upper benefit ceiling was raised but the percentage earnings replacement ratio for low earners remained at the level set in 1967. The proposed Wechselmann Bill only concerned unemployment insurance legislation but before it was put to parliament it was integrated into a wider bill that also legislated public and private placement provisions and the structure of the employment service.[17] The latter provisions had been discussed by the labour market partners in the ad hoc 'contact group', which had been called by the labour minister.

The employment service issue caused little conflict between employers and unions. Once it had been decided that placement provision by the insurance funds should be abolished and once it had been decided that labour market policy should not be a prerogative of local government, employers and unions experienced no difficulties in agreeing that they should be the dominant organisations in the employment service. Noting that the new structure gave only very limited influence to local government, local government representatives tried to raise a debate, arguing once again that placement provision ought to be transferred to local government. Yet at that stage the bourgeois labour minister 'did not even care to debate with the local government associations' and simply reported that the contact group wanted 'a national unitary system under the auspices of the state' (Sonne Nørgaard 1997, p. 343).

The new legislation was passed with near unanimity in parliament; only three left-wing MPs abstained. This did not mean that there was full consensus about the bill. Whilst there was little disagreement about the main principles, substantial disagreements erupted concerning the details of the benefit proposal which was included in the bill. Whilst during step two of the reform process it was mainly the skilled workers unions which had voiced criticism, it was now mainly the unskilled workers who were aggrieved in that they felt that raising the upper benefit ceiling would mainly benefit high earners. The Social Democrats tried to mobilise the peak organisation of the labour movement (LO) in a campaign against the proposal but without any success (Buksti and Sørensen 1971, p. 23, Hornemann Møller 1986, p. 110). In the end they felt they had no other option than voting for a bill which the unions had had a major influence on and which established a whole new set of principles for labour market policy.

The benefit issue was raised again after the Social Democrats came to power following the election in autumn 1971. With the support of the Socialist Peoples Party and against strong opposition from the bourgeois parties, the benefit earnings replacement ratio for low earners was raised in 1972 to 90 per cent of previous earnings, waiting days reduced and benefit duration increased. The Socialist Peoples Party demanded 'full compensation', by which they meant a ratio of 100 per cent, whilst the bourgeois parties thought it to be more appropriate if the ratio remained at the existing 80 per cent.[18] At the same time and based on recommendations by the Social Reform Commission a wider reform of short-term cash benefits was implemented which led to a more simplified and unified benefit structure. Instead of the previous highly disparate rates, all short-term benefits – sickness, maternity, accident and unemployment – have from then on been granted at the same rate.

Summary: the constitution of Danish labour market policy

With the 1970 and 1972 reforms what might be termed the constitutional phase of Danish post-war labour market policy was completed. Although the details have changed, the main structures which were introduced in these reforms have remained in operation ever since. In November 1972 Denmark ratified the 1948 ILO Employment Service Convention and thereby signalled its full acceptance of the Philadelphia model of labour market policy.

The reforms were the results of a long process of negotiations where all actors changed strategy on at least one occasion. Disagreements between the actors had little to do with disagreements about high principles but were determined by strategies aiming at securing important power bases within the social administration structure. Indeed, the process itself can be described as a scramble to secure such power bases.

The Social Democrats originally wanted to pursue a piecemeal approach to social administration reform which would have kept important institutional power bases intact but were forced into a more wide ranging reform by the initiatives of the bourgeois parties and in particular the Liberal party. Once the process could no longer be controlled and the contours of the new system were clarified, the party began to embrace reform, even though the party's power base in the sickness organisations had to be surrendered. The bourgeois parties – champions of a Beveridge-style unitary system of social administration – did not implement unitarism in full when they had the chance. Their very demand for a unitary system with a base in local government administration needs to be viewed against the background of the Liberal party's traditional strength in local government. Trade unions and the Association of Unemployment Insurance Funds had to surrender insurance fund placement provision; employers had to accept the continuation of trade union linked unemployment insurance.

With the exception of the peculiar case when the Social Democrats decided to abstain from voting for a bill they themselves had proposed a few months earlier, all legislation on social administration reform was passed unanimously. Sabotaging a necessary reform on the basis of simple institutional self-interest appear to have been something none of the parties could bring themselves to do – even though the Association of Sickness Insurance Funds and the Social Democratic representative on the Social Reform Commission did their best in trying to provoke a confrontation. Insurmountable disagreements only emerged concerning benefit generosity. It is therefore correct when Poul Nyboe Andersen, one of the strong men in the bourgeois government 1968-1971, states that with respect to social reform the difference between the bourgeois and Social Democratic parties amounted to 10 per cent (Petersen 1998, p. 279).

The result of the process was the replacement of a fragmented administrative structure with a fairly systematic dual structure consisting of on the one hand the employment service and the unemployment insurance funds and, on the other, local government social services and security.

The public employment service that was created was a reformed directorate model. The main new element was the introduction of a network of 27 county level and 305 local placement offices to replace the hitherto existing 31 public offices and 3796 unemployment control branches of the unemployment insurance funds.[19] Furthermore, new tripartite national and county level advisory boards (arbejdsmarkedsnævn) were created which strengthened the role of the labour market partners in policy making and implementation. Finally, more comprehensive mobility allowances were introduced.

At the central government level, few changes were introduced after the establishment of a separate 'Labour Department' in 1963. The devolved Swedish-style structure, which the Kirstein Committee had hoped for, was not implemented. Policy making responsibilities remained firmly located in the labour department; the directorate remained a machinery of delivery; the functions of the new boards were largely advisory. Furthermore, as we have seen, both the Kirstein Committee and the Borreschmidt group argued that a substantial functional concentration of labour market policy might be beneficial. Yet also after the reform, the Danish labour market policy administration remained a very slim service and there is no evidence that any concentration of responsibility was implemented.[20] Many core labour market policy functions remained located in the ministries for education and social affairs.

This absence of a functional concentration of labour market policy at the central level was subject to a stinging criticism when in 1974 it was the turn of Danish labour market policy to be examined by the OECD Manpower and Social Affairs Committee. The OECD examiners felt that a completely different administrative machinery was needed in order to strengthen labour market policy and they went as far as to propose a complete overhaul of Danish central government and administration. 'The OECD examiners point out that there are different ways to arrive at this administrative structure: the existing Ministry could be strengthened and developed; another well established Government department like Education and Finance could be given responsibility for manpower; a new Ministry could be created; or a tripartite policy-making and executive agency could be set up' (OECD Observer 1974, p. 7). We do not know how the Danish government received this unusually bold criticism. Certainly, the government did not follow the OECD advice.

In the Danish context the root problem of the new structures was viewed as being in a quite different policy area. In creating a dual structure of placement and social service provision, the problem of establishing adequate rehabilitation structures had been granted very little priority. Whilst the core labour force may have benefited, one of the weakest groups in the labour market was the biggest loser as a result of the Social Democratic strategy of separating placement service reform from the wider social reform. The strain on public budgets resulting from the 1972 cash benefit reform also put restrictions on the development of adequate social service provisions, including rehabilitation measures.

The situation was not helped by the fact that in developing its proposals for further social service reform, the Social Reform Commission continued to pursue its own reform logic in spite of that an important precondition for its preferred local government model no longer existed as a result of the placement service reform. In its second report on social service reform, the commission proposed the abolition of the existing 12 rehabilitation centres and the transfer of their functions to the new local government social service departments. In spite of criticisms from several sources,[21] the proposal was translated into legislation in the Social Support Act of 1974. This increased instead of reduced co-ordination problems in rehabilitation provision in that the placement service now needed to collaborate with 275 local social services departments and several thousand social workers instead of 12 centres and a few hundred rehabilitation consultants (Valbak 1988).

The new unemployment insurance system reduced the functions of the insurance funds to the collection of contributions and to the payment of benefits in cases of unemployment (Kuhlmann 1974, p. 28). All discretion of the funds with respect to contribution and benefit rates was abolished in that these rates were largely standardised across the various individual unemployment insurance schemes.[22] Furthermore, the government assumed responsibility for the deficits of the individual schemes, and therefore for the deficits of the system as a whole. Thus with the reform, all aspects of 'risk-rating' were abandoned. Differences and changes in unemployment and therefore in demand for insurance benefits no longer lead to differences and changes in contribution rates. Yet the voluntary nature of the system and the ties between unions and unemployment insurance remain. The insurance funds (of which there were 55 in 1973) continue to be organised along lines of trade union demarcation.

Finally, the benefit structure was changed substantially. The old grading of benefits according to family status and the means-tested family benefits were replaced with a standard rate. In the literature there is much confusion about whether the benefit schedule that was introduced is earnings-related or flat-rated. This has also implications for the understanding of the policy process in that the bourgeois parties led by the Liberals and inspired by Beveridge demanded the institution of a national minimum (grundsikring) whilst the Social Democrats demanded a Bismarckian style earnings-related schedule.

The Danish benefit schedule provides an example of how futile it is to discuss benefits on the basis of grand principles without the necessary further specifications in that it can be viewed both as a flat-rated and as an earnings-related benefit schedule. In 1973 claimants in the lower part of the earnings distribution received 90 per cent of previous earnings in benefits. However, there was a maximum rate of 696 kroner per week (Rold Andersen 1973, p. 226). This benefit schedule can be viewed as an earnings-related schedule with a low upper ceiling.[23] On the other hand the schedule can also be viewed as flat-rated with low earners receiving a reduced (earnings-related) amount so as to avoid adverse incentive effects caused by benefits being higher than earnings.[24] Hence both the Liberals and the Social Democrats can claim that their ideas from the beginning of the 1960s were implemented with the cash benefit reforms in the late 1960s and early 70s. One can then discuss the appropriate rates and as we have seen this was indeed subject to heated discussions.[25] But the fact remains that the schedule can be viewed as both a Beveridge-Liberal and a Bismarckian-Social Democratic one.

Notes

1 The Philadelphia active labour market policy model can be found in Toft (2000). The related recommendations were the 'Employment (Transition from War to Peace) Recommendation' and the 'Public Works (National Planning) Recommendation'. In the same session an 'Income Security Recommendation' was also passed.

2 The Socialist Peoples Party was only founded in 1956 following the Russian invasion of Hungary. It has been called Europe's first Euro-Communist Party.

3 See Danish Government 1962a, 1962b, 1964a, 1964b, 1966, 1968, 1969, 1970.

4 Hornemann Møller bases this on an interview with Kirstein from 1980.

5 For example, the Social Democratic Prime Minister, Viggo Kampmann, who was a trained economist, discusses in Kampmann (1963) macro-economic and incomes policy but does not mention at all a real or potential role of the placement service in this context. The leading mainstream Danish labour economic textbook (Rold Andersen and Kjerkegård 1969) deals with labour market adjustment but does not argue that adjustment policies would make for example incomes policy less important. In this mainstream Danish politics and academics followed their Swedish counterparts in that Rehn's ideas about the substitution of labour market policy for expansionary macro-economic policy and incomes policy were never followed by Swedish policy makers (see Björklund 1982).

6 The official party history states that the initiative came from Bundvad who wished to be relieved of some of his workload (Krag and Andersen 1971, p. 258; The authors J. O. Krag and K. B. Andersen served as Prime Minister and as Minister respectively in several Social Democratic governments). This is plausible in that complex pension legislation was coming up. The establishment of an independent Labour Department may also have played a role, though there is no direct link between department and ministerial administrations. As we have seen, a minister may be responsible for more than one independent department. Finally, although it can not be proved, pressures from trade unions and anticipated troubles relating to the work of the Kirstein Committee most probably played a role. Bundvad, whose career included a lengthy spell as a high school teacher, did not have the close ties to the unions as Dinesen, who also appears to have had a higher standing within the party. The official book on the history of the ministry of labour, written by two civil servants, describes Bundvad as 'a solid and regarded party soldier'. Dinesen, by contrast, is described as a skilled and knowledgeable leader 'whose insights and diligence gave him a central and influential position within the government' (Hartvig Pedersen and Holmqvist-Larsen 1994, pp. 105-6).

7 Thomsen and Jørgensen are the official historiographers of the Association of Unemployment Insurance Funds writing the histories of the association at its 40th respectively 50th anniversary. Even though their works do not live up to the usual academic standards, their presentation on this point seems very plausible.

8 Per Kirstein can possibly be said to belong to this reformist intellectual group within and around the Social Democratic party, though we do not know for sure whether or not he was a party member.

9 Originally Kaj Andresen, a Social Democratic MP was appointed to chair the commission but he withdrew when he became a Minister for Housing in the Social Democratic minority government after the 1964 election. Why Seierup was then appointed is not clear. He was a Social Democrat but certainly no party soldier and proved difficult to control. His loyalty was directed towards genuine reform rather than towards the tactics of the Social Democratic party leadership.

10 More precisely, the task of the Commission was firstly to investigate the possibility of a simplification and enhancement of efficiency in social administration; secondly, to investigate the extent to which it would be possible to adjust social security and services to the modern aims of prevention, rehabilitation, security and well-being; thirdly to consider if a revision of the financing of social security and services would be advisable. Furthermore, it was also stated that the Commission was free to take up and investigate other issues which it felt would be of significant importance for the best possible design of social security and services (Danish Government 1964b).

11 Three research reports were published on the basis of this research but they only arrived in 1970-71 when the first Report from the Commission had been published and the first Reform Commission Bill on the governance of the social services had been passed by parliament.

12 This is not to say that in different circumstances the sickness insurance organisations could not have been reformed and that Denmark could have developed the sort of Sickness Insurance Boards which exists in Sweden. However, at a minimum this would have required that the Social Democrats would have pursued a completely different strategy right from the early 1960s.

13 The deportation rhetoric emerged again in the early 1970s in the context of Danish entry into the European Common Market. Opponents of entry argued that unemployed Danish workers could be forced by the public employment service to search for jobs in and hence face deportation to 'Europe'. (According to the opponents, Denmark did not belong to 'Europe'). Of course this never happened. On the contrary, in the 1990s Danish placement officers had to find ways of curbing young Danes' desire to search for jobs in Greece in the summer whilst bringing their generous unemployment benefit with them. On the other hand, part of the blame for the emergence of this crazy rhetoric has to be put on the Kirstein report with its strong emphasis of internationalisation and Danish entry into the European common market constituting a rationale for the establishment of a Danish 'Employment Service'.

14 The group did not visit Stockholm but did visit the employment office in Helsingborg. They also visited the employment office in Flensborg, but there is no evidence that the German system provided the group with much inspiration.

15 In an annex to the Borreschmidt report it appears that in Denmark 19 bodies under 6 ministries were involved in matters relating to employment policy. Even though in Sweden not all of the functions that were managed by these bodies were integrated in the Employment Service, it constituted nonetheless a much higher degree of fragmentation than in Sweden. The annex was meant to illustrate a problem, and the group

did not propose that all these functions be integrated into a Danish Employment Service.

16 This was part of wider strategy of the Social Democrats during the first years of the bourgeois government trying to discredit the government's intentions regarding cash benefit reform. During those years the Social Democrats several times submitted proposals in parliament for highly inflated and immediate benefit increases which the government of course could not accept. (A Social Democratic government would also not have been able to implement these demands) (see Christensen 1998, pp. 151 and 157, Petersen 1998, p. 281).

17 In the final bill, unemployment insurance provisions appeared as Section III. This section was identical to the Wechselmann Bill proposal, which in turn had been written on the basis of the said technical review. Section I legislated public and Section II private placement provisions. The only difference between the Wechselmann Bill and the proposal of the 'contact group' concerned the composition of a new unemployment insurance tribunal (Ankenævnet for Arbejdsløshedsforsikringen). The Wechselmann report and the contact group suggested that the tribunal be composed of two employer and union representatives along with a neutral chairman. But the government bill changed the composition by including two bureaucrats instead of the second employer and union representatives (Sonne Nørgaard 1997, p. 345).

18 Of course, if income tax and travel to work and other costs are taken into consideration, an 80 per cent earnings replacement ratio can also under certain circumstances be said to provide 'full compensation'.

19 Figures refer to March 1966 and March 1973 and are from the relevant annual reports of the labour directorate (Arbejdsdirektoratet 1967, 1973). The new system followed the new county and local government area divisions, though a few counties and local government districts had more than one office.

20 It is difficult to follow in detail the extent of restructuring of responsibilities in central government during the late 1960s and early 70s. However, Hartvig Pedersen and Holmqvist-Larsen, the official historians of the Ministry of Labour, do not mention any changes in the area of labour market policy (1994 chapter 3).

21 For example, Jørn Henrik Petersen, the well-known social policy scholar, reviewing the proposals found: 'I must admit that I find the arguments for the abolition of the rehabilitation centres 'thin' and have a feeling that particular biases of one kind or the other have had an influence on the proposal. Whilst a lot could be said for the abolition of the sickness organisations, the same is not in my opinion true with respect to the rehabilitation centres' (Petersen 1972, p. 268).

22 The costs of administration are carried by the insurance funds so that there are still some differences in rates of contribution between funds arising from this factor.

23 All earnings-related benefit systems have upper ceilings but they are placed at different levels. For example, the German ceiling is placed much higher up on the earnings structure than the Danish.

24 If low earners received the maximum rate they would have a replacement rate in excess of 100 per cent.

25 As we have seen bourgeois parties thought that 80 per cent would be more appropriate but the Socialist Peoples Party thought that 100 per cent would be the only appropriate rate. The Social Democrats got their way and the system settled on 90 per cent which is the schedule which still exists to day. The bourgeois governments of the 1980s did not change the 90 per cent rate but reduced the real value of the upper ceiling quite dramatically in that for a long period the ceiling was not raised in spite of considerable price and wage increases.

References

Arbejdsdirektoratet (1967), 'Beretning om arbejdsanvisningen og arbejdsløshedsforsikringen m. m. for regnskabsåret 1965-66', *Socialt Tidsskrift*, Afdeling C, vol. 43, pp. C1-C119.

Arbejdsdirektoratet (1973), 'Beretning om arbejdsformidlingen og arbejdsløshedsforsikringen m. m. for regnskabsåret 1972-73', *Socialt Tidsskrift*, Afdeling C, vol. 49, pp. C181-C263.

Björklund, Anders (1982), 'Rehn/Meidners program och den faktiska politiken', Delegationen för arbetsmarknadspolitisk forskning (ed.), *Arbetsmarknadspolitik under debatt*, Liberförlag, Stockholm, pp. 15-34.

Buksti, Jacob A. and H. Sørensen (1971), *Reformen af arbejdsløshedsforsikrings- og arbejdsanvisningslovgivningen 1968-71 med særligt henblik på fagbevægelsens rolle*, Århus University Department of Political Science.

Christensen, Jacob (1998), *Socialpolitiske strategier 1945-1972*, Odense Universitetsforlag, Odense.

Danish Government (1962a), *Administrationsudvalget af 1960. 1. Betænkning*, Betænkning nr. 301, Copenhagen.

Danish Government (1962b), *Administrationsudvalget af 1960. 2. Betænkning*. Administrationen af arbejds- og sociallovgivningen, Betænkning nr. 320, Copenhagen.

Danish Government (1964a), *Den danske arbejdsanvisnings struktur, funktioner og virkemidler*, Betænkning nr. 345 (Kirstein report), Copenhagen.

Danish Government (1964b), *Betænkning over forslag til folketingsbeslutning om forberedelse af en socialreform*, Annex 1 in Danish Government 1969, (The Social Reform Commission mission statement), Copenhagen.

Danish Government (1966), *Foreløbig betænkning afgivet den 19. oktober 1966 af Udvalget af 1964 om arbejdsløshedsforsikringen*, Folketingstidende, Tillæg A: Forelagte Lovforslag, 1966-67: Column 1211-1226, (First, preliminary, Wechselmann report), Copenhagen.

Danish Government (1968), *Betænkning vedrørende spørgsmål i forbindelse med de offentlige arbejdsanvisningskontorers overtagelse pr. 1. april 1968 af de funktioner, der i henhold til lov om arbejdsanvisning og arbejdsløshedsforsikring m. v. påhviler de anerkendte arbejdsløshedskasser med hensyn til kontrol med og anvisning af arbejde til ledige medlemmer*, Folketingstidende, Tillæg A: Fremsatte Lovforslag, 1967-68: Column 2211-2292. (Borreschmidt report), Copenhagen.

Danish Government (1969), *Socialreformkommissionens 1. betænkning. Det sociale tryghedssystem. Struktur og dagpenge*, Betænkning nr. 543 (First report from the Social Reform Commission), Copenhagen.

Danish Government (1970, *Forslag om revision af arbejdsløshedsforsikringen. Afsluttende betænkning, afgivet af det af arbejdsministeriet den 9. april 1964 nedsatte udvalg*, Betænkning nr. 551 (Final Wechselmann report), Copenhagen.

Elm Larsen, Jørgen and Fritz von Nordheim Nielsen (1985), 'Det danske dagpengesystems storhed og fald', in Henning Jørgensen and Jens Chr. Tonboe (eds), *Fagbevægelse, stat og kommuner*, Aalborg Universitetsforlag, Ålborg, pp. 38-76.

Esping-Andersen, Gösta (1990), *The Three Worlds of Welfare Capitalism*, Polity Press, Cambridge and Oxford.

Folketingsårbog 1967-68.

Folketingsårbog 1969-70.

Grønnegård Christensen, Jørgen (1993), *Efter almindelige administrative principper: Efterkrigstidens centraladministration*, Århus University Department of Political Science.

Hartvig Pedersen, Jesper and Niels Henrik Holmqvist-Larsen (1994), *Arbejdsministeriet. Et rids af fortid, opgaver og organisation*, Arbejdsministeriet, Copenhagen.

Hedborg, Anna and Rudolf Meidner (1984a), *Folkhemsmodellen*, Rabén & Sjögren. Stockholm. German version, (1984b), *Modell Schweden. Erfahrungen einer Wohlfahrtsgesellschaft*, Campus Verlag, Frankfurt/New York.

Hornemann Møller, Iver (1981), *Klassekamp og sociallovgivning 1850-1970*, Socialistiske Økonomers Forlag, Copenhagen.

Hornemann Møller, Iver (1986), *'Arbejderflertallet' og 70'ernes socialreform*, Socialistiske Økonomers Forlag, Copenhagen.

Janoski, Thomas (1996), 'Explaining state intervention to prevent unemployment: The impact of institutions on active labour market policy expenditures in 18 countries', in Günther Schmid, Jacqueline O'Reilly and Klaus Schömann (eds), *International Handbook of Labour Market Policy and Evaluation*, Edward Elgar, Cheltenham, pp. 697-724.

Jørgensen, Hans (1997), *50 års samvirke. 1947-1997*, Arbejdsløshedskassernes Samvirke, Copenhagen.

Kampmann, Viggo (1963), 'Indkomstpolitik og helhedsløsning' *Socialt Tidsskrift*, vol. 39, pp. 205-16.

Kirstein, Per (1958), 'Nogle betragtninger vedrørende dansk beskæftigelsespolitik siden 1945', in Nationaløkonomisk Forening (ed.), *Festskrift til Frederik Zeuthen*, Copenhagen, pp. 177-93.

Krag, Jens Otto and Knud Børge Andersen (1971), *Kamp og Fornyelse. Socialdemokratiets indsats i dansk politik. 1955-1971*, Fremad, Copenhagen.

Kuhlmann, Stig (1974), *Danske arbejdsmarkedsforhold*, Arbejdsministeriet, Copenhagen.

OECD (1974), 'Danish Labour. The need for an Active Manpower Policy', *The OECD Observer*, vol. 12, no. 69, pp. 5-7.

Petersen, Jørn Henrik (1972), 'Socialreformkommissionens 2. Delbetænkning. Indhold og vurdering', *Socialt Tidsskrift*, vol. 48, pp. 215-30 and 265-83.

Petersen, Klaus (1998), *Legitimität und Krise. Die politische Geschichte des dänischen Wohlfahrtsstaates 1945-1973*, Verlag Arno Spitz, Berlin.

Rold Andersen, Bent and Else Marie Kjerkegård (1969), *Holdepunkter i arbejdsmarkedspolitikken*, Gads Forlag, Copenhagen.

Rold Andersen, Bent (1973), *Grundprincipper i Socialpolitikken*, Nyt Socialt Bibliotek, Det Danske Forlag, Albertslund.

Scharpf, Fritz W. (1987), *Sozialdemokratische Krisenpolitik in Europa*, Campus Verlag, Frankfurt/New York (English translation 1991, Crisis and Choice in European Social Democracy, Cornell University Press, Ithaca).

Socialt Tidsskrift (1963), 'Særnummer om arbejdsformidlingen', *Socialt Tidsskrift*, vol. 39, no. 3-4, pp. 65-116.

Sonne Nørgaard, Asbjørn (1997), *The Politics of Institutional Control: Corporatism in Danish Occupational Safety and Health Regulation & Unemployment Insurance, 1870-1995*, Politicas PhD series, Århus University Department of Political Science.

Toft, Christian (1993), 'Social security reform in unitary Britain', University of Wales, SABE Research Paper, 93/32.

Toft, Christian (1995), 'State action, trade unions and voluntary unemployment insurance in Great Britain, Germany, and Scandinavia, 1900-1934', *European Economic Review*, vol. 39, pp. 565-74.

Toft, Christian (2000), 'Gösta Rehn and the Philadelphia model of active labour market policy. A critical assessment', Mimeo, Max Planck Institute for the Study of Societies, Cologne.

Thomsen, Paul (1987), *40 års samvirke. 1947-1987*, Arbejdsløshedskassernes Samvirke, Copenhagen.

Valbak, Åge (1988), 'Idé og virkelighed – revalideringsarbejdets udvikling og vilkår i tiden efter bistandsloven' in Hans Ole Jönsson and Kirsten Lange (eds), *Revalidering – igen*, Nørhaven A/S, Viborg, pp. 38-51.

Westergård, Kaj (1971), *Socialreformundersøgelserne Bind III: De sociale ydelser*, Teknisk Forlag, Copenhagen.

PART 4
European Perspectives

Chapter 11

Rehn-Meidner and Austro-Keynesianism: Two Post-Keynesian Roads to High Employment[1]

Markus Marterbauer

Introduction

For decades full employment was given priority in economic and social policy in Austria and Sweden. Both countries were relatively successful in this respect. In Austria, full employment was able to be maintained until the beginning of the 1980s. Its 1999 unemployment rate of 4¼ per cent of the total labour force is still one of the lowest in the European Union. The employment rate (employed persons in relation to the population aged between 15 and 64) is about 70 per cent, nearly ten percentage points above the EU average. Youth unemployment is the lowest in Europe (4 per cent) and long-term unemployment is about a quarter of total unemployment. This rather bright picture of the Austrian labour markets is overshadowed, however, by continually rising unemployment in the 1990s. Furthermore, there is considerable hidden unemployment (particularly among those people over the age of 55 who are in early retirement schemes). The female employment rate is rather low and precarious employment is increasing. In Austria, there is little tradition of active labour-market policy.

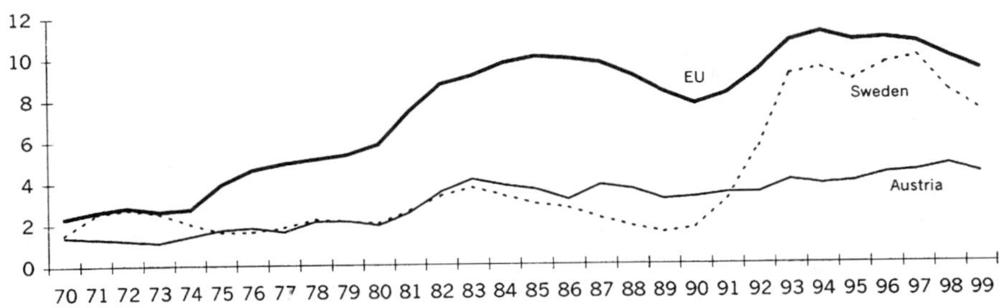

Sources: OECD, WIFO.

Figure 11.1 Unemployment rate. Per cent of total labour force

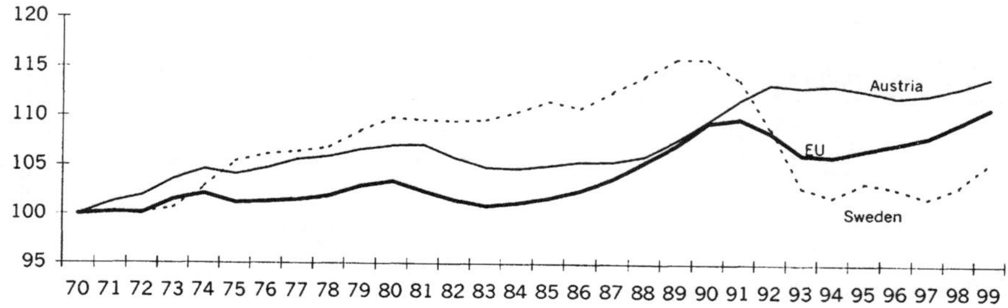

Sources: OECD, WIFO.

Figure 11.2 Civilian employment. 1970 = 100

Sweden was able to maintain full employment until 1990. In the deep recession between 1991 and 1993, when real GDP shrank by 5 per cent, unemployment increased dramatically to a level of about 10 per cent. The economic upswing starting in 1998, however, has lead to a considerable reduction in the rate of unemployment (7¼ per cent in 1999). Among the European economies, Sweden has continuingly shown one of the highest labour-market participation rates; in 1990, the total labour force amounted to 81 per cent of the working age population. During the recession this level decreased to 70 per cent. Nevertheless, women still had a high participation rate and not just in the public-sector area. Furthermore, high employment rates in the public sector (more than one-quarter of total employment) resulted in Sweden having the highest private-sector employment (of the 15 to 64 year old population) of all European countries. The comprehensive welfare state (e.g. full coverage for day-care centres and kindergartens) encouraged high participation rates, especially for women, in the private as well as in the public sector. In the 1980s, up to 56 per cent of the working age population was employed in the private sector (26 per cent in the public sector), whereas the EU average was 50 per cent (11 per cent in the public sector).

This relatively favourable outcome concerning labour market data in both countries is the result of a distinct policy strategy over the last few decades which gave priority to full employment. This policy strategy could be characterised as following the post-Keynesian tradition – referred to as 'Austro-Keynesianism' (Arestis 1986) and the 'Rehn-Meidner Model' (Tichy 1984). This article compares the main aspects of macroeconomic policy and their connection to employment developments between the two models.

In both countries, there has been a basic theoretical assumption resulting from empirical experience: the existing capitalist economies based on private ownership and free markets are essentially unstable. The instability of a free market economy is mainly determined by the instability of private investment, which is attributable to volatile business expectations. As employment and unemployment are mainly the result of macroeconomic developments (and social trends), labour markets are directly influenced by macroeconomic instabilitites. Therefore, a deep scepticism existed towards a theoretical position which sees full employment as the automatic outcome of well-functioning, unregulated factor and goods markets. This understanding led to the development of specific institutional and political frameworks for public policy intervention in favour of stabilising expectations and confidence of investors and consumers.

The institutional and political environment of the two economies have many points of similarity. The social democratic parties have been hegemonic for a long time. In Sweden, the Socialdemokratiska Arbetarepartiet (SAP) has been in power since 1932 (with three short breaks in 1936, between 1976 and 1982, and between 1991 and 1994, when bourgeois governments were in office). In Austria, the Socialistische Partei Österreichs (SPÖ) – after 1991 known as the Sozialdemokratische Partei – has been a member of each government since 1945 (except currently and 1966-1970) and has held the office of chancellor ever since 1970. In both countries, comprehensive welfare states which guarantee social security for the whole labour force were established after World War II, and public expenditure in relation to GDP is above the OECD average. The core groups of interest representation (trade unions and employers' organisations) have high organisation rates and rather centralised forms of organisational structure. The corporatist regime allows wage policy to be a macroeconomic policy variable, although incomes policy with state intervention in the wage negotiations was not established either in Sweden or in Austria. Both countries are small, open economies with high export quotas (Sweden 40 per cent of GDP, Austria 41 per cent), where the competitiveness of the export industry on world markets is an important determinant of macroeconomic development.

The main purpose of the Austro-Keynesian model and the Rehn-Meidner model was to combine full employment with price stability. Austrian economic policy of the 1970s and 80s was a pragmatic concept of 'muddling through' the instabilites of the world economy – it was only declared to be 'a model' ex post (Seidel 1982). It combined Keynesian elements – especially referring to fundamental Keynesian notions such as uncertainty and volatility of expectations – with Austrian specifica: corporatist institutions and stable currency policy. The Swedish model – named after the two leading labour union economists, Gösta Rehn and Rudolf Meidner – was initially (ex ante) designed for an overheated economy in the postwar period (Meidner, Rehn 1953). It was therefore not 'Keynesian' with respect to its focussing on specific problems. The Rehn-Meidner model contains a restrictive general fiscal and monetary policy and expansionary selective instruments. Solidarity wage policy with formidable goals concerning income distribution, as well as active labour market policy, have played an important role in this concept. Despite the shared full-employment/price-stability purpose, the strategies of macroeconomic policy in Austria and Sweden have been quite different.

The core elements of Austro-Keynesianism – which Tichy (1984) called an

Table 11.1 Macroeconomic development

	1970/1979			1980/1989			1990/1999			1999		
	Austria	Sweden	EU	Austria	Sweden	EU	Austria	Sweden	EU	Austria	Sweden	EU
				Annual percentage changes								
Gross Domestic Product	+4.0	+2.4	+3.3	+2.1	+2.0	+2.2	+2.2	+1.3	+1.8	+2.2	+4.0	+1.9
Inflation	+6.1	+8.6	+9.7	+3.8	+7.9	+7.3	+2.4	+3.5	+3.3	+0.5	+0.3	+1.3
				As a percentage of GDP								
Gross fixed capital formation	25.1	21.1	23.2	22.2	19.4	20.5	23.5	15.9	19.4	24.3	15.3	18.8
General government financial balance	-0.6	+2.6	-2.0	-3.1	-1.6	-4.1	-3.2	-3.6	-3.8	-2.1	+1.9	-1.0
				Per cent of total labour force								
Unemployment rate	1.6	2.1	3.7	3.3	2.6	8.8	4.0	7.3	9.8	4.3	7.3	9.3

Sources: OECD. WIFO.

Table 11.2 The labour market in 1998

	Employment (per cent of employment)		Employment rate (per cent of working-age population)				Unemployment rate (per cent of labour force)				
	part time	temporary	total full-time equivalent	total	male	female	total	male	female	long-term	youth[1]
Austria	15.8	7.8	65.0	70.1	80.1	60.1	4.7	3.9	5.6	1.4	3.8
Sweden	23.9	12.9	62.8	70.3	73.2	67.2	8.3	8.6	8.0	3.1	7.5
EU	17.4	12.8	55.7	61.1	71.1	51.2	10.0	8.6	11.8	4.9	9.3

[1] Per cent of working age population

Source: European Commission, Employment in Europe, 1999.

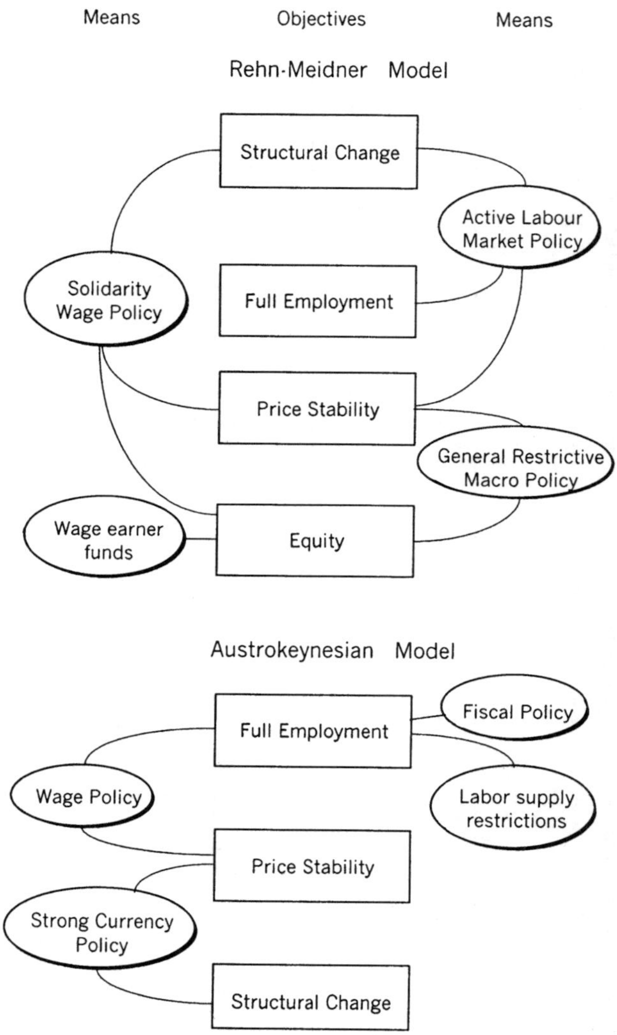

Figure 11.3 Rehn-Meidner Model and Austro-Keynesian Model

'... unconventional assignment of instruments to goals' – have been: a demand-oriented fiscal policy to stabilise the business cycle and boost growth and employment; a currency policy stabilising the exchange rate of the Austrian schilling to the German mark to fight inflation, stabilise expectations and implement transformation pressure on the economy; and a macroeconomically-oriented wage policy by the social partners to survey the wage-price spiral and secure the competitiveness of the economy. The isolated expansionary and anticyclically-oriented fiscal policy of Austro-Keynesianism has been handled more cautiously in the 1980s and, especially, the 1990s due to international economic developments and European regulations. Nevertheless, the strong-currency policy and the macro-economically-oriented incomes policy have been maintained.

In Sweden, on the other hand, solidarity wage policy has been the most important tool not only of redistribution, but also of structural adjustment. Fiscal and monetary policy have not been able to fully realise – in accordance with the Rehn-Meidner model – their restrictive stance since the 1970s. They have mainly been determined by fluctuations in the business cycle or in the balance of payments development.

Several post-Keynesian elements can be discerned in the macroeconomic strategies of both Sweden and Austria. First, there is the strategic role of investment for macroeconomic development. In Austria, the encouragement of private investment has always been seen as an important role of economic policy. Several instruments have been employed to stabilise the expectations of investors. In Sweden, the wage-earner funds debate could be interpreted as an – albeit failed – attempt to advance Keynesian 'socialisation of investment'. Second, there is the attempt to stabilise aggregate demand by fiscal policy. This has been an explicit purpose of Austrian economic policy. The Rehn-Meidner model favoured restrictive fiscal policy, but the size of the public sector in both countries has led to high elasticity of the budget and to economic growth. Third, we come to the importance of incomes policy. Although incomes policy has not been implemented in a traditional post-Keynesian tripartite way in either Sweden or Austria, wage policy has fulfilled important tasks at a macroeconomic level. Fourth, we have the attempts of both countries to handle the balance of payments restrictions, even if implemented with extremely different instruments.

The rise and decline of the Swedish model

Solidarity wage policy – equality and transformation

The Swedish system of centralised wage bargaining was introduced in the mid-fifties and became more and more elaborate in the 1960s. It was based on two factors: the extremely high degree of organisation of the labour market parties (the blue-collar trade union Landsorganisationen – LO – and the entrepreneurs' organisation Svenska arbetsgivareföreningen – SAF) and the 1938 'Saltsjöbaden Agreement', which stated that labour market conflicts should be resolved through negotiated agreements and not by legislation. In contrast to the Austrian model of wage policy and the Keynesian notions on incomes policy, wage policy in the Rehn-Meidner model has not been an instrument of anti-inflationary policy. It argues (Meidner, Rehn 1953; Erixon 1994) that inflation in an overheated economy calls for restrictive macroeconomic policy. Instrumentalising incomes policy would be ineffective, a threat to tariff autonomy and a source of conflict within the trade unions. Wage policy in Sweden has, however, primarily been seen as an instrument of income equalisation – 'equal pay for equal work' – and structural transformation. Wage differences should reflect skill and training but not the profitability of the firms.

Solidarity wage policy in reality was designed to reduce wage differentials between different sectors and regions of the economy, and between men and women. It has been criticised as promoting 'equal pay for every type of work'. A detailed system of constantly lifting the lowest contractual wages has led to a very even distribution of wages. It has also exerted a strong squeeze on profits and productivity pressure on the least productive sectors. Many firms – e.g. the textile industry – were driven out of existence. On the other hand, centralised wage policy has favoured the high-productivity industries, making huge profits. Wage drift has been a continuous problem under centralised bargaining. It accounts for about half the total post-war wage increases in Sweden. The importance of central agreements is therefore somewhat overstated in economic literature.

During the period of fixed exchange rate, in the context of a Bretton-Woods system, wage policy was also implicitly oriented towards competitiveness. The 'Scandinavian model of inflation' in its normative interpretation defined a 'room' for wage increases – the sum of labour productivity growth in the tradables sector and inflation on the world markets. Incomes policy has been ensuring that the improvement in Sweden's competitiveness was not eliminated immediately by the strength of high wage claims after the devaluation of 1982.

The year 1983 was a turning point for the wage negotiation system and the model as a whole. The employers' organisations began to leave corporatist institutions (e.g. in manpower administration, in safety and health matters and in government commissions of various kinds) and central wage negotiations. They proposed a decentralised system of sector and enterprise level negotiations allowing for increasing wage differentials between individuals. With the end of centralised wage negotiations and a corporatist system of economic and social policy, Sweden lost an important tool of policy making. The effects have been disastrous. In the boom period of the second half of the 1980s, huge nominal wage increases in the dried-up labour markets, leap-frogging and a high wage drift contributed considerably to the acceleration of inflation rates. Between 1991 and 1993, the government intervened in the bargaining process and gave a mediation commission (the

'Rehnberg Commission') a mandate to bring down wage inflation. Since then, the employers' organisation SAF has not taken part in central wage bargaining. Collective wage bargaining on a national level has come to an end.

Active labour market policy – still 'best practice' in Europe

In the Rehn-Meidner model, active labour-market policy is in charge of organising the structural, educational and regional adaptability and mobility of the work force. Labour market policy in the Swedish context has three important tasks. First, a highly efficient labour market service intensifies and speeds up the placement process of the unemployed. Sweden shows a very decentralised, personal and budget-intensive organisation of the labour market service. Second, there is an active qualification and education policy, seen as a structural measure, which facilitates adaptability of the unemployed in accordance with labour demand developments. Third, work-provision measures, by means of wage subsidies or public works programmes, have anticyclical tasks, on the one hand, and include handicapped people in the 'work line' of the Swedish model, on the other hand.

Evaluations of labour market policies (Björklund 1993, Calmfors 1994) have shown positive ratings for placement efforts concerning fast and flexible reactions to local labour market challenges. Labour market training has a favourable influence on the matching process, on effective labour supply, productivity, and the welfare of the unemployed. Recent empirical studies (Ackum Agell 1995, Ackum Agell et al. 1995) have raised some doubt about positive income and employment effects for participants in labour market training.

Active labour market policy – constantly covering 2 to 3 per cent of the workforce – has been the main determinant of the Swedish success in providing a flexible effective labour supply in a dynamic economic environment. But labour market training has also shown to be an inefficient instrument in combatting cyclical unemployment in the 1990s. Labour market policy measures were extended to 5 per cent of the workforce, which resulted in a shift towards cheap, but less efficient demand-oriented measures (public work programs). Huge public efforts in retraining and employing people, however, have had positive effects in terms of prohibiting the emergence of long-term unemployment and providing an effective labour supply (with an anti-inflationary impact) in the upswing.

Fiscal policy – a by-product of cyclical instability?

Fiscal policy in the Rehn-Meidner model has been part of a restrictive economic policy, fulfilling mainly anti-inflationary tasks. The contractive orientation had led to considerable public surpluses and high tax rates during the 'golden age' of the Swedish model in the 1950s and 60s. The expenditure side of the public budgets has been oriented mainly towards providing high quality and evenly distributed public services.

However, the development of fiscal policy during the last decades has been showing a very high cyclical dependency and often was too expansionary from a Rehn-Meidner perspective. High tax and expenditure rates result in a public budgets being highly sensitive to variations in the business cycle. During cyclical upswings and booms, the Swedish budget has shown considerable surpluses (about 6 per cent of GDP in 1989, when the economy was considerably overheated), whereas in deep recessions public deficits have tended to explode. Net lending of the public sector deteriorated in the period of economic crisis between 1976 and 1982 by 12 per cent of GDP and in the recession 1991 to 1993 by 15 per cent of GDP. Public budgets, on the one hand, stabilise the business cycle in Sweden but, on the other hand, the alarming proportions of the budget deficits make discretionary measures for budget consolidation necessary.

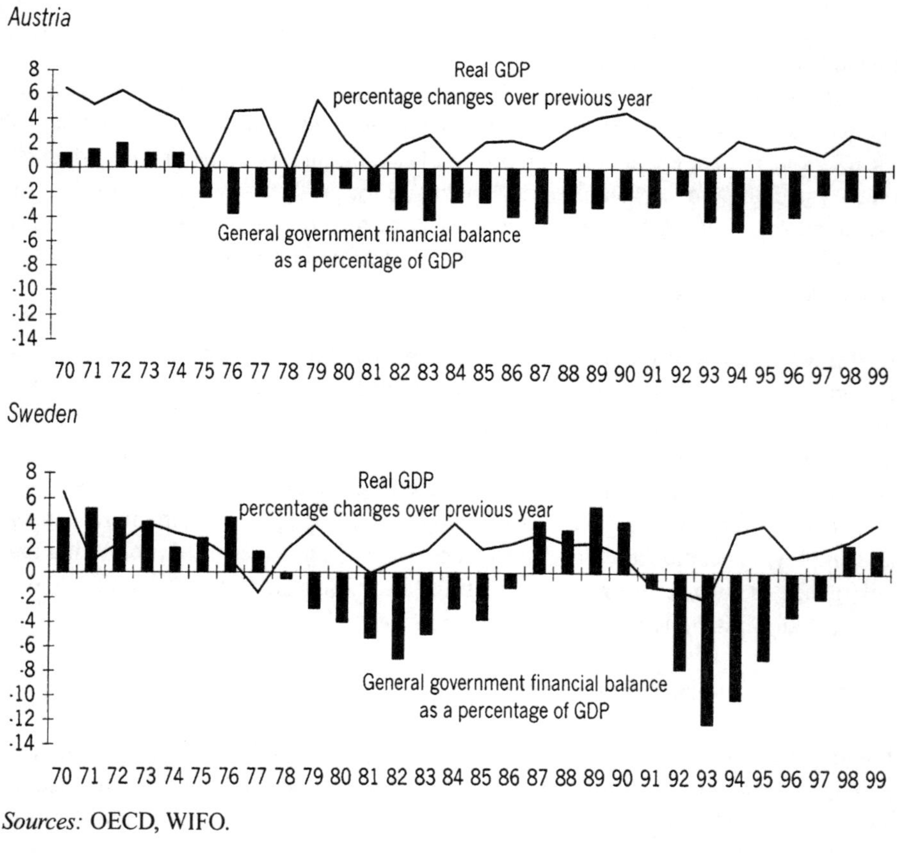

Sources: OECD, WIFO.

Figure 11.4 Real GDP growth and general government financial balance

Fiscal policy was quite expansionary in the second half of the 1970s, when the conservative government was unable to cope with the problems of international economic turmoil. In the second half of the 1980s, with an overheated economy and inflation pressures, political constraints meant fiscal policy was not able to take the needed restrictive stance. It was only the new social democratic government in 1994 which shifted to restrictive fiscal policy, resulting in public budget surpluses in 1998 and 1999.

A failed attempt to socialise investment

'Wage-earner funds' (löntagarfonder) were not part of the Rehn-Meidner model. The concept, however, can be interpreted in a post-Keynesian way. The discussion started in the mid-seventies. The solidarity wage policy of LO had by then led to huge profits in the big firms and thus favoured undesirable wealth concentration, wage drift and leap-frogging between the sector unions. An LO working group, led by Rudolf Meidner, proposed the introduction of collective capital ownership. Part of the share capital of the firms – dependent on the amount of profits – should be transferred by obligatory new emissions from the owners to funds, which were dominated by the employees. After long discussions, wage-earner funds were implemented in 1984, but the construction of the model did not have very much in common with the original proposals. Nevertheless, Arestis (1986) characterised the socialisation of investment by the introduction of wage-earner funds as being of '...paramount importance and ... [constituting] ... the backbone of post-Keynesian economic policies... [in Sweden]'. The funds then were financed by a profit tax and contributions by employees. They were part of the capital-based line of the pension system (ATP). The funds invested in the shares of Swedish firms, but they had an upper threshold for investment (8 per cent of the total shares). In 1990 the wage-earner funds were liquidated and the accumulated capital was shifted into new funds for research.

Although the concept of wage-earner funds in theory fitted quite well into the post-Keynesian Swedish model, in practical policy it posed considerable problems. Serious controversies within the labour movement and between labour and capital occurred. Centralised bargaining was made more difficult because anti-corporatist elements in business were strengthened.

Monetary policy without direction

Exchange rate policy in Sweden was often instrumentalised to ease the macro-economic pressure when the burden from wage increases was too high and the international competitiveness of export industries was endangered. The Swedish krona has been undergoing devaluation since the end of the Bretton-Woods system (especially in the periods 1976-1982 and 1992-1995) and has lost more than 70 per cent in nominal terms (and some 45 per cent in real terms) versus the Austrian schilling.

In 1982, the incoming Swedish social democratic government depreciated the krona by 16 per cent, which was the starting point of macroeconomic consolidation. Real-wage adaptability proved to be high in this period as the trade unions – closely linked politically to the government – allowed nominal wage moderation to result in downward real-wage adjustment (until 1985). Expansionary monetary policy was successful until 1986. The export-led recovery of economic growth resulted in a return to full employment. However, the devaluation proved to be far too great, especially in combination with a fiscal policy not sufficiently restrictive to meet the requirements of the Rehn-Meidner model. The overheating of the economy started in the export sector.

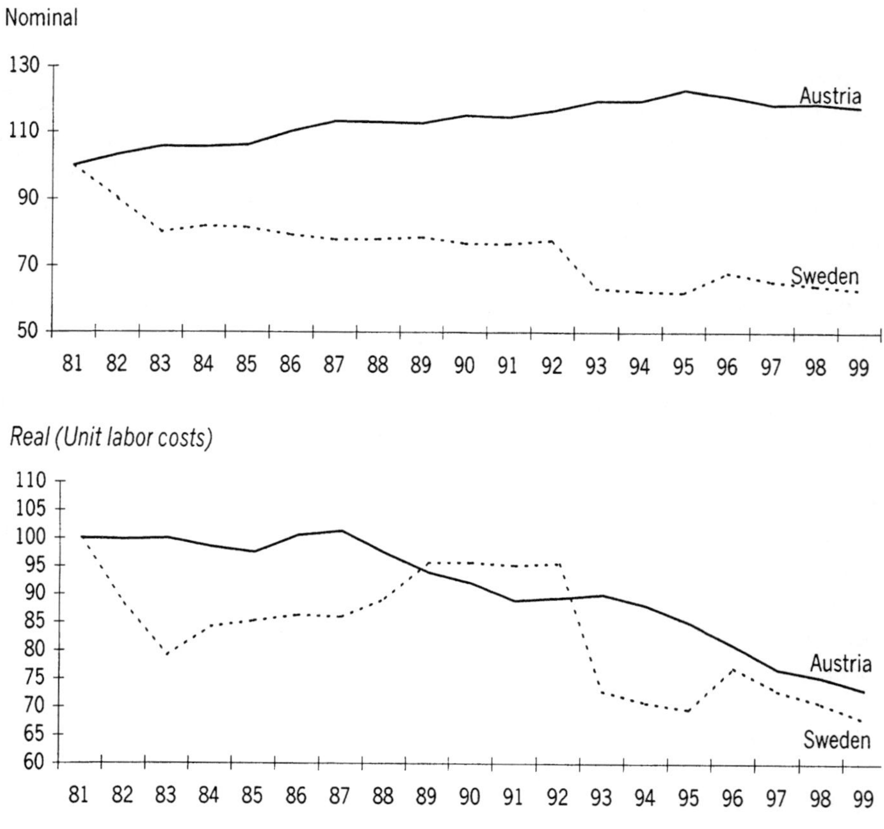

Source: IMF.

Figure 11.5 Effective exchange rates. 1981 = 100

One further element of monetary policy contributed essentially to the overheating. A miscarried deregulation of the credit markets, starting in 1985, led to the emergence of a speculative bubble in financial and real estate markets. The abandoning of credit ceilings was reinforced by the existing possibilities for tax-deductions for interest expenditure. A negative real interest rate, after taxes, led to a fast expansion of private sector indebtedness, a boom on real estate and capital markets, and to a huge private demand expansion in general, accompanied by rising inflation. Again, due to political constraints, fiscal policy was not able to implement the necessary restrictive stance. A public surplus of 4 per cent of GDP and the unstable political situation of a minority government did not allow a tighter budgetary policy. Monetary policy failed to increase interest rates and to initiate a sufficient appreciation of the currency. The burst of the speculative bubbles, connected with balance sheet adjustments of firms and households and the ever-deteriorating competitiveness of the export industry, resulted in the deepest recession since the early thirties. The government tried to renew confidence in the Swedish krona by linking it to the ECU in 1991. This policy failed, however, and a currency crisis in autumn 1992 resulted in Sweden abandoning the fixed exchange rate system. Within one year, the Swedish krona depreciated by 25 per cent and was at the mercy of the waves of international currency speculation, along with high long-term interest rates in real and nominal terms (see Lindbeck 1992).

Austro-Keynesianism – macro-economic policy in favour of full employment

Expansionary fiscal policy stabilising aggregate demand

In Austria, demand management has been seen as having two important tasks in stabilising the business cycle: on the one hand, it has been used to mitigate cyclical fluctuations of the economy from a short-term perspective, and, on the other, as a long-term instrument for stabilising business expectations and fostering investment and growth.

From a short-term cyclical perspective, the most important stabilising factors stem from the built-in flexiblity of Austria's federal budget and the comprehensive welfare state. Relatively high tax and high contribution rates to the social security system, as well as extensive social security outlays – total receipts of the public sector amounted to 51 per cent in 1999, total expenditure to 53 per cent – work as automatic stabilisers, which ensure significant anti-cyclical effects. In addition, during the recessions of 1975, 1978 and 1981 there was discretionary fiscal action concerning infrastructure investment, as well as other public outlays such as subsidies to nationalised and other industries, combined with labour hoarding in the nationalised industries.

Encouraging private investment has – in a Keynesian tradition (Smithin 1996,

p. 57) – always been seen as a crucial task of economic policy in Austria. One important instrument has been demand management, as a steady rise in effective demand is able to stabilise investors' expectations, leading to higher levels of investment. Furthermore, an extensive system of tax incentives and subsidies, such as accelerated depreciation, tax credits, low-interest loans and export guarantees, has been instrumentalised for strengthening private investment and exports. The Austrian investment quota stands at 24 per cent of GDP, considerably higher than the EU average (18 per cent) or the Swedish quota (15 per cent).

The attempts of economic policy to stabilise expectations and therefore economic development led, in contrast to other European countries (including Germany) and the US, to a rather low variability of output, private consumption and investment (Tichy 1986, Hahn and Walterskirchen 1992). Compared to Germany, or especially Sweden, recessions were less severe in Austria. Better performance in recessions is the most important characteristic of Austrian macroeconomic development; resulting in lower employment losses and unemployment increases. An important part of current, relatively low unemployment in Austria can therefore be traced back to the successful prevention of unemployment hikes in the era of international economic turmoil – especially in the 1970s. In spite of the active and expansionary fiscal policy in the 1970s, total net lending of the Austrian public sector has been lower than the EU average. While Austrian public expenditure has been spent on stabilising business cycles and on enhancing economic growth, other countries have had to pay for rising unemployment.

After the political shift to conservative governments in the US, the UK and Germany, however, the implementation of monetaristic and supply-side oriented

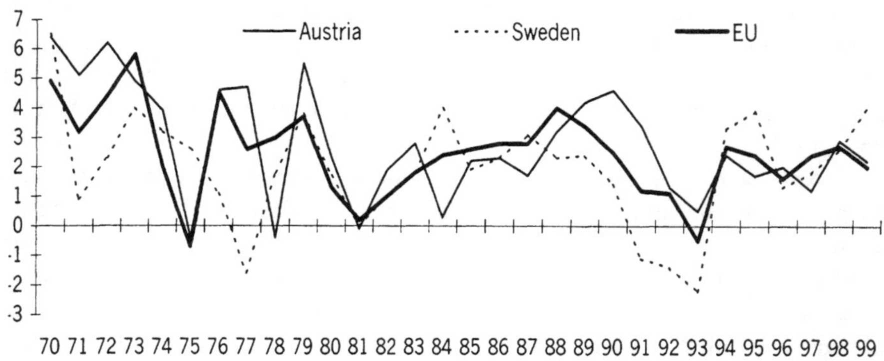

Source: OECD, WIFO.

Figure 11.6 Real GDP. Percentage changes over previous year

economic policy in Europe led to a steady lack of effective demand, as well as to rising unemployment rates all over the industrialised countries. This also had consequences for Austria as the openness of the economy allowed no uncoupling from the international trends. Fiscal policy passed over to a restrictive stance in 1983, although unemployment was rising in that period. Due to the importance of the automatic stabilisers, however, fiscal policy still played its part in softening recessions, as for instance in 1993. In 1996 and 1997 the Maastricht criteria for the entering into European Monetary Union made necessary an extensive consolidation package, with some negative effects on aggregate demand and employment (Marterbauer and Walterskirchen 1999). Budget consolidation has been remaining the most troublesome element of economic policy in the years afterwards.

Strong-currency policy stabilising expectations

The Austrian schilling has been pegged to the German mark since the mid-seventies. That means that Austria has never used the exchange rate instrument for short run employment purposes. This fact seems – at least in its isolated form – not to be very Keynesian. Hard-currency policy was, however – taking into account the conditions of a small open economy – rather adopted as a tool for stabilising business expectations and reaching price stability. It therefore could be characterised as reducing uncertainty.

Hard-currency policy in Austria, suggested by the trade unions, was supported by the social partners, both industry and labour. Stable exchange rates have stabilised the expectations of the exporters and have, in the long run, led to closer trade relations with the main trading partner – the share of exports to Germany from the total exports of goods amounts to about one third. Effective exchange-rate appreciation has led to losses in the export industry's competitiveness in the short run. However, in the long run, this strategy has promoted the restructuring process of the economy and, as a consequence, increases in labour productivity in the highly exposed manufacturing sector have been exceptionally high compared to the main OECD trading partners. In terms of promoting the restructuring process and of strengthening productivity growth, Austria's strong currency policy has the same effects that wage policy was supposed to have under Rehn-Meidner. Although the fixed exchange rate has led to lower nominal wage increases, due to the necessity of maintaining the competitiveness of the export industry, real wage increases were not affected.

By stabilising the expectations of exporters and investors, the Austrian exchange rate policy has therefore been another instrument which has given economic policy a long-term perspective. It has also stabilised the expectations of capital markets, a fact which became more and more important when capital market integration was intensifying in the 1980s and 90s. With a credible exchange rate link, Austria never faced harmful speculation against the schilling and therefore enjoyed low long-term nominal interest rates, in comparison to other European countries, such as Sweden. However, the decision to keep the schilling-DM rate fixed has, under the conditions of liberalised capital markets, dissolved the room of manoeuverability for autonomous monetary policy: Austrian monetary policy has been more or less entirely determined by the German Bundesbank. This was particularly painful when the Bundesbank – especially between 1991 and 1995 – favoured high interest rates for fighting inflation without any regard for growth or effects on employment.

Trade unions have always supported a strong-currency policy and promoted it by a moderate nominal wage policy. That was especially apparent as long as they could rely on fiscal policy securing full employment, but even afterwards there has been no doubt about this particular orientation.

Macroeconomically-oriented incomes policy in the system of economic and social partnership

The third and most important cornerstone of Austro-Keynesianism is the corporatist model of incomes policy. Based on economic and social partnership, incomes policy has been the most essential factor in making strong-currency policy feasible and keeping unemployment low (Walterskirchen 1997). The social partnership system is commonly seen to have brought prosperity and social stability to the country (Guger 1992).

The scope of Austrian economic and social partnership is much wider, however, than a post-Keynesian style institution of wage bargaining would suggest. It is a system of voluntary and informal, yet firmly institutionalised, cooperation between labour, business and the government which is involved in all important aspects of economic and social policy. The institutional core of the partnership is formed by the Council of Workers' Chambers, the Federal Chamber of Commerce and the Presidential Conference of Chambers of Agriculture, each of them based on compulsory membership, as well as the Trade Union Federation, which has a voluntary membership – yet represents some 45 per cent of Austrian employees. The core of the system is not the formal institutions, but rather the informal meetings which create a climate of consensus and which harmonise the expectations of those actively involved.

Incomes policy is not a short-term manoeuvre to cope with accelerating inflation, as in other countries; it has a long-term and macroeconomic perspective. There is no formal national wage round or official wage guideline. Wage negotiations take place at the branch level, but are informally coordinated. Wage increases are remarkably uniform, although they leave room for wage-drift at company level. This means that in industries with high productivity growth and strong unions the effective wage increases are higher than in branches with low productivity and weak unions. In fact, Austria has relatively high interindustrial wage differentials. The Austrian experience shows that large wage differentials – which are often seen as instrumental for labour market flexibility and productivity growth in the international discussion – have rather hampered the process of structural adjustment by keeping labour and capital too long in marginal production and impeding the process of reallocation (Guger 1998).

Austrian wage policy has, in general, been macroeconomically-oriented for a long time. There is an implicit consensus between the social partners, as far as distributional stability between labour and capital is concerned, that wage growth is supposed to compensate for inflation and long-run productivity increases. But wage policy was also explicitly dedicated to counter-cyclical orientations (in the 1960s), to current-account considerations (in the 1970s), to promoting the restructuring process in the nationalised industries (in the 1980s) and to compensating for exchange rate appreciation (in the 1980s and 90s). Wage policy has always taken the development of the labour market into consideration. In the last two decades, real wage growth has therefore fallen significantly behind the increase in productivity.

Labour supply regulation and public sector employment

Labour supply policy has always played an important role in Austria. It is widely acknowledged that labour supply developments are of considerable importance for employment and unemployment patterns. One of the characteristics of the Austrian labour market is a strong labour force reaction towards employment changes. Early retirement policies were implemented in the 1980s in the form of easing conditions for receiving disability pensions and 'special allowances' for certain groups of the older unemployed. In particular, employers and trade unions have been making such arrangements in decaying firms. This policy was successful in lowering unemployment among older adults and in allowing for smooth labour force adaptation in crisis branches – e.g. the nationalised steel industry in the 1980s. But this use of early retirement programmes also led to early pension entry age (57 years on average) and was a rather costly way of reducing unemployment – higher pension contributions from employees and employers were necessary and subsidies from the public sector to the pension system had to be increased. Consequently, the reform of the pension system in 1997 started to reduce incentives for early retirement.

The entrance of foreign labour, especially from Southern and Eastern Europe, has always been restricted and has been seen as a discretionary tool of labour market policy. Foreign labour supply is strictly regulated – however, some 8 per cent of the workforce are foreigners, one of the highest rates in Europe. Trade unions are especially cautious as to the impact on the labour market of the European Union's expansion to the east.

In the last decade, rising public employment also eased the labour market situation. In the 1990s, two-thirds of the increase in employment took place in the public sector (Walterskirchen 1997). This is credited to the fact that the most dynamic service sectors – education, health, and other social services – are mainly dominated by the public sector. The share of public sector employment is about 21 per cent.

The two models and the internationalisation of the economy

Sweden and Austria have been characterised by common goals in economic policy; the most important one being full employment. Both countries have favoured a cooperative model of policy-making. However, the assignment of policy instruments to goals has been quite different. In the environment of liberalised capital markets the Austrian strategy of fixing the exchange rate and instrumentalising wage policy for securing competitiveness seems to have been more successful than the Swedish approach, where regular depreciations of the currency helped to regain competitiveness, while nominal wage increases have been higher than in trading partner countries. The stable macroeconomic development of Austria is the most prominent outcome of this relatively successful policy orientation.

Until the early 1980s the Swedish economy – characterised inter alia by a weak exchange rate, highly regulated financial markets and centralised wage negotiations – did quite well in securing full employment. But it adapted quite inefficiently in the 'new' environment. Liberalisation and deregulation of international financial markets have led to a dominance of financial market interests versus real economy interests. The Swedish orientation on uncoordinated expansionary monetary policy did not only fail internally, but also led to an extremely unstable external monetary environment for economic policy. This resulted in considerable cyclical instabilities, huge budget deficits and high unemployment. It coincides badly with a far reaching loss of economic policy credibility on international financial markets, which became 'the rulers of the game'. In a world of financial market dominance over real economic interest and objectives, a policy regime like the Austrian one, which has been especially successful in stabilising the monetary environment, seems to be more appropriate. The policy specification of 'strong-currency policy' has short-term costs but appears to contribute to high macroeconomic stability in the long run.

For Austria, the smaller space to manoeuvre in anticyclical fiscal policy proved to be the most important restraint for employment policies in the last fifteen years. Anticyclical macroeconomic policy was important in Austria and Sweden for prohibiting the development of cyclical unemployment, which in other European countries led to the emergence of structural unemployment, due to persistence effects. Austria secured macroeconomic adjustment through the expectation-stabilising instrument of corporatism, centralised wage negotiations and stability-oriented fiscal policy. Sweden relied on monetary and exchange rate policy, when corporatism was weakened. National economic policy is increasingly restricted in its room for manoeuvre with regard to anticyclical policy, not only by the liberalisation of factor and goods markets, but also by European regulations. The so-called 'stability and growth pact' for fiscal policy of EMU member states is putting considerable pressure on fiscal policy.

Wage policy has always been of high importance in employment developments in Austria and Sweden. In both countries, the institutional background of wage policy is formed by corporatism. Corporatist regulatory systems in small European countries seem to have done quite well in stabilising the expectations of economic actors, orienting wage policy to macroeconomic objectives, and prioritising the full employment goal. Especially in countries with strong trade unions, coordinated wage negotiations on a central level are able to reduce macroeconomic wage pressure and help to maintain full employment. The price-wage spiral following the steps towards decentralised wage negotiations in Sweden seem to have been part of the characteristics of the bubble economy. The stability of the Austrian institutional system allows nominal wage policy to be a macroeconomic instrument in favour of the full employment objective in the context of a strong currency and liberalised financial markets. However, there has been a significant change in the governance structure of the economy – national economic policy lost influence in favour of 'the markets' – and the increase in the relative mobility of capital vis-a-vis labour in the process of economic integration and globalisation has shifted power in favour of business.

Both countries have been, especially after their accession to the European Union in 1995, reorienting important elements of economic policy. In Austria fiscal policy has mainly been oriented towards budget consolidation and less toward employment promotion. On the other hand, active labour market policy has been getting new stimulus from the European Social Funds and the National Employment Action Plans. With no Austrian tradition of training policies, the introduction of these policies in Austria can be seen as an adaptation of the Swedish model. Public expenditures in this area have been increasing from 6 billion Austrian schilling in 1996 to 11 billion. In 1999, 18 per cent of the unemployed took part in training programs in 1999, and the government has set a goal of reducing the unemployment rate to 3 per cent of the labour force in 2002.

In Sweden economic policy orientation has changed considerably in the 1990s. The European Union's credo of 'sound public finance and price stability' as the main macroeconomic goals has been implemented in Swedish policy. In 1998 public households for the first time since 1990 have been showing a surplus and inflation has been dampened to levels of around 1 per cent. Sweden has no trouble in meeting the EMU criteria. Due to an upswing in internal and external demand even the unemployment rate started to decline. The level of 7 per cent in 1999, however, was still considerably higher than in Austria.

Note

1 The author thanks Alois Guger, Henry Milner, Eskil Wadensjö, Ewald Walterskirchen and the discussants at the EAEPE-Conference in Lisbon, 1998 for valuable comments.

References

Ackum Agell, Susanne (1995), 'Swedish Labour Market Programs: Efficiency and Timing', *Swedish Economic Policy Review*, vol. 2, pp. 65-98.

Ackum Agell, Susanne, Anders Björklund and Anders Harkman (1995), 'Unemployment Insurance, Labour Market Programs and Repeated Unemployment in Sweden', *Swedish Economic Policy Review*, vol. 2, pp. 101-28.

Arestis, Philip (1986), 'Post-Keynesian Economic Policies: The Case of Sweden', *Journal of Economic Issues*, vol. 20, pp. 709-23.

Björklund, Anders (1993), 'The Swedish Experience', in Karsten Jensen and Per Kongshøj Madsen (eds), *Measuring Labour Market Measures, Proceedings from the Danish Presidency Conference 1993*, Ministry of Labour, Copenhagen, pp. 243-64.

Calmfors, Lars (1994), 'Active Labour Market Polic y and Unemployment – A Framework for the Analysis of Crucial Design Features', *OECD Economic Studies*, No. 22.

Erixon, Lennart (1994), 'A Swedish Economic Policy. A Revindication of the Rehn-Meidner Model', Institutet för Arbetslivsforskning, Working Paper No. 20.

Guger, Alois (1992), 'Corporatism: Success or Failure? Austrian Experiences', in Jukka Pekkarinen, Matti Pohjola, Bob Rowthorn (eds), *Social Corporatism – A Superior Economic System?*, Clarendon Press, Oxford, pp. 338-76.

Guger, Alois (1998), 'Economic Policy and Social Democracy: The Austrian Experience', *Oxford Review of Economic Policy*, vol. 14, pp. 40-56.

Hahn, Franz and Ewald Walterskirchen (1992), '"Stylized Facts" der Konjunkturschwankungen in Österreich, Deutschland und den USA', *WIFO Working Papers,* Nr. 58.

Lindbeck, Assar (1997), 'The Swedish Experiment', *Journal of Economic Literature*, vol. 35, pp. 1273-319.

Marterbauer, Markus and Ewald Walterskirchen (1999), 'Macroeconomic Effects of Fiscal Consolidation Policy in the EU', *Austrian Economic Quarterly*, vol. 4, pp. 105-14.

Meidner, Rudolf, Gösta Rehn et al. (1953), *Trade Unions and Full Employment*, Report to the LO Congress 1951, Stockholm.

Seidel, Hans (1982), 'Der Austro-Keynesianismus', *Wirtschaftspolitische Blätter*, vol. 29, pp. 11-15.

Smithin, John N. (1996), *Macroeconomic Policy and the Future of Capitalism*, Edward Elgar, Cheltenham.

Tichy, Gunther (1984), 'Strategy and Implementation of Employment Policy in Austria', *Kyklos*, vol. 37, pp. 363-86.

Tichy, Gunther (1986), 'Die Amplitude der österreichischen Konjunkturschwankungen im internationalen Vergleich', *Empirica*, 1986, vol. 13, pp. 69-96.

Walterskirchen, Ewald (1997), 'Austria's Road to Full Employment', *WIFO-Working Paper* 89.

Chapter 12

Gösta Rehn, the Swedish Model and the Dutch Miracle

Jelle Visser

Introduction

Would Gösta Rehn have approved of the Dutch miracle? Colin Crouch raised the question during the 1999 SASE conference in Vienna. Both Colin and I met several times with Gösta, as members of a European team working on a book in which we tried to document how trade unions and wage bargainers had responded to the 'challenge of flexibility' (Baglioni and Crouch 1990). The combination of what he preferred to call the 'flexilife' idea and labour market adjustment had been an old theme of Rehn from his days in the Organisation of Economic Co-operation and Development (OECD 1972; Rehn 1973, 1984). But it had fallen on barren soil in the labour movement. In the 1980s, unfortunately, flexibility had become a theme of the political right and was almost entirely defined by the needs and strategies of management.

Would Rehn have liked the Dutch employment miracle of the 1990s, based on a combination of wage moderation, tight fiscal and monetary policies, social security and labour market reform, work sharing through the promotion of part-time employment, tax breaks and subsidized low-paid employment (for a full description: Visser and Hemerijck 1997)? I cannot tell for sure, but I do know that Rehn was extremely critical of the 'old' Dutch model. He was appalled by the adjustment policies, which he observed in the early 1980s in the Netherlands and other mature welfare states (and would be repeated, a decade later, in Sweden). These policies were based, in his summary, on 'high rates of interest, high and non-productive expenditure for compensation to the unemployed, and high unit costs through low-capacity utilisation. Thus the anti-inflationary effects depend solely upon wage restraint forced upon workers through unemployment. This is a very costly method for fighting inflation, in both economic and social terms' (Rehn 1987, p. 72).

He never understood nor liked the passive policies, directed at income replacement rather than services, of the Dutch social democrats in power in the

1970s. I remember his scorn for Joop den Uyl (the Labour Party leader of the time), when den Uyl defended the policy entitling unemployed workers to refuse a 'suitable job' (passend werk) if it was not located within a 30 km distance of their present home. To Rehn, this was a perversion of a social democratic policy of social progress and protection, which, he affirmed, should strengthen rather than weaken incentives for change and adjustment among workers. In the series of studies, which Rehn and his colleagues at the OECD conducted in a number of European countries, the one on the Netherlands was highly critical, as it uncovered the almost complete lack of training, regional development and mobility supporting instruments in Dutch public manpower policy (OECD 1967; Rehn 1967). But this critique fell on deaf ears at a time when the country was enjoying full employment for adult males, when redundant miners or textile workers were being sent into retirement and when married women were withdrawing from the labour market almost without exception.

The Netherlands was light years away from the idea of 'active' or 'activating' social and labour policies. Indeed, the main response to the economic shocks of 1967-68, 1973-74 and 1980-81 had been a policy of reducing labour supply, mainly through by encouraging older workers to leave the labour market, partly through the indiscriminate use of a very generous disability pension system (Aarts and de Jong 1996). It was not until the end of the 1980s that Dutch policy makers, stimulated by the Council for Scientific Advice to Government Policy, began to study the active labour market policies in other countries, beginning with Sweden (WRR 1987, 1990). In the 1990s there was a paradigmatic shift in labour market and social policy towards the active welfare state (Visser and Hemerijck 1997).

In the following pages I shall first offer a brief overview of recent changes in the Dutch labour market, followed by a discussion of the policies behind these changes. After that overview I return to my opening question: How do these policies and outcomes compare to the Swedish Model as advocated by Rehn?

The Dutch labour market: from crisis to miracle

Fifteen years ago, the Dutch labour market was in a very depressed state. Using the new definition of unemployment, nearly 600,000 people, more than 10 per cent of the labour force was unemployed. (Under the old definition the figures would have been 800,000 or 13 per cent. The new definition follows ILO-standards and requires the unemployed to be available to take the job within the reference period. About one-third of the unemployed according to the old definition were not available or ill prepared to take a job within short notice.) This indicated, if nothing else, a severe problem of 'inactivity' in the Dutch labour market. An almost similar proportion had left employment due to illness, disability or early retirement in advance of the legal retirement age of 65. One of every four out-of-school youth under the age of 25 was

Table 12.1 A summary of the Dutch labour market 1970-1996

	1970	*1984*	*1996*	*annual % change 1970-84*	*annual % change 1984-96*
Participation rate (%)					
Total	57.3	54.6	63.5	-0.2	0.7
All 15-24 years	58.9	42.0	45.0	-1.3	0.3
Women 25-49 years	23.5	38.2	61.9	1.1	2.0
Men 25-49 years	96.9	92.2	93.2	-0.4	0.1
All 50-64 years	49.6	37.5	41.6	-0.9	0.3
Employment (>1 hour)					
Jobs	5,469,000	5,718,000	6,982,000	0.3	1.8
Labour years	4,763,000	4,672,000	5,503,000	-0.1	1.5
Labour hours (x1.000)	9,559,000	8,386,000	9,581,000	-0.9	1.2
Employment (>12 hours)					
Industry and agriculture	2,183,000	1,560,000	1,571,000	-2.4	0.1
Private services	1,704,000	1,810,000	2,493,000	0.4	3.0
Public and subsidised services	919,000	1,273,000	1,369,000	2.4	0.7
Full-time jobs	3,742,000	3,497,000	3,648,000	-0.5	0.4
Part-time jobs (>12 hours	635,000	1,079,000	1,844,000	3.9	4.6
Atypical jobs	219,000	354,000	723,000	3.5	6.1
Low-paid jobs (<2/3 median)	460,000	347,000	–	-3.9	–
	–	415,000	524,000	–	2.4
Labour conditions					
Real wage rate (1970=100)	100	137	147	2.3	0.6
Wage distribution (interquartile)	0.454	0.399	–	-1.8	–
	–	0.418	0.462	–	1.0
Hours per year (full-time job)	2,007	1795	1,741	-0.8	-0.3
Unemployment	44,000	591,000	440,000	20.4	-2.4
Share long-time unemployed (%)	9	53	49	3.1	-0.3
Vacancies (x 1000)	52,000	31,000	69,000	-4.6	6.9

Source: Author's calculations from Central Bureau of Statistics data and Social-Cultural Report 1998.

unable to find a job. The employment/population ratio of the Netherlands had dropped below 50 per cent and was one of the lowest in Europe.

The first half of the 1980s was the culmination of a decade of employment stagnation (see Table 12.1). It was also a turning point. Looking back from the perspective of today, we can observe a reversal of trends in a number of important indicators. Labour participation has increased among all age groups. Most spectacularly participation of women between the ages of 25 and 49 has increased. The average rate of job growth has been rising during the past decade and a half at a rate of 1.8 per cent per year, accelerating to 3.5 per cent in 1997 and 3.0 per cent in 1998. This is no less impressive than the American 'jobs machine' and many times better than the European average (0.4 per cent) during the same period. It remains so even when we take into account the fact that many of these jobs are part-time and the annual working time of full-time workers has fallen by 0.3 per cent per year since 1984. If employment is expressed in full-time equivalents or in hours worked rather than in jobs or persons, employment increased with an average rate of 1.2 per cent per year, which is still three times the European average.

The Netherlands can be considered the world's first part-time economy (Freeman 1998; Visser 1999). Part-time jobs account for three-quarters of the job growth since 1984. Of the total increase in employment with 1.2 million persons between 1988 and 1997, two-thirds were working part-time (defined as jobs of less than 35 hours per week, this may include a small number of shift workers). Employment growth is driven by strong labour force growth, 1.4 per cent per year between 1982 and 1996, compared with 0.5 per cent in the European Union. This reflects relatively rapid population growth (the birth rate in the Netherlands declined later than in other European countries) and a catching-up of the low female participation rate to European averages. In the period considered here, the Netherlands experienced the fastest rise in the employment rate of women in any OECD country.

Part-time employment ratios for women show that the Netherlands (with 36.4 per cent of all women between the age of 15 and 65 working in a part-time job) has overtaken the leading positions of Norway (31.5 per cent), Sweden (27.5 per cent) and Denmark (23.4 per cent) (OECD figures for 1996). With regard to full-time employment of women, however, little has changed. The full-time employment ratio of women in the Netherlands (18.6 per cent) is half, or less, the ratio in Norway (37.4 per cent), Sweden (43.1 per cent) and Denmark (43.1 per cent), and has hardly changed since 1970 (Visser 1999). Hence if one measures the total input of paid labour by women in terms of full-time equivalents (counting part-time jobs as half-time jobs), the Netherlands remains at the bottom end of the European list.

Returning our attention to Table 12.1, we find that sectoral employment trends in the Netherlands went in almost opposite directions before and after 1984. In the 1970s the subsidised sector (health, education) and government employment witnessed the strongest growth (2.4 per cent per year, on average), whereas private sector employment stagnated. Employment levels in industry fell steeply (-2.4 per cent) and employment growth in private services (trade and transport, financial and personal services, hotels and restaurants) was faint (0.4 per cent). After 1984 the picture is very different. Job decline in industry and agriculture has stopped; we now find a pattern of 'jobless growth', combining a strong export performance and productivity increases with more or less stagnant employment (0.1 per cent). In services the picture is different. Jobs in private services have increased at a rate of 3 per cent per year, absorbing nearly all the new entrants in the labour force, especially women. We note that, with an annual growth of 0.6 per cent, a much smaller contribution, though still significant, came from the public and subsidised sector. (The government absorbs 13 per cent of total employment, a much lower proportion than in other European countries and seemingly at odds with the high share of public expenditure in the Netherlands. The explanation is that many 'public' services, in health, social welfare, education, broadcasting, and the arts, are organised by 'voluntary associations' under public regulation and with public subsidies. The 'quartiary' sector of public and subsidised services accounts for about a quarter of total employment).

Further contrasts between the two periods under consideration concern wage and equality trends. After 1979 real wage growth came to a standstill and in the early 1980s there was even a small decline. Beginning with the Wassenaar agreement between the central organisations of trade unions and employers at the end of 1982, trade unions have made wage restraint their official policy. This policy was continued, with a brief interruption around 1990, until today and was partly made possible by a reduction of taxes in support of the purchasing power of workers. As more households have two (or rather one-and-the-half) earners, household income and domestic consumption have risen in real terms, but income differences between households (of different composition) as well as between individuals (especially between those with and without employment) have increased. The post-war trend towards greater earnings equality came to a halt in the early 1980s and was reversed (Table 12.1). Earnings have grown more unequal, a trend that is found in most developed industrial countries and is not particularly pronounced in the Netherlands, compared to the UK or the US (OECD, 1996). The number of low-paid jobs has increased, partly as the result of deliberate policies to create more employment opportunities for low-skilled workers with little job experience. Finally, unemployment has fallen from its very high levels in the mid-1980s. At the end of 1999 the number of unemployed fell under 200,000 for the first time since 1979. The standardised unemployment rate – based on ILO criteria – dropped to 4 per cent in 1998 and stood at 3.3 per cent in the last quarter of 1999, which is the lowest unemployment rate in Europe but for Luxembourg.

The low open unemployment rate, combined with the appearance of difficult-to-fill vacancies in a number of regions and jobs, suggests that the Dutch economy is presently running close to its full-employment rate. In many sectors employers report problems of recruitment and some have started to hire Belgian and German workers. There are also signs of unions stepping up wage pressures, after a long period of almost zero real wage growth. There are still considerable problems of hidden unemployment, though. Of every two persons between the age of 55 and 65, only one participates in the labour market. The government is considering repealing the executive order of 1984, which exempts the older unemployed (aged 57.5 and older) from job search. With the recent influx of women around the age of 35 to 40 in the system, the current number of people on full- or part-time disability pensions has again risen dangerously close to the one million figure, a figure that prompted such drastic political intervention in the beginning of the 1990s. And while the number of long-term unemployed people is falling rapidly, among those remaining unemployed half are without a job for one year or longer. This reflects passive policies of the past, and places a considerable challenge on labour market programs. Unemployment among unskilled and immigrant workers has also decreased, but remains at a much higher level (two to three times above the national average).

Three policy changes

Although it attracted international attention only in the 1990s, the 'Dutch miracle' has its basis in policy changes in the 1980s. The recession following the second oil shock was exceptionally severe. The restrictive macroeconomic policies of the U.S. and Germany in the wake of the second oil shock increased the financial liabilities of Dutch firms and caused a spate of bankruptcies and factory closures. Between 1981 and 1983 300,000 full-time jobs in industry were shed. Unemployment soared to a rate of 10,000-15,000 per month and seemed unstoppable. With rapidly rising (international) interest rates, and falling profits, private sector investment fell to an all-time low. The public-sector deficit peaked at 6.6 per cent of GDP in 1982. The trade unions lost almost one-fifth of their members and nearly one-quarter of those remaining were out of work, on social benefits or retired (Visser 1990).

In this situation, there was 'a change in policy and mentality', based on the awareness that 'a limit was reached' (Visser and Hemerijck 1997, p. 13). The crisis created a sense of urgency and triggered social learning and policy change after a decade of stalemate. The three main changes underlying the remarkable 'employment revival' (Auer 1999) are in my view (1) wage moderation, combined with and in response to the submission of monetary policy to the Bundesbank (far in anticipation of EMU), (2) fiscal consolidation, social security and labour market reforms, based on a new balance between market incentives, private responsibilities and public tasks, and (3) a continued but gradual process of 'centralised decentralisation' in collective bargaining over wages, working hours and working conditions.

Wage moderation

In 1974, in response to the first oil crisis, the Centre-Left government had opted for a Keynesian strategy of fiscal stimulation, setting the stage for a corporatist policy package, exchanging fiscal reflation for wage restraint. But the radicalised Dutch unions wanted more reforms in economic policy and corporate governance than the government, with reluctant support of its Christian coalition parties, could offer. In 1974 and 1976 the government imposed a wage and income freeze, but its effects were futile. After 1977 a Centre-Right government tried to govern without incomes policies, but resorted to intervention in wage setting in 1979, 1980, and 1981. The short-lived participation of the Social Democrats in the government in 1981-82 was again marred by disputes with the unions, this time over attempts to brake rising absenteeism due to illness.

Thanks to its gas exports, the Netherlands did not suffer from a balance of payments constraint, but it paid the price of a structurally overvalued guilder. An expansionary course, based on public borrowing, was therefore quite feasible, but on condition that unions held back wages. Without restraint and with profits under pressure, Dutch products would price themselves out of the market, with disastrous consequences for employment in a small and open economy even more dependent on exports than Sweden. The Unions began to appreciate these facts by 1978 or 1979, but it was not until 1982 that the situation was ripe for a policy change.

Beginning with the main trade union in industry, which suffered the closing down of an entire industry (shipbuilding), Dutch union leaders recognised that for a higher level of investment, essential for the creation of more jobs and the struggle against unemployment, there had to be a higher level of profits and, hence, a lower wage share. This view became the basis for a sustained policy of wage moderation, beginning with the central agreement of Wassenaar in 1982. In that agreement the unions accepted a temporary decline in real wages for the purpose of a recovery of profits and investment as the main method of stopping the decline in employment. Employers lifted their veto of a cost-neutral reduction of working hours from 40 to 38 weekly hours. The agreement was the beginning of a sustained policy of wage moderation and was described by the Dutch Central Planning Office as 'Holland's single most important weapon in international competition' (Visser and Hemerijck 1997, p. 26).

There had been attempts at wage moderation before. In 1979 a central agreement had in the last minute been wrecked by the opposition of unions representing low-paid workers. The difference, in 1982, was that the hard currency stance of the Dutch Central Bank, and behind it the Bundesbank, no longer left room for doubt. Earlier in the year the patched-up coalition of Social and Christian Democrats had foundered and the new Centre-Right coalition had announced a 'no nonsense' policy of fiscal consolidation. The government had already decided that it would suspend the cost-of-living indexation in wage agreements and social benefits, and freeze minimum wages, social benefits and public sector wages. The unions were in no position, morally or otherwise, to protest. Both unions and employers were sick of recurrent government intervention, and preferred a deal between them. The response to the Wassenaar agreement was swift. In less than a year, two-thirds of all collective agreements were renewed, mostly for two years, during which the payment of price compensation was suspended and a 5 per cent reduction of working hours took place (Visser 1990).

After the Wassenaar agreement, the powerful Labour Minister convinced the Cabinet, against the advice of the Central Bank and the finance ministry, to let the value of the guilder slip by 2 per cent against the Deutsche mark in the EMS currency alignment of January 1983 – a decision that was soon regretted when financial markets drove up interest rates as an extra risk premium. Later in the year, the Dutch monetary authorities announced in 1983 that henceforth the guilder was to be pegged to the D-mark. Exchange rate policy would now be decided in Frankfurt. Inflation fell to zero in the mid-1980s and has, until recently, disappeared from the country's concerns. The strict exchange rate policy exerted disciplinary influence on wage setting, while, in turn, wage moderation enabled the Central Bank to credibly stick to its non-inflationary targets. Low inflation allowed unions to drop cost-of-living adjustments in (multi-annual) wage agreements.

The turnaround in employment growth came later and benefited mainly newcomers to the labour market. Unemployment did not start to fall until the late 1980s. The reduction of working hours had an additional work-sharing effect, but the largest boost to employment came from the rapid expansion of part-time jobs, most of which went to married women and young people. Unskilled youth, ethnic minorities and older workers who had lost their jobs in the 1980-81 crisis filled the ranks of the long-term unemployed and many never found their way back to the labour market. The growth in part-time jobs was not the result of policy changes, but originated in behavioural changes of women. In the absence of day-care facilities, part-time work became the dominant 'coping' strategy of working women whose increased educational attainments made the century-old tradition of withdrawing from the labour market upon marriage and motherhood more and more costly and anachronistic. In health, education and social services, as well as in central and local government, women wanted to switch from full-time to part-time jobs, in order to combine work and motherhood, and to keep their jobs or maintain seniority. At the time it was a much-welcomed means for employers to reduce excess capacity or adjust to budget restrictions. In later years, part-time work became a means to fill the widening and variable gap between the reduced working hours of workers and the longer operating time of firms and offices (Visser 1999).

Fiscal consolidation, welfare and labour market reforms

In the 1970s the main rise in government spending was directed at expanding welfare programs, reflecting in part a concession to the solidaristic preferences of the unions. In 1974 the minimum wage and, indirectly, public-sector salaries and social security benefits were indexed to private-sector wage increases. Youth minimum wages were sharply increased and indexed as well. Most collective agreements contained automatic cost-of-living adjustment escalators. The result was that pay increases in the private sector automatically translated to increased public sector outlays. It made the government a prisoner to the outcome of negotiations in the private sector and an interested party in wage negotiations, which, unavoidably, thus became tripartite (Hemerijck 1995).

After the Wassenaar agreement, with private sector bargaining out of its hands, the government used the opportunity to sever the 'automatic linking' of public sector wages to contractual wages, a system which had been established in 1962. Unlike Sweden, the approximately 800,000 Dutch civil servants were legally excluded from the right to strike and from collective bargaining, and until 1982 their wages had 'followed the trend' set by private-sector wage contracts. When the government decided to lower nominal public sector wages by 3.5 per cent in 1984, after a freeze in 1983, the public sector unions organised the largest-ever strike. Abandoned by the private sector unions and under siege from a hostile public opinion, they lost the battle but gained a victory of sorts when the judiciary acknowledged, citing the European social charter, the right to strike of civil servants. After another intervention by the International Labour Organisation, which had been appealed to by the unions, the government announced a change in the law. In a stepwise process, civil servants and employees in subsidised services have been granted the right to bargain. Since 1993, wages and conditions in the public sector have been determined through negotiations, at the same time differentiation by sector (central government, local government, police, education, etc.) has been allowed as well as a modest degree of decentralisation by establishment (municipality, university, etc.). During the 1983-93 period wage moderation has been much more severe in the public sector than in the private sector (Hartog 1999). The effect was mainly shouldered by new entrants (women, young people) whose entry wages were lower.

By lowering the minimum wage in 1984 and by de-linking its increase from private sector wage developments, the growth in social security spending was slowed down. The statutory minimum wage serves as the anchor for the universal old age pensions, legally guaranteed minimum benefits, and social assistance (the lowest level of which is set at the 'social minimum' or 70 per cent of the minimum wage). The (absolute and relative) reduction of the minimum wage did affect mostly people dependent on benefits (single mothers without a job, the long term unemployed, disabled workers with insufficient insurance coverage, and retired workers without supplementary pension schemes). Workers with jobs covered by collective agreement usually move up one or two scales above the minimum wage. Consequently, the percentage of adult workers with a minimum-wage job dropped after 1983 from 10 to 3 per cent. However, the minimum wage lowering was greatest where it applies mainly to young workers who receive a percentage of the adult minimum wage, beginning with 60 per cent for those age 16 and rising with age.

In 1987 the government implemented its long-announced overhaul of employee insurance laws, tightening the eligibility conditions for unemployment and disability, and lowering legally guaranteed benefits from 80 to 70 per cent of last-earned wages. In part, these effects were compensated through collective bargaining. These measures halted the rise in the social security spending, but the number of claimants kept mounting. Under the increased competitive pressures of the 1980s, many firms had channelled less productive and expensive, mostly older, workers out of the labour market into unemployment or disability. There was a clear moral hazard, since the insurance costs were borne by all firms and, should funds run out, by the taxpayer (Aarts and de Jong 1996). The rising insurance premiums resulted in higher social security contributions, while the wedge between total (wage and non-wage) labour costs and take-home pay increased. This engendered a vicious circle of 'welfare without work', of firms seeking to match rising costs through layoffs, leading to higher social charges, and so forth (Esping-Andersen 1996).

It soon became increasingly obvious that firms, with the complicity of social security administrators, were reducing slack while externalising the costs of adjustment, leading to an ever-growing volume of claimants. After the so-called 'system reforms' of 1987, the government had promised 'peace on the social security front', but it was not to be. The route through sickness and disability was the way of least resistance for Dutch employers. In the 55-64 age group, recipients of a disability benefit outnumbered workers with a job by 1986, and in 1990 the total number of disability claimants approached the unimaginable figure of one million.

In the late 1980s, policy-makers became aware that the low level of labour market participation was the Achilles' heel of the extensive but passive Dutch system of social protection. This diagnosis inspired the Christian-Social government (1989-94) and the two Social-Liberal governments (1994-98, 1998-) to recast the balance between active and passive policies. In late 1993, the social partners endorsed the new approach. In their central agreement, called 'A New Course', they cited increased participation in the labour market as the main criterion by which to design or judge wage, working hours, social security and labour market policies (Visser and Hemerijck 1997, p. 181).

The Social Democrats had made the re-establishment of the linkage between wages and benefits a condition for their return in the government, after the general elections of 1989. But in coalition negotiations with the Christian Democrats they had been forced to concede that the policy of fiscal consolidation and lowering of the public sector debt, begun in 1982, had to continue. This condition in the coalition contract became a constraint when the initial boom following German unification changed into a recession. While the EMU criteria of Maastricht (1991) gave additional ammunition to the proponents of tight fiscal and budgetary policies, the Social Democrats, led by former union leader and Wassenaar negotiator, now

Finance Minister Wim Kok, found no escape from seeking to reduce the cost of social security, preferably by slowing down the number of claimants rather than breaking an electoral promise and reduce the level or duration of social benefits. The continued increase in disability claims, despite the system reforms of 1987, caught them wrong-footed. Only by drastically changing the rules of the game (reducing the benefits for those in the system despite electoral promises and principles) could the disability crisis be solved, with dire electoral consequences. In 1994 the elections were lost and it was only because the Christian Democrats did even worse that Kok was able to negotiate and lead a new coalition government, this time with the Liberal Right. In the meantime, in a spectacular parliamentary inquiry, the unions and employer organisations were blamed for mismanagement and abuse of the social security programs. This has since resulted in a series of reforms which strengthen state supervision and reduce the involvement of the 'social partners'. In addition, through a privatisation of sickness (wage continuation) insurance and a moderate degree of experience rating in disability insurance, more market pressures have been introduced in the social security administration.

Having come in on a program of welfare reforms, designed to lower the attractiveness of these programs for those with access to the labour market, the Social Democrats condemned themselves to a policy of 'jobs, jobs, and more jobs'. This became the rallying slogan of the first Social-Liberal government and made its imprint on all kinds of labour market policy initiatives. There was a new focus on active labour-market policies. After long and tiresome preparations, taking almost a decade, the public employment service had been reorganised in 1991, brought under tripartite control and, in part, devolved to the regions. A critical evaluation after four years led to another overhaul in 1996 and provided a policy window for issue-linkage between labour market and welfare policy. As a result of the strengthening of 'activating' measures in unemployment insurance and social assistance, municipalities and social insurance organisations have a budget to buy placement and training activities from the employment service. Starting in the year 2000 the employment service is expected to compete with private providers, such as the temporary-work agencies. The so-called 'Melkert-jobs' (named after the Social-Democratic Minister in the 1994-98 Cabinet) are permanent jobs in the public sector set aside for unemployed youth and for the long-term unemployed. Additional job programs now absorb around 2 per cent of total employment. Next, the government has introduced several kinds of employment subsidy schemes based on a reduction of social security contributions paid by employers. Employment subsidies can add up to 25 per cent of the annual wage, and subsidy schemes cover as many as one million workers. Inwork benefits have become a permanent feature of the Dutch tax system, increasing the pecuniary advantages of work and lowering some of the worst benefit traps in the system.

Labour market flexibility is an integral part of the new labour market policy mix. Legislation removing constraints on shop opening hours, business licenses, temporary job agencies, working time, and dismissal law consolidate this development. While the unique system of administrative dismissal controls has been retained, procedures have been simplified and negotiated layoffs, with severance payments, play a very large role. In 1995 unions and employers signed the first collective agreement for workers on temporary contracts, introducing a right of continued employment and pension insurance after four consecutive contracts or 24 months of service. It prepared the ground for the central agreement on 'Flexibility and Security' of 1996, which, in turn, paved the way for the overhaul of Dutch dismissal protection law in 1999. This 'flexicurity' law (Wilthagen 1998) is a compromise, not just between employers and employees, but also within the unions between workers with and without stable jobs. The incremental individualisation of the tax system since 1984, the improved possibilities to switch from full-time to part-time jobs, and the removal of all remaining elements of discrimination of the basis of working hours, have contributed to a 'normalisation' of part-time employment (Visser 1999).

Centralised decentralisation

The Wassenaar agreement of 1982 was the beginning of an organised process of decentralisation, with more scope for market influences, but still with a significant role for the central organisations. Elsewhere, evaluating its 'constitutive' impact on labour relations, I have compared Wassenaar with Saltsjöbaden (Visser 1998). The first and perhaps most important element of the agreement was the re-establishment of bilateral relations and bipartisan autonomy in wage setting by the social partners. Indeed, by showing a (at the time still modest) degree of 'partnership', after more than a decade of conflict over ends and means, the central organisations of unions and employers managed to keep the state out of a policy domain which they had since 1962, when the statutory wage policy instituted in 1945 collapsed, reclaimed as their own. Until the late 1970s they had either not trusted each other enough to do business without the state, or had expected to achieve more through legislation.

After Wassenaar the Netherlands ended its attempt to run an incomes policy which it had been doing since 1945, initially through state-imposed guidelines, later through tripartite negotiations. Formally there is no Tariffautonomie in the Netherlands. But the revised Wage Act of 1987 tightened the conditions, which allow the government to intervene and impose a wage freeze of up to 18 months in case of a major economic crisis, in recognition of the newly found partnership in responsibility of the central union and employers associations. In 1993, when Dutch exports once again suffered and unemployment rose steeply in the EMS crisis, the government did send a bill to parliament sufficiently impressing upon the social partners the need for self-restraint. It is unlikely that this could be repeated today. While parliament and government have reduced the autonomy and role of social partners in the administration of social security, the principle of 'free' collective bargaining is undisputed and guarded as sacrosanct by the social partners. In a number of sectors and for about half a million workers in retail, construction and small firms in industry, the negotiating parties depend on government support for the extension of their agreements to non-organised employers. Attempts to end this practice, or in any case to make extension conditional upon the content of agreements (whether or not they contain 'good practice' clauses such as extra training for ethnic minorities, lower 'entry' wages for inexperienced workers, or dispensation rules for starting firms) have been more or less been abandoned after a show of goodwill by the social partners in the mid 1990s. The state is very reluctant to involve itself again in policing collective bargaining in substantive terms and lacks the monitoring and sanctioning capacity needed for effective steering.

The Wassenaar agreement delivered restraint across the entire economy, something which would have been welcome, but did not happen, during the stagflation crisis of the 1970s. On occasion, such generalised (or macroeconomic) restraint may still be necessary, as was the case in 1992 and 1993, when an adjustment to the changing terms of trade and conditions of competitiveness following the EMS crisis was called for. After some cajoling, the central organisations responded with a recommendation to cease wage negotiations during the first two months of 1993, extending existing agreements and giving negotiators time to take account of the new international situation and lower demands (which had been based on forecasts of a more buoyant economy). As a result, at the end of 1993 they signed a new central agreement combining wage restraint with decentralisation.

Over and above the orchestration of a rapid and general response to changing external conditions or shocks, which under EMU is as important as it ever was, central agreements must set the stage for differentiation across sectors. The Wassenaar agreement began the process by keeping the government out, since governments, for reasons of distributional justice and informational short-comings, find it extremely hard to run a differentiated incomes policy (the Dutch government had tried, back in the early 1960s, and miserably failed, see Windmuller 1969). The second contribution of the Wassenaar agreement was that it contained a general recommendation on desirable behaviour by wage negotiators rather than a specific ceiling or maximum wage norm, as had been the custom on previous (failed) occasions. The problem with such a norm is that it tends to become a standard or minimum, because no union negotiator can afford to come home with less (Visser 1990).

The most important change that came at the time of the Wassenaar agreement, was the de-coupling of public-sector wage setting, affecting 800,000 civil servants and 700,000 'trend followers' in subsidised services. Inter-sectoral differentiation of wages, reflecting differences in profitability and productivity, becomes increasingly important for employment. Problems of uncertainty are better solved at a lower level, provided the negotiators have sufficient trust that mistakes can still be corrected in the next round. Even with broadly similar sectoral trends in profits or productivity, sectoral negotiators find themselves occasionally confronted with bottlenecks in the labour market, to which they want to apply specific solutions. Thus, in metal engineering, quality upgrading may require higher wages in order to attract or keep higher skilled workers, whereas in banking, with relative high wage levels and job security, but with structural overcapacity, unions and staff may prefer worksharing solutions through shorter working hours and a slow-down in wage growth. In the Netherlands, sectoral differentiation is enhanced through different agreements applying to large and small firms, as is the case in engineering and will be the case in banking. Moreover, multinational firms usually negotiate their own agreements, with tacit or open co-ordination in the employers associations.

In the 1970s agreements were often only different in name, while their contents were copied from one company or sector to another. There is some evidence that diversity has increased in the 1990s (Hartog 1999). With the New Course agreement of 1993, decentralisation has been deepened by adding an individual or group dimension to many collective agreements. In some cases this means more involvement of workers and local union representatives in the actual negotiations. In other cases we find a stronger association of wages to productivity or profits, or some element of variable effort-related remuneration. Increasingly, unions have accepted the introduction of annual accounts of working hours, with savings plans and some scope for individual pension schemes. The central organisations of unions and employers guide the process mainly by providing a climate of trust and by co-ordinating policies with the government through the Foundation of Labour and in the tripartite Social-Economic Council. This creates ample opportunities for issue linkage and for compensating policies in exchange for unwanted but unavoidable concessions. Since 1982 the Foundation has published some 100 guidelines, opinions, and agreements, mostly offering recommendations on best practice, or possible trade-offs, to human resource directors and union representatives involved in negotiating around 1000 collective agreements covering around 80 per cent of all employees. Co-ordination works mainly through moral persuasion, between and within the central organisations. (Note that, unlike government statutes or collective agreements, central agreements have no legal status and cannot be the basis for claims in court. Under Dutch legislation collective agreements overrule individual labour contracts and create legally binding obligations and rights for the contracting parties; the infringement of a government statute creates a punishable offence.)

Evaluation

After this overview of the Dutch employment recovery in the 1990s and the policies behind it, I now return to the opening question. What would Gösta Rehn have thought of it? How does it compare to the Swedish Model that he advocated?

If we limit ourselves to comparing recent developments in the Dutch and

Swedish labour markets, there is little question that the Dutch have done much better (see Table 12.2). Sweden is still far ahead when we compare employment ratios, of men and women, or of older workers, but the gap has narrowed considerably since 1990, because relative levels of inactivity have risen in Sweden and fallen in the Netherlands.

Eklund (this volume) has made a distinction between the original Rehn-Meidner model of the 1950s and the actual development of the Swedish Model in later years (on the same point, see Lundberg 1985). According to Eklund, Rehn summarised his model in four main points: a tight fiscal policy to fight inflation; a selective labour market policy, rather than general demand reflation, to fight unemployment should retrenchment and fiscal tightness cause problems in the labour market; an active labour market and welfare policy to push workers to new job opportunities and move people out of unemployment; and a solidaristic wage policy (i.e. equal pay for equal work) as a matter of egalitarian principle and as an instrument to speed up structural transformation by not allowing inefficient firms, based on low pay, to stay in the market.

Table 12.2 Sweden and the Netherlands compared

Employment growth	1983-93	1994	1995	1996	1997	1998
Netherlands	1.8	-0.1	2.4	2.0	3.4	3.0
Sweden	-0.6	-0.9	1.6	-0.6	-1.1	1.5
Unemployment rate	1983	1990	1995	1996	1997	1998
Netherlands	9.7	6.2	6.9	6.3	5.2	4.0
Sweden	3.7	1.7	8.8	9.6	9.9	8.3
Employment population ratio	Men 15-65			Women 15-65		
	1983	1990	1998	1983	1990	1998
Netherlands	69.1	74.3	79.9	34.7	46.9	59.4
Sweden	84.7	85.2	73.5	75.5	81.0	69.4
Older males 55-65	Employment ratio			Unemployment rate		
	1983	1990	1998	1983	1990	1998
Netherlands	50.5	33.5	46.0	6.7	3.2	2.0
Sweden	73.9	74.4	65.8	4.0	1.3	7.8
Incidence part-time employment	% of male employment			% of female employment		
	1983	1990	1998	1983	1990	1998
Netherlands	5.6	13.4	12.4	44.7	52.5	54.8
Sweden	–	5.3	05.6	–	24.5	22.0

Source: Data from OECD, *Economic Outlook* and *Employment Outlook*, various years. Unemployment rates are standardised; part-time employment refers to jobs of less than 30 hours per week.

The differences with current Dutch policies are slight in the case of the first three points in this list, although one does not yet see a strongly developed selective or regional labour market policy in the Netherlands, addressing the persistent inter-regional imbalances and the problem of an overheated labour and housing market, and therefore congested traffic system, in the Randstad (the urban agglomeration of Holland and Utrecht). The main difference, one that Rehn would have no doubt criticized, is the absence of a solidaristic wage policy in the Netherlands. This is not because the unions, or the Social Democratic party, have abandoned egalitarian objectives. We must simply observe that, being a minority, their preferences, even if they were strongly egalitarian, would count less. Dutch unions are nowhere near the powerful position of Swedish unions; they are internally divided among different ideological currents, organise only a quarter of wage and salary earners, and must deal with a well-organised and highly international capitalist class. We also observe an attenuation of the egalitarian drive in the Dutch labour movement since the 1970s and more room for meritocratic principles, stressing equality of opportunity rather than equality of outcomes.

But it is fair to say that Dutch unions have never embraced the economic logic behind solidaristic wage policy as defended by Rehn and Meidner, not even in the times of full employment when such a policy of modernisation seemed within reach. The active labour-market policy, needed to help and promote adjustment among workers, was entirely absent, as was the required regional or selective dimension (OECD 1967). The Dutch unions and the Social Democrats chose fiscal expansion in response to international shocks (as did Swedish policy makers). No longer able to deliver wage restraint, they had to suffer the consequences of monetary restraint, with the large economic and social costs that came with it.

Before one starts to praise the Dutch miracle of the 1990s, one should first acknowledge that the social and human costs of the mistakes of the 1970s, the drastic monetary and fiscal corrections, and the wage moderation induced by high unemployment have been very high – as predicted by Rehn in his 1987 article. To get it right again has taken the Netherlands more than 15 years, reaping the benefits (but not the costs) of German unification and a combination of policy changes that turned out fortuitous (Hemerijck and Schludi 2000). As Wassenaar negotiator and current prime minister Kok has admitted, much harm would have been prevented had the agreement been reached some years earlier. Implicit in my argument is that the (half-way) solidaristic wage policies of the Dutch trade unions in the 1970s would have been a better (Keynesian) response to the crisis, had they been combined with restraint, a softer monetary stance and a Swedish-type active and selective labour market policy. Hence, the Dutch economy of the 1970s would have been well-served with a greater dose of the Rehn-Meidner Model.

Does this mean that a solidaristic wage policy is still preferable, or feasible, today? Rehn saw large wage inequalities, unrelated to permanent differences in risk or skill, as an inefficient method of convincing workers to move from declining to expanding industries, with the danger of jealous wage competition between workers. In a full employment economy this would increase the risks of cost-push inflation. Unlike Beveridge, he believed that asking unions and workers to show voluntary restraint under these circumstances (full employment and wage inequalities related to profits and labour demand) would be 'futile' (Rehn 1987, p. 67). We cannot yet tell from the Dutch developments in the 1990s, that this prediction must be rejected. The economy has only recently moved to a condition of full employment and wage inequalities, though rising, have been checked through collective bargaining. The next two or three years should tell us more.

Even if we suppose that Rehn is right – coming from Sweden he certainly did not write about the 'new economy' without business cycles, no overheating and powerless unions – one would have to ask whether the degree of centralisation of wage setting, needed for a solidaristic wage policy, would be feasible or desirable. I tend to believe that the post-Fordist economy, with its much larger degree of heterogeneity and variability among firms and workers, has to live with a more differentiated and flexible path than in earlier decades, with the consequence of larger earnings differentials. Whether the widening differences in income can be mitigated through taxation is a question that I cannot discuss here. Rehn saw unemployment as wasteful – an inefficient and inhuman means of controlling inflation. I think that it follows that a low-wage sector of (domestic) service, absorbing people who would otherwise be unemployed, is to be preferred to inactivity, or to a large informal economy in the shadow of the law and beyond the reach of the tax office. Wage differentiation may help and in my view it has helped in the Dutch case. But that is of course not the end of the story. Once the unemployment problem is 'solved', will we then be stuck with a permanent 'low wage – bad jobs' sector? Will the people in these jobs be given a chance to move on? If wage differentiation, not based on skills or risks but on profits or labour demand, 'freezes' the economic structure by 'extra taxes on the "good" (through high wages) and subsidies to the "bad" (in the form of low wages)' (Rehn 1987, p. 77), it lowers the (future) welfare of all and should be reconsidered or, at least, mitigated by other policies.

References

Aarts, Leo and Philip de Jong (eds) (1996), *Curing the Dutch Disease*, Avebury, Aldershot.

Auer, Peter (1999), *Employment Revival in Europe, Labour Market Success in Austria, Denmark, Ireland and the Netherlands*, ILO, Geneva.

Baglioni, Guido and Colin Crouch (eds) (1990), *European Industrial Relations. The Challenge of Flexibility*, Sage, London.

Eklund, Klas (this volume), 'Gösta Rehn and the Swedish Model. Did we follow the Rehn-Meidner Model too little rather than too much?'

Esping-Andersen, Gösta (1996), 'Welfare States Without Work. The Impasse of Labour

Shedding and Famialism in Continental Welfare States', in Gösta Esping-Andersen (ed.), *Welfare States in Transition. National Adaptation in Global Economies*, Sage, London, pp. 236-57.

Freeman, Richard (1998), 'War of the models: Which labour market institutions for the 21st century?', *Labour Economics*, vol. 5, pp. 1-24.

Hartog, Joop (1999), 'Country Employment Policy Reviews: The Netherlands', Paper for the ILO Symposium 'Social Dialogue and Employment Success', Geneva, 2-3 March.

Hemerijck, Anton (1995), 'Corporatist Immobility in the Netherlands', in: Colin Crouch and Frank Traxler (eds), *Organized Industrial Relations in Europe. What Future?* Avebury, Aldershot, pp. 183-226.

Hemerijck, Anton and Martin Schludi (2000), 'Policy Adjustments under External and Internal Constraints', in Fritz W. Scharpf and Vivien A. Schmidt (eds), *Welfare and Work in the Open Economy: Diverse Responses to Common Challenges in Twelve Countries*, Oxford University Press, Oxford, vol. 2.

Lundberg, Erik (1985), 'The Rise and Fall of the Swedish Model', *The Journal of Economic Literature*, vol. 23, pp. 1-36.

Rehn, Gösta (1967) 'Manpower Policy and European Unemployment', *The OECD Observer*, no. 31, pp. 15-18 and 31-4.

Rehn, Gösta (1973) 'For Greater Flexibility in Working Life', *The OECD Observer*, no. 62, pp. 3-7.

Rehn, Gösta (1984), 'The Wages of Success', *Daedalus,* no. 113, pp. 137-68.

Rehn, Gösta (1987), 'State, Economic Policy and Industrial Relations in the 1980s: Problems and Trends', *Economic and Industrial Democracy*, vol. 18, pp. 61-79.

OECD (1967), *Manpower Policies in the Netherlands*, OECD, Paris.

OECD (1972), *New Patterns of Working Time,* OECD, Paris.

OECD (1998), *Trends and Driving Forces in Income Distribution: summary of key findings of an OECD study*, Paris, mimeo.

Visser, Jelle (1990), 'Continuity and Change in Dutch Industrial Relations', in Guido Baglioni and Colin Crouch (eds), pp. 199-240.

Visser, Jelle (1998) 'Two Cheers for Corporatism, One for the Market', *British Journal of Industrial Relations*, vol. 36, pp. 269-92.

Visser, Jelle (1999), 'The First Part-time Economy. Does it Work?', AIAS-CESAR research paper, Amsterdam.

Visser, Jelle and Anton Hemerijck (1997) *'A Dutch Miracle'. Job Growth, Welfare Reform and Corporatism in the Netherlands*, Amsterdam University Press, Amsterdam.

Wilthagen, Ton (1998), 'Flexicurity: A New Paradigm for Labour Market Policy Reform?', Discussion Paper FS I 98-202, Wissenschaftszentrum Berlin für Sozialforschung.

Windmuller, John P. (1969), *Labor Relations in the Netherlands*, Cornell University Press, Ithaca, NY.

WRR (1987), *Activerend Arbeidsmarktbeleid* (Activating Labour Market Policy), The Hague, Report to the government.

WRR (1987), *Een Werkend Perspectief* (A Perspective of Work), The Hague, Report to the government.

Chapter 13

Assessing the Influence of Gösta Rehn in France

Dominique Anxo, Christine Brossier, Bernard Gazier[1]

Introduction

The influence of Gösta Rehn on French social and economic policy debate appears to have been deep, though discrete. Looking for evidence of direct and wide diffusion of his ideas and proposals in France proves disappointing. A review of the literature shows that very few references in French are to be found (see bibliography). Even when taking the indirect route of looking for references to Scandinavian social orientations, the result is not much more satisfying. Internationally, the name of Gösta Rehn is directly connected to the so-called 'Swedish Model', but few in France, even in well-informed milieus, clearly associate his name to this model, and fewer know of the 'Rehn-Meidner Model' as such.

In fact, Rehn lived nc fewer than twelve years in France, where he was head of the OECD Directorate of Manpower and Social Affairs (1962 – 1974), and was involved in various activities and networks in this country during this period and subsequently. Analysing in detail such a complex set of actions and connections would be the only correct approach, but is beyond the scope of our short essay. Our aim is, more modestly, and according to the information we were able to gather,[2] to provide some insight into the immediate and lasting consequences of Rehn's active presence in France, focusing on certain key topics and networks.

Our contribution is divided into four sections. First we consider the various channels through which Rehn participated in French social debates and policy decisions and how these took up the main themes he developed. In our second section we examine his influence on some aspects of labour market policy in a broad sense. Third, we focus on the issue of working time, which has received specific attention in France. In our last section, we broaden the perspective with a few remarks on the role played by the 'Swedish model' in France.

Channels and subjects

At least three different channels of influence can be identified:

1) As a member of the OECD staff, Gösta Rehn initiated research programs, proposals, and symposia, on various topics and issues, such as active labour market policy, training and retraining, lifelong learning, and working time flexibility. Under his direction, the OECD held a number of meetings with the active participation of social partners, as well as experts from national governments and administrations. As a matter of course, these activities involved French trade union members,[3] employers and experts. Later, Rehn participated as an expert himself for certain OECD reports, some of which were co-ordinated by French experts. This channel of influence can be termed as international and technical. Through it, certain French specialists in industrial relations, labour market policy and training institutions gained a detailed knowledge of his works and proposals.
2) As a political and union activist, Rehn met a number of French activists during a period characterized by vivid political debates about desirable social institutions, the future of capitalism and socialism, and the question of self-management ('autogestion'). He participated in their discussion networks through various 'think tanks', political-ideas 'clubs', non-profit networks, and political party meetings. This channel was more general in terms of ideas and more specific in terms of networks. It depended on contacts with specific organizations more or less sympathetic to the ideas and experiences promoted by Rehn. In the French case, the main organization involved was the socialist party and, to a lesser extent, the non-communist unions, CFDT and FO.[4]
3) Gösta Rehn was able, in a discrete way, to influence certain top-level political decision-makers through continuing dialogue and collaboration, as well as interventions at critical moments. This channel of influence is personal, and was contingent on opportunities and trust. Here three names can be cited in particular: Jacques Delors, Michel Rocard and Dominique Strauss-Kahn. Most significant is the fifty-year long dialogue between Rehn and Delors. At the beginning of the 1950s, Delors, then a young union expert on economic questions at the Christian trade union CFTC (which later became the secular CFDT), met Rehn in Sweden. He immediately realized the importance of the emerging 'Swedish model' and the two developed a relationship based on personal friendship and shared views of social and economic issues.

As a man of action as well as a social thinker, Rehn simultaneously developed these three channels, and was able to reinforce each of them by the others. The main sources associated with the three channels described above which we have used to look at Rehn's contributions are:

a) OECD publications, reports and activities,

b) Interventions, articles, interviews in academic journals and political reviews and articles about him in newspapers,[5]
c) Personal statements about specific events and policies.

As a point of departure, we note that Rehn's influence, at least during his presence in France and despite the relationship established with Jacques Delors, was not associated with any general discussion on the advantages and drawbacks of the 'Swedish model'. During the 1960s and 70s, French policy debate on the left was dominated by the perspective of a rupture with capitalism and search for an original way – which in 1978 brought the alliance of the Socialist and Communist parties. Debate on such a 'model' came more to the fore during the 1980s, when the rupture perspective was abandoned and unemployment was soaring in France while Sweden seemed to be completely immune. Hence, we shall first focus on specific policy themes and topics specifically advocated by Rehn, and then introduce the 'Swedish model'.

Active labour market policy and collective bargaining

How might some features of the Scandinavian experience be adapted to a Latin, state dominated country? Rehn's Sweden sought to combat inflation through an ambitious active labour market policy designed to complement wage bargaining. Such a policy encompassed mobility and training schemes, and wage subsidies for the hard-to-place, and was part of a new relationship between the social partners. In contrast, in France the policies remained separate, and implementation of each was crucially associated with state intervention. The first debate to be initiated was over income policy; it was followed by training, and, last, by 'active labour market policy'.

The wage-inflation nexus: delayed influence

During the 1950s and 60s, Rehn made numerous important contributions on the subject of wage inflation. These were available in French, for example through the ILO channel (*Revue internationale du travail* 1959). The main thesis was twofold:

1) Keynesian effective demand management brought a danger of fostering cost-inflation through wage drift that had to be eliminated. And the solution proposed by Rehn was to develop an active labour market policy, with wage subsidies and occupational and geographical mobility measures. Thus, expanding demand beyond a given point in order to keep unemployment low was unnecessary to avoid the specific drawbacks of an expansive macroeconomic policy, namely labour shortages with inflationary consequences. In addition, the application of the egalitarian principles underlying the solidaristic wage policy meant that it was not necessary to develop wage inequality in order to foster worker reallocation from 'sunset' to 'sunrise' industrial firms.

2) In a small open economy like Sweden, it was possible to build on the distinction between a protected sector and a sector exposed to international competition, with important consequences as regards wages. Some inequality rewarding particular efforts made in the exposed sector could be tolerated, but the gains from exports had to be redistributed to the whole economy.

From this came the idea of centralised and co-ordinated wage bargaining with wages in line with the sum of productivity growth in the export-oriented sector and world inflation.

This line of thinking was not followed in France due to two factors. First, it was associated with Swedish specificities, such as labour shortages and high mobility costs. Second, the main bargaining tradition in France, the very opposite of the Swedish one, was characterised by dispersed, rival and highly militant trade unions, some of them espousing radical political projects. Moreover, French industrial relations were characterised by unstable bargaining processes and the trade unions were accustomed to present strong claims with little co-ordination with employers. This contrasts sharply with the Swedish experience.

Consequently, the main solution explored in France was the so-called 'income policy', advocated for example by Jacques Delors during the 1960s and 70s. This policy consisted of the application of state-fixed norms strongly urged upon the social partners before the bargaining process began. Such ex-ante wage moderation is closer to the Dutch experience[6] and quite different from the Swedish debate on ex-post absorption via specific taxes of any excess of distributed purchasing power. The 'income policy' was sharply criticized by the unions and the left-wing political parties, and not implemented as such during the 1960s and 70s.

It was later, in a different context (one of deep monetary and external trade crisis) at the beginning of the 1980s, that Delors succeeded, as finance minister, in promoting ex-ante wage moderation and breaking the inflationary spiral in France.[7] It was only during the 1980s that the understanding that France was also an open economy came to be commonly accepted.

Training efforts and industrial relations

Gösta Rehn's influence is clear in one specific field where relatively early initiatives were taken in France. This was the promotion of retraining and lifelong learning as a policy device aimed at reconciling efficiency and equity and the adaptation of workers to changing market conditions.

Through the OECD seminars, he contributed indirectly or directly to a number of thematic or national reports on the promotion of 'active manpower policy', with training,[8] placement, hiring subsidies and mobility incentives and an insistence on the active involvement of social partners. He served as a consultant for the UK, Germany, and Japan - but not France (1973).[9] He was, in fact, a forerunner in developing a form of benchmarking on these matters, through international comparisons identifying problems as well as successes.

In some respects French policy developed in accordance with these ideas, through the actual implementation of this policy began before Rehn's arrival in Paris. The French public employment agency was created at the beginning of the 1960s. Rehn's main influence was through his efforts at involving the social partners in the conception and implementation of the vocational training system. At the end of the 1960s, after the Grenelle Agreement (*Les Accords de Grenelle* – the main result of which was a massive wage increase) the French social partners collectively bargained over training and retraining issues.

We should at this point return to the dialogue with Delors, who was associated with a number of OECD reports during the 1960s as an expert on the 'Commissariat Général du Plan', a French agency fostering long-term predictions and social dialogue. The crucial period was 1969-1971 when Delors, serving as counsellor to Prime Minister Chaban-Delmas, promoted important reforms under the rubric 'Nouvelle Société'. Before accepting the position, Delors had presented to Chaban-Delmas a program delineating the reforms needed to modernize France. The context was highly specific: one year after the 'May 68 events' and the student revolt, some type of new social action deal seemed possible, even if power remained in the hands of the conservative or centrist Gaullists. For a left-wing activist and policy expert such as Delors, this was an opportunity to translate ideas into policy initiatives. In the action program, approved by the prime minister, entitled 'Note on social policy',[10] a key paragraph concerned 'the implementation of an active employment and training policy', which was presented as urgent:

> ... the immediate implementation of an active employment and professional training policy. As regards employment service, we have unfortunately ten years of backwardness compared to great modern nations. We have to change our rhythm by a spectacular program of development of placement and orientation services, and by the amplification of the effort to ensure six months paid vocational training. The trade unions must be closely associated to the conception and implementation of this policy.[11]

A concrete result of such a policy was the 1971 law on occupational training, often referred to as the 'Delors law', which relied on the previous agreements with the social partners. However, it differed from the orientation proposed by Rehn. The law stipulated that firms had to spend a given percentage of their wage bill in training and retraining their workforce, or to pay it to the government in order to develop training for the employees. So we observe, as for income policy, a French program, adapted to the French particularities, with negotiations backed up by state intervention. The law was seen as one of the main tools for adapting the labour force to the new constraints faced by the economy.

The Delors-Rehn dialogue took another early and concrete form with the presentation of the 'training voucher' during the years 1973-74 through the social discussion club *Echanges et projets*. At the same time the shared idea of a 'time bank' emerged (see below).

More generally, both during his short but intense participation in the Chaban-Delmas government and later on, Delors promoted 'social dialogue', opening new dimensions for French industrial relations. He explicitly acknowledged the importance of the Scandinavian experience and later welcomed the 'Scandinavian idea of industrial democracy'.[12] Thus the modernizing process of the industrial relations in France, from confrontation and protest with little coordination, toward more effective social dialogue and negotiations, can in part be ascribed to the influence of Gösta Rehn.

'Activating' labour market policies? Delayed influence

Finally, another discussion related to employment policy came to the fore, namely over the 'activation' of labour market policy. The main issue was whether to increase the share of 'active measures'. During the 1980s and 90s, a period plagued with massive and lasting unemployment in France (over 10 per cent), the debate focussed on the more favourable Swedish unemployment performance. While active labour market expenditure accounted for two thirds of total labour market expenditure in Sweden, in France it was only one third.

Several efforts were made in France to increase the share of active policy, but without considering the other elements of the Swedish model or of Rehn's proposals. These efforts had some limited success in the 1990s, as the share of the active components rose toward 40 per cent.

The French governments gave much attention and placed much hope on wage subsidies, either targeted on specific disadvantaged groups, or aimed at lowering the labour cost of the low-skilled workforce. As we know, marginal employment subsidies were long advocated by Rehn.

Rehn's influence was delayed and somehow paradoxical, because the problems he was initially concerned with were the lack of qualified labour force and the mobility/inflationary nexus, while it was in a totally different labour market context that a more comprehensive and active labour market policy was discussed in France.

Working time policy: towards a society of free choice

Working time policy was a major concern for Gösta Rehn. As early as in the mid-1940s, he proposed to implement a system of time banks to limit short run employment fluctuations over the business cycle (Rehn 1944 and 1988). But the major contribution to the subject of working time remains incontestably his seminal article from 1972 when he was Director for Manpower and Social Affairs at the OECD in

Paris. In this pioneering work, *Prospective View on Patterns of Working Time*, Rehn sets out his ideas as to how working time policy should cope with the major transformations experienced by industrialized countries. The article constitutes a plea for the implementation of a policy, which promotes individual flexibility over the life cycle in the regulation and allocation of time between gainful employment, study and leisure.

For Rehn, the wide range of individual preferences as regards the reduction and flexibility of working time points in the direction of more flexible adaptations of working time over the life cycle. While general and uniform reductions of working time were undoubtedly necessary in the past,[13] the need for flexibility, reflecting various household situations and working conditions, cannot be satisfied only by standardized or statutory regulations giving little room for individual differentiation. Both economic efficiency and the heterogeneity of individual preferences require differentiation and variability in working time patterns.

According to Rehn, the traditional division of time between periods of education, paid employment and retirement reflects a social order and concept of work organization increasingly unsuited to the major features of post-industrial societies. In contrast to the prevailing piecemeal view of time allocation, he favoured a holistic approach, recommending the implementation of a single comprehensive and co-ordinated system for financing all periods of non-paid time. He proposed the introduction of general income insurance combined with access to individual drawing rights.[14] Furthermore this system should provide a high degree of interchangeability in the allocation of time over the life cycle. Hence, for Rehn, individual freedom in allocation must be guaranteed through the application of a universal citizen right, complemented by an integrated system of income transfers. The financing of income transfer between the various periods of paid employment and other social activities (leisure, education, training, retirement, etc) should be based on a general income insurance fund financed out of social contribution taxes. In other words, the financing of pensions, leave periods and training should be consolidated into an integrated social insurance system. In terms of social justice, the general and compulsory membership of all individuals in the proposed financing system, individual drawing rights appear to be more equitable since everyone contributes to the financing of such system, each individual is the main beneficiary of his own contribution.[15] Technically, the system of income insurance and drawing rights cover all periods of non-work: the payment out of current income to cover the cost of pensions for old age and disability, of various forms of leave of absence (parental and educational leaves, sabbaticals etc), would be administrated by a single central fund and be registered by computer on each individual account. Every year each citizen could get access to his account together with information about the current state of his drawing rights and the conditions for their utilization.

Independently of the social desirability of such a system, Rehn argued that the ongoing transformation of modern societies requires both a greater differentiation in working time patterns and a system of income transfer between periods of directly productive paid work and other social activities in each individual's life. Since the publication of his seminal paper, most industrial societies have experienced a marked trend towards a *diversification, decentralisation and individualisation* of working time patterns. Over the last two decades, the profound changes in household[16] and demographic structure have created new needs and also new challenges. The globalisation process and the intensification of competition have had a large impact on production methods and work organisation. Modifications in consumer behaviour and product diversification have meant that an increasing number of enterprises have gradually abandoned Taylorist methods of mass production. The introduction of these new methods (just in time, lean production, etc) has been reflected by a gradual abandonment of traditional ways of adjusting employment and by a much more flexible organisation of work and working time. These changes often make the conventional weekly standard of working time obsolete and are forcing enterprises to rethink the ways in which they regulate working time. In a growing number of enterprises, strict control of working hours is being replaced by performance monitoring. These modifications often give employees much more freedom in choosing their working hours.[17] These new trends therefore reflect the transition from a relatively standardised work organisation structure and working time patterns to more complex and more diversified structures (see Anxo and O'Reilly 2000).

These new trends also coincide with the emergence of the so-called information and knowledge-based economy, which obliges both individuals and firms to reconstruct their competence more frequently than before. Such accelerating changes call for new strategies. The new economy put pressures on adaptability in terms of occupational mobility and recurrent training. Rehn's thirty-year-old proposal is thus well in line with the major transformation of modern post-industrial societies. The implementation of drawing rights is not only beneficial for the individual but also for the economy as a whole since the application of a universal citizen right to recurrent periods of education has an overall productivity enhancing effect. The system promotes investment in human capital and improves the efficiency of the matching process in the labour market.[18]

Promoting flexibility in working life appears also to be a major concern in the European Union. Enhancing working time flexibility is a key issue in efforts to improve the employment content of economic growth. Following the conclusions of the Extraordinary European Council on employment in Luxembourg in 1997, the Council adopted a Resolution on guidelines for employment, intended to improve enterprises' and workers' capacities for adaptation. In order to promote a more modern labour organisation, the social partners are exhorted to negotiate, at the appropriate level, agreements to introduce flexible and innovative methods of labour organisation to reconcile enterprises' need to be competitive with employee preferences over the division of time between work, leisure and education. This quest for new forms of negotiated flexibility could, for instance, take the form of agreements over the reduction of working time, the annualisation of working hours, the reduction of overtime, the development of part-time work, 'lifelong' education and career breaks. Even if these initiatives can be seen to be roughly in line with earlier Rehn proposals, they are still piece-meal measures and not part of an integrated model combining reforms of social insurance and the allocation of time.

The rising imbalances and slackening-off of growth brought about by the first oil crisis led to a lively and polemical debate in a number of European countries about reducing unemployment by a general reduction in working time. In some EU member states, trade union organizations and governments took a favourable attitude towards the reduction of working time, hoping for net job creation or at least for a curb on rising unemployment. In this respect France constitutes a good illustration. During the last decades, French working time policy has been characterized by a set of measures aiming to reduce labour supply[19] and by various statutory reductions of working time in order to combat mass unemployment. Even though his drawing rights system could also be used to promote temporary reduction of working time (by providing income maintenance for the hours not worked and by giving financial incentives[20] to stimulate the temporary reduction of working time for vocational or academic studies), Rehn consistently opposed any general statutory reduction of working time to resolve imbalances in the labour market. He remained convinced that unemployment depends on other factors than the length of the standard workweek and that there is no clear-cut correlation between countries' level of unemployment and the length of working time. The impact of a statutory reduction of working time is, inter alia, highly dependent upon the conditions under which it is implemented and also upon the strategy of the players involved. Hence, for Rehn, the conditions under which a general statutory reduction of working time might have a long-term impact on employment and unemployment are very restrictive. It is therefore not surprising that he was opposed to the French statutory working time reform initiated in 1981/82 ('39 hours paid as 40').[21] Delors, then minister of finance in the Mauroy government, asked him to write a short position paper against such a reform. He wrote it together with Jarl Bengtsson but the arguments were not fully accepted by the government. It must, however, be noted that the proposal to further reduce weekly working time (35 hours in 1985) was postponed.

At first sight, thus, the influence of Rehn's proposals appears limited: a comprehensive and integrated policy of time allocation does not seem to be at the top of the French political agenda. Nevertheless, his ideas on time flexibility have, over time, gained more support. French efforts to promote the emergence of a negotiated flexibility, concretised by the recent modification of the working time law, combined with a system of financing incentives, are partly in line with Rehn's objective of increasing the variability of working time and reconciling firms' competitive constraints with employees' preferences over working time patterns, but are still far from an overall societal project aiming to promote a society of free choice. It should, nevertheless, be added that some elements of Rehn's proposal are now, at the turn of the century, under active discussion at government and expert levels.

Two related examples can be mentioned here. 1) The 1998 'Supiot report',[22] written by a French labour law specialist on the future of industrial relations in Europe, insisted on the contrast between 'passive protection' and 'active security', and developed solutions in terms of new rights to be given to the workers through a system of vouchers. Such an approach (thirty years later) followed Rehn's well-known distinction between 'security under the shell' vs. 'security through the wings'.[23] 2) Rehn's pioneering view on time allocation is close to the concept of Transitional Labour Markets developed by Schmid and Gazier.[24] One of the central issues in the theory of the Transitional Labour Market is promoting individual freedom of choice in the allocation time over the life cycle. From an organizational, social and income distribution point of view, Transitional Labour Markets appear to be a combination of gainful employment and other useful social activities, a combination of paid work, transfer payments and contracted entitlements for transitional employment over the life cycle.

The Swedish model

We can now turn to the 'Swedish model' and its perception and fate in France. We noted that during the 1960s and 70s most French policymakers and thinkers (with the exception of Jacques Delors and Michel Rocard) were simply not interested in such a model.[25] The main references on the left were the (more or less fading, but still maintained) notion of a socialist revolution and a clear break with capitalist society. Certain Italian experiences and ideas were much more attractive than those of Sweden, which seemed too timid and intrinsically reformist. Indeed, Sweden was little known (and prejudices abounded). As noted above, the social dialogue also was weak, discontinuous and eruptive, while the left-wing parties were completely excluded from executive power. Still, at the end of the 1970s, Rehn succeeded in arranging a meeting between Francois Mitterrand, then first secretary of the Socialist Party, and Olof Palme.[26]

We mentioned that during the 1980s the perception changed dramatically,[27] when the employment performances of Sweden contrasted with France's persisting problems. The 'model' became an object of debate and research, and the main principles elaborated by Rehn and Meidner came to the fore. The political context also changed radically: the long lasting government experience of the Socialist Party, with little progress toward any rupture with capitalism and high unemployment, coupled with the advancing European project and 'globalisation', led to the expression of more reformist (realistic?) aspirations and more attention paid to Scandinavian experiences and achievements.

In this new context, measures more or less derived from Rehn became fashionable. Michel Rocard, after he became prime minister in 1988, implemented a 'continuing education voucher' that can be seen as taking up the proposals Delors and Rehn made at the beginning of the 1970s.

In sum, the influence of Gösta Rehn in France, while discreet, has nevertheless been significant. Rehn actively contributed to many of the important labour market policy debates in France, and, while it may be difficult to trace exactly the path of his influence, his contacts with a number of prominent figures, in particular Delors and Rocard, had an impact on policy development in France. Those who met Rehn in France were struck by the exceptional strength and originality of his personality, his powers of persuasion, and his continual effort to find ways of combining social justice with economic efficiency. Perhaps most impressive is how many of his ideas, including especially active labour market and flexible working time policy, though developed in the 1940s, are still viewed as modern and progressive today.

Notes

1 Dominique Anxo is associate professor of economics, University of Göteborg and director of the Centre for European Labour Market Studies (CELMS); Christine Brossier is head of the documentary centre of the 'Maison des Sciences Economiques', University Paris 1; Bernard Gazier is professor of economics, University Paris 1, and director of the MATISSE, University Paris 1 and CNRS. The authors would like to thank Donald Storrie for helpful comments.

2 Our thanks go to Danielle Rehn, Jarl Bengtsson (Counsellor, Centre for Research and Innovation in Education, OECD), and Robert Cottave (expert at the Force Ouvrière trade union.) who provided key information. Our special thanks go to Jacques Delors who agreed to be interviewed (March 20, 2000). This article owes much to his information and analyses.

3 Not from the CGT, Confédération Générale du Travail, however, which had no access to the OECD meetings.

4 In particular André Bergeron from FO (Force Ouvrière) and Eugène Descamp from the CFTC-CFDT (Confédération Française des Travailleurs Chrétiens, Confédération Française Démocratique du Travail).

5 In the documentary centre of the newspaper *Le Monde*, on the whole sympathetic with Rehn's ideas, there exist only three articles about him (1973, 1978 and 1996). This situation is a good illustration of Rehn's low visibility in French information networks.

6 During the 1950s, three 'income policy' experiences were developed: the first one, bilateral and bargained, was in Sweden; the second, trilateral, and involving the state as well as social partners, was in the Netherlands, and the third, which turned out to be a failure, in the UK.

7 In our interview, Delors declared that he would have preferred to attain that result through the concertation of the social partners.

8 During the 1960s, Delors, invited by Rehn, participated in OECD experts groups on education and wrote a number of reports.

9 The commissioned experts were Charles Steward, Deputy Assistant Secretary for International Affairs, Department of Labour, USA, and Joseph Deroo, Directeur à l'Administration de l'Emploi du Ministère Belge de l'Emploi et du Travail. The French delegation comprised Joseph Fontanet, then minister of labour, and a number of members of the cabinet and the administration of the ministry.

10 Delors (1975), pp. 333-9.

11 Delors (1975), p. 334.

12 Delors (1975), p. 279.

13 For Rehn statutory regulation or collective agreements on working time remains, of course, a guarantee against the negative externalities associated with long working hours.

14 The proposed system of drawing rights included the possibility of advance credit, which can be drawn upon before any fees have been paid.

15 As stressed by Rehn under due actuarial account of the risk sharing involved.

16 In particular, the increased feminisation of the labour force and the related shift from the single male breadwinner household to dual earner households.

17 From the point of view of employees, while it is true that diversified forms of flexible working hours give them greater freedom of choice, it should also be borne in mind that the development of some forms of working time seems also to exacerbate duality between labour market segments and increase gender segregation. Flexible working time is often associated with lower pay levels and with less stable employment relationships. Thus, in parallel with the upturn in flexible forms of working time there has also been an increase in fixed-term employment contracts.

18 As mentioned earlier, the idea of a training voucher was also explored at the beginning of the 1970s by Delors within the framework of 'Echanges et projets' club. The reference given for 'Club Echanges et projets' is a book published in 1980, but the ideas circulated within this club at the beginning of the 1970s (suggested by Jacques Delors; our interview).

19 In particular, an ambitious program of early retirement and training measures targeted at young people.

20 As a supplement to the drawing rights.

21 And, of course, the recent statutory reduction introducing the 35 hours (the so-called Aubry Law) still motivated primarily as a means of reducing unemployment.

22 Supiot (1999).

23 For a French version, see Rehn (1978), p. 316.

24 Schmid and Gazier (2000). For a French overall presentation of Transitional Labour Markets, see Gazier (1998).

25 Very early, Rocard took a favourable view of the Swedish model in an interview in *Lui, le magazine de l'homme moderne* (1970). Even if Delors was also sympathetic, he felt that any attempt to adopt the Scandinavian model in France was unrealistic (comment made during our interview).

26 Interview of Jarl Bengtsson, March 2, 2000.

27 An illustration of the changing perception may be found in the anthology *La socialdémocratie en questions* (1981), published by the French socialists, which aimed at discussing the whole span of European experiences.

References

Anxo, Dominique and Jacqueline O'Reilly (2000), 'Working Time Regimes and Transitions in Comperative Perspective,' in Jacqueline O'Reilly, Inmaculada Cebrian and Michel Lallement (eds), *Working Time Changes: Social Integration through Transitional Labour Market*, Edward Elgar, Cheltenham, pp. 61-90.

Club Echanges et Projets (1980), *La révolution du temps choisi*, Albin Michel, Paris.

Delors, Jacques (1975), *Changer*, Grasset, Paris.

Drouin, Pierre (1973), 'L'ennui, le vice et le besoin', *Le Monde*, 31 mars.

Gazier, Bernard (1998), 'Ce que sont les marchés transitionnels', in Jean-Claude Barbier and Jérôme Gautié (eds), *Les politiques de l'emploi en Europe et aux Etats-Unis*, Presses Universitaires de France, Paris, pp. 339-55.

Groupe de concertation 'Minima sociaux, revenus d'activité, précarité' (2000), *Rapport final*, Commissariat Général du Plan, Paris.

La social-démocratie en questions (1981) (various authors), Editions de la Revue politique et parlementaire, Paris.

Le Monde (1978),'Le BIT préconise les congés payés à la carte', 19-20 mars.

Lui, le magazine de l'homme moderne (1970), 'Tête-à-tête avec Michel Rocard' (interview by Pierre Démeron), January, no 72, pp. 5-16.

OECD (1973), *Manpower Policy in France,* Paris.

Peltier, Benoit (1996), 'Gösta Rehn. Un économiste suédois brasseur d'idées', *Le Monde*, 14 décembre.

Rehn, Gösta (1944), '3 månaders semester som medel mot arbetslöshet I och II', *Fackföreningsrörelsen*, vol. 24, part 1, pp. 110-7, 126-32.

Rehn, Gösta (1972), 'Prospective View on Patterns of Working Time', Manpower and Social Affairs Directorate, OECD, Paris.

Rehn, Gösta (1977), 'Towards a Society of Free Choice', in Jerzy J. Wiatr and Richard Rose (eds) *Comparing Public Choices.* Ossolineum, Wroclaw, pp. 121-57.

Rehn, Gösta (1978), 'Vers une société de libre choix (temps de travail et temps de loisir)', *Droit Social,* Juillet-Août, pp. 314-32.

Rehn, Gösta (1988), *Full Sysselsättning utan Inflation. Skrifter i urval*, Tiden Förlag, Stockholm.

Revue Internationale du Travail (1959), 'Négociations sur les salaires et politiques des salaires en Suède' (no author indicated), vol. LXXX, no 4 and 5.

Schmid, Günther and Gazier, Bernard (forthcoming), *The Dynamics of Full Employment.* Social Integration by Transitional Labour Markets, Edward Elgar, Cheltenham.

Supiot, Alain (1999), *Au delà de l'emploi*, Flammarion, Paris.

Chapter 14

Missed Opportunities: British Social Democracy and the Rehn Model, 1951-1964[1]

Mark Wickham-Jones

Introduction

Between 1951 and 1964, the British and Swedish labour movements advocated different economic programmes which were designed to meet different goals and were based on contrasting conceptions of social democracy. The Swedish Social Democratic Party (SAP) and the Swedish Confederation of Trade Unions (LO) adopted, gradually, the core measures of the model designed by Gösta Rehn and his co-author economists at the LO. The programme was based on three features: deflationary demand management, active labour market measures and a solidaristic wages policy. The policy platforms of both the British Labour party and the Trade Union Congress (TUC) were at odds with each of these aspects of the Rehn model. Labour advocated a straightforward Keynesian economic strategy in which aggregate levels of demand management would ensure full employment (Wickham-Jones 1996, pp. 34-52). The party eschewed measures to improve the operation of the supply side of the economy, such as re-training for the jobless (King 1995, pp. 28-30, 161-2). It proposed to control inflation through a mix of physical controls, economic expansion and moral exhortation. For the most part, the TUC endorsed this programme which was also dominant within the theoretical discourse surrounding social democratic politics. In the first (and full) edition of *The Future of Socialism*, the most influential text of post-war British reformism, Anthony Crosland, endorsed Keynesianism, rejected a wages policy and did not discuss training (Crosland 1956).

In the 1960s, the programme of the British labour movement was reorientated. The realignment involved the advocacy of incomes policy and improved training facilities. Such measures were part of a turn towards planning launched by both the Conservative government and the Labour opposition in an attempt to improve the growth rate of the British economy. Neither the incomes policy nor the training measures that Labour articulated were part of an integrated social democratic strategy as were the measures of the Rehn model. Indeed, when Labour did study such measures, separate policy-making committees discussed them. Incomes policy was designed to insure a planned growth of wages. It did not challenge wage differentials or promote structural economic adjustment as did the Swedish variant. Labour's training measures were not seen as a necessary complement to tackle the 'islands of unemployment' resulting from tight fiscal policy (LO 1953, p. 92). The programmes of Labour and the TUC remained essentially Keynesian. The new policies were designed as part of a modest indicative planning initiative in which the government would map out the higher aggregate levels of demand, investment and output that were desired.

In this article I discuss some of the reasons why the Swedish and British Labour movements adopted such different policy platforms. My objective is to assess why Labour and the TUC did not take up the kind of platform designed by Gösta Rehn and his colleagues in the early 1950s. I realise that this goal may seem futile: to study how two distinct reformist movements responded to the situation in which they found themselves and examine some of the ways in which those responses differed might beg too many questions. Nevertheless, there are important similarities. Although very different in size, Sweden and the United Kingdom were amongst a handful of democratic states in Europe to emerge from the Second World War without having undergone the experiences of either occupation or territorial conflict. Both Sweden and Britain were industrialised nations (more so than Ireland, for example), with a similar per capita income, and both had social democratic governments in the late 1940s. Labour had been elected to office in Britain in 1945; in Sweden, the SAP had been in power since 1932 (with a brief break in 1936). Both had faced inflationary problems in the aftermath of the war: between 1948 and 1950 the labour movement in each had accepted wage restraint in response to economic difficulties (LO 1953, pp. 16-7). By 1950 both the LO and the TUC were hostile to further wage restraint of the kind that had been implemented thus far.

In the 1950s and early 1960s many commentators assumed that aspects, at any rate, of the Swedish model could be applied to the British polity. Gösta Rehn took such a view, perhaps partly for political reasons. He argued, 'My views were even more applicable to England than to Sweden with our a little more centralised unionism. Thus I would say that the need to put the brakes on wages through financial policy, instead of through wage restraint, is even more apparent in England than here' (Rehn 1950a, p. 2). Rudolf Meidner and Rehn discussed the British situation in their respective contributions to the 1952 collection *Wages Policy under Full Employment* (see Rehn 1952, p. 36 and Meidner 1952, p. 26). On the British side, a Labour delegation to Sweden concluded, 'There are many similarities between the Swedish Social Democratic Labour Party and the British Labour Party.'[2]

A variety of academics and commentators argued along similar lines. B. C. Roberts drew a series of parallels between the British and Swedish trade union movement (Roberts 1956). Michael Shanks's volume, *The Stagnant Society*, emphasised the need for the United Kingdom to reform wage bargaining along Swedish lines, so too did Jack Cooper's pamphlet for the Fabian society (Shanks 1961 and

Cooper 1963). In 1958, after a discussion of the Swedish and Dutch experience, Thomas L. Johnston claimed, 'It seems obvious that we in Britain have something to learn from the European approach' (Johnston 1958, p. 144). Writing later John D. Stephens concluded, 'Around 1950, the ideologies of Swedish and British social democracy were more similar than they had been before or would be subsequently' (Stephens 1979, p.146). In a similar vein, Andrew Martin and George Ross (1999, p. 8) asserted that, in the 1940's 'many elements for a "Swedish deal" were present in the United Kingdom.[3] It has been a common assertion amongst academics that senior figures within the British Labour party during the 1950s wanted to emulate Swedish reformism. Perry Anderson labelled Sweden as 'Mr. Crosland's dreamland' (Anderson 1961, pp. 4-12).

The central aim of this article is to examine the limited influence that the Swedish model had in shaping British social democracy over the fifteen years or so from 1951. I discuss four reasons that may explain why Labour failed to espouse the kind of measures associated with Swedish reformism. In the second section, I look at relations between the two countries to assess the extent to which the Rehn model was disseminated within the United Kingdom. In the third section, building on this point, I address the nature of policy-making within the Labour party and TUC. Many commentators have noted the British labour movement's insular nature (Wickham-Jones 2000). In this context, I ask how open was policy-making to outside influences? In the fourth and fifth sections, I assess arguments that were put forward by reformists in Britain when rejecting the Swedish model. I divide these into two broad kinds, structural claims and agent-orientated criticisms. Structural reasons, discussed in the fourth section, concern a variety of institutional impediments to the adoption of Swedish-style policies by the Labour party that were identified by reformists in the United Kingdom. Agent-orientated criticisms, discussed in the fifth section, relate to the objectives of the policies outlined by Rehn and others, and their performance in practice. I ask how attractive was the Rehn model to members of the British labour movement. Finally, in my conclusion, I draw these themes together and consider what the preceding discussion suggests about the nature of the reformist project in the United Kingdom in this period.

The dissemination of the Rehn model

The Labour Party and the TUC enjoyed good relations with the SAP and the LO during the 1950s.[4] For the most part, the parties and union organisations were in frequent and straightforward contact with each other. Many of these, however, concerned relatively low-level and mundane matters such as facilitating exchanges of grassroots party and union members. There were, of course, more significant contacts. In 1954, Hugh Gaitskell visited Sweden, and Tage Erlander, the Swedish prime minister, attended Labour's annual conference at Scarborough.

Between 1951 and 1964 only one party delegation and one TUC group visited Sweden to study its social democratic arrangements. The party trip took place in August 1951, before the LO Congress in September that year. It noted the 'influence and authority' of the movement's central organisations and concluded, 'Sweden provides many lessons which other nations might well learn, mark and inwardly digest.'[5] It did not spell out the nature of those lessons and the visit was accorded the briefest of references in Labour's 1952 annual report. A further party delegation visited Denmark, Sweden and Norway in May 1963 specifically to discuss the European Free Trade Area. Of course, fraternal delegates were sent regularly to conferences of the SAP and the LO. During the 1963 visit, wider discussions took place on a variety of issues, including incomes policies (Report 1963, p. 6). The delegation's report noted, 'There is a feeling amongst the Scandinavian Social Democratic Parties that there are not enough visits from leading Labour party figures ... Their governments have a wealth of experience (particularly Sweden) which the Labour party would do well to study' (Report 1963, p. 2). The secretary of one local Labour party wrote to head office in 1960, suggesting that 'on the face of it, we should have more to learn from the Swedish than the other European Labour parties' (Sweeny 1960).

A TUC delegation visited Sweden in October 1962 at the invitation of the LO. There were clear differences within the group about what lessons might be drawn from Swedish experience. A report, based on two internal papers, was published in May 1963. The TUC wanted to look at what was the basis for union centralisation, what determined good industrial relations, and how the national interest could be reconciled to that of individual union members. It concluded, 'Clear and precise answers were not obtained to each of these questions' (TUC 1962a, p. 1). Although the 1963 trip to Sweden represented a serious initiative in looking at social democratic arrangements, little came of it. The report was mentioned at the 1963 Congress where some hostility was expressed towards Scandinavian reformism.

How well received in Britain were the ideas set out by Rehn and his colleagues in the 1951 LO report and elsewhere? The 1951 report was abridged and translated into English in 1953. A collection of articles on the issues surrounding the report was translated and published in 1952, edited by Ralph Turvey, who was one of the few economists to read the draft of Crosland's 1962 collection, *The Conservative Enemy*. Academically, it was reasonably well received. One reviewer of the volume commented that 'Rehn's proposals are original and ingenious. But they imply an overwhelming amount of state control and still depend in some degree on voluntary restraint of trade unions.'[6] Rehn's approach was 'stimulating and provocative'. In the *American Economic Review*, Melvin W. Reder noted, 'Rehn, however, is more willing to take the risks of living with Leviathan' (Reder 1953, p. 715). Incidentally, Reder reported that he had seen an alternative translation of Rudolf Meidner's chapter in the collection (itself an indication of interest in the approach). He noted that an omission in the published version of Meidner's chapter 'quite altered' it.

Meidner's advocacy of a 'planned agreement policy, which would not exactly mean centralized actions for increased wages but central influence on the claims of the different unions' had been deleted (Reder 1953, p. 715). The reviewer in *Economica* concluded, 'The constructive suggestions all come from Mr. Rehn' (Morgan 1952, p. 443).

Aside from the translation of its 1951 report, the LO throughout the 1950s disseminated a regular bulletin on economic and political developments in Sweden (LO 1948-63). Although the bulletin did not lay out the Rehn model as a set of propositions, it did detail the kind of policies on wage setting and the labour market being advocated by the LO and being implemented by the SAP government. The report went to both the Labour party and the TUC. The TUC sent Tom Eccles as a delegate to the 1951 Congress at which the LO report was debated and his report referred to the discussions on wage setting. The experience does not appear to have had much impact on his outlook: at the 1952 TUC Congress, he spoke in favour of free collective bargaining (TUC 1952, p. 486).

The key features of the Rehn model were laid out in an internal Labour party memorandum in 1956, a summary of a Socialist International conference. It accepted that one means, amongst others, to secure price stability 'is through the acceptance of a rather lower level of demand for labour without departing from the objective of full employment policy; this would mean tackling what would be merely local pools of unemployment by other means.'[7] Similar wording cropped up later: 'The resulting islands of unemployment should then be treated as special areas.' The phrase 'islands of unemployment' was taken from the LO report (the phrase was also used later by Meidner).[8] Crosland cited the 1953 translation in his discussion of wages in *The Future of Socialism* as an 'excellent discussion of this point, and indeed of the whole question of wages policy' (Crosland 1956, p. 451). His conclusion was rather different to that articulated by the LO. High profits would undermine, he noted, wage restraint. He concluded that in such circumstances restraint would have to be abandoned. The LO position, of course, proposed to tackle the high surplus accruing to employers through a profits squeeze whilst maintaining some form of restraint.

Senior figures within the British Labour movement were well informed about the details contained in the 1951 report. Gösta Rehn had written to the secretary of the TUC research and economics department in September 1950, outlining the key features of his approach. He was prompted to do it following the rejection of the General Council's support for the Labour government's wage restraint at the Blackpool congress. He summarised his position:

> [For] a more definitive solution of the wages and prices stabilisation problem in full employment, we – the trade unions – take some money from profits, the government takes some of the money from us through diminishing of subsidies or increase of taxes in order to keep general purchasing power in line with real economic possibilities; thus lack of

> consumers' purchasing power makes it impossible for entrepreneurs – at least in part – to increase prices enough to compensate themselves for all of the increased wage costs… I am only afraid that this policy will not be carried through with enough audacity (Rehn 1950b, p. 2).

Rehn called for wage increases for the low paid and concluded, 'There should be no support for those demanding simply a restoration of the old set of differentials.' He hoped that the Congress decision 'will force English economic policy in "my" direction'.

On behalf of the TUC, D. Bowers, secretary of the research and economics department, was unimpressed by Rehn's ideas, replied that such views 'may well be completely valid for the Swedish economy, but I can foresee some difficulties in the way of their application here' (Bowers 1950a, p. 1). In place of the kind of measures Rehn proposed, Bowers predicted that there would be a return in the United Kingdom to the kind of direct controls utilised during the Second World War. When Rehn responded at some length to Bowers' criticisms, the TUC official was blunt to the point of rudeness: 'I fear I must call a halt at this point' (Bowers 1950b, p. 1).

Labour's insular policy-making

Academic commentators have often noted the internalised nature of Labour party politics. An example of that insularity is to be found in the party's policy-making process during the 1950s and into the 1960s. Few Labour party documents looked at the experience of social democratic parties abroad. Policy-making committees did not discuss, for the most part, the policies articulated by other reformist parties. A draft pamphlet, 'What about Wages?' produced in May 1951, while Labour was in government, did look at the record of other countries in designing incomes policies. It did not address the Swedish case. In Norway, it noted, 'This policy seems to have worked very well.'[9] It was the last paper to look at the use of wages policy and the nature of anti-inflation measures elsewhere.

The only internal document to discuss the features of the Rehn model during the 1950s was the report of the Socialist International experts' conference in 1955. It laid out the key proposals in clear fashion: 'Equal pay for equal work can itself be a useful instrument for distributing the labour force. It obliges all firms, whatever their efficiency, to pay an identical rate for the job. Inefficient firms cannot survive by paying low wages.'[10] It continued, 'A low cost, low-profit economy should be aimed at, accepting the consequences that marginal firms will be forced out of business.'[11] The memorandum simply reported the conference: it did not associate the above directly with the Swedish LO. It made a few critical comments about different positions but did not seek to analyse them. The paper did not feed into the party's policy-making machinery.

When the party finally turned back to examine incomes policies in the early 1960s, such measures were couched in national terms. The papers laid before Labour's finance and economic policy sub-committee did not address either Swedish experiences or those of social democrats elsewhere. In designing an incomes policy on which to fight the 1964 general election, Labour's economic policy committee was not influenced by Swedish arrangements. Such measures were never discussed.

The conclusion that Labour's failure to learn from Sweden was a reflection of its internalised nature may reflect an over-emphasis upon the formal policy-making processes of the party. It is possible that outside the sub-committees of Labour's National Executive Committee and away from the work of the party's research department, Swedish experiences were discussed. Most of the party's economic policy documents resulted, however, from the initiatives of the sub-committees and the research department. Drafts from these were formalised, approved and sent to the annual conference for confirmation. In any case, there is limited evidence of an alternative, more open, policy-process being in existence alongside the more formal, closed, set of formal procedures. To be sure, leading figures within the party did discuss economic matters outside of committees. But such activities were not isolated from formal policy-making; rather they represented a continuation of it. A series of private party seminars, including shadow chancellor James Callaghan at Nuffield College, Oxford during 1962-63, discussed economic matters, including papers from the finance and economic policy sub-committee (Morgan 1997, pp. 173-9). At the time, Hugh Gaitskell, as party leader, did express some interest in Scandinavian mechanisms. He told Callaghan, 'What I have in mind, of course, is the whole question of incomes policy. Somebody ought to be studying pretty seriously the Swedish and Dutch systems and considering the possibilities of applying them here' (Williams 1979, p. 674). Callaghan's reply was indicative of the party's outlook: he 'seems to have interpreted this as an inquiry about the group's work in general' (Morgan 1997, p. 179). He claimed that they had been looked at and that little could be done until the party was in office. Around the same time, Gaitskell told Alistair Hetherington that the ground had been prepared for an incomes policy (Hetherington 1962).

Aside from discussion over incomes policy, it should be noted that Labour's policy making was less internalised during the early 1960s. Some of the memoranda on planning looked at experiences elsewhere. Thomas Balogh, an economic adviser, noted Japan and France's success; 'It would be foolish to imagine that Britain could obtain equal success just by establishing a planning agency' (Balogh 1962, p. 3; Neild 1962). He argued, however, that lessons could be learnt. Around the same time, a couple of internal papers examined social security provision in Belgium, Germany and the United States alongside Sweden.[12] Later documents looked at taxation and at housing finance in Sweden.[13] As a final contrast with incomes policy, on training Labour did note, in detailing the difference between

Britain and Sweden in terms of the numbers involved, the apparent success of foreign arrangements.[14] Another document stated, 'our effort pales into insignificance when compared with the activity abroad, particularly in Sweden and the USA ... We can learn much from foreign experience, particularly that in Sweden.'[15] Even so, Labour's training proposals in 1964 revolved around economic expansion and not the reskilling needs of those out of work. They did little to challenge the prevalent voluntarism of British industrial relations (King 1995, pp. 129-33). A delegation of trade unionists, civil servants and employers to Sweden in 1961 reported, 'The team members were most impressed by the size of the training programme, its flexibility and its comprehensiveness in providing for the needs of so many different age groups and categories' (Delegation to study training, 1961, pp. 2-3).

Unlike the Labour party, the TUC did look in detail at Swedish reformism as an integrated package. Two background papers were produced, one before and one after the union delegation had visited in October 1962. In January 1963 the TUC economics committee debated at length the draft report. Some members of the delegation argued that the trip had been useful 'in stimulating constructive thinking about the problems of British trade unions' (TUC economics committee 1963a, p. 23). Overall, however, 'Different members had reached differing views both about the merits of the Swedish system and about the lessons which British trade unionists might draw. To some the differences between the two systems were more apparent than the similarities' (TUC economics committee 1963a, p. 23). The newspaper *Tribune* reported, 'The TUC leaders were impressed with what they saw and heard in Sweden. But they were not blinded.'[16] It described efforts to mimic Swedish arrangements as 'extraordinary rubbish'. Frank Cousins, leader of the Transport and General Workers' Union and a member of the delegation, was critical of Swedish industrial relations, though much more positive about the links between social democratic policy and the trade unions (Goodman 1979, pp. 353-4).

It was agreed that a report should be published: 'great care should, however, be taken in drawing conclusions about the extent to which aspects of the Swedish system were applicable in Britain: it was always unwise, and could be dangerous, to assume that what worked satisfactorily in one country could be imitated in another' (TUC economics committee 1963a, p. 24). When published, the report stated that members of the delegation 'were not looking for, and certainly were not offered, a formula for reproducing in Britain the Swedish pattern of trade unionism or industrial relations' (TUC economics committee 1963a, p. 1). During 1963, the TUC economics committee went on to look at Swedish arrangements, concluding, 'It is doubtful whether it is ever profitable to copy another country's institutions, but some general lessons about the institutional arrangements which would be necessary for the development of incomes policy may be drawn from Dutch and Swedish experience' (TUC economics committee 1963b, p. 7; see also p. 6). Clive Jenkins claimed in *Tribune* that the TUC was influenced by the LO's 1961 report (as well as Catholic social thought) in drafting its supplementary report, *Economic Development and*

Planning, for the 1963 Congress.[17] The TUC report did touch on the demands of structural change but did not outline the kind of strategy that Rehn and others had advocated in Sweden. The Congress rejected one paragraph of the report, which hinted at an organised wages policy. Though some TUC officials were interested in closer arrangements with a Labour government, they did not look towards Sweden and its social democratic strategy but rather towards a more generic conception of corporatism in which unions would be accorded some status in the formation and implementation of public policy.[18]

This discussion of policy-making with the labour movement indicates that, though social democrats in Britain were aware of the central features of the Rehn model, those policies had little impact on the economic measures that they designed. I next turn to possible explanations for this position.

Structural obstacles

The most common reason given by social democrats and trade unionists in Britain as to why the Swedish approach was inappropriate concerned structural differences between the two polities (TUC economics committee 1963a, p. 23). Wages policies worked in Sweden because the union movement was concentrated in a relatively small number of unions and because power was centralised in a strong central authority, namely the LO. In the United Kingdom both conditions were missing. The absence of a central authority meant that a wages policy could not be negotiated and implemented. This problem was noted by many trade unionists during the wage restraint of 1948-50, though they did not then compare British experience with that of Sweden. L. C. White told the 1948 TUC Congress, 'We may as well face the fact quite squarely that the TUC has no authority and very little influence over the wages policies of the affiliated unions' (TUC 1948, p. 485). The 1949 TUC report on the economic situation noted, in similar fashion, 'In matters of wage determination the powers of the Trade Union Congress will be limited' (TUC 1949, p. 548). A year later the General Council report was pessimistic, 'It was impossible for a voluntary association such as the TUC to maintain indefinitely a rigid policy of wage restraint' (TUC 1950, p. 260). In their correspondence, D. Bowers told Gösta Rehn, 'There is no machinery for a central control of wages policy in the trade union movement, nor are unions prepared to give such powers to the TUC' (Bowers 1950a, p. 2). When the TUC economics committee debated Swedish reformism in 1963, some members argued that 'the general differences in structure, history and economic background made it impossible to draw from this situation conclusions applicable to Britain' (TUC economics committee 1963a, p. 23). As well as noting structural problems, members of the TUC economics committee praised the sense of common identity in Sweden: 'The real difference lay in the sense of common purpose that pervaded the Swedish movement: in this sense there was no British trade union movement – only a collection of unions' (TUC economics committee 1963a, p. 23). Further reference was made to the way that Swedish situation had been shaped by thirty years of social democratic government.[19] Writing in *Tribune*, Jack Jones, a union leader, referred to 'the peculiar conditions of Sweden.'[20]

Similar points were made within the Labour party. The draft 1951 pamphlet on wages claimed, 'It is important though to note the big difference in the structure of the Norwegian trade union movement and the British movement.'[21] The summary of the experts' conference at which features of the Rehn model were laid out concluded, 'In many countries such a system would be more difficult to operate, because of more complicated union structure or greater diversity within their trade union movement.'[22]

The structural argument did not concern just the nature of the union movement, but also the status of employers' organisations. In the 1950s employers in Britain were as fragmented as the unions: there were two peak organisations, the Federation of British Industry and the British Employers' Confederation. Both were weak. The lack of a single employers' body with authority weakened the argument of those seeking centralised negotiations over such issues as wages and training. In 1962, in response to a question from Rehn, a British Ministry of Labour official scoffed at the idea of co-ordinated employer support for training as a 'hopeless daydream which is only dreamed by impractical theoreticians.'[23]

A further structural dimension concerned the relationship between the unions and the Labour party. The unions founded the party and continued in the 1950s to dominate many aspects of the party, including the voting procedure at the annual conference. In effect, this compact gave the unions a veto over certain areas of policy including incomes policy and training (see Minkin 1980). The result made policy formation in these areas difficult: the TUC was essentially a reactive body in designing macroeconomic strategy but the Labour party could not proceed in certain policies without support from its affiliated unions. A TUC representative on the science and industry sub-committee warned, 'Concerning adult training, I think that it would be most advisable to consult trade unions before formulating any detailed policy in this field' (Winnard 1963, p. 2).

Although the structural objections to the British labour movement copying Swedish social democratic arrangements have some force and were made frequently in the early 1960s, there are three significant problems with this approach. The first is that the structural argument under-estimated the agency enjoyed by social democrats. There was a sense of fatalism about the claim that the United Kingdom could never replicate Swedish policies because of a series of impediments. The criticism did not assess what might be done to tackle those obstacles. In this sense, reformism might have been more dynamic. A TUC memo in 1950 noted, 'Scandinavian unions are prepared to adjust themselves to changing circumstances.'[24] Some members of the TUC economics committee 'took the view that, given the will, there was no reason why British unions should not accept the desirability of giving the TUC more power to take decisions in the common interest' (TUC economics committee 1963a, p. 23). The Swedes, it was argued, had adopted the centralised structure: 'The Swedish trade union structure had been consciously adapted to its present form and purposes in accordance with a clear philosophy of trade unionism' (TUC economics committee 1963a, p. 23). A British movement could do likewise.

The second objection challenges the contrasting extent to which the British labour movement was fractured and the Swedish one centralised. Gösta Rehn asked Bowers, 'I wonder if not the English arbitration system is much more effective instrument (for calming down a movement for wage increases tending to run crazy) than our TUC centralisation, which should not be too over-rated in this respect. Our industrial unions are rather self-governing institutions, too' (Rehn 1950a, p. 2). (British arbitration was abandoned in 1951.) With reference to Britain, one union leader, Bryn Roberts, claimed that 'The majority of members in a given industry rarely decide policy; policy is more often decided by small sections within the several competing unions within the industry' (Roberts 1951, p. 16). A TUC background paper doubted the extent of centralisation in Sweden: 'It is highly probable that the LO takes care not to strain too far the limits of tolerance of its affiliated unions and of the membership at large. In matters of structure it proceeds with caution and by persuasion' (TUC 1962b, p. 12). The draft TUC report noted, 'the LO is susceptible to pressure from groups of trade unionists' (TUC 1962a, p. 1). It was pointed out that 'Swedish unions had to justify themselves to their members' (TUC economics committee 1963a, p. 23).

The third objection is that neither the Labour party nor the TUC were consistent in their application of the claim that structural obstacles prevented them from looking to Sweden. If Swedish-style policies were held to be inappropriate because of the fractured nature of the union movement and the lack of a centralised union authority, then so too were any policies which required such preconditions. If the Rehn model was ruled out on these grounds, so too was any use of incomes policy other than the most dirigiste form in which the government determined directly the level of wages. All incomes policy with any voluntary element would founder, by this logic, on the lack of a centralised and disciplined union movement. Equally, if the kind of incomes policy that Labour adopted in the early 1960s, was a feasible one, so too were the measures put forward by Gösta Rehn and his colleagues in the 1950s. Indeed, the Swedish model might appear more attractive than those measures that Labour did adopt, given its carefully designed theoretical nature and its linkage to a social democratic economic strategy. The structural argument, from this perspective, fails to explain why Labour did not follow the Swedish model.

The objectives and outcomes of Swedish reformism

Alongside arguments about the structural obstacles to the adoption by British social democrats of the kind of policies articulated by Swedish reformists was a second broad form of objection. Some critics of the Swedish model focused on its goals, others on its performance during the 1950s to argue that the British labour movement should choose not to adopt such policies because they were undesirable ones.

In terms of aims, some trade unionists objected to the close relations between employers and unions that the Rehn model proposed would help settle wages. At the TUC Congress in 1963, A. W. Day told the audience that he found the Norwegian variant of this approach to contain 'a degree of co-operation and collaboration which to me was quite frightening' (TUC 1963c, p. 376). The idea that a centralised union organisation should negotiate with similar body representing employers over wages challenged a long held attachment to localised free collective bargaining. Many unionists believed that any intervention in wage setting process was unwarranted. In 1950 the TUC General Council report insisted that 'wages policy was not to be imposed by the government and the machinery of voluntary negotiation had to be preserved' (TUC 1950, p. 267). This line of criticism of the Rehn model was made by Labour's summary report of the Socialist International experts' conference: 'The major obstacle to the introduction of a national wages policy in most countries, however, is the fear that it would deprive the trade unions of their traditional functions.'[25] Jack Jones was scathing, 'Acceptance of the "official" point of view of the Swedish trade unions for application in this country would mean disarming the well organised trade unionists' (*Tribune*, 21 June 1963).

Members of the TUC economics committee were concerned by the extent to which the national interest could be reconciled with the interests of union members. Members should come first. Jones argued, 'The suggestion that profitable employers ought not to be pressed to make concessions in relation to their "ability to pay" would be regarded by many of us here as giving opportunities to such employers to evade reasonable obligations to their workers' (*Tribune*, 21 June 1963). The TUC's pamphlet on Sweden reported:

> It [the LO] regards rising living standards, full employment, economic expansion and reasonable price stability as being indissolubly joined, and accords to the achievement of this group of objectives a higher priority than it gives to some other aims to which British trade unions have traditionally been attached, for example the preservation of the existing structure of the trade union movement, the autonomy of affiliated unions and job security. There is no simple explanation of why attitudes should be so different (TUC 1963a, p. 14).

Eric Heffer, elected a Labour MP in 1964, claimed later that Michael Shanks's advocacy of Swedish industrial relations helped to delegitimise the work of British trade unions (Heffer 1973, p. 33).

A core feature of Rehn's approach was the need for high levels of labour mobility to improve the economy's performance (and to ensure full employment). British unions were dubious about the benefits of increased labour mobility. The TUC background paper on Sweden commented, 'An important factor in the bargaining strength of a union is its ability to limit entry into the job' (TUC 1962b, p. 12). Swedish unions lacked, it noted, such powers. In similar vein, in the Swedish labour market there was no 'guarantee that each worker will keep his existing job' (TUC 1962a, p. 2). A TUC meeting in 1964 noted, 'It was argued that it was unrealistic to expect working people to abandon protective practices unless they were assured of security.'[26] Jack Jones commented acerbically, 'The Swedish trade unions clearly believe in trying to make capitalism work, they accept the rationalisation of industry' (*Tribune*, 21 June 1963). A further difference concerned differentials. The Rehn model proposed that differentials should be eroded. Many unions in Britain remained committed to them. During wage restraint in the late 1940s, the TUC General Council report recognised 'the need to safeguard those wage differentials which are an essential element in the wages structure of many important industries' (TUC 1948, p. 290). The summary of the Socialist International experts' conference stated, 'It is clear that wage increases of this type can only work when there is agreement over differentials.'[27] At the same time, members of the TUC trip to Sweden were concerned by the lack of commitment given by the LO to the redistribution of incomes and to the extension of nationalised industries (TUC economics committee 1963a, p. 23).

Aside from differences over the goals adopted by the Swedish social democrats, there were doubts about the performance of the Rehn model in practice. The background paper for the TUC trip to Sweden in 1962 noted 'mixed success' in economic performance: 'In the last decade the Swedish economy has grown at the respectable, though not striking rate of about 3.5 per cent per annum, which is rather more than the 2.2 per cent achieved in the UK but less than those of W. Germany, Italy or the Netherlands' (TUC 1962b, p. 1). Although the model was designed to achieve solidaristic wages, some commentators noted that in its flexibility it often resulted in high levels of wage drift. Such wage drift was problematic: it reimposed differentials and fuelled inflation.[28] The TUC estimated that more wage increases resulted from wage drift than from central wage negotiations (TUC 1962b, p. 10). One paper noted that 'over the last decade there does not appear to have been any more compression of differentials in earnings in Sweden than in Britain' (TUC 1963b, p. 4). Wage drift reduced the LO's influence on national economic developments (TUC economics committee 1963a, p. 23). To the extent the low paid were better off, the TUC argued, 'It is doubtful whether the cause of this was the pursuit of high wage solidarity rather than the economic circumstances prevailing in particular industries' (TUC 1962b, p. 11). The 1963 report noted, 'It is significant that the LO has to some extent redefined solidarity' (TUC 1963a, p. 12).

Economists were also concerned by the impact that the profits squeeze would have on investment levels. Bowers wrote to Rehn, 'In the end the government will be providing all the funds for investment. This may be a desirable objective in the long-run but as a short-term prospect it would certainly evoke the strongest opposition from British industrialists (Bowers 1950a, p. 2). Rehn responded, 'May I add what seems to me most peculiar ... On the one hand you cannot – for the sake of co-operative effort for higher output – hurt the industrialists through a policy that would make profit margins smaller ... on the other you now provoke a most furious uproar among these industrialists through a nationalisation of steel' (Rehn 1950a, pp. 2-3).

Conclusions

Between 1964 and 1979 Labour governments in Britain struggled to find some sort of accommodation with the trade union movement over wages. Such initiatives did not prove successful. Though at times they hinted at Swedish style arrangements, they were essentially reactive, part of a process of crisis management. From the very beginning of its discussions the 1964 Labour government told the TUC that an incomes policy was absolutely vital given the United Kingdom's dire economic situation. The planned growth of incomes that such a measure was meant to secure was downgraded and the policy was never linked to social democratic goals. In the early 1970s, Labour and the unions negotiated a Social Contract in which policies would be traded for some of wider considerations on the part of organised labour in wage setting. It was the most elliptical of agreements. Quite what action the unions would take was ill defined: it was a vague statement and different parties to it drew radically different conclusions. In any case, in office after 1974, Labour once again resorted to wage restraint as a means of controlling price increases in a hostile economic environment (see Wickham-Jones 1996, pp. 70-1, 129-32, and 150-4).

In 1979, after the collapse of Labour's last attempt to secure wage restraint, the Conservative party was elected to office under Mrs Thatcher. It was to be eighteen years before Labour would form a government again and by then its model of social democracy would be very different (though the party did look at wages policies again in the late 1980s and early 1990s). The Swedish model itself, of course, went through a variety of changes during the late 1960s and 1970s. Its implementation was controversial and open to interpretation to the extent it conformed to the original ideas laid out by Gösta Rehn. By the late 1970s it was in severe difficulties and, in the 1980s was, effectively, abandoned. Nevertheless, its record during the post-war era should not be underestimated: for much of this period the Swedish economy outperformed the British, especially in terms of its ability to tackle unemployment (see table one). It did so whilst securing a range of egalitarian outcomes (see the discussion in Goodin et al. 1999, pp. 80-6). Moreover, the capacity of Swedish reformism to negotiate a transition to the kind of arrangements that predominate currently in the political economies of advanced industrial capitalism can be contrasted with the devastating change experienced in the United Kingdom's deindustrialisation during the 1980s.

Table 14.1 A Comparison of Sweden and the United Kingdom

	Average percentage rate of growth in GDP per annum		
	1950-73	1973-94	
Sweden	3.7	1.4	
UK	3.0	1.7	
	Average percentage rate of price increases per annum		
	1950-73	1974-83	1983-1993
Sweden	4.7	10.2	6.3
UK	4.6	13.5	5.2
	Average percentage rate of unemployment per annum		
	1950-73	1974-83	1984-93
Sweden	1.8	2.3	3.2
UK	2.8	7.0	9.6

Source: Maddison (1995), pp. 83-4 and 23.

Let us recapitulate. I have looked at four reasons why Labour did not seek to emulate Swedish style social democracy. First, I have suggested that the British and Swedish movements enjoyed good relations and that British reformists were aware of the model of social democracy laid out by Gösta Rehn and others. Poor dissemination does not explain Labour's failure to take up Swedish ideas. Second, I have argued that the Labour party and the TUC did not explore in any depth the possibility of adopting Rehn's measures. In part this decision reflected the insularity of Labour's policy-making process, itself a manifestation of the internalised nature of the party. (One does not need, however, to conclude from this discussion that the party's was completely isolated from Europe: it simply indicates that the Labour's policy-making process seldom looked to the experiences of continental reformists.) At this time, the early 1960s, there was less awareness of Britain's relative economic decline: policy-makers had less of an incentive to look elsewhere for ideas. Third, I have addressed the argument that structural differences between Britain and Sweden prevented Labour from adopting the policies advocated by the LO. I have rejected this argument because it ignores the possibility of structural adjustment and exaggerates the constraints on social democratic actors. Most importantly, structural obstacles cannot explain how Labour's policy was shaped in the early 1960s, since the same arguments could be applied to the policies that the party did adopt. There is no doubt, however, that this view was held by many trade unionists. Fourth, I have indicated that British reformists, including many trade unionists were hostile to the objectives articulated by Rehn's approach and had doubts about its practical efficacy in a British context. Moreover, many within the labour movement had serious reservations about the kind of goals the Swedish model entailed. My account thus emphasises the second and fourth explanation.

One other point should be noted. Labour's close relations with the unions may have inhibited the party's policy-making in the 1950s and 60s. Whether the trade union influence on the party's programme was quite as strong as has been suggested by some commentators is another matter. The party was able, after all, to reach some agreement with reluctant unions over incomes policy by the time it entered office in 1964. British unions were, by and large, reactive to economic events. In 1956, Bryn Roberts criticised the TUC for its failure to look at the economic situation analytically: 'The Council is, of course, continuously examining the economic situation and it may well decide to undertake some kind of special survey, but it appears unlikely that it will make a study of the situation comparable to the one made by the Swedish Federation of Labour, mentioned earlier which resulted in a 255-page report' (Roberts 1956, pp. 17-18). It is striking, though, that British unions proved to be more open than the Labour party in studying economic and industrial patterns in other countries at this time. This openness is evidenced in the TUC visit to Sweden in 1962. John D. Stephens concludes rightly that Labour failed as an innovative party in this period (Stephens 1979, p. 148). On the one occasion that the party sketched out the Rehn model, it implied that such 'experimental approaches' would not be possible for the United Kingdom: 'Where bitter memories of mass unemployment still linger anything that suggests a retreat from full employment [as deflationary demand management did] will not receive serious consideration. In practice this policy would run up against severe difficulties.'[29] Once Labour had adopted a version of Keynesian social democracy, the party proved to be unimaginative and atheoretical in considering further amendments to the strategy, despite the emergence of difficulties with it.

Discussion of Swedish-type arrangements divided British trade unionists. There is little doubt that the failure of union leaders and members of the TUC economics committee to reach agreement about what might be learnt from Sweden limited the possibilities of the British labour movement designing such a strategy itself. Internal division jeopardised policy coherence. Whether a bolder and more innovative Labour party could have provided the lead in adopting the kind of reformist measures advocated by Rehn is an open question. The subsequent attempts of British social democrats to design a coherent and plausible economic strategy either in terms of reformulated revisionism or in the form of renewed commitment to intervention and public ownership enjoyed little success during the 1960s and 1970s. The rejection of the Rehn model by British social democrats owed much to their limited perception of its goals and potential. In place of a coherent social democratic strategy, Labour used incomes policies as an attempt to restrain wage inflation, a choice with disastrous consequences for the labour movement. From this perspective, the failure to learn from Sweden should be taken not as waking up from a hopeless dream but as missing a real opportunity.

Notes

1 The author thanks Bernard Alford, Stefan Berger, Rodney Lowe, Kenneth O. Morgan, Roger Middleton, Hugh Pemberton, and Andrew Thorpe for comments and help with sources. He also gratefully acknowledges help from the Harold Wincott Foundation and the Arts and Humanities Research Board of the United Kingdom. Responsibility, as ever, is his.
2 Delegation to Sweden 1951, p. 12.
3 For example, Howell 1980, p. 193.
4 For an important account of Labour's links with European Social Democracy, see Berger (2000).
5 Delegation to Sweden 1951, pp. 11 and 14.
6 *Journal of Political Economy* (1952, p. 178).
7 'Experts' Conference of the Socialist International' 1956, p. 17.
8 LO 1953, p. 92; Meidner 1993, pp. 211-28.
9 'What about wages?' 1951, p. 10.
10 'Experts' Conference of the Socialist International' 1956, p. 18.
11 'Experts' Conference of the Socialist International' 1956, p. 19.
12 'Study Group on Security and Old Age' 1961; 1962; and 'Pensions in Germany' 1962.
13 'The Taxation of Wealth in Sweden' 1963; 'Housing Finance in Sweden' 1964.
14 'Industrial Training' 1963, p. 2.
15 'Industrial Training for Adult Workers' 1964: p. 3; see also pp. 4-5.
16 'Sweden and the TUC', *Tribune*, 17 May 1963.
17 *Tribune*, 13 September 1963.
18 See the discussion in Panitch 1976, especially pp. 49-51.
19 *Tribune*, 17 May 1963.
20 *Tribune*, 21 June 1963.
21 'What about wages?' 1951, p. 24.
22 'Experts' Conference of the Socialist International' 1956, p. 18.
23 Quoted by Swenson 1996, p. 22.
24 'Wage and Price Regulation in Finland, Denmark and Sweden' 1950, p. 3.
25 'Experts' Conference of the Socialist International' 1956, p. 18.
26 TUC special economics committee 1964, p. 17.
27 'Experts' Conference of the Socialist International' 1956, p. 18.
28 'Incomes policy: An Appraisal' 1962, p. 10.
29 Experts' Conference of the Socialist International' 1956, p. 20.

References

Note: *Labour party internal memoranda are to be found in the Labour Party Archive (LPA) at the National Museum of Labour History, Manchester, United Kingdom. TUC papers and minutes are to be found at the Modern Records.*

Anderson, Perry (1961), 'Sweden: Mr. Crosland's dreamland', *New Left Review*, vol. 7, pp. 4-12.

Balogh, Thomas B. (1962), 'Notes on Economic Planning', RD 195/January 1962, LPA.

Berger, Stefan (2000), 'Labour in Comparative Perspective', in Duncan Tanner et al. (eds) *Labour's First Century*, Cambridge University Press, Cambridge, pp. 309-40.

Bowers, D. (1950a), letter to Gösta Rehn, 14 September 1950, MRC, MSS 948.5 (1), Sweden.

Bowers, D. (1950b), letter to Gösta Rehn, 12 October 1950, MRC, MSS 948.5 (1), Sweden.

Cooper, Jack (1963), *Industrial Relations: Sweden shows the way*, Fabian Society, London.

Crosland, C. Anthony R. (1956), *The Future of Socialism*, Jonathan Cape, London.

Crosland, C. Anthony R. (1962), *The Conservative Enemy*, Cape, London.

Delegation to Sweden (1951), 'Report', NEC/12 December 1951, Sweden 1948-63, international department files, LPA.

Delegation to study training (1961), Report, 19-25 March 1961, MRC, MSS 292B/557.37/3.

'Experts' Conference of the Socialist International' (1956), memorandum, Re. 17/January 1956, LPA.

Goodin, Robert E. et al (1999), *The Real Worlds of Welfare Capitalism*, Cambridge University Press, Cambridge.

Goodman, Geoffrey (1979), *The Awkward Warrior*, Davis-Poynter, London.

Heffer, Eric S. (1973), *The Class Struggle in Parliament*, Victor Gollancz, London.

Hetherington, Alistair (1962), 'Meeting with Mr Gaitskell', 7 June 1962, Hetherington papers, London School of Economics.

'Housing Finance in Sweden' (1964), memorandum, RD 722. /March 1964, LPA.

Howell, David (1980), *British Social Democracy*, Croom Helm, London.

'Incomes policy: An Appraisal' (1962), memorandum, RD. 370/December 1962, LPA.

'Industrial Training' (1963), memorandum, RD. 432/March 1963, LPA.

'Industrial Training for Adult Workers' (1964), memorandum, RD.629/April 1964, LPA.

Johnston, Thomas L. (1958), 'Wages Policies Abroad', *Scottish Journal of Political Economy*, vol. 5, pp. 26-44.

Journal of Political Economy (1952), anonymous review of Ralph Turvey (ed.), Wages Policy Under Full Employment, vol. 61, p. 178.

King, Desmond S. (1995), *Actively Seeking Work?*, University of Chicago Press, London.

LO (1948-1963), 'Information to foreign countries', series III, international department files, LPA.

LO (1953), *Trade Unions and Full Employment*, LO, Stockholm.

Maddison, Angus (1995), *Monitoring the World Economy*, OECD, Paris.

Meidner, Rudolf (1952), 'The dilemma of wages policy under full employment', in Ralph Turvey (ed.), *Wages Policy Under Full Employment*, London, William Hodge and Co., pp. 16-29.

Meidner, Rudolf (1993), 'Why did the Swedish Model Fail?', *Socialist Register*, pp. 211-28.

Minkin, Lewis (1980), *The Labour Party Conference*, Manchester University Press, Manchester.

Morgan, E. Victor (1952), review, *Economica*, vol. 19, p. 443.

Morgan, Kenneth O. (1997), *Callaghan A Life*, Oxford University Press, Oxford.

Nield, Robert (1962), 'Economic Planning in the Light of French Experience', RD 202/January 1962, LPA.

Panitch, Leo (1976), *Social Democracy and Industrial Militancy*, Cambridge University Press, Cambridge.

'Pensions in Germany' (1962), memorandum, RD199/January 1962, LPA.

Reder, Melvin W. (1953), review, *American Economic Review*, vol. XLIII, pp. 714-17.

Rehn, Gösta (1950a), letter to D. Bowers, 21 September 1950, TUC archive, MRC, MSS 292/948.5 (I), Sweden.

Rehn, Gösta (1950b), letter to Ted Fletcher, 9 September 1950, MRC, MSS 948.5 (1), Sweden.

Rehn, Gösta (1952), 'The problem of stability: An analysis and some policy proposals', in Ralph Turvey (ed.), *Wages Policy Under Full Employment*, William Hodge and Co., London, pp. 30-54.

Report (1963), research department memorandum RD 494/June 1963, LPA.

Roberts, Bryn (1951), 'The Case in Favour', *Fabian Journal*, pp. 15-17.

Roberts, Bryn (1956), 'Trade Unions in the Welfare State', *Political Quarterly*, vol. 27, pp. 6-18.

Russ, George and Andrew Martin (1999), 'European Unions Face the Millenium', in Andrew Martin and George Russ et al, *The Brave New World of European Labour*, Berghahn Books, London, pp. 1-25.

Shanks, Michael (1961), *The Stagnant Society*, Penguin Books, Harmondsworth.

Stephens, John D. (1979), *The Transition from Capitalism to Socialism*, Macmillan, Basingstoke.

Study Group on Security and Old Age (1961), 'Comparative Study of Social Security Provisions in Belgium, Germany, Sweden and USA', RD. 190/December 1961, LPA.

'Study Group on Security and Old Age' (1962), memorandum, RD. 198/January 1962, LPA.

Sweeny, Denis (1960), letter to Morgan Phillips, 22 December 1960, Sweden 1948-63, international department files, LPA.

Swenson, Peter (1996), 'Employers Wanted the Welfare State', paper presented at the American Political Science Association annual meeting, San Francisco.

'The Taxation of Wealth in Sweden' (1963), RD 508/July 1963, memorandum, LPA.

TUC (1948), *Annual Report*.

TUC (1949), *Annual Report*.

TUC (1950), *Annual Report*.

TUC (1952), *Annual Report*.

TUC (1962a), 'Draft Report of Visit to Sweden', economics committee, 3/1, 1962, MRC, MSS 292B/560.1/5.

TUC (1962b), 'Industrial Relations and Wages Policy in Sweden', economics committee 1/1, 1962, MRC, MSS 292B/560.1/5.

TUC (1963a), *Sweden – its unions and industrial relations*, London, TUC.

TUC (1963b), 'Incomes, Costs and Prices', MRC, MSS 292B/560.1/7.

TUC (1963c), *Annual Report.*

TUC economics committee (1963a), minutes, 9 January 1963, MRC, MSS 292B/560.1/5.

TUC economics committee (1963b), minutes, 10 April 1963, MRC, MSS 292B/560.1/6.

TUC special economics committee meeting (1964), minutes, 7 December 1964, MRC, MSS 292B/560.1/9.

'Wage and Price Regulation in Finland, Denmark and Sweden' (1950), memorandum, MRC, MSS 292/948.5 (1).

'What about wages?' (1950), R.46/May 1951, LPA.

Wickham-Jones, Mark (1996), *Economic Strategy and the Labour Party*, Macmillan, Basingstoke.

Wickham-Jones, Mark (2000), 'An Insular Party? Labour's Century in Comparative Perspective', *Renewal*, vol. 8, p. 15-25.

Williams, Philip (1979), *Hugh Gaitskell*, Jonathan Cape, London.

Winnard, D. (1963), 'Suggested Amendments to Revised Paper on Industrial Training', RD 453/April 1963, LPA.

Bibliography of the Writings of Gösta Rehn

Eskil Wadensjö

Introduction

Gösta Rehn was not a traditional academic. His academic publication profile is not the customary one of papers mainly published in scientific journals or as books or chapters of books published by scientific publishers. He has published in that way also, but the main part of his published works consist of other types: articles in journals and newspapers, reports to governmental committees and authorities, reports to international organisations and reports both to and for the Social Democratic party and trade union organisations. Although this makes them more difficult to locate, hopefully this bibliography will facilitate the work of those who want to look for his publications.

Gösta Rehn started publishing early. He began writing short pieces already in 1934 for *Folket*, a local newspaper (these articles are not included in this bibliography). In 1936, while studying at the School for Social Work, and studying economics at Stockholm Högskola (the present Stockholm University) at the same time, he began writing in *Clarté* (a left-wing journal where he was one of the editors for two years) and *Metallarbetaren*, a weekly journal for the members of the metalworkers' union. In 1937 to 1939 he wrote 66 articles in *Metallarbetaren* and 13 in *Clarté*. Almost all of the articles were on economic policy or on the economic situation. Two topics, which Gösta Rehn came to concentrate on in the years to come, were the focus of several articles: the regulation of working hours and business cycle policy.

Gösta Rehn resigned as the editor of *Clarté* in the autumn of 1939, and some months later left the Clarté-organization due to a political split between social democrats and communists in the organization. In 1939 he started to write in *Fackföreningsrörelsen*, the journal of LO (the confederation of blue-collar unions in Sweden) and from 1940 in *Socialdemokraten*, a main Social Democratic newspaper. Gösta Rehn started to do some work for LO already in 1940 and became a full time

LO-economist in 1943. Most of the publications in the 1940s are reports on economic issues written for LO, and articles in newspaper and journals related to LO and the Social Democratic Party. Some of the reports are descriptions of the economic development but quite a few deal with the issues that Gösta Rehn later become well-known for: flexibility of working hours, and analysis of how to combine low inflation and full employment. He also contributed one article to *Ekonomisk Tidskrift* (now the Scandinavian Journal of Economics) and participated in the debates of the Swedish Economic Association, which were published in the same journal. The first article on the Rehn-Meidner model was published in the Social Democratic journal *Tiden* in 1948.

Gösta Rehn continued to write for LO until the beginning of the 1950s, but in 1952 he began work for a governmental committee and directly after its completion went on to another committee, both on different aspects of stabilisation of the business cycle. He was on leave from LO between 1952 and 1958. During that time he wrote articles in different journals and newspapers and also memos for the internal debate in the Social Democratic Party. In August 1959 Gösta Rehn was appointed head of economic affairs branch of the Ministry of Finance. He stayed there for three years and wrote a number of papers for the ministry while also continuing to write articles for journals (including economic journals published in Swedish) and newspapers. In the 1950s he also published some articles in edited books and scientific journals in English.

In 1962 he was appointed Director of Employment and Social Affairs Secretariat at the OECD in Paris. His publications during the following 12 years were mainly related to his work for OECD, but he continued to take part in the Swedish debate. In the 1960s his OECD studies were mainly on labour market policy, and in the 1970s he started to write extensively on working hours, advocating a more flexible working hours regime.

In the mid-1970s he returned to Sweden as professor at the Swedish Institute for Social Research. He continued to write on flexible working hours and labour market policy. In addition to the earlier issues, he started to write on recurrent education and also about a new policy for combining full employment and price stability – marginal employment subsidies.

In a formal sense Gösta Rehn retired in 1979, but in practice he continued working as usual for many years – his last article was published in 1995. He wrote articles for scientific journals, articles in books, articles in other types of journals and newspapers, and he also wrote memos for internal discussions in the Social Democratic Party.

Up to 1963 the main part of Gösta Rehn's publications were in Swedish. From the mid-1960s to his return to Sweden in 1975, he wrote mainly in English. When back in Sweden he continued writing in English although many publications from that period are in Swedish (as well as other languages). In practice, everything written by Gösta Rehn is possible to understand for those who are knowledgeable of both English and Swedish.[1] For those who do not understand Swedish, it is not possible to follow the development of the ideas (many of the ideas of later years are discussed in a less detailed way already in the 1930s and the 1940s – before the Rehn-Meidner model was presented). It is also impossible to follow his intense and long-term efforts to influence the Swedish economic policy. Nevertheless, it is possible to get a good grasp of his basic ideas in English. Gösta Rehn was eager to get his ideas accepted and he believed that repetition and presentation to different groups on different occasions was a good pedagogical devise.

Three collections of articles by Gösta Rehn have been published. The first one in 1952 is a selection and translation by Ralph Turvey of the articles in which the Rehn-Meidner model was first discussed. It contains two of Gösta Rehn's articles. Another volume, in Swedish, edited by Eskil Wadensjö, Åke Dahlberg and Bertil Holmlund contains 30 articles and also an earlier version of his bibliography. This volume, Full sysselsättning utan inflation (Full employment without inflation), was published in 1988 in honour of Gösta Rehn's 75th birthday. A third volume was published in Spanish in 1989 – Ensayos sobre política de emploe activa – and contains 8 articles by Gösta Rehn from different periods of his career.

[1] All items in this bibliography are included in a special collection at Stockholm University Library.

Books, articles in journals and newspapers, memoranda, etc.

1936

1. 'Dit befolkningsfrågan hunnit', *Clarté*, vol. 13, no. 6, pp. 17-22

2. 'En köpkraftsteori' (review of Axel Uhlén's book Kris, köpkraft, reallöner), *Metallarbetaren*, no. 48, pp. 5-6

1937

1. *Clarté*, vol. 14
1.1 'Sexualradikalismen segrar', no. 1, pp. 8-11
1.2 '40-timmarsveckan', no. 7, pp. 4-7
2. *Metallarbetaren*
2.1 'Högkonjunktur', no. 2, p. 2
2.2 'Ett genmäle' (by Axel Uhlén with reply from Gösta Rehn), no. 3, p. 14
2.3 'Skatten är aktuell', no. 5, p. 7
2.4 'Levnadsstandarden', no. 6, p. 2
2.5 'Professor Ohlin och samhället' (review of Bertil Ohlin's book Fri eller dirigerad ekonomi), no. 7, p. 21
2.6 'Levnadsstandarden' (continued from no. 6) no. 8, p. 2
2.7 'Dyrtid i sikte?', no. 10, p. 2
2.8 'Vårt lands utrikeshandel', no. 12, p. 2
2.9 'Vårt lands utrikeshandel II', no. 14, p. 2
2.10 'Nordiskt samarbete', no. 16, p. 2
2.11 'Livsmedelspriserna', no. 18, p. 2
2.12 'Arbetslöshetspolitik i högkonjunktur', no. 20, p. 2
2.13 'Hur skall det gå med konjunkturen?', no. 22, p. 2
2.14 'Sparsamhet på avbetalning', no. 24, p. 2
2.15 'Socialpolitik 1937', no. 26, p. 2
2.16 'Socialpolitik 1937 II', no. 28, p. 2
2.17 'Socialpolitik 1937 III', no. 30, p. 2
2.18 'Kring 40-timmarsfrågan', no. 32, p. 2
2.19 'Kring 40-timmarsfrågan II', no. 34, p. 2
2.20 'Lönen stiger – i utlandet', no. 37, p. 2
2.21 'Kring 40-timmarsfrågan' (comments on the debate, including a reply from Gösta Rehn), no. 38, p. 6
2.22 'Järnvinsterna', no. 39, p. 2

2.23 'Kring 40-timmarsfrågan' (two comments on the debate, including a reply from Gösta Rehn), no. 39, p. 67
2.24 'Räkna kallt', no. 42, p. 2
2.25 'Studera ekonomi', no. 43, pp. 8-10
2.26 'Indexmystiken', no. 44, p. 2
2.27 'Levnadskostnaderna', no. 46, p. 2
2.28 'En ful figur', no. 48, pp. 2 and 15

1938

1. *Clarté*, vol. 15
1.1 'Konjunkturläget och budgeten', no. 1-2, pp. 8-11
1.2 'Den svenska skolan inom nationalekonomin', no. 1-2, pp. 23-6
1.3 'Krisdiskussionen redan glömd?' (review of Gunnar Dahlberg and Herbert Tingsten's book Svensk politisk uppslagsbok), no. 1-2, pp. 28-9
1.4 'Internationell diskussion', no. 5-6, pp. 28-9
1.5 'Klassintressena i jordbrukspolitiken' (review of Gunnar Myrdal's book Jordbrukspolitiken under omläggning), no. 7, pp. 12-13
1.6 'Köpkraftssvindelns sammanbrott' (on France) no. 9, pp. 6-10
1.7 'Köpkraftssvindelns sammanbrott' (replies and an answer from Gösta Rehn), no. 11-12, pp. 25-7
2. *Metallarbetaren*
2.1 'Tulltaxan', no. 3, pp. 15-16
2.2 'Teoretiskt om tullar', no. 5, p. 2
2.3 'Tullpolitikens verkningar', no. 7, p. 2
2.4 'Ekonomisk spådomskonst', no. 10, p. 2
2.5 'Det står och väger', no. 12, p. 2
2.6 'Österrikes erövring', no. 14, p. 2
2.7 'Frankrike', no. 16, p. 2
2.8 'Folkfrontens verk', no. 18, p. 2
2.9 'Folkfrontens bekymmer', no. 20, pp. 2 and 14
2.10 'Kan prisstegring vara bra?', no. 22, p. 2
2.11 'Jordbrukshjälpens framtid', no. 24, p. 2
2.12 'Inför en ny världskris?', no. 26, p. 2
2.13 'Diskussionsinledning...', no. 30, p. 2
2.14 'Vi behöver praktisk teori', no. 33, p. 2
2.15 'Friheten naggas i kanten', no. 37, p. 2
2.16 'Arbetsglädje och arbetsresultat', no. 39, p. 2
2.17 'Om kapital', no. 42, p. 2
2.18 'Rationalisering', no. 44, p. 2
2.19 'Hårt spel' (review of Stefan Szende's book Maktspelet kring Donau) no. 44, p. 10
2.20 'Idyll och kanoner' (short book reviews) no. 45, p. 12

2.21 'Vår tids gåta', no. 46, p. 2
2.22 'Varför krisen kommer', no. 48, p. 2

1939

1. *Clarté*, vol. 16
1.1 'Socialpolitik och lönepolitik', no. 3-4, pp. 16-18
1.2 'Debatt om lönepolitiken' (a critical comment by Lennart Björk with an answer from Gösta Rehn), no. 5, pp. 11-14
1.3 'Krigsekonomi' and 'Den franska erfarenheten' (short book reviews), no. 6, p. 15
1.4 ''Tiden', Clarté och tiden', (comments to an editorial by Torsten Gårdlund in 'Tiden') no. 7-8, pp. 31-2
2. *Metallarbetaren*
2.1 'Konjunkturrapport', no. 1, p. 2
2.2 'Om vi skulle dela lika', no. 4, p. 2
2.3 'Ekonomi och samhälle' (review of Wagner-Zellhof's book I världshushållningens labyrinter), no. 5, p. 12
2.4 'Vill Wigforss svälta ut oss?', no. 7, p. 2
2.5 'Ödesfrågan och råvarorna' (book reviews of Fritz Sternberg: Hur länge kan Hitler föra krig? and John Vogt: Mens våpnene hviler), no. 8, p. 4
2.6 'På väg mot planhushållning', no. 9, p. 2
2.7 'Reformism', no. 12, p. 2
2.8 'Nyttan av höga skatter', no. 16, p. 2
2.9 'Att lära av motståndaren', no. 19, p. 2
2.10 'Tysk ekonomi', no. 23, p. 2
2.11 'Ekonomi bakom taggtråd', no. 24, p. 2
2.12 'Idyll i skugga', no. 26, p. 2
2.13 'Krigstidens löner', no. 36, p. 2
2.14 'Krisnämnderna', no. 39, pp. 2 and 14
2.15 'Problem i krisen', no. 47, p. 2
2.16 'Vem betalar?', no. 49-50, p. 25
3. 'Genève och världsutvecklingen' (about ILO), *Fackföreningsrörelsen*, vol. 19, part 2, pp. 77-85
4. 'Svar om Genève' (a reply to Sven Andersson 'Den internationella socialpolitikens problem' Fackföreningsrörelsen, vol. 19, part 2, pp. 352-6), *Fackföreningsrörelsen*, vol. 19, part 2, pp. 451-2
5. 'The Structure and Development of Swedish Economic Life', pp. 134-55 in *The World Economic Situation:* International Survey and Reports from national centres affiliated to the IFTU, International Federation of Trade Unions, Paris

1940

1. *Socialdemokraten*
1.1 'Underskott i folkhushållet I' 1940.12.07
1.2 'Underskott i folkhushållet II' 1940.12.12
2. 'Krigsekonomi och välfärdspolitik', Discussion in Fackligt Forum 1940.12.06

1941

1. *Fackföreningsrörelsen*, vol. 21
1.1 'LO-chefen om löneproblemen', part 1, pp. 89-91
1.2 'Lönepolitik och prisreglering', part 2, pp. 196-200
1.3 'Böndernas kompensation', part 2, pp. 301-17
2. 'Väsentligheterna i lönepolitiken', *Metallarbetaren*, no. 5, p. 6
3. 'LO-chefen om löneproblemen', *Socialdemokraten*, 1941.01.19
4. LO press information, series I
4.1 'LO:s krav på skärpt priskontroll', no. 10, 1941.02.17
4.2 'Lettlands arbetare under sovjetvälde I', no. 39, 1941.05.03
4.3 'Lettlands arbetare under sovjetvälde II', no. 40, 1941.05.03
4.4 'Demokrati i Sovjet-Lettland', no. 41, 1941.05.08
4.5 'Fängelse för att man överger sin arbetsgivare', 1941.05.26

1942

1. 'Kapitalinkomsternas utveckling under kriget', *Ekonomisk tidskrift*, vol. 44, no. 1, pp. 66-79
2. *Fackföreningsrörelsen*, vol. 22
2.1 'Review of Stefan Szende's book I guldets trollkrets', part 1, pp. 287-8
2.2 'Review of Kurt Stechert's book Tre gånger mot England', part 1, pp. 487-8
2.3 'Landsorganisationens framställning om förbättrad levnadskostnadsberäkning', part 1, pp. 97-100
2.4 'Krisbördornas fördelning', part 1, pp. 145-9
2.5 'Kriskonjunkturskatten', part 1, pp. 193-6
2.6 'Gratisaktiernas praktiska innebörd' (unsigned article), part 1, pp. 278-85
2.7 'Arbetslönerna och inflationen', part 2, pp. 53-60
3. *Krisbördornas fördelning*, Information och argument no. 1, LO, Stockholm
4. *Metallarbetaren*
4.1 'Krisbördornas fördelning', no. 9, p. 2
4.2 'Kapitalinkomsterna under kriget', no. 12, p. 2
5. Contibution to the debate in connection with Harald Cramér, 'Levnadskostnadsindex under kristid' 1942.12.17 *Nationalekonomiska föreningens förhandlingar 1942* (Proceedings of the Swedish Economic Association 1942), Gösta Rehn pp. 90-3

6. LO press information, series I
6.1 'Kapitalinkomsterna under kriget', no. 10, 1942.02.24
6.2 'Kapitalägarnas vinster under krisen', no. 11, 1942.02.27
6.3 'Bönderna och krisbördan', no. 12, 1942.03.05
6.4 'Jordbrukarnas kompensation för dyrtiden', no. 16, 1942.03.10
6.5 'Exempel på ekonomisk upplysning', no. 20, 1942.03.24
6.6 'Ekonomiska allvarsord', no. 41, 1942.05.21
6.7 'Skall man ljuga i klasskampen?', no. 53, 1942.07.03
6.8 'Amerikansk bok om våra kollektivavtal' (review of Paul Norgren's book The Swedish Collective Bargaining System) no. 87, 1942.09.08

1943

1. *Metallarbetaren*
1.1 'Bättre metoder för indexberäkningen', no. 8, pp. 181 and 184
1.2 'Ny dag och Gösta Rehn', no. 24-25, p. 18
2. 'Konsumtionsreserverna: Övriga konsumtionsvaror', Supplement 1b, The Labour movement's committee for planning of the post-war period. Proceedings from a meeting 25-31 July 1943
3. Gösta Rehn and Carl Björk, 'Motion om nordiskt samarbete', Motion no. 4 to the SSU Congress, The Labour Movement Archives
4. *Socialdemokraten*
4.1 'Kominterns likvidering – socialdemokratins radikalisering' 1943.05.29
4.2 'Ny Dag kontra Gösta Rehn' 1943.06.02
4.3 'Clartédebatten' (answer to a reply by Sven Linderot in the same issue) 1943.06.17
5. *Fackföreningsrörelsen*
5.1 'Kommunisterna, bolagsvinsterna och lönepolitiken', part 1, pp. 263-4
5.2 'Inkomstutvecklingen under kriget', part 1, pp. 504-9
5.3 'Inkomstutvecklingen under kriget II', part 1, pp. 550-5
5.4 'Inkomstutvecklingen under kriget III' and 'Kommunistiska fakta', part 2, pp. 8-20
6. LO memorandum (the research department)
'P.M. med jämförelse mellan lantarbetares och industriarbetares reallöner' 1943.11.18

1944

1. LO memorandum (the research department)
1.1 'Lönestatistiken för 1943 mm' 1944.10.07
2. 'Tre månaders semester!', *Frihet*, no. 2, p. 15
3. '3 månaders semester som medel mot arbetslöshet I och II', *Fackföreningsrörelsen*, vol. 24, part 1, pp. 110-17 and 126-32

4. *Så är det!* Kommunistiska standardlögner vederlagda, Aktuella frågor no. 2, LO, Stockholm
5. 'Svar på 'Socialdemokratiska sifferkonster...' (Reply to 'Socialdemokratiska sifferkonster. Svar på förtal', Arbetarekultur 1944, which was a reply to 'Så är det!'), *Fackföreningsrörelsen*, vol. 24, part 1, pp. 580-8
6. 'När man inte...', *Metallarbetaren*, no. 39, p. 12
7. Comments on the debate in connection to Arthur Montgomery, 'Arbetslönerna efter kriget' 1944.04.27 *Nationalekonomiska föreningens förhandlingar 1944* (Proceedings of the Swedish Economic Association 1944), Gösta Rehn pp. 70-2
8. LO press information, series I
8.1 'Kommunistisk sifferlek', no. 58, 1944.04.25
8.2 'Cassel och efterkrigsprogrammet', no. 60, 1944.05.08
8.3 'Kommunistisk räknekonst', no. 83, 1944.06.15 and no. 114, 1944.09.13
9. 'Tremånaderssemestern och kritiken' (reply to 'Tre månaders semester för varje sexårsperiod' i Aftontidningen 1944.01.23), *Aftontidningen* 1944.01.26

1945

1. LO memoranda (the research department)
1.1 'Översikt av uppgjorda avtal t.o.m. 20.2.45' 1945.02.22
1.2 'Översikt av uppgjorda avtal t.o.m. 23.4.45' 1945.04.25
1.3 'Löneutvecklingen sedan krigsutbrottet för vuxna manliga löntagare' 1945.07.12 (Arbejderbevaegelsens Bibliotek og Arkiv, Denmark)
1.4 'Timförtjänster i olika dyrortsgrupper år 1943. Jämförelse mellan reella förtjänsterna i de olika dyrortsgrupperna med hjälp av 1941 års dyrortsundersökning' 1945.10.06
1.5 'Timförtjänster 1939, 1943 och 1944 enligt Socialstyrelsens statistik. Beräkning för 1945 enligt avtalen' 1945.10.15
1.6 'Översikt av avtalsläget och arbetarpartens förslag hösten 1945' 1945.12.12
1.7 'Löneläget i olika dyrortsgrupper 1944. Socialstyrelsens preliminära statistik' 1945.12.12
2. *Sant och osant i ekonomidebatten* (reply to 'Socialdemokratiska sifferkonster. Svar på förtal', Arbetarekultur 1944), Aktuella frågor no. 3, LO, Stockholm
3. *Fackföreningsrörelsen*
3.1 'Penninglönernas stegring 1939-1945', vol. 25, part 2, pp. 524-7
3.2 'Löneolikheterna 1944 och 1945', vol. 25, part 2, p. 545
3.3 'Ekonomisk översikt. Iakttagelser i lönestatistiken', vol. 25, part 2, pp. 601-3
4. 'Preliminär lönestatistik 1945' LO's research department. Expanded reprint of the articles in *Fackföreningsrörelsen* 1945, no. 48 and 49
5. LO press information, series I
5.1 'LO och abortfrågan', no. 26, 1945.02.09

1946

1. LO memoranda (the research department)
1.1 'Synpunkter på frågan om produktionsnämndernas uppgifter' 1946.01.15
1.2 'PM angående löneutvecklingen' 1946.04.23
1.3 'Avtalsöversikt' 1946.04.23
1.4 'Kort PM till höstens lönefråga' 1946.07.20
1.5 'Preliminär lönestatistik 1946' 1946.08. 10
1.6 'Relativa löneläget 1945' 1946.09.25
1.7 'Avtalsläget' 1946.10.09
2. *De 27 punkterna,* Studieplan no. 62 ABF, Stockholm
3. *Kvinnoarbetet och kvinnolönerna*, Studieplan no. 64 ABF, Stockholm
4. 'Full kompensation?', *Metallarbetaren* no. 21, p. 12
5. LO press information, series I
5.1 'Har vi fått tillbaka 1939 års reallöner?', no. 79, 1946.05.11
6. 'Kvinnoarbetet och kvinnolönerna', *Förbundskamraten*, no. 6, pp. 138-9 and *Mål och Medel*, no. 6, pp. 166-8
7. 'Vår reallön', *Mål och Medel*, no. 6, p. 163
8. 'Gallup om Oms', *SIA* (Skogsindustriarbetaren), no. 25-26, pp. 2, 10 and 30
9. Comments in the debate at the LO congress 1946 pp. 84-6, 87 and 92 in the 13th ordinary congress of LO 7-13 September 1946. Minutes, Stockholm

1947

1. LO memoranda (the research department)
1.1 'Avtalet om företagsnämnder. Redogörelse för den omfattning i vilken förslag om avtalets tillämpning framförts till motparten' 1947.02.15
1.2 'Relativa löneläget 1945 (definitiva siffror)' 1947.02.18
1.3 'Lönespridningen bland LO:s medlemmar 1946' 1947.02.22
1.4 'Utlåtande över preliminärt utkast till utredning om den kemisk-tekniska industrien. (De Förenade Förbunden)', August
1.5. 'Kommentarer till sysselsättningsutvecklingen inom industri och hantverk 1947' 1947.10.10
2. 'Synpunkter på den ekonomiska utvecklingen 1947-48' (The Labour Movement Archives; Ernst Wigforss' documents) 1947.05.21
3. *Nationalekonomiska föreningens förhandlingar 1947* (Proceedings of the Swedish Economic Association 1947)
3.1 Comments on the debate in connection to Eli Heckscher's lecture 'De nya skatteförslagen' 1947.01.14, Gösta Rehn p. 31
3.2 Comments on the debate in connection to Erik Lundberg, 'Inflationsfaran och den ekonomiska politiken' 1947.03.28, Gösta Rehn pp. 53-5 and 60-1
4. 'Översikt av remissyttrandena över skatteförslaget' (during a period of three months Gösta Rehn served at the Ministry of Finance in the capacity as expert in writing the tax

proposal) (The Labour Movement Archives; Tage Erlander's documents)
5. 'Synpunkter på frågan om vinstbegränsande fondavsättningar i proportion till företagens löneutgifter' (The Labour Movement Archives; Tage Erlander's documents) 1947.09.29

1948

1. 'Arbetsmarknaden', Chapter V in *Konjunkturläget hösten 1947*, Meddelanden från Konjunkturinstitutet, Serie A:15, Stockholm
2. *Kommunisterna om pris- och lönestoppet*, Aktuella frågor no. 5, LO, Stockholm
3. 'Det ekonomiska läget', *Morgontidningen* 1948.05.13
4. LO memoranda (the research department)
4.1 'Ny PM om steriliserad lönehöjning' 1948.10.01
4.2 Rudolf Meidner and Gösta Rehn 'PM om eventuella inslag i det ekonomiska programmet hösten 1948' 1948.10.08
4.3 'Ekonomisk översikt till representantskapet 10.11.48', 1948.11.06
4.4 'Problem och program för lönestatistisk undersökning 1948-49', 1948.12.28
5. '... några artiklar i aktuella ekonomiska ämnen' (Inkomstutvecklingen för olika folkgrupper 1939-1948; Prisstabiliseringens möjligheter; Inkomstbegränsning för andra folkgrupper), LO press information 1948.12.06
6. *Stabiliseringslinjen*, Aktuella frågor no. 13, LO, Stockholm 1948
7. 'Ekonomisk politik vid full sysselsättning', *Tiden*, vol. 40, pp. 135-42
8. 'Statistiken rörande sysselsättningen inom industrien' 1948.02.10, Memorandum for Arbetsmarknadsstatistikkommittén (the committee on labour market statistics) 1948.12.30
9. LO press information, series I
9.1 'Ekonomisk stabilisering – ett löntagarintresse', no. 142, 1948.11.18
10. Memoranda for SAP/LO (The Labour Movement Archives; Tage Erlander's documents)
10.1 'PM om eventuella inslag i det ekonomiska programmet hösten 1948' 1948.10.08
10.2 'PM om innebörden i olika alternativ för bestämning av jordbrukarnas inkomstläge under nästa produktionsår' 1948.10.16
10.3 'Översikt av pågående arbete och utredningar i samband med det ekonomiska programmet' 1948.11.01
10.4 'Reviderat utkast till ekonomiskt program', no date
10.5 'Answers to Questionnaire on Economic Planning' for 'Conference on Administration of Nationalized Industries', London, December 1948
11. *Det ekonomiska läget*, Information och Argument. LO propagandarådet
12. Review of Gustaf Åkerman's book Engelsk arbetslöshet och arbetslöshetspolitik, *Ekonomisk Tidskrift*, vol. 50, pp. 179-84

1949

1. LO memoranda (the research department)
1.1 'Löneutvecklingen inom industri mm 1939-49' 1949.08.15
1.2 'Anm. till beräkningen av justeringsbehovet i lönekostnadsposten' 1949.08.21
1.3 'Försök till vissa justeringar i jordbrukskalkylens lönekostnadspost' 1949.08.21
1.4 'Hur borde jordbrukskalkylens lönepost ha räknats våren 1949?' 1949.08.24
1.5 Nils Kellgren and Gösta Rehn, 'Några slutsatser från löneenkäten till förbunden' 1949.09.10
1.6 'PM med vissa allmänna synpunkter på den aktuella ekonomiska politiken' 1949.10.15
1.7 'Översikt av svaren på cirkulär 1.819' (angående ev undantag från avtalsprolongationen) 1949.10.24
1.8 'Problems of Industrial Democracy and Full Employment. Sweden', Comisco Expert Conference, September 1949, Örenäs
1.9 'Wages and Prices in Full Employment', Comisco Expert Conference, September 1949, Örenäs
2. 'Fullsysselsättningens löneproblem', *Fackföreningsrörelsen*, vol. 29, part 2, pp. 461-70
3. LO press information, series I
3.1 'Kommunistargumenten mot LO I', no. 47, 1949.03.29
3.2 'Kommunistargumenten mot LO II', no. 48, 1949.03.30
3.3 'Churchill och Ny Dag i samma fallgrop', no. 125, 1949.10.03
4. 'PM angående ev. acciser på vissa investeringsmaterial' (The Labour Movement Archives; Tage Erlander's documents) 1949.02.08

1950

1. 'Lönerna och inkomstutvecklingen' Chapter X in *Konjunkturläget hösten 1949*. Meddelande från Konjunkturinstitutet Serie A:17 Stockholm
2. LO memoranda (the research department)
2.1 'PM om prisutvecklingen 1950-51' 1950.09.23
2.2 'Översikt över prishöjningar 1950/51' 1950.09.24
2.3 'Synpunkter på prisutvecklingen 1950-1951' 1950.10.11
2.4 'PM till exportavgifterna på skogsprodukter' 1950.11.02
2.5 'Survey of Nationalized Industries in Sweden' Memorandum for COMISCO meeting (The Labour Movement Archives; Tage Erlander's documents)
3. 'Lönepolitiken och fullsysselsättningen' (a reply to Erik Lundberg, 'Lönepolitik under full sysselsättning', pp. 43-61 in the same issue), *Ekonomisk tidskrift*, vol. 52, pp. 62-7
4. LO press information, series II
4.1 'Vår ekonomi just nu', no. 2, 1950.01.12
5. Memoranda for SAP/LO (The Labour Movement Archives; Tage Erlander's documents)
5.1 'PM om arbetarpensioneringen som instrument i den ekonomiska politiken på lång sikt' 1950.05.24

5.2 'Fortsättning på PM den 24.5.50 om arbetarpensioneringen' 1950.05.26
5.3 'Folkpartiet och kommunisterna hand i hand' 1950.05
5.4 'Folkpartiet och löneutvecklingen' 1950.06.16
5.5 'PM nr 2 om exportavgifterna' 1950.11.18
6. 'Indirekta företagsskatter för ekonomisk stabilitet', *Morgontidningen* 1950.10.12

1951

1. Gösta Rehn and Per Åsbrink, 'Full sysselsättning utan inflation', Memoranda for the meeting of Nordiska Samarbetskommittén in Stockholm 17 and 18 February 1951

2. Contributions to the debate on the LO congress 1951 pp. 186-188, 201, 227-32, 235, 263-4 in Landsorganisationen i Sverige, 14th ordinary congress, 8-15 September 1951. *Minutes*, Stockholm
3. 1949 års skatteutredning. *Betänkande ang. den statliga direkta beskattningen.* SOU 1951:51
3.1 Kapitel VII 'Direkt och indirekt beskattning'
3.2 Special remarks by Henriksson and Rehn, pp. 270-5
3.3 Special remarks Åkerström, pp. 303-14 (a footnote in the remarks as well as material in the National Archives show that this is part of a draft of Chapter VII written by Gösta Rehn)
4. LO memoranda (the research department)
4.1 'Förutsedda och inträffade prisstegringar från september 1950 till juni 1951' 1951.01.03
4.2 'Diskussionspromemoria om pensionsutredningens betänkande' (förberedelse till LO:s remissyttrande) 1951.03.13
4.3 'Synpunkter på den ekonomiska politiken 1951' 1951.04.20
4.4 'Om allmän pensionsförsäkring' (Förslag till Statsrådet och chefen för Kungl. Handelsdepartementet) 1951.04.30
4.5 'PM inför överläggning den 4 maj 1951' (mellan regeringen och LO) 1951.05.02
4.6 'PM om vissa specialfrågor. Anm. till statsinkomstberäkningen för 1951/52' 1951.05.09
4.7 'PM för överläggning den II maj 1951' 1951.05.10
4.8 'Bilaga till PM för överläggning den 11 maj 1951' 1951.05.10
4.9 'Om allmän pensionsförsäkring' (Förslag 2 till Statsrådet och chefen för Kungl. Handelsdepartementet) 1951.05.12
4.10 'PM för ordförandekonferensen den 12 juni 1951' 1951.06.08
4.11 'Utkast till en realekonomisk beräkning av utrymmet för lönestegring 1952 mm' 1951.08.31
4.12 'PM till överläggning med regeringen 1951.11.07' 1951.11.07
4.13 'Indexavtal och subventioner' 1951.11.19
4.14 'Redovisning av den penninglönestegring som erfordras för en viss reallönestegring

utifrån nuvarande läge m.m.' 1951.12.14

5. 'Betänkande med förslag till förordning angående inskränkning i rätten att uppspärra armbågar vid folkträngsel' (contribution to the debate on Tage Lindbom's book Efter Atlantis), *Morgontidningen* 1951.12.20

6. 'Mysteriet med de uppspärrade armbågarna' (reply to 'Ur expertisens tankevärld', an editorial in Aftontidningen 1951.12.26), *Aftontidningen* 1951.12.30

7. *LO, Fackföreningsrörelsen och den fulla sysselsättningen* (the study was done by a committee with Nils Goude as chairman. It was mainly written by Rudolf Meidner, Gösta Rehn, Nils Kellgren and Arne Henrikson from LO's research department)

8. Memoranda for SAP/LO (The Labour Movement Archives; Tage Erlander's documents)

8.1 'Den ekonomiska situationen m.h.t. pris- och löneutvecklingen' 1951.03.25

8.2 Gösta Rehn and Nils Kellgren, 'Den ekonomiska situationen april 1951 II. Sammanfattning och förslag' 1951.04.01

8.3 'Utkast till PM inför ev. disk. m. reg.' 1951.04.15

9.1 'Anteckningar från sammanträde på Rosenbad tisdagen den 19 juni 1951 mellan representanter för RLF and lantbruksförbundet (inbjudare) och landsorganisationen', 1951.06.21

9.2 'Anteckningar från sammanträde mellan bondeförbundets ledning och landsorganisationen på Mjölkcentralen onsdagen den 20 juni 1951', 1951.06.21

1952

1. 'The Problem of Stability' and 'Reply to Erik Lundberg' (translated and to some extent revised versions of 'Ekonomisk politik vid full sysselsättning' Tiden 1948 and 'Lönepolitiken och fullsysselsättningen' Ekonomisk tidskrift 1950) in Ralph Turvey (ed.), *Wages Policy Under Full Employment*, William Hodge & Co., London, pp. 30-54 and 72-9

2. LO memoranda (the research department)

2.1 'PM med vissa kompletteringar till expertkommitténs beräkningar rörande indexeffekten av lönehöjningar' 1952.01.03

2.2 'Kommentar till direktör Kugelbergs radioanförande' 1952.01.14

2.3 'Lönestegringen 1951-52' 1952.02.01

3. 'Amerikanska fackföreningar', *Metallarbetaren*, no. 35-36, p. 12

4. Memoranda for Penningvärdeundersökningen:

4.1 'Lönepolitiska frågeställningar' 1952.02.19

4.2 'Not' 1952.08.13

4.3 'Inledning till betänkande' 1953.02.27

4.4 'Om definition av uttrycket full sysselsättning' 1953.03.24

4.5 'Politiska premisser' 1953.03.29

4.6 'Lönerna och fullsysselsättningen' December 1954

5. 'Osams med Wigforss!' (one in a series of articles on Ernst Wigforss: Socialism i vår

tid. The other articles were by Tage Erlander, 'Tage Erlander om "Wigforss-kursen", in no. 21; Torsten Eliasson, 'Slut på defensiven' in no. 23; Anatol Renning, 'Wigforss och Atlantis' in no. 24 and Ernst Wigforss' final comment 'Dolken i skidan, Rehn!' in no. 25-26), *Frihet*, no. 22

6. LO press information, series I

6.1 'Den amerikanska stålstriden – en kamp mellan staten och kapitalet. I', no. 88, 1952.07.22

6.2 'Den amerikanska stålstriden. Argument kring profilerna. II', no. 89, 1952.07.23

6.3 'Stålstrejkens eftermäle', no. 93, 1952.08.11

6.4 'Gengångare från Vilda Västern', no. 94, 1952.08.12

6.5 'Rättelse' (till no. 93, 1952.08.1 1) no. 95, 1952

6.6 'Fackföreningsrörelsen och politiken', no. 96, 1952.08.15

6.7 'Den statliga lönekontrollen. I', no. 99, 1952.08.20

6.8 'Fackföreningskunskap på universitet', no. 105, 1952.09.01

7. LO press information, series II

7.1 'Amerikas fackföreningar 1952', no. 26, 1952.08.01

7.2 'Amerikas fackföreningar II', no. 28, 1952.08.09

8. 'PM med förslag om sysselsättningsutjämningsfond' 1952.09.24 (The Labour Movement Archives; Tage Erlander's documents)

9. 'Lönepolitiska frågeställningar', 1952.02.19

1953

1. 'Regleringsväsen, finanspolitik och arbetsmarknadsproblem'. Discussion on Erik Lundberg's book 'Konjunkturer och ekonomisk politik'. Other comments by Carsten Welinder, Erik Dahmén, Ivar Sundbom and Erik Lundberg, *Ekonomisk tidskrift*, vol. 55, pp. 271-90

2. 'När är folkomröstning demokratisk?', *Aftontidningen* 1953.05.26

3. 'Folkomröstning och propaganda' (reply to editorial by Herbert Tingsten in Dagens Nyheter with this title 1953.05.29; Tingsten answered in the same issue), *Dagens Nyheter* 1953.06.04

4. 'Folkomröstning och propaganda. Slutreplik till prof. Tingsten', *Aftontidningen* 1953.06.08

5. 'Kring folkomröstningen I: logik och polemik' (reply to Herbert Tingsten's summary of a radio debate with Gösta Rehn published in Dagens Nyheter 1953.07.28 'Principiellt för, praktiskt mot' and 1953.07.29 'Värdet av folkomröstning'), *Aftontidningen* 1953.08.08

6. 'Kring folkomröstningen II: logik och politik', *Aftontidningen* 1953.08.09

7. 'Småkolonier i privathem bättre än "anstaltsvård"' (comments on Ture Gerdes, 'Jag tvivlar på skollovskolonierna!', Aftontidningen 1953.08.06), *Aftontidningen* 1953.08.11

8. 'Pressfrihet och rättvisa', *Ny Tid* 1953.10.03, *Oskarshamns Nyheterna* 1953.10.03 and *Östgöten* 1953.10.07
9. 'Reflexioner om "köpkraft"', *Fackföreningsrörelsen*, vol. 33, pp. 340-6
10. 'Organisationerna och friheten', *Tiden*, vol. 45, pp. 517-25
11. 'Kortare arbetstid eller löneökning?' (comments on Anatol Renning 'Lönen och "kakan", Metallarbetaren no. 40), *Metallarbetaren*, no. 45, pp. 6-7
12. 'Den triumferande kyrkan' (about the Helander case), *Aftontidningen* 1953.12.29
13. 'Han trollar med hjärnan. Dag Hammarskjöld, FN:s nye generalsekreterare, presenteras av Gösta Rehn', *Vi* 1953.04.17
14. 'Inkomsternas fördelning i Sverige' (review of Ragnar Bentzel's book Inkomstfördelningen i Sverige), *Vi* 1953.05.08
15. *LO, Trade Unions and Full Employment* (revised English version of 'Fackföreningsrörelsen och den fulla sysselsättningen' 1951),
16. 'De svåra alternativen: Kortare arbetstid eller löneökning?', *Metallarbetaren*, no. 45

1954

1. 'Angående kollektivanslutningen (i anslutning till diskussion den 13.1.54)', Memorandum (LO's archives)
2. 'Lönerna och inflationsrisken', Memorandum 1954.10.30
3. 'Den ekonomiska politiken och frågan om arbetstidsförkortning' (reply to Per Prydz, 'Kortare arbetstid eller löneökning?' in Metallarbetaren no. 49, 1953 which was critical of Gösta Rehn's article with the same name in Metallarbetaren no. 45, 1953), *Metallarbetaren*, no. 5, p. 8

4 The Labour Movement Archives; Tage Erlander's documents

4.1 'Lönesituationen hösten 1954'

4.2 'Förslag till utformning av regler för fördelning av ett statens upplysningsanslag vid folkomröstning'

5. 'Reformistisk förnyelse', Memorandum 1953/54
6. Memorandum on the 'wage drift' in Sweden, January (SAF Library)

1955

1.1 'Kommentarer till Bent Hansen: Rehns politik', Memorandum

1.2 'Angående Rehns linje' Memorandum to Bent Hansen

2. 'För en ny internationalism', *Värmlands Folkblad* 1955.04.27 and *Östergötlands Folkblad* 1955.05.02.
3. 'På tal om under' (contribution to a debate on the economic development in West Germany which took place in several newspapers), *Morgon-Tidningen* 1955.06.17
4. Memoranda for SAP/LO

4.1 'Extra PM om påbörjande av pensionsförsäkringens fondbildning 1956' 1955.11.09 (The Labour Movement Archives; Tage Erlander's documents)

4.2 'Utkast till rundabordsuppgörelse om den ekonomiska politiken för 1956' 1955.11.20

1956

1. Bent Hansen and Gösta Rehn, 'On Wage-Drift. A Problem of Money-Wage Dynamics', in 25 *Economic Essays in Honour of Erik Lindahl*, Ekonomisk Tidskrift, Stockholm, pp. 87-138

1a. Bent Hansen and Gösta Rehn, 'Försök till statistisk belysning av löneglidningens orsaker' Revised translation to Swedish of 'On Wage Drift' in 25 *Economic Essays in Honour of Erik Lindahl*, (The Labour Movement Archives)

1957

1. 'Unionism and the Wage Structure in Sweden', in John Dunlop (ed.), *The Theory of Wage Determination.* Proceedings of a conference held by the International Economic Association (includes several interventions made by Gösta Rehn at the debates), Macmillan, London, pp. 222-37
2. 'Löneglidningen, ett centralt problem i vår ekonomi', minutes of a debate between Curt-Steffan Giesecke and Gösta Rehn chaired by Torsten Gårdlund on the conference 'Vårt ekonomiska läge 1957' 1957.02.13 (the debate is not included in the conferece volume)
3. 'Hata inflationen!', Tiden, vol. 49, pp. 104-12
4. 'Replik från Rehn' (reply to an editorial 'En ropandes röst' in Eskilstuna-Kuriren 1957.03.06), *Eskilstuna-Kuriren* 1957.03.16
5. 'Inflationspolitiken än en gång', *Eskilstuna-Kuriren* 1957.03.19
6. 'Svar till hr Wedén och EK', (comments to 'Käppen och moroten' Eskilstuna-Kuriren 1957.03.19 and the editorial 'På arbetsgivarlinjen!' Eskilstuna-Kuriren 1957.03.20; reply by Sven Wedén, 'Tänk om vi hade...' Eskilstuna-Kuriren 1957.04.03), *Eskilstuna-Kuriren* 1957.04.01
7. 'Swedish Wages and Wage Policies', *The Annals of the American Academy of Political and Social Science,* vol. 310, pp. 99-108
8. Memoranda for *Stabiliseringsutredningen*:

   A. Erfarenheter av utvecklingen sedan 1939

      1) Den institutionella ramen för lönepolitiken (1957.10.04)

      2) Översiktlig återblick på lönepolitiken under fullsysselsättningsperioden (1957.03.13)

   B. Problemanalys

      1) Frågeställningar och begreppsbestämningar (1957.05.11)

      2) Lönebegreppet

      3) Begreppen lönepolitisk återhållsamhet och aggressivitet

      4) Lönemultiplikatorn

      Inledning till löneteorin (1957.02.26)

      Bent Hansens förslag till styrning av löneutvecklingen

Förenklad teori för bevarandet av stabil prisnivå och lugn löneutveckling vid full sysselsättning (1957.02.26)
Lönedifferenser som metod för styrning av arbetskraftsströmmarna (1957.02.26)

9. 'Lagpension med valfrihet', *Stockholms-Tidningen* 1957.10.15
10. 'Vem skall betala för de barn som skall betala våra pensioner', *Morgon-Tidningen* 1957.12.04
11. 'Reform av pensionsreformen?' (The Labour Movement Archives; Tage Erlander's documents) 1957.02.11
12. 'Pensioner och barn', Memorandum, October 1957
13. 'Pensionskostnadernas fördelning och familjepolitiken', Memorandum, November 1957

1958

1. 'Formuleringsförslag, valet 1958', Memorandum, September 1958 (the typed version is dated Jan. 12 1959)
2. 'Utkast till en "kompromiss"', 1958.02.23
3. 'Ett par frågeställningar inför kommande valstrider kring pensionsfrågan', 1958.03.22
4. Debate in connection with Ulrich Herz, 'Arbetslöshet i nytt perspektiv', *Ekonomisk revy*, vol. 15, pp. 727-30 (Gösta Rehn's intervention)
5. 'Wage Drift in Sweden', European Productivity Agency (EPA). Trade Union Research and Study Departments. International Trade Union Conference. Vienna 9-12 December 1958

5a. 'Le glissement des Salaires en Suede', (the version in French of Wage drift in Sweden)

6. Comments on the debate in connection with Bertil Olsson, 'Arbetsmarknadspolitikens betydelse i nuvarande konjunkturläge' *Nationalekonomiska föreningens förhandlingar 1958* (Proceedings of the Swedish Economic Association 1958), Gösta Rehn, pp. 92-4
7. Erland von Hofsten and Gösta Rehn 'Ny giv åt barnfamiljerna', *Vi*, no. 2, pp. 8-9 and 35-6
8. 'Pensionsutskottet och överkompensationen', Memorandum 1958.04.22

1959

1. 'Amerikansk kritik av överflödssamhället' (review of John Kenneth Galbraith's book The Affluent Society), *Fackföreningsrörelsen*, vol. 39, part 1, pp. 6-12
2. 'Pensionsreformens praktiska resultat beskrivet t ex vid ett val- eller fackföreningsmöte år 1970', Memorandum (no date, 1959) (Lund University Library; Ernst Wigforss' documents)
3. 'Reformistisk förnyelse I och II', *Tiden*, vol. 51, pp. 135-45 and 196-208
4. *Arbetet*

4.1 'Nästa stora socialreform' 1959.09.05

4.2 'Välfärdspolitiken inför den unga generationen' 1959.09.06

5. Intervention in the debate in connection with Ulrich Herz, 'Välstånd contra välfärd? Socialpolitiken i nytt utgångsläge', *Nationalekonomiska föreningens förhandlingar 1959* (Proceedings of the Swedish Economic Association 1959), Gösta Rehn pp. 76-7 and 79
6. 'Den nya arbetsmarknadspolitiken' (also as an expanded reprint), *Svensk sparbankstidskrift*, vol. 43, pp. 215-22
7. 'Förslag till programkommittén', Memorandum 1959.02.13
8. 'Samhällsekonomiska synpunkter på näringslivets lokalisering', Memorandum for a study of societal relocalisation 1959.12.11
9. 'Samhället fungerar bakvänt', *Frihet*, no. 6

1960

1. 'Angående metoderna för val av organisatoriska och offentliga förtroendemän', Proposal for a motion to Social Democratic party congress in 1960; the motion was not accepted by the local party organisation in Solna (Gösta Rehn lived in a Solna and was member of that local party organization) (Lund University Library; Ernst Wigforss' documents)
2. 'Det offentliga sparandet', *Svensk sparbankstidskrift*, vol. 44, pp. 61-70
3. 'Synpunkter på läget och den ekonomiska politiken 1961', Memorandum 1960.12.11
4. Memoranda, Ministry of Finance, Department of Economic Analysis (The Labour Movement Archives; Tage Erlander's documents)

4.1 Rein Hinno and Gösta Rehn, 'Den statliga arbetskraftsbegränsningen sommaren 1960 (tom 15 september)' 1960.10.25

4.2 'PM om begränsningen av den statliga arbetskraftsanvändningen' 1960.10.27

5. 'Bruttobeskattning' pp. 31-7 in *Framtidens företagsbeskattning*, minutes of the discussion on pp. 52-60. Presentations and discussions at an SNS conference. Studieförbundet Näringsliv och Samhälle, Stockholm

1961

1. 'The Case for Expansion of Labour Market Policy as an Instrument of Economic Progress', Paper for the meeting of Senior Economic Advisors ECE – 20-24 March 1961
2. Comments on the debate in connection to Bent Hansen's lecture 'Löner och priser', *Nationalekonomiska föreningens förhandlingar 1961* (Proceedings of the Swedish Economic Association 1961), Gösta Rehn pp. 113-15, 121-4 and 125
3. 'Arbetsmarknadspolitik som samhällsidé', pp. 74-94 in Olle Svensson (ed.), *Femton år med Tage Erlander*. Tiden, Stockholm
4. 'På väg mot en rationell finanspolitik' pp. 76-92 in *Idé och handling* (In honour of Wigforss' 80th birthday on 24 January 1961), Tiden, Stockholm

5. 'Den irrationella finanspolitiken' (comments on Carsten Welinder, 'Mot en rationell finanspolitik' Ekonomisk Revy no. 4, which was a critique of Gösta Rehn's article in *Idé och handling*), *Ekonomisk Revy*, vol. 18, pp. 335-8
6. 'Modern konjunkturpolitik', *SACO tidningen*, vol. 8, pp. 79-82 and 101-7
7. 'Company Taxation: Recent Reforms and Discussions in Sweden', (Memorandum prepared for a visit by Goldberg, the head of U.S. Department of Labor), Ministry of Finance 1961.03.27
8. Gideon Nitare and Gösta Rehn 'Investment Reserves Allowances in Swedish Fiscal Policy', Memorandum. (AMS and Ministry of Finance) 1961.06.05
9. Gösta Rehn and Lennart Klackenberg, 'Notes on Swedish anti-cyclical policy', Memorandum, Ministry of Finance, 1961.09.30

1962

1. 'Nationalbudgeten och konjunkturpolitiken', *Skandinaviska Banken Kvartalsskrift*, vol. 43, no. 2, pp. 37-45
2. 'Stadsplaneärende i Solna', *Stockholms-Tidningen* 1962.02.26
3. 'Demokrati och stadsplaner', *Stockholms-Tidningen* 1962.04.25
4. 'Manpower Adaptability and Economic Growth', *The OECD Observer*, no. 1, pp. 14-18
5. Memoranda for the Social Democratic party

5.1 'Rätten till förtida pensionsuttag' 1962.01.31
5.2 'Fallet med den lurade invaliden' 1962.02.03
5.3 'Tillägg om förhandspensioneringens inadvertenser' 1962.02.05

1963

1. Erik Lundberg and Gösta Rehn, 'Employment and Welfare: Some Swedish Issues', *Industrial Relations*, vol. 2, no. 2, pp. 1-14
2. 'Integration Between Social Legislation and Manpower Policy', OECD Memorandum 1963.02.12

1964

1. 'Vägar till valfriheten', *Stockholms-Tidningen* 1964.10.06
2. 'The Workings of an Active Manpower Policy', *The OECD Observer*, no. 8, pp. 3-7

1965

1. 'Labour Market Adjustment Policies – Trends and Perspectives in Manpower Policy'. Conference on Poverty in America. Berkeley, February 26-28

2. Special remarks to the report of 1960 års arbetsmarknadsutredning *Arbetsmarknads-politik*, SOU 1965:9, pp. 547-9
3. 'The Workings of Active Manpower Policies in Europe', Speech at the Department of Labor, USA

1966

1. 'An Account of Progress in Manpower Policies', *The OECD Observer*, no. 21, pp. 3-10

1967

1. 'Manpower Policy and European Unemployment', *The OECD Observer*, no. 31, pp. 15-18 and 31-4
2. 'Amended version of G. Rehn's main intervention at the International Institute for Labour Studies' Symposium on the Labour Market and Inflation', October 1966, 1967.02.20
3. OECD, *Manpower Policies and Problems in Austria* (F. Denis, K. Holler and Gösta Rehn examiners)

1968

1. 'Pension Intricacies', Memorandum, OECD 1968.12.19

1969

1. *On Incomes Policy*, Papers and Proceedings from a Conference in Honour of Erik Lundberg. SNS, Stockholm (several shorter comments, and one longer, pp. 163-8)
2. 'Förslag angående sysselsättningspolitiken 1969-70', Memorandum 1969.04.14
3. 'Economic Implications of Training Programmes', OECD, 1969.01.21

1970

1. 'Nyare tendenser i arbetsmarknadspolitik', *Vårt ekonomiska läge 1970* , pp. 119-42
2. 'Förslag till justering av nuvarande regler för förtida pensionsuttag', Memorandum to the Minister of Social Affairs and the Prime Minister 1970.01.02
3. 'Manpower lessons from Europe', paper for British Institute of Management, National Conference on the Management of Britain's Human Resources in the 1970's, London, 11 March 1970
4. 'A Note on the Political Presentation of Manpower Policy', Memorandum, OECD 1970.07.01

5. 'Trends and Innovations in Manpower Policy 1967-69', Third Report on Implementation of the Recommendation on Active Manpower Policy by the Manpower and Social Affairs Committee, OECD
6. OECD, *Manpower Policy in the United Kingdom*, (J.C. Donovan, H. Ernst, E. März and Gösta Rehn examiners)
7. 'Social- och arbetsmarknadspolitik enligt OECD', Speech, 15 October 1970
8. 'Kommentar till Riksförsäkringsverkets förslag om vidgad förtidspensionering', 1970-71

1971

1. 'Varför hata inflationen?', *Svensk sparbankstidskrift*, vol. 55, pp. 267-71
2. 'Skiss till extra åtgärd i sysselsättningspolitiken' (Memorandum to Palme, Sträng etc.) 1971.11.26

1972

1. 'Bertil Olsson, 60 år, en kraftkarl med tur', *Byggnadsindustrin*, vol. 42, no. 39, pp. 23-4
2. 'General observations about future work', OECD-memorandum (undated, most likely 1972)
3. 'OECD Tasks and Priorities in the 1970s', Memorandum, OECD 1972.02.10
4. 'Prospective View on Patterns of Working Time', OECD International conference on New Patterns in Working Time, Report no. 1 B. September

1973

1. 'Die Gesellschaft der freien Wahl' in *Beiträge zu einer Theorie der Sozialpolitik* Festschrift für Elisabeth Liefmann-Keil zum 65. Geburtstag, Duncker & Humblot, Berlin, pp. 317-51
2. 'Relationen mellan avgång från anställning (retirement) och pensionering; Flexibel pensionsålder', in Yngve Zotterman (ed.), *Pensionering och sysselsättning: aktivering av äldre*, Allmänna förlaget, Stockholm, pp. 106-19
3. 'Manpower Policy as an Instrument of National Economic Policy' in Seymour L. Wolfbein (ed.), *Manpower Policy Perspectives and Prospects* (papers on the occasion of the tenth anniversary of the Manpower Development and Training Act of 1962), Temple University, Philadelphia
4. 'For Greater Flexibility of Working Life', *The OECD Observer*, February, pp. 3-7
5. 'Die Verbindung von Arbeit, Bildung und Freizeit – Ein Modellvorschlag', *Gewerkschaftliche Monatshefte*, vol. 24, July
6. 'Recent Trends in Manpower Policy', *European Yearbook*, vol. XXI, pp. 82-112

7. 'Förslag om revalvering' Memorandum, 1973.10.04
8. 'Long-term Programme for the Manpower and Social Affairs Committee', OECD 1973.10.10
9. OECD, *Manpower Policy in Japan*, (C.D. Stewart, H. Knolle and Gösta Rehn examiners)
10. 'Ge oss flexliv', *Vi*, no. 50/51

1974

1. 'Måste vi leva med inflationen?' (panel debate with several participants), *Vårt ekonomiska läge 1974*, pp. 101-40
2. 'Vägar till frihet och självansvar' (series of articles in connection with Göran Palm's Bokslut från LM and Anders Leion's Den svenska modellen), *Metallarbetaren* no. 35, pp. 4-5 and 10; no. 39, pp. 6-7; no. 40, pp. 6-7; no. 41, p. 6
3. 'Towards Flexibility in Working Life', *Universities Quarterly*, no. 3, pp. 276-86
4. OECD, *Manpower Policy in Germany*, (Alfred Bernfeld, Leo Klassen and Gösta Rehn examiners)
5. 'Towards Flexibility in Working Life' in Selma J. Muskin (ed.), *Recurrent Education*, Georgetown University conference on recurrent education, Washington DC, National Institute of Education, pp. 177-86
6. 'Sysselsättningsutredningen inför de marginella grupperna', Memorandum, 1974.05.05
7. 'Towards a Society of Free Choice', Paper for OECD Experts Meeting on Life-Long Allocation of Time, 12-14 November 1974
8. 'Några kommentarer till forskningspolitiska programförslaget, version December 74', 1974.12.27

1975

1. 'Fortsatt kommentar till SAP-forskningsprogramförslaget. Ang. 4.6 (sid. 26): En demokratisk forskning' 1975.01.07
2. 'Framtidens arbetsmarknadspolitik i Sverige och utlandet' in *Rätten till Arbete*, Föreningen Sveriges Socialchefers konferenstryck. Speech, 26 September 1975
3. Short summary of Gösta Rehn's introduction 'Vad har avtalsrörelsen lärt oss?' at Arbetsmarknadsstämman, 11 October 1975
4. 'Kan vi göra om arbetslivet?' (reply to criticism of earlier articles in Metallarbetaren), *Metallarbetaren*, no. 4, pp. 12-13
5. 'Manpower Policy in the Fight against Stagflation', pp. 12-35 in Seminar Proceedings from the conference on Active Labor Market Policy in Selected Countries. Berlin, April 24-26

5a. 'The Fight Against Stagflation' (revised version of Manpower Policy in the Fight against Stagflation) August 12

6. 'Så räddas jobben vid nästa vågdal', *Arbetet* 1975.10.02

7. 'Sysselsättningspremier som inslag i arbetsmarknadspolitiken', Bilaga till Arbetsmarknadsgruppens rapport för Sysselsättningsutredningen. 1975.08.01
8. 'Flextid och flexliv' Introduction and comments in the debate, (Nationalekonomiska föreningens förhandlingar) *Ekonomisk Debatt*, vol. 3, no. 1, pp. 72-81 (introduction), 84-6 and 87-8
9. 'Some Thoughts on Employment Policy in the OECD Area During 1975 and later years' (consultant's contribution to ILO preparation of World Employment Conference)
10. 'Sysselsättningspolitiken inför 1976', Memorandum 1975.11.02
11. 'Introductory thoughts concerning a new Recommendation on a Strategy for Employment Policy' Memorandum, OECD, 1975.12.03

1976

1. 'Framtidens arbetsmarknadspolitik i Sverige och utlandet' in *Rätten till Arbete*, Föreningen Sveriges Socialchefer. Stockholm 1976
2. 'Reflections on the seminar on Growth without Inflation' (Kiel, 28 June 1976)
3. 'På väg mot bättre invandrarutbildning (Europarådets konferens om invandrarutbildning)', *Invandrare och minoriteter*, vol. 3, no. 2, pp. 9-13
4. 'Hata inflationen ännu mera', *Tiden*, vol. 68, pp. 355-61
5. 'Recent Trends in Western Economies: Needs and Methods for Further Development of Manpower Policy', in US National Commission for Manpower Policy, Special Report No. 10: *Re-examing European Manpower Policies*, pp. 53-71
6. 'The Policies for Equal Opportunity', ICSW – XVIII International Conference on Social Welfare: The Struggle for Equal Opportunity. San Juan, Puerto Rico, July
7. Introduction to a discussion on Jan Bröms's paper 'Om selektiv politiks generella verkningar på den industriella utvecklingen', in *Erfarenheter av blandekonomin* (Papers and discussions at the Dahmén-symposiet on the Swedish mixed economy), Saltsjöbaden 18-19 October 1976, Skandinaviska Enskilda Banken, Stockholm, pp. 174-80
8. 'Recurrent Education in internationaler Sicht', *Erwachsenbildung in Österreich*, vol. 27, pp. 401-8

1977

1. 'Samhällsekonomiska synpunkter på aktivering av äldre', in Carl Ström and Yngve Zotterman (eds) *Arbete och sysselsättning för de äldre*, Liber förlag, Stockholm, pp. 184-90
2. 'Framtidens arbetsmarknadspolitik' (introduction and comments in the debate), (Nationalekonomiska föreningens förhandlingar) *Ekonomisk Debatt*, vol. 5, pp. 116-23 (introduction) and 131-4

2a. 'Framtidens arbetsmarknadspolitik', The Swedish Institute for Social Research, (expanded version of the article published in Ekonomisk Debatt)

3. 'Finansministrarna, LO-ekonomerna och arbetsmarknadspolitiken', in Jan Herin and Lars Werin (eds), *Ekonomisk debatt och ekonomisk politik, nationalekonomiska*

föreningen 100 år, Norstedts, Stockholm, pp. 201-27
4. 'Arbetsmarknadspolitik', in Lars Hjalmarsson (ed.), *Ekonomisk politik inför 1980-talet*, Tiden, Stockholm, pp. 67-99
5. 'Towards a Society of Free Choice', in Jerzy J. Wiatr and Richard Rose (eds), *Comparing Public Choices*, Ossolineum, Wroclaw, pp. 121-57
6. 'Attainment and Maintenance of Full Employment', Symposium on the European Social Charter and Social Policy Today, Strasbourg 7-9 December
7. 'The Role and Problems of Government Policies', EurCult Foundation, Fere-en-Tardenois, April 1977

1978

1. 'Myter om rörlighetspolitiken', *Dagens Nyheter* 1978.04.01
2. 'Employment Premiums in Economic Policy' PM för 'Group of Independent Experts' EEC, Brussels June 1978
3. Special remarks to Sysselsättningsutredningen's partial report *Arbete åt handikappade* SOU 1978:14
4. Special remarks to Sysselsättningsutredningen's partial report *Regionalpolitiska stödformer och styrmedel* SOU 1978:62
5. Contribution to the debate in connection with Stephen Marris 'En presentation av McCracken-rapporten: mot full sysselsättning och prisstabilitet', *Ekonomisk Debatt*, vol. 6, Gösta Rehn pp. 132-9, 147-8 and 151
6. 'Den förhärdade reformismen är vårt öde', Contribution to the debate in connection with John T Dunlop, 'Nya villkor för ekonomisk-politiskt beslutsfattande', *Ekonomisk Debatt*, vol. 6, pp. 571-6
7. Letter to Stephen Marris (also distributed to other participants in the meeting of the Manpower and Social Affairs Committee, 1 December 1978)
8. 'Vers une société de libre choix' (Temps de travail et temps de loisir), *Droit Social*, no. 7-8, pp. 314-32
9. 'Le Travail: Privilège, droit ou obligation', in *La sécurité d'emploi*, Les Presses de l'Université Laval, Québec, pp. 155-65
10. 'Full Employment without Inflation. (Draft presentation of some fundaments)', August 1978
11. 'Contribution to the Discussion on Temporary Employment Subsidies'. For OECD working party on employment. Preliminary Annex to MAS (78) 21, 5 November 1978
12. 'Workers can be choosers. In defence of free choice in working life', *The Unesco Courier*, November 1978

1979

1. 'Sweden: Active Manpower Policies'. Paper for conference on Critical Economic and Work Force Issues Facing Western Countries, Washington D.C., 5-6 December 1979

1980

1. Gösta Rehn and K. Helveg Pedersen *Education and Youth Employment in Sweden and Denmark*. Carnegie Council on Policy Studies in Higher Education, Berkeley
2. 'Inflationen kan stoppas!', *LO-tidningen*, no. 49
3. 'Mit Expansionskostensenkung gegen die Stagflation. Beschäftigungsprämien in der Wirtschaftspolitik', *Mitteilungen aus der Arbeitsmarkt- und Berufsforschung*, vol. 13, pp. 543-51
4. 'Expansion Against Stagflation – Some Unorthodox Reflections Based on the Swedish Experience', *Working Life in Sweden*, no. 18, July
5. 'Idéutvecklingen', in *Lönepolitik och solidaritet*. Contribution to the debate at the Meidner seminar 21-22 February 1980, LO, Stockholm, pp. 22-69
6. 'Financing Recurrent Education by a System of Individual Drawing Rights'. Paper for CERI conference on The Costs of Financing of Recurrent Education. Bremen, 30 September 1980

1981

1. 'Anti-inflationary Expansion Policies (With Special Reference to Marginal Employment Premiums). Report to the Commission of the European Communities. 1981. Also with supplement 1982: 'Marginal Employment Subsidies: Experiences and Reflections'. – There is also a French version of main report, 'Politiques d'expansion anti-inflationistes'
2. 'Den svenska välfärdsstaten: uppgång, kris och framtidsutsikter', *Katsaus* 1-1981, pp. 20-38
3. 'För en ny historisk kompromiss', *Aftonbladet* 1981.01.21
4. 'Om vargar och rödluvor' (reply to 'Vargens lockrop', Svenska Dagbladet 1981.01.22 which was a critique of 'För en ny historisk kompromiss'), *Svenska Dagbladet* 1981.01.27
5. 'Kasta inte sten i Nirvanas hus!', *Svenska Dagbladet* 1981.02.11
6. 'Skärpning i krisprogrammet!', *Aftonbladet* 1981.07.27
7. 'Vinsterna måste få stiga? Ja, men bara där det gör någon nytta!', *Stockholms-Tidningen* 1981.09.28
8. 'Frihet från inflation villkor för fulla sysselsättningen', *Dala-Demokraten* 1981.10.23
9. 'Hata inflationen III', *Tiden*, vol. 73, pp. 205-18
10. 'Utländska erfarenheter av sysselsättningsstöd', (Memorandum to Expertgruppen för marginella expansionsstöd (The group for a study of marginal expansion subsidies) 1981.01.20
11. 'Discussant's Comments', in Bertil Gardell and Gunn Johansson (eds), *Working Life*, John Wiley & Sons Ltd., Chichester
12. 'Inflationsbekämpning genom förbilligad produktionsökning' (for the Social Democratic party group on the economic crisis), April 1981

13. 'Inflationsbekämpning genom förbilligad produktionsökning (continued)' (for the group on the economic crisis), April 1981
14. 'Synsätt på äldreomsorg och kostnader', 1981.12.31

1982

1. Sten Johansson, Gösta Rehn and Krister Wickman 'Ett recept för provisoriska löntagarfonder', *Stockholms-Tidningen* 1982.04.02
2. 'Some Theoretical and Practical Aspects of Inequality Reduction' Expert Meeting on the Methods of Reducing Economic and Associated Socio-Cultural Inequalities, held in Stockholm 30 August-3 September. UNESCO
3. 'Låt företagen slippa arbetsgivaravgiften!', *Dagens Nyheter* 1982.12.18
4. 'Expansion mot inflation', *Administrations-TEMA* no. 1, pp. 14-15 and 48
5. 'Kommentar till budgeten: varning för självmord av fruktan för döden', *Tiden*, vol. 74, pp. 5-8
6. 'Koordination und Selektion im Bildungs- und Beschäftigungssystem Schwedens', in Ludwig Bussman (ed.), *Abstimmungs- und Auswahlprobleme im Bildungs- und Beschäftigungssystem*. Duncker & Humblot, Berlin, pp. 305-42
7. 'PM till partiledningen SAP' (on the economic policy) 1982.01.21
8. Gösta Rehn and Birger Viklund 'Labor Year Book 1981/82'. Arbetslivscentrum
8a. Gösta Rehn and Birger Viklund 'Svezia. Verso una svolta del modello svedese: I fondi di capitale dei lavoratori', in Guido Baglioni and Ettore Santi (eds), *L'Europa Sindicale nel 1981*, Società Editrice il Mulino, Bologna (Italian version of 8), pp. 193-285
9. 'Attackerna mot arbetsmarknadspolitiken', 1982.09.12
10. 'Lönepolitiskt undantagstillstånd?', SNS 14 December 1982

1983

1. 'Gösta Rehn vädjar till budgetreportrarna', *Stockholms-Tidningen* 1983.01.10
2. 'Journalister – rapportera bättre om budgeten', *Aftonbladet* 1983.01.10
3. 'En utmaning – från Gösta Rehn till nationalekonomerna', *Stockholms-Tidningen* 1983.02.15
4. 'The Debate on Employees' Capital Funds in Sweden', The Commission of the European Communities, Brussels, August
5. 'Den stora skolreformen' in Documentation from the seminar on *Den stora skolreformen*, SAF, pp. 47-52
6. 'Individual Drawing Rights', pp. 67-79 in Henry M. Levin and Hans G. Schütze (eds), *Financing Recurrent Education: Strategies for Increasing Employment, Job Opportunities and Productivity*, Sage, Beverly Hills
7. Gösta Rehn and Birger Viklund 'Labour Year Book 1982/83', Arbetslivscentrum

7a. Gösta Rehn and Birger Viklund 'Svezia – per un riformismo più avanzato senza compromesso di classe', i *L'Europa sindicale nel 1982*. Società Editrice il Mulino, Bologna (Italian version of Labour Year Book 1982/83), pp. 183-230
8. 'Economic Preconditions for a Lasting Consensus', Contribution to the Debate at the Lisbon Conference on Incomes Policy. March 1983
9. 'Experiences of Centralised Bargaining in Sweden', Swedish Institute for Social Research seminar paper. July 1983
10. 'The Debate on Employees' Capital Funds in Sweden', For the Commission of the European Communities, Brussels. August 1983

1984

1. 'Ofattbara miljarder', *Stockholms-Tidningen* 1984.01.19
2. 'Cooperation Between the Government and Workers' and Employers' Organizations on Labour Market Policy in Sweden' (in a version in French as 'La politique du marché du travail en Suède: Le lieu d'une cooperation entre le gouvernement et les partenaires sociaux') revised English version in 1986, The Swedish Institute, Stockholm
3. 'The Wages of Success', *Daedalus*, vol. 113, no. 2, pp. 137-168
4. 'The Role of Training in the Active Labour Market Policy – The Swedish Example' Conference of Greater London Training Board, May 10
5. 'The Active Labour Market Policy: a Historical Review', in *Beleid in de Tijd*, 's-Gravenhage, pp. 113-121
6. Comment (to a presentation by Barbosa de Melo), in Anibal A. Cavaco Silva, *Economic and Social Partnership and Incomes Policy*, Faculdade de Ciéncis humanas da universidade catolica portoguesa, Lissabon, pp. 165-73
7. 'Memoire à l'intention de diverses personnes concernées par les réformes d'imposition et la politique de l'emploi en France', 17 July 1984
8. 'La politique du marché du travail en Suède: le lieu d'une coopération entre le gouvernement et les partenaires sociaux', in *Les stratégies de reprise*, AEP

1985

1. Review of Hansson, Holgersson and Åberg's book Hur ska vi ha det med jämlikheten?' *Ekonomisk Debatt*, vol. 13, pp. 374-8
2. 'Erlander beredde väg för en ny modell', *Dagens Nyheter* 1985.07.28
3. 'Swedish Active Labor Market Policy: Retrospect and Prospect', *Industrial Relations*, vol. 24, no. 1, pp. 62-89
4. 'Is Job Sharing and the Shortening of Working Hours an Alternative to the Payment of Unemployment Benefits?' Symposium on the Grants Economy, Augsburg Sept/Oct.
5. 'Ska facket hålla nere lönerna?', *Aftonbladet* 1985.11.16
6. 'På väg mot valfrihetens samhälle' (a translated and revised version of 1977:5), Delfa. Delegationen för arbetstidsfrågor. Stockholm, March 1985

7. Gunnar Myrdal, Gösta Rehn, Krister Wickman, Jan Tinbergen and Pierre Uri 'För en anti-inflatorisk expansionspolitik' (a memorandum intended for the socialist political parties in the industrialized countries)

1986

1. 'Hur bädda för en antiinflatorisk inkomstpolitik?', in *Förhandlad inkomstpolitik?* Fackföreningsrörelsens institut för ekonomisk forskning, Stockholm, pp. 71-89
2. 'Free Choice and Flexibility in Working Life', *Inside Sweden*, no. 5

1987

1. 'State, Economic Policy and Industrial Relations in the 1980s: Problems and Trends', *Economic and Industrial Democracy*, vol. 8, pp. 61-79
2. 'Lönepolitiken – modell 1947?', *Aftonbladet* 1987.09.25
3. 'Alternativ megoldások a munkanélküliség ellen', *Fórum Tervgazdasági*, no. 4, pp. 14-23
4. 'Economia e attori nell'europa degli anni '80', in Guido Baglioni and Carrado Squarzon (eds), *Stato, politica economia e relazioni industriali in Europa*, Franco Angeli, Milano, pp. 98-119

1988

1. *Full sysselsättning utan inflation.* Skrifter i urval (Full employment without inflation. Selected works) edited by Eskil Wadensjö, Åke Dahlberg and Bertil Holmlund, Tiden, Stockholm
2. 'Vem ansvarade för flyttlasspolitiken?', *Dagens Nyheter* 1988.01.17
3. 'Reminiscences of the Stockholm School' and 'Swedes versus Marxists', mimeo, 1988.05.06

1989

1. 'The Swedish Experience', Socialist Solutions..., Givat Haviva, January 1988. Version February 1989
2. 'Flexibility and Free Choice in Working Life', paper for Gerontology Congress, Acapulco 1989
3. 'Ett lärorikt misstag i sysselsättningspolitiken', *Aftonbladet*, 1989.06.18
4. 'Mer än en framgångshistoria: Dra lärdom av misstagen', *Arbetarhistoria*, vol. 52, no. 4, pp. 8-11
5. 'Falsk bild av arbetslösheten i Sverige och världen', *Ekonomisk Debatt*, vol. 17, pp. 571-3

6. *Ensayos sobre política de empleo activa.* Coleccion Economia Del Trabajo no. 37. Ministerio de Trabajo y Seguridad Social, Madrid
7. 'En rättvis och flexibel tilläggspension', The Swedish Institute for Social Research, Working papers no. 7/1989

1990

1. 'Kritik av en drömbok. 90-talsprogrammet borde konkretiseras', *Arbetet*, 1990.09.14
2. '90-talsprogrammet, diskussion', *Arbetarhistoria*, no. 1-2, pp. 43-4
3. 'Inte klasskamp – bara evig kamp mot inflationen', *Aftonbladet*, 1990.03.31
4. 'Klara jobben utan inflation', *Aftonbladet*, 1990.08.20
5. 'The Future of the Welfare State', For PSOE conference on the Future of Socialism, Sevilla, December 1990
6. Gösta Rehn and Birger Viklund, 'Changes in the Swedish Model', Arbetslivscentrum
7. 'Análisis general de la economía sueca y su desarrollo', *Sistema*, no. 94-95, pp. 19-30

1991

1. 'Oerhört dyrt, Calmfors', *Aftonbladet*, 1991.04.06
2. 'Gösta Rehn bemöter Bööks kritik "Löntagarna uppfann själva rörligheten"', *Arbetet* 1991.09.17
3. 'Skäms dom inte?', *Aftonbladet* debatt, 1991.07.15
4. 'Sweden's Active Labor Market Policy', International Symposium on State, Labor and Capital. Seoul, December 1991

1992

1. Rudolf Meidner and Gösta Rehn, 'Fel metod mot arbetslöshet', *Dagens Nyheter* 1992.05.09

1993

1. 'Socialdemokratin inför verkligheten' (galley proof; never published) ISBN 91-7604-054-2
2. 'Bakvänt Wibble', *Dagens Nyheter* 1993.02.25

1995

1. 'Le modèle suédois: l'expérience passée et les perspectives d'avenir', in Diane-Gabrielle Tremblay (ed.), *Concertation et performance économique: vers de nouveaux modèles?*, Presses de l'Université du Québec, Sainte Foy (Québec), pp. 25-34

Presentations and interviews with Gösta Rehn

1. 'Bohemisk ekonom. Tidens porträtt', *Tiden* 1948, vol. 40, no. 4
2. Allan Lundberg: 'Gösta Rehn på gaffeln' (interview with Gösta Rehn), *Industria* 1956 no. 1, pp. 69-70, 85
3. 'Ett tillrättaläggande' (a correction of an interview in Industria), *Fackföreningsrörelsen* 1956, vol. 36, Part 1, p. 557
4. 'Får vi kvar arbetslöshet i högkonjunktur?' (interview with Gösta Rehn), *Veckans affärer* 1968, vol. 4, no. 29, pp. 16-18
5. Thor Brunius: '"Livsarbetstidens" lämpliga utnyttjande – stor framtidsfråga inom OECD' (interview with Gösta Rehn), *Kontorsvärlden* 1970, no. 10, pp. 16-17
6. 'Färsk doktorshatt – sprängfylld med idéer' (interview with Gösta Rehn), *Arbetsmarknaden*, no. 28, 27 September 1971
7. Sven Thiessen: 'Nya riktlinjer för framtidens arbetsmarknad' (interview with Gösta Rehn), *Arbetaren* 1972, no. 33/34, p. 8
8. 'Ekonomerna: Avgiftsbeläggning kan ge stora rationaliseringsvinster' (interview with Erik Höök and Gösta Rehn), *Administrations-TEMA* 1974, no. 2, pp. 4-6
9. 'Ökat statsstöd för nya jobb. 80-tal med flexliv', *Dagens Nyheter* 1974.03.18
10. Peeter-Jaan Kask: 'Flexliv – framtidens alternativ?' (interview with Gösta Rehn), *Arbetet* 1974.03.21
11. Åke Olsson: 'Det är förnuftigt att satsa stora pengar på att skaffa jobb åt folk' (interview with Gösta Rehn), *Aftonbladet* 1975.03.08
12. Lillemor Thalin: 'Hårdare styrning krävs' (interview with Kjell-Olof Feldt and Gösta Rehn), *Dagens Nyheter* 1975.04.08
13. Nils Kellgren: 'Rätt till arbete och flexliv' (interview with Gösta Rehn), *Vår industri* 1975, vol. 4, no. 11, pp. 28-31
14. Jan Gillberg: 'Gösta Rehn och marknadsförarna i "ohelig allians"', (interview with Gösta Rehn), *Svenska Marknaden* 1976, no. 3, pp. 4-8
15. 'Statlig premie för nya jobb. Dyrbara omvägar till sysselsättning', (interview with Gösta Rehn), *Dagens Nyheter* 31 December 1977
16. 'The Crisis of the Swedish Welfare State' (interviews with Gösta Rehn and others), *Challenge* 1980, vol. 23, July/August
17. Gunnar Hagtorn: 'Utbudsstimulans behövs – men gör mer!' (debate between Gösta Rehn and Karl-Olof Faxén), *Veckans affärer* 1981, no. 36, pp. 38-9 and 41
18. Hans Bergström: 'Miljarder till dödsdömda en ekonomisk tragedi' (interview with Gösta Rehn), *Nerikes Allehanda* 1982.01.05
19. Brita-Lena Ekström: 'Mängdrabatt till företagen ger fler jobb' (interview with Gösta Rehn), Svenska Dagbladet 1982.07.19
20. Göran Sten: 'Gösta Rehn: mer anti-inflatorisk expansionspolitik' (interview with Gösta Rehn), *LO-tidningen* 1983, no. 1/2, p. 11

21. Berndt Ahlqvist: 'Ekonomisk tillväxt kräver nya instrument' and 'Svenska modellens fader föreslår nytt recept mot inflation' (interview with Gösta Rehn), Arbetet 1984.05.18 and *Stockholms-Tidningen* 1984.05.20
22. Stig Tegle and Mats Isaksson: 'Löner och priser: handla, predika inte!' (interview with Gösta Rehn), *Socialistiskt Forum* 1986, no. 1/2, pp. 16-18
23. Anders Nordström: 'Gösta Rehn skapade den svenska modellens profil. Regeringen misslyckades bekämpa inflationen' (interview with Gösta Rehn on the policy of the Social Democratic party), *LO-tidningen* 1989, no. 35, pp. 4-5

Notes on the Authors

Dominique Anxo is director of the Centre of European Labour Market Studies and Associate Professor at the Department of Economics, University of Göteborg. His research interests fall into the areas of labour economics and industrial relations, gender and time use studies and evaluation of labour market policy.

Anders Bäckström is an economist at LO (the Swedish Trade Union Confederation) where he has been since 1970. He has represented LO in various official national and international bodies. He is presently Labour attaché at the Swedish Embassy in Germany.

Christine Brossier is currently head of the documentary unit, Maison des Sciences Economiques, Paris 1 University. A specialist in labour and employment, she previously worked at the CEREQ (Centre d'études et de recherches sur l'emploi et les qualifications).

Klas Eklund joined Skandinaviska Enskilda Banken (SEB) as Chief Economist in 1994. In the 1980s he worked in the Ministry of Finance (as Deputy Under-Secretary of State) and in the Cabinet office (as economic adviser to the Prime Minister). In 1989-90 he was the Secretary of the Social Democratic Party's programme commission for the 1990s.

Lennart Erixon has been Associate Professor at Stockholm University since 1993. Erixon has two main research interests, growth economics and Swedish economic policy. He has collaborated with social scientists from other Nordic countries in his work on Swedish growth and stabilisation policy.

Heikki Ervasti was Research Fellow (Academy of Finland, University of Turku) 1993-96 and has been Assistant Professor since 1997. His main research interests include comparative analyses of labour market and unemployment in Scandinavian countries and public opinion on the welfare state.

Bernard Gazier is Professor of economics at the Paris 1 University and Director of the research team MATISSE. He is a specialist in labour economics, and most of his recent work is devoted to employment policies and labour market reform ('transitional labour markets').

Geir Høgsnes is Professor in the Department of Sociology, University of Oslo. For many years he was a researcher at the Norwegian Institute for Social Research, ISR. His publications have focused on changes in bargaining structure and developments in the relative wages of groups of employees in different sectors of the labour market.

Sven Jochem has been Assistant Professor/Lecturer (Wissenschaftlicher Assistent) at the Centre for Social Policy Research, Bremen University since October 1997.

Frode Longva is researcher at Fafo Institute for Applied Social Science in Oslo. His research interests and publications focus on the sociology of labour markets, industrial relations and further education and training.

Markus Marterbauer is economist at the Austrian Institute of Economic Research (WIFO), and was previously Lecturer at the Vienna University of Economics and Business Administration. His main research areas are national economic policy and employment policies. He has published several papers comparing Swedish and Austrian economic policy.

Henry Milner is Professor of political science, Vanier College, Visiting Professor, Department of Political Science at Umeå University in Sweden, and Adjunct Professor, Department of Political Science, Université Laval. He is co-editor of Inroads, a Canadian journal of opinion and policy. He has published several studies on Sweden.

Christian Toft has worked at universities in Denmark, Britain, Germany and Italy. He is now a Visiting Fellow of the Max Planck Institute for the Study of Societies in Köln, Germany. His main area of research is comparative public policy with special emphasis on policy choices in the area of social security and labour market policy.

Axel van den Berg is Professor and Chair of the Department of Sociology of McGill University. He has been a Visiting Research Fellow at the Swedish Institute for Social Research in Stockholm. His recent research has focused on the sociology of labour markets, the relation between sociology and economics and contemporary sociological theory.

Jelle Visser is Professor of empirical sociology and chair of sociology of labour and organization at the University of Amsterdam, where he directs the Amsterdam Institute for Advanced Labour Studies (AIAS). He is associated with the Max Planck Institute for the

Study of Societies in Cologne. He has published books on trade unions and the 'Dutch miracle'.

Eskil Wadensjö has been Professor of labour economics at the Swedish Institute for Social Research, Stockholm University since 1980 and Dean of the Faculty of Social Sciences, Stockholm University since 1996. He was president of the European Association of Labour Economists (EALE) 1993-1999. His main research interests are labour economics and the economics of social policy.

Mark Wickham-Jones is Senior Lecturer in politics at the University of Bristol. He is currently researching the UK Labour Party's relationship with European social democracy.